CHINESE LAW
IN IMPERIAL
EYES

A STUDY OF THE WEATHERHEAD EAST ASIAN INSTITUTE
COLUMBIA UNIVERSITY

STUDIES OF THE WEATHERHEAD EAST ASIAN INSTITUTE
COLUMBIA UNIVERSITY

The Weatherhead East Asian Institute is Columbia University's center for research, publication, and teaching on modern and contemporary East Asian regions. The Studies of the Weatherhead East Asian Institute were inaugurated in 1962 to bring to a wider public the results of significant new research on modern and contemporary East Asia.

A Study of the Weatherhead East Asian Institute, Columbia University

For a list of selected titles, see page 401.

Li Chen

CHINESE LAW IN IMPERIAL EYES

Sovereignty, Justice, & Transcultural Politics

COLUMBIA UNIVERSITY PRESS   NEW YORK

Columbia University Press
Publishers Since 1893
New York   Chichester, West Sussex
cup.columbia.edu

Library of Congress Cataloging-in-Publication Data
Chen, Li, author.
Chinese law in imperial eyes : sovereignty, justice, and transcultural politics / Li Chen.
pages   cm. — (Studies of the Weatherhead East Asian Institute,
Columbia University)
Includes bibliographical references and index.
ISBN 978-0-231-17374-2 (cloth)—ISBN 978-0-231-17375-9 (pbk.)—
ISBN 978-0-231-54021-6 (e-book)
1. Law—China—History. 2. Sociological jurisprudence—China—History.
3. Extraterritoriality. 4. Sovereignty. 5. Criminal law—China—History.
6. Da Qing lü. 7. Justice, Administration of—China.
I. Title.

KNN440.C445   2016
349.5109'033—dc23
2015003030

Cover design: Lisa Hamm

*Cover image: View of the foreign factories at Canton, ca. 1805. Oil paint,
watercolor, gouache, glass, enamel; image 15½ x 23½ in. (39.3 x 59.7 cm), Chinese artist.
Gift of Misses Aimee and Rosamond Lamb. Courtesy of Peabody Essex Museum, E78680.*

This book is dedicated to my parents.

CONTENTS

Acknowledgments

O ver the years, I have incurred innumerable debts in completing this book. I cannot list in the space available here all the people and institutions whose help improved this book one way or another, but I am grateful to all of them for their generosity and kindness.

I am very fortunate to have had Madeleine Zelin as my mentor for all these years, and I cannot thank her enough for her guidance and unwavering support. In writing this book, I have also benefited enormously from the inspiration and scholarship of other superb scholars, including Partha Chatterjee, Myron Cohen, Wm. Theodore de Bary, Nicholas Dirks, David Engel, JaHyun Kim Haboush, Robert Hymes, Dorothy Ko, Eugenia Lean, Lydia Liu, Jonathan Ocko, and Guobin Yang.

A number of colleagues and friends generously volunteered their time to offer feedback on different parts or versions of the book manuscript. Besides those mentioned, I am truly grateful to Zvi Ben-Dor Benite, Takashi Fujitani, and Teemu Ruskola, and the anonymous reviewers for this book. Their feedback have profoundly shaped this book. I presented chapters of this book at numerous conferences and institutions, including Beijing University, Central University of Nationalities (Beijing), Columbia University, Duke University, Harvard University, Qinghua University, SUNY Buffalo Law School, University of Chicago, University of Helsinki, University of Toronto, and University of Utah Law School. I thank all the organizers and commentators, including Pär Cassel, Pamela Kyle Crossley,

Linda Feng, Joshua Fogel, Yi Evie Gu, Douglas Howland, Yonglin Jiang, Joan Judge, Michelle King, Jed Kroncke, John H. Langbein, Yue Meng, Peter Perdue, James Philips, Janet Poole, Johanna Ransmeier, Scott Relyea, Andre Schmidt, Guoquan Sen, Yanhong Wu, Yiching Wu, Lisa Yoneyama, and Yurou Zhong.

At various stages of this project and my career, I received a lot of feedback and encouragement from my friends at Columbia University, including Daniel Asen, Adam Clulow, Alexander Cook, Martin Fromm, Michael Hill, Collin Jaundrill, Jimin Kim, Jisoo Kim, Elizabeth Lacouture, Fabio Lanza, Georgia Mickey, Thomas Mullaney, Rebecca Nedostup, Alyssa Park, Tian Huan, Man Xu, and Lei Xue. I am also indebted to many other colleagues in Chinese studies, including William Alford, Gregory Blue, Timothy Brook, Thomas Buoye, Chen Hwei-syin, Chiu Pengsheng, Deng Jianpeng, He Zhihui, James Hevia, Jed Kroncke, Lai Junnan, Margaret Kuo, Geoffrey MacCormack, Michael Ng, Billy So, Matthew Sommer, Su Yigong, Janet Theiss, Wang Zhiqiang, Pierre-Étienne Will, Robin Yates, You Chenjun, and Taisu Zhang for sharing their work or wisdom, which have helped me bring this project to its completion. I am thankful especially to Jérôme Bourgon for allowing me to access his collection of visual material and use three images as illustrations in this book.

This book has been greatly improved by the stimulating conversations I had with scholars in the fields of international law, comparative legal history, South Asian studies, new imperial history, or sociolegal studies. I thank particularly Antony Anghie, Lauren Benton, Ritu Birla, Lindsay Farmer, Karen Knop, Martti Koskenniemi, Liliana Obregón, Bruce Smith, Mariana Valverde, and James Q. Whitman.

I started full-time teaching at the University of Toronto, where many colleagues have provided an unusually supportive environment over the past five years. I would like to particularly thank department chairs Daniel Bender, William Bowen, and Madhavi Kale for providing the financial support and mentorship that have been crucial to my research projects and career development. It has also been a great pleasure to work with a number of other scholars, including Katherine Blouin, Michael Gervers, Donna Gabaccia, Franca Iacovetta, Russel Kazal, Hui Kian Kwee, Tong Lam, Jeffry Pilcher, Bhavani Raman, Stephen Rockel, Natalie Rothman, Jayeeta Sharma, and Nhung Tuyet Tran.

Research for this book was conducted with the help of many people at libraries and archives in Beijing, London, Taibei, and elsewhere, particularly those at the Academia Sinica, Beijing University, Chinese Academy of Social Sciences, Columbia University (especially Charlene Chou, Wang Chengzhi, and Zhang Rongxiang), Harvard University, Leeds University, University of Illinois, and University of Toronto (especially Lucy Gan and Stephen Qiao). My research assistants, Erik Chen, Elizabeth Cinco, Jackson Guo, Weiting Guo, Surayya Khan, Peng Chuhang, Sana Samdani, Yu Wang, and Shirley Xie, provided much-needed help for this project.

An earlier version of some parts of chapter 1 was published as "Law, Empire, and Historiography of Sino-Western Relations: A Case Study of the Lady Hughes Controversy," *Law and History Review* 27, no. 1 (2009): 1–53; a few passages in the introduction and chapter 5 appeared in my article "Universalism and Equal Sovereignty as Contested Myths of International Law in the Sino-Western Encounter," *Journal of the History of International Law* 13, no. 1 (2011), 75–116; and a few paragraphs in chapter 4 were included in a chapter in *The Scaffold of Sovereignty: A Global Interdisciplinary Approach*, edited by Zvi Ben-Dor Benite, Stefanos Geroulanos, and Nichole Jerr (New York: Columbia University Press, forthcoming). I thank Cambridge University Press, Brill, and Columbia University Press for permission to use them here.

I am grateful to Columbia University, the University of Toronto, the Connaught Fund, and the Social Sciences and Humanities Research Council of Canada for funding my research. I also express heartfelt appreciation to the Schoff Fund of the University Seminars at Columbia University for a generous subvention grant for this book's publication. Material in this book was presented to the Early Modern China Seminar and the Modern China Seminar at Columbia University. The help of Ross Yelsey at the Weatherhead East Asian Institute at Columbia University and of Anne Routon, Whitney Johnson, and Leslie Kriesel at Columbia University Press have made the production process of this book a wonderful experience. Frank Chow's feedback has immensely improved the clarity of arguments in this book, and copyeditor Mike Ashby's extraordinary patience and attention to detail have helped me avoid embarrassing errors or omissions. I appreciate all their work for making the book better than it was.

I would never have had the opportunity to become a historian without the support of my parents, Zhang Zhirong and Liu Zuojin, and other family members and friends back in my hometown. Finally, this book would certainly not have been possible without all the love, patience, and sacrifice of my wife, Ruoyun Bai, and our two sons, Anthony and Aaron Chen. A scholar of Chinese media and culture at the University of Toronto, Ruoyun has not only done everything that I could have expected from the most loving wife but has also been my most valued, intellectual interlocutor and honest critic.

CHINESE LAW
IN IMPERIAL
EYES

INTRODUCTION

Toward the end of 2009, a diplomatic controversy erupted between China and Britain. A fifty-three-year-old Pakistani Briton named Akmal Shaikh was executed for smuggling four kilograms of heroin into northwestern China in 2007. The Chinese courts had rejected British requests for clemency or medical assessment of the alleged mental disorder of the accused (who had previously been convicted by a British law court for a different offense). British Prime Minister Gordon Brown and his colleagues in foreign affairs condemned the Chinese execution "in the strongest terms" as an act unacceptable "by any standards of human rights" in the twenty-first century. British media denounced it as a "barbaric act" and "medieval rough justice" of a country "still stuck in the dark ages." The perceived lack of political liberalization and rule of law in general were cited to show that a Westerner could not expect a fair trial in China and did not deserve death in the Chinese form, regardless of the crime. Stressing that the seized heroin could kill 26,000 individuals and damage numerous families, the Chinese government insisted that the defendant's rights had been properly respected and that foreigners should not interfere with its "judicial sovereignty" and independence. Many foreign and Chinese commentators noted the uncanny similarities between the dispute of 2009 and the First Opium War in 1839–1842 in their primary concerns: a contraband drug, Chinese law and sovereignty, sentiments about humanity and justice, perceived cultural differences, and international power politics.[1] Few realized that this was the first Chinese execution of a

European in more than half a century, and of a British national under Chinese law since the *Lady Hughes* case of 1784, in which a British sailor was executed for killing two local Chinese in Guangzhou (Canton).[2] More intriguingly, the Chinese and British rhetorical strategies and the underlying issues in 2009 can be traced back to the *Lady Hughes* and other Sino-Western legal disputes in the eighteenth century. Despite the lapse of two centuries separating the two cases and the *vastly different* circumstances underlying them, the dominant narrative seems not to have changed a bit: that of an innocent foreigner falling victim to Chinese despotism or barbarity. Eighteenth-century images of Chinese law have survived, and so has the power of a peculiar case to evoke a discursive chain regarding law, national sovereignty, cultural identity, and international relations.

This book investigates how such images of China or Chinese law were created and how and why they acquired extraordinary and lasting power in the context of Sino-Western encounters from approximately the 1740s through the 1840s. By studying a series of pivotal moments of Sino-Western contact and conflict during this period that culminated in the famous First Opium War, I examine the *formation and transformation* of Western knowledge and perception of Chinese law and society over time. I argue that the resulting Western discourse of China and Chinese law was not only central to many of the disputes that structured the trajectory of modern Sino-Western relations but also a key site at which the cultural and national boundaries were constructed or negotiated.

Several excellent studies have dealt with some of the related issues or sources recently; drawing on their insights, this book examines a different set of questions from substantially different perspectives.[3] First of all, it concentrates on the *century-long* period of Sino-Western, especially Sino-British, encounters before 1842, a formative century that has profoundly shaped modern Sino-Western relations but has received inadequate attention among scholars of China since the 1930s.[4] Second, instead of studying this period as a diplomatic, intellectual, or literary history, this book provides an integrative, critical analysis of the *archival, popular, intellectual, and political* dimensions of the Sino-Western encounter to historicize the processes of knowledge production and transcultural boundary making in the age of empire. A central concern of the study is to find out whether such a multidimensional interdisciplinary study may shed new light on the history of

Sino-Western contact or other transimperial encounters. This book makes no pretension of being a comprehensive history of this period. Instead, using a combination of case studies and selected themes and events to slice through history temporally and spatially, it hopes to *illustrate* the complex power dynamics in the contact zones of empire that have created some of the still influential ideas of Sino-Western difference, identities, and modernities at a time when these ideas remained seriously underdeveloped, contradictory, or contested.

This book builds on critical scholarship in multiple disciplines to explore the intersection of the discourse of Chinese law and society, Euro-American modern transformation, and imperial ideology and practice. In the next few sections, I situate this study within the recent literature on Chinese law and Sino-Western relations, and then explain several key concepts and analytical approaches used in this book. I also connect this study with the broader historiography of modern imperialism, liberalism, and international law. The last section introduces some of the arguments of the succeeding chapters of this book.

CHINESE LAW AND SINO-WESTERN RELATIONS IN RECENT SCHOLARSHIP

For over two centuries, the dominant Western discourse about the law of imperial China was informed by a set of interrelated and often *contradictory* characterizations. The internal fissures of this discourse are analyzed in detail in the next few chapters, but it may be useful to highlight some of its most popular tropes here. On the one hand, Chinese society was said to be governed by the terror and caprice of a despotic ruler without any rational or fundamental law. This eighteenth-century view then led subsequent intellectuals to argue that late imperial Chinese judges decided cases according to Confucian moral precepts and personal sentiments rather than written law. On the other hand, China was portrayed as a country where all human actions were controlled by meticulous, overrationalized laws and regulations, with no room for the development of individuality or historical self-consciousness. As a result, Chinese law, if there was any at all, was dismissed as inherently incapable of protecting property, rights, and freedom or promoting justice, rule of law, and societal progress. The implications of these views were not limited to the Chinese legal system. Rather, they were frequently cited as conclusive or self-sufficient proof about the presumably stagnant, arbitrary, irrational, or backward nature of the entirety of Chinese civilization. As such, China's judicial institutions and practices rendered China an illegitimate regime pursuant to the liberal theories of civilization and modernity derived from the eighteenth-century European Enlightenment. This has often led to the denial of China as one of the sovereign subjects of the modern world and international law from the eighteenth through the twentieth centuries.[5]

Over the past three decades, a rapidly growing body of research on Chinese legal tradition should have provided enough evidence to lay to rest such stereotypes of Chinese law and society. In contrast with the conventional wisdom, these recent studies have shown that the formal judicial system in serious cases was generally regulated by codified laws and procedures; that legal institutions, knowledge, and instruments (such as "contracts") were widely utilized by ordinary people to serve their interests in everyday life; and that the state-society relationship, within and outside the formal legal system, was far more complex and dynamic than assumed by the earlier depiction of late imperial China as an unchanging Confucian society or one of Oriental despotism.[6]

Showing Chinese law and society to be different from the earlier Western representations can be very useful but in itself is insufficient to undo the latter's legacy if we want to study Chinese law or history on its own terms. For one thing, many of the key legal concepts and categories used in the recent revisionist scholarship, such as "civil law," "criminal law," or "contract law," are borrowed from Western legal systems and may be accompanied by normative assumptions that unwittingly perpetuate nineteenth-century discourses of cultural hierarchy or Chinese backwardness.[7] At the same time, to dismiss the traditional Western views of Chinese law and society as simply Orientalist stereotypes without examining their actual formation and operation is to commit the same kind of essentialism as earlier Orientalists did in dehistoricizing and desocializing the objects of inquiry and discourse from their historical specificities. Moreover, as Shu-mei Shih, Arif Dirlik, Ruth Rogaski, and Teemu Ruskola have recently pointed out, Chinese reformers and intellectuals themselves have often practiced self-Orientalism in their efforts to reform Chinese literature, politics, society, and law over the past century.[8] In the meantime, given that contemporary China's law and government still appear so different from what are presumed to be the *modern* legal and political systems in the West, it is little wonder that many of the eighteenth- or nineteenth-century Western representations of China have persisted in one form or another. For instance, social scientists and political pundits still frequently describe China as a "lawless" country ruled by Communist authoritarianism and plagued with transgressions of international laws and conventions concerning human rights, intellectual property, international trade, cyberspace, and maritime borders.[9] Needless to say, this book is not to deny or gloss over the issues of political oppression, brutal state violence, corruption, social inequality, or ineffective law enforcement in past or present China. However, the popular tendency to turn specific institutional or socioeconomic problems into grounds for claiming transhistorical Sino-Western dichotomies or hierarchies requires more careful analysis and rethinking.

As noted earlier, I study the modern Western representations of Chinese law and society as *both produced by and productive of* the historical processes and forces that shaped the Sino-Western encounter during the eighteenth and nineteenth centuries. It is therefore important to explain how this book is related to the prior scholarship on early modern Sino-Western relations. Influenced by earlier narratives, pioneering historians such as Hosea Morse (1855–1934), Earl Pritchard (1907–1995), and John Fairbank (1907–1991) established a framework for twentieth-century Western scholarship on China, dominant almost until the early 1990s, by interpreting the Sino-Western conflicts in the previous two or three centuries as inevitable clashes of two incommensurable civilizations.[10] As Fairbank famously put it, events such as the 1784 *Lady Hughes* case, the Macartney Embassy of 1793 to China, and the First Opium War were ultimately attributable to the inability of late imperial China—stuck in its Confucian and Sinocentric tradition and tributary system—to effectively respond to the "civilizing" impact of modern (Western) capitalism, diplomacy, culture, technology, and so on.[11] Over the past few decades, this framework has come under severe criticism, although its influence remains strong among some academics and hardly diminished among the general public. In refuting the

Euro-Americentric assumptions of this earlier theory, historians such as Paul Cohen and William Rowe have adopted the "China-centered" approach to study the vitality and rationality of Chinese indigenous institutions, actors, and socioeconomic practices in explaining modern Chinese history.[12] More recently, James Hevia has shown the Macartney Embassy to be not "an encounter between civilizations or cultures, but as one between two imperial formations," with competing ideologies, interests, and ambitions.[13] In his monumental study of the Second Opium War in 1856–1860, John Wong likewise criticized the tendency to use such a "vague general concept" as cultural clash instead of the specific economic interests, personalities, domestic politics, and diplomacy of imperialism to account for such an event.[14] Lydia Liu's more recent analysis of the semiotics and politics of translation in nineteenth-century Sino-British relations led her to conclude unequivocally, "Civilizations do not clash, but empires do."[15] In other words, it was *historically specific* social, ideological, political, and economic factors, rather than the inevitable clash of supposedly incompatible civilizations, that drove competing empires into military conflicts such as the two Opium Wars.

In the meantime, many historians in post-1949 China, influenced by Marxism or nationalism, tended to reduce Sino-Western relations during this period to little more than aggression toward and exploitation of a pre-industrial "feudal" society by foreign imperialism and capitalism.[16] Since the start of the reform and opening policy in 1978, some Chinese historians have echoed Fairbank's thesis in seeing the nineteenth-century Sino-Western conflicts as the results of cultural misunderstanding while blaming the ruling elites' "backward" mentality and policies in the Qing dynasty (1644–1911) for China's "belated modernization."[17] Much of the recent Chinese scholarship on this topic is still influenced to varying degrees by a teleological notion of history that privileges the modern nation or party state in recasting the last 170 years or so as a progressive trajectory of national humiliation, awakening, revolution, and revival.[18] As a result, alternative narratives of China's historical experience with modernity or encounters with foreign powers have often been marginalized or repressed through what Prasenjit Duara has called the practice of "bifurcation" of nationalist historiography.[19]

CONTACT ZONES, BOUNDARY MAKING, AND LEGAL ORIENTALISM REVISITED

The revisionist scholarship on the clash of empires provides a much-needed antidote to the reductive culturalist interpretations of the Sino-Western conflicts informed by the clash-of-civilizations thesis in traditional historiography. What has not yet received enough attention is the question of *why and how* instances of the clash of empires came to be understood as examples of the clash of civilizations in the context of Sino-Western relations. One of my goals is to examine this question in order to better understand the complicated and changing relationship between imperial and colonial archives and modern historiography of Sino-Western conflicts, including the *Lady Hughes* case and the Opium Wars. In the meantime, I believe it also worth noting that the history of the Sino-Western encounter is not simply a history of clashes. Conflicts and collisions documented in prior scholarship coexisted with negotiations, compromises, and transcultural engagements between the Chinese and their Western counterparts during the eighteenth and nineteenth centuries.[20] It is equally problematic to view the Sino-Western relationship during this period as *dominated* by the Western empires just because China was later reduced to a "semicolony" after the Opium Wars. This retrospective projection of Western domination to the pre-1840 period has obscured the Western empires' long struggle for recognition and security in China before and, to a lesser extent, after 1840.

The tendency to focus on the "intractable conflict" between cultures and the presumption of Western domination is also reflected in Mary Louise Pratt's famous conceptualization of the imperial or colonial "contact zones" in the eighteenth and nineteenth centuries. In her pathbreaking study *Imperial Eyes: Travel Writing and Transculturation*, Pratt defines "contact zones" as "social spaces where disparate cultures meet, clash, and grapple with each other, often in highly asymmetrical relations of domination and subordination—like colonialism, slavery, or their aftermaths as they are lived out across the globe today."[21] As a key feature of the contact zone, "transculturation" has been used by Pratt and other scholars to highlight the fact that colonized people creatively appropriated elements of the metropolitan culture to develop a hybrid or new culture rather than just being passively assimilated or acculturated into the dominant culture.[22] Cultural difference and Western domination are often the points of departure for their analysis of the imperial contact zone or transculturation, not the subjects of their inquiry.

When applied to the Sino-Western encounter, nevertheless, their useful analysis of the contact zones and transculturation requires significant modification. First of all, I argue that the widely claimed clash of civilizations or cultural incommensurability between China and the Western countries must be examined as a historical phenomenon and discursive construct rather than taken for granted. As Natalie Rothman and other historians have recently shown, cultural difference "is not a pregiven fact but part of an ongoing process of boundary maintenance that unfolds in specific sites and institutions" through the mediation and articulation of cultural brokers or "transimperial subjects" in the contact zones.[23] Part of this book explores how Sino-Western cultural boundaries were asserted and negotiated through the discourses of law, justice, sentiment, and sovereignty. Second, it is also important to bear in mind that the Chinese government maintained a dominant position in deciding the terms of the Sino-Western economic, cultural, and political relationships for almost three centuries before the First Opium War. In consequence, the British and other Westerners in China often felt vulnerable or humiliated for much of that period. This sense of insecurity and insult, in conjunction with their imperial ambitions and interests, constantly shaped their routine interactions in the Sino-Western contact zones. Finally, as chapter 3 shows, the focus on conflicts and Western domination has missed another sort of transculturation in the Sino-Western contact zones, in which the presumably dominant European cultures actually appropriated various ideas from China, including ideas of Chinese legal and political institutions, *as exemplary models or cautionary foils*, for transforming or "modernizing" their own societies. Other scholars have also shown the considerable influence of the Sino-Western contact on European science and technology, philosophy, arts, literature, and other sociocultural aspects in the seventeenth through the nineteenth centuries.[24] In this sense, what Pratt and others have called transculturation should be understood as a two-way process. It is important to recognize this in order to challenge the Eurocentric narrative of global modernity.

Understood this way, this modified concept of contact zones provides us with a valuable analytical perspective for reassessing the nature and effects of the historical formation, transformation, and operation of modern Western knowledge of Chinese law and society. In many ways, such knowledge production constituted "Orientalism" for Edward Said, or what Teemu Ruskola has more recently called "legal Orientalism." Said's enormous contribution to postcolonial critiques of empire and cultural imperialism has been well documented. Like numerous other studies over the past four decades, this book is considerably indebted to his insights on how imperial cultures or imperial structures of feeling were formed and mobilized in legitimating or sustaining colonial power. These issues are analyzed in this book as well. Besides the fact that China rarely figures in his analysis due to his different research focuses, Said's theorization of Orientalism as an internally coherent and an externally totalizing or hegemonic discourse of the Western will to dominate requires reconsideration in the Sino-Western context.[25] Said did place more emphasis on the agency of non-Western societies in his later work, although he remained convinced that "there was little domestic resistance to these [Western] empires" and that "there was virtually unanimity [in the West] that subject races should be ruled."[26] The internal consistency and uniformity thus ascribed to Western imperial cultures during this period may have the unintended effects of reinforcing the imperial powers' otherwise contested or precarious claim to legitimacy and ideological hegemony. As I have explained earlier, the European discourse of China or Chinese law under study here developed before the structure of European domination over China was formed and consolidated, this discourse was internally fractured and incoherent, and the British or other Euro-Americans often lacked "a consolidated vision" among themselves about China or Chinese law, as will be seen in the debates over the First Opium War.[27] This is not to downplay the enormous discursive power and oppressive effects of Orientalism in shaping Western imperial ideologies and practices in relation to China and other countries in the past few centuries. Rather, by not "homogeniz[ing] a power relationship whose limitations and contingencies need to be examined" in a specific historical context, such as the Sino-Western encounter before 1840, we may place ourselves in a better position to interrogate the history and legacy of various imperial formations.[28]

Instead of treating Orientalism as something unilaterally imposed on the Orient by Western powers, Arif Dirlik has suggested that it can be more fruitfully understood as "the product of an unfolding relationship" between Western and non-Western peoples in the contact zones. This unfolding relationship presumes participation of non-Western actors, while the presence of contact zones "implies a distance, a distance from the society of the Self, as well as of the Other," thus decentering the production of Orientalism from the total control of the dominant imperial powers. For Dirlik and other scholars, attending to the shifting sites of knowledge production and to the shifting balance of power (witness the recent rise of China and India in relation to the Western countries) is crucial for grasping the historical role and operation of Orientalism in the past and present.[29] Drawing on Ruskola's recent analysis of American legal Orientalism mostly in the post-1842 period, my study focuses more on the dynamics, contingencies, and tensions of the unfolding Sino-Western relationship in various contact zones in the crucial century before 1842 through the lens of law, cultural boundaries, and transnational politics.

In this book, I use the term "contact zones" to refer to not just the physical and social spaces in which Chinese and Western persons and things meet but also the cultural and discursive spaces in which Chinese and Western ideas, languages, perceptions, and sentiments come to influence or constitute each other. It is by attending to these different interlocking contact zones that we may be able to develop a more accurate or nuanced picture of how the modern Sino-Western cultural or racial boundaries have been asserted, contested, or normalized, both intellectually and institutionally.[30]

It is important to stress the heterogeneity among the Western states and actors in their motives or policy strategies toward China even though they might all play a part in shaping the discourse of China or seek concessions from China for themselves. The terms "West(ern)," "Europe(an)," or "Euro-America(n)" are sometimes used in this book partly because the source materials themselves used such broad terms in relation to China or other non-Western countries. Otherwise, I use some of these terms *only in the geographical sense*—just as other scholars use "transatlantic"—to refer to the relevant countries located in those regions or continents such as France, Britain, Germany, Portugal, Italy, Spain, the Netherlands, and the United States, without implying their social, cultural, or political homogeneity. It is beyond the scope of this book to flesh out all the internal dynamics of both sides of the Sino-Western encounter, and chapters 1 and 5 can make only a limited attempt in that direction, but such pluralities and complexities must be kept in mind when studying any transcultural or transimperial contact. Needless to say, not all the findings concerning the Sino-British encounter are applicable to China's relationship with another country. However, given that Britain was the most powerful Western country and played the leading role in shaping Sino-Western relations during most of the time of the eighteenth and nineteenth centuries, even the chapters that focus more on the Sino-British relationship might prove useful for understanding the major events or general patterns of the Sino-Western encounter during this period.

To sum up, by historicizing the transnational representations of Chinese law and society, this book studies the construction of cultural difference and identity as an *unfolding process of boundary making* in the Sino-Western contact zones, with a shifting balance of power. In this book, I understand identity and subjectivity not as givens but as constituted through both discursive and material practices. Stuart Hall's analysis of these two concepts is particularly pertinent for our discussion. For Hall, identity is "the meeting point" between the practices that interpellate us or speak to us "as the social subjects of particular discourses" and "the processes which produce subjectivities [and] which construct us as subjects" that can be spoken to. "Identities are thus points of temporary attachment to the subject positions which discursive practices construct for us."[31] A great deal of postcolonial scholarship has shown that Orientalism as a discourse of power and cultural hierarchy helped turn the West or Occident into the "sovereign subject" that claimed authority, power, and legitimacy, and the Orient into its nonspeaking "subaltern" Other.[32] If that were the case, our critical reexamination of the Western discourse of China or Chinese law would contribute to what Michel Foucault has described as the task of "depriving the subject (or its substitute) of its role as the originator [of history and meaning] and of analyzing the subject as a variable and complex function of discourses" and historical contingencies.[33] Furthermore, the modern identities of Chinese and Western law and societies are mutually defined. As Ruskola has reminded us, Western law and Chinese law do not exist in isolation of each other but exist "in both Chinese and Western imagination and are intersubjectively linked," both forming "part of a global discourse of legal modernity."[34]

The story of the Western discourse of Chinese law in the eighteenth and nineteenth centuries is also part of the larger history of empire and international law that transitioned from doctrinal recognition of territorial sovereignty to Western practice of extraterritoriality in China and other countries in East and Southeast Asia by treatises and gunboat diplomacy after the First Opium War. Hence, it is worth noting what we mean by "sovereignty" in this study. Sovereignty is one of the most crucial, ambiguous, and contested concepts in modern political theories. With no need to enter that debate here, I use the term "sovereignty" in this book, on the one hand, to simply refer to the supreme authority of an independent state or imperial formation to rule or administer matters within the geographical boundaries, however loosely defined, under its effective control. In principle, this would include the power to decide how *and* whether to make and enforce domestic law, enter international treaties, and make war and peace with other states. On the other hand, I also understand sovereignty more broadly as a social, cultural, or legal construct that claims higher authority for a state or imperial formation over another state or political community through practices or discourses of language, law, ritual, religion, cultural imperialism, and so on.[35] More specifically, the Qing conception of sovereignty was complicated by the Manchu rulers' remarkable adeptness in appropriating and appealing to a variety of religious, ethnic, and cultural traditions to consolidate their rule over a vast multiethnic colonial empire and extend their influence over China's "tributary" states.[36] James Hevia has suggested that the Qing rulers developed a system of "interdomainal sovereignty" to incorporate the "lesser lords" of the borderland ethnic regimes, such as the Mongols and Tibetans, and of other smaller "tributary" states into a hierarchical imperial power structure headed by the Manchu emperors. Pär Cassel has further argued that the Qing government practiced "legal pluralism" in adapting its judicial system to the governance of its different ethnic groups and frontier situations.[37] As this book also shows, there were substantial differences and similarities in the sovereign thinking and practices of the Qing, British, and other Western colonial empires during this period under study, and the differences do not warrant an a priori conclusion that the Qing practices were antithetical to "modern diplomacy" and thus caused the Sino-Western conflicts under study in this book. Moreover, the Qing authorities sometimes exercised or claimed sovereignty without necessarily resorting to what might be considered as indispensable prerogatives of sovereignty in the West, such as *strict enforcement* of its law against all foreign offenders within its territory. It is also important to keep in mind the significant tensions between the Qing central government and local officials in terms of what they deemed necessary or effective in safeguarding Qing sovereignty and interests against the foreigners. What were true with the Qing policies concerning other frontiers or political communities might not be true with southern China or with the Sino-British or Sino-Western relationship.[38]

CENTRALITY OF LAW TO MODERN COLONIALISM AND IMPERIAL IDEOLOGY

So why law? Law (including international law) played a crucial role in shaping the ideologies and practices of modern Western empires and in displacing many moral questions that necessarily arose in the course of imperial expansion. Legal anthropologist Martin Chanock's statement that "[t]he law was the cutting edge of [European] colonialism, an instrument of the power of an alien state and part of the process of coercion" captures only part of law's significance in modern world history from the fifteenth century onward.[39] Although the early modern European empires differed from one another in many ways and changed considerably over time and space, law remained central to imperial projects. Together with the discourses of Christianity and civilization, law was both a cornerstone of colonial empires such as Portugal, England (later Britain), France, and the Netherlands— regulating imperial projects and interstate relationships—and a key source of their legitimation over the next few centuries. From the beginning, law helped alleviate the classical concerns about the corrupting effects of imperial expansion and the injustice of dispossessing others.[40] Founders of the Portuguese and Spanish empires turned to the universal jurisdiction of God and the Roman papacy as the basis of their legal claims to the non-European "New World."[41] Thus, in 1455 Pope Nicholas V (r. 1447–1455) granted the king of Portugal and his heirs an exclusive right to "invade, search out, capture, vanquish, and subdue all Saracens and pagans whatsoever, and other enemies of Christ wheresoever placed," and to enslave them and appropriate their dominions and possessions. Besides Africa, the Indies, which were understood to include China and the Spice Islands, were frequently mentioned in such papal bulls or edicts.[42] After Spain sponsored Christopher Columbus's famous "discovery" of America in 1492, another papal bull and its derivative treaty divided the non-Christian world between Spain and Portugal in 1494.[43]

As shown by Anthony Pagden, Robert Williams, and other historians of empire, European powers such as France, England, and the Netherlands might compete fiercely with the Iberian empires, but they frequently invoked similar doctrines of the universality of Christian civilization to justify their colonial ventures in the West and East Indies.[44] For instance, the letters patent of King Henry VII of England (r. 1485–1509) for John Cabot's voyage to North America in 1496 adopted the language of the papal bull of 1455 noted above.[45] These presumptions also shaped the beginning of European colonial ventures in Asia after the 1520s. Like the English (1600) and Dutch (1602) East India Companies, the French East India Company of 1664 was authorized by its royal charter to wage war and negotiate treaties with Asian states and to take the property, dominion, and other sovereign rights in all places that it conquered, purchased, or found "deserted or possessed only of Barbarians."[46] Thus, the discourse of law often served as the primary justification for overseas expansion to promote universal civilization and humanity (through commerce and evangelism), even as it simultaneously excluded other societies from this expanding European community or Christian empire (*imperium Christianum*).[47]

Scandals of colonial corruption and illegality and intra-European conflicts also led European jurists like Spanish theologian Francisco de Vitoria (also given as Victoria) (ca. 1483–1546) and Dutch diplomat Hugo Grotius (1583–1645) to develop the law of nations (jus gentium) through a theory of increasingly secularized natural law. While acknowledging the capacity of Amerindians for *universal* human reason and sovereignty, Vitoria in the 1530s defended the Spanish legal title to the American colonies on the grounds that Spain had natural-law rights to free trade, travel, and preaching of Christianity and therefore to colonize the "hostile" natives under the doctrine of just war (*bellum justum*) or to rescue the natives from rulers who were tyrannical or condoned cannibalism.[48] About eighty years later, Grotius echoed Vitoria's natural-law doctrines in defending the right of the Dutch Republic to the maritime trade of the East Indies against the Iberian monopoly. He contended that the Asian countries' sovereign rights could not be taken away by the Iberians according to the doctrine of discovery or papal grants and that those countries were free to trade or contract with the Dutch.[49] To protect the growing Dutch interests in America and Asia, however, Grotius also agreed that Christian states could wage a just war to punish native tyrants, cannibals, pirates, and those who mistreated their parents or foreign settlers.[50] These legal and ideological innovations could not resolve the differences and conflicts even among the European powers themselves. During the seventeenth and eighteenth centuries, the French, Dutch, British, and Iberians deployed a host of frequently contradictory arguments for their competing claims to colonial possessions and privileges, on the basis of discovery of *res nullius* (nobody's property), purchase, concession, conquest by just war, or prescription (continuous usage creating property rights or even legal titles).[51]

The so-called first European empires (1490s–1830s), which focused more on evangelization or territorial conquest and settlements, laid the ideological foundation for the second European empires in Asia and Africa (1730s–1990s), which tended to prioritize commerce and indirect rule, and law remained crucial for displacing or redefining the "tensions of empire" in the latter phase of European expansion.[52] Many Enlightenment thinkers— such as Benjamin Constant (1767–1830), Denis Diderot (1713–1784), Marquis de Condorcet (1743–1794), and David Hume (1711–1776)—wrestled with the contradiction between the ideals of universal justice, liberty, and progress and the exclusionary practices of slavery or colonialism.[53] Just as the discourses of liberalism, sentimentalism, civilization, and modernity would evolve over time to address some of these ideological or geopolitical changes, theorists of the law of nations, which became better known as international law in the nineteenth century, invented new doctrines of sovereignty, just war, and international relations to provide a much-needed legal order or legal fiction for a conflict-ridden colonial world.[54] I explore these issues in the last three chapters of this book. Where colonial control was not yet feasible in an Asian or African country such as China, Japan, Vietnam (Annam) or Thailand (Siam), the Euro-Americans often sought legal immunity from local jurisdiction, in addition to the privileges of free trade or preaching. For many British explorers, who had come to see their expanding empire as "Protestant, commercial, maritime and free" by the 1730s,[55] having access to their own legal system and protection not only provided the best protection of their rights to liberty and free trade but was also part of their national or cultural identity. Besides the impeachment of Governor-General Warren Hastings for corruption and maladministration of British India in the 1780s to 1790s, the widely reported trials of the British governor of Trinidad in 1806 and of Jamaica in 1866 testified to the continued emphasis on the legality and legitimacy of the imperial project even as these instances betrayed the huge gap between the metropolitan ideals of liberty and rule of law and the colonial practice of despotic rule and terror.[56] Contrary to the once popular assumption that Western imperialism or colonialism cared little about legality or morality, the discourse of law frequently served to provide both legal and moral defenses of empire, as we shall see in chapters 1 and 5.

Besides providing a semblance of ideological coherence and moral legitimacy for the imperial enterprise, law was also essential for classifying and maintaining the desired cultural, social, or racial boundaries. As noted earlier, Europe's overseas expansion was legally predicated on certain notions of hierarchy between Christian Europeans and non-Europeans, who were considered "infidels," "barbarians," or "outlaws of humanity."[57] This logic of simultaneous inclusion and exclusion later also informed the modern Western liberal theories about "citizenship, sovereignty and [political] participation" in metropole and colony alike in the nineteenth and twentieth centuries.[58] Postcolonial scholars and new imperial historians remind us that "questions of difference, its ascription and maintenance among colonizers as well as colonized, were also central to colonial projects and imperial visions."[59] This desire to maintain boundaries while promoting ideas of universal liberty and natural rights generated what Frederick Cooper and Ann Stoler have called "a most basic tension of empire."[60] In this sense, law helped alleviate some tensions of empire even as it was creating new ones. This book will show that the Western discourse of Chinese law was instrumental in reinforcing the Sino-Western or Sino-British dichotomy and provided the much-needed grounds for Western extraterritoriality and for making China an exception to international law in the nineteenth century. It was for these reasons that the discourse of law, including Chinese and international law, acquired such cultural and political force and strategic importance in the period under study. In this sense, the chapters that follow form a case study of *the imperial formation of law and the legal formation of empire.*

THE PRECARIOUS LEGAL STATUS OF WESTERNERS
IN SOUTHERN CHINA FROM 1520 TO 1840

If the Europeans depended on papal grants, discovery, conquest, or the law of nations to justify their colonial expansion or settlement overseas after the 1490s, China presented a very different kind of challenge. Instead of enjoying free access to its markets and resources, or even imposing their own terms upon the Chinese, the Europeans remained in a precarious and reportedly undignified situation for the next few centuries. Europeans arrived in China soon after Vasco da Gama (ca. 1460–1524) rounded the Cape of Good Hope and reached India in 1498. As early as 1508, King Manuel of Portugal sent Diogo Lopes de Sequeira (1465–1530), the future viceroy of the Estado da India, to Malacca to learn about Chinese customs, products, military, and territory.[61] Initially the Iberians approached China with the same conquistador mentality that they had brought to the New World, claiming as the Portuguese did in 1514 that they had "discovered China" (*discoperto la Cina*), a large empire with the world's greatest wealth and "white" people just like the Europeans. Unlike in other places where they had landed, however, they found that the Chinese government had strict laws and policies to guard against foreign incursion even though the people reportedly desired peace and friendship with the European visitors.[62] For nearly three centuries, despite various proposals and attempts to subdue or open China by force, the Europeans (and the Americans after 1784) never managed to obtain the same kind of territorial or legal concessions from China that they enjoyed elsewhere.[63] The Portuguese did obtain a local official's consent to erect a temporary shelter at Macao in the mid-1550s and then expanded it into a fortified settlement with a population of several thousand Portuguese, Malaccans, Indians, Africans, and Chinese by 1585, allegedly governed by the laws and jurisdiction of Portugal without subordination to the Chinese.[64] However, they continued to pay 500 taels of silver for the land lease every year until after the First Opium War. They and other Europeans were aware that the Chinese never formally relinquished sovereignty or jurisdiction over Macao until the end of the nineteenth century.[65] The Dutch, Spanish, and English who arrived in the sixteenth and early seventeenth centuries also failed to significantly improve their legal status in China.[66]

Western access to China for missionary purposes or lucrative trade thus hinged largely on the goodwill and policy considerations of the Chinese authorities at the central and local levels. Foreign policies of the late Ming dynasty (1368–1644) and of the Qing dynasty (established by the Manchus in 1644) were shaped by a combination of economic, cultural, and political considerations, including concerns about imperial sovereignty and security. From the 1560s through the 1610s, a series of memorials from Guangdong provincial officials warned the Ming emperors that the illicitly established Portuguese settlement in Macao would cause serious trouble in the future as the foreign residents became more numerous and defiant every day, posing a threat to China's territory and governance.[67] By the 1610s, however, it had become practically difficult and ideologically inconsistent with the policy of pacification and compassion toward foreigners—which can be called the *huairou* doctrine—to forcibly demolish the Macao settlement. Local officials who emphasized the economic benefits of foreign trade then prevailed in the policy debate, provided that the Westerners were placed under closer surveillance.[68] From the 1610s to the 1640s, the Ming government promulgated a series of laws and regulations controlling the size and conduct of the foreign population in Macao and restricting their contact with the local people and officials.[69] These measures conceptually informed the basic regulatory framework regarding the Western sojourners in the next two centuries.

After conquering all of Ming China, the Qing government decided to lift the legal ban on maritime trade in 1685 to improve "the national economy and welfare of the country" (*guoji minsheng*), but it also reinstated the Ming policy that all foreigners must leave Guangzhou after each trading season to prevent their entrenchment.[70] Although the Kangxi emperor (r. 1661–1722) was relatively open-minded toward Western learning, science, and Christianity, he also echoed the late-Ming concerns about the potential Western threat when he stated in 1716, "I can foresee that China may be plagued by the [European] countries of the Western Ocean hundreds of years later" (*Haiwai ru xiyang deng guo, qianbai nian hou, Zhongguo kongshou qilei*).[71] During the first half of the eighteenth century, continuing reports of Europeans' illegal conduct and threat to the security of the empire's coastal frontiers (*haijiang*) led the Qing authorities to further restrict the physical and social space of the contact zone in southern China. For instance, in 1724, the Portuguese were ordered to register all their twenty-five ships and forbidden to add any ship or person to the existing population in Macao, which then had 3,567 Europeans and 2,524 Chinese. Except their supercargoes, all crew members of European ships at the anchorage of Huangpu (Whampoa) were forbidden to go ashore to wander around, and the foreign traders could deal directly only with officially licensed Chinese Hong merchants (*hangshang*) and interpreters (*tongshi*) for services and business. A set of eight regulations were issued in 1735 to prevent smuggling, evasion of customs duties, and illicit contact between local people and foreigners.[72] The Qing attitudes, as John Cranmer-Byng and John Wills have recently put it, were "those of watchfulness but general confidence in the ability to keep control," until a rapid growth in the number of foreigners led to more restrictive regulations in the 1750s.[73]

Fearing that another Macao would spring up in eastern China after the British kept sending ships to trade in Zhejiang province despite legal prohibitions and official remonstrations, the Qing court decided to confine all foreign trade to Guangzhou in 1757. Under this so-called Canton System, Westerners would stay in the foreign "factories" (leased houses for residence and storage) outside the city wall of Guangzhou to do business with the Hong merchants during the trading season, and movements of foreign goods and persons were under the surveillance of customs tollhouses, military forts, and a few thousand troops along the Zhu (Pearl) River down from Guangzhou.[74]

Besides such restraints, the foreigners in southern China were placed in a legally ambiguous and problematic situation. They were in principle subject to Chinese jurisdiction according to both Chinese law and the law of nations, and Euro-Americans were indeed executed for homicides in about half a dozen cases. In general, the Chinese government recognized the Western officials stationed in southern China only as representatives of their respective trading communities or firms (such as the different East India Companies)—thus giving them some power and responsibilities for controlling their subordinates or compatriots in China—but not as consuls or ambassadors with legal immunity and acting on behalf of *an equal sovereign state or government* with a formal diplomatic relationship with China.[75] Although the European officials had obtained substantial leeway when dealing with disputes and certain crimes among their people in China by the late eighteenth century through different tactics, their embarrassing

legal and political status made many of them feel that their lives and property were constantly exposed to the danger of the arbitrary and corrupt
power of the Chinese authorities. Even the Portuguese in Macao were not
saved from the frequent reprimands and threats of the Qing officials.[76]

This rather peculiar situation caused a lot of frustration and anxiety
among the Euro-Americans, who did not doubt the superiority of their
nations' power and culture and who had expected legal immunity from Oriental jurisdictions. Peter Marshall, a renowned British imperial historian,
has recently noted that even in the late eighteenth century, Britain's relationship with China was "a clear illustration of the limits on British political
or commercial influence in Asia outside India. The Chinese government
was not prepared to make political concessions. The East India Company
was only granted access to the single port of Canton, where the Company
had no exemption from strictly imposed regulations. Commercially, the
British were only of marginal importance to the Chinese."[77] To seek China's
formal recognition of their national character or sovereign status, and in
turn to obtain legal, diplomatic, and commercial privileges through international treaties or other means, was therefore one of the main goals of
the more ambitious Western empire builders. For instance, it was observed
around 1830 that Britain's valuable commercial and political relationship
with China had long rested on a most humiliating, transient, and "extremely
precarious" foundation.[78] For the British government, the First Opium War
was waged to place its relationship with China on "a solid and improved
footing" by demanding "redress for the past and security for the future."[79]
These institutional conditions of the Sino-Western contact zones affected
the resulting representations of Chinese law and society.

Before concluding this introduction, let me briefly outline the chapters
that follow. The next five chapters are organized around the interrelated
archival, intellectual, popular, and official domains of the production, circulation, consumption, and codification of the knowledge of Chinese law
mostly from the 1740s to the 1840s. By analyzing the official and alternative records of a series of Sino-Western legal disputes in southern China
from 1740 to 1839, particularly the most famous one, the *Lady Hughes* case
in 1784, chapter 1 explores how certain representations of Chinese law
and government came to acquire authority in Western imperial archives,
official narratives, and modern historiography. Some newly discovered or

rarely used archival sources in Chinese and European languages enable us to cross-examine the traditional accounts of these events. The findings challenge the still-dominant view of these disputes as proof of the presumed clash of legal cultures that led to the First Opium War and foreign extraterritoriality in 1843–1943. Furthermore, there is evidence of constant negotiation and accommodation between Chinese and foreign officials, whose personal interests and agendas often affected the immediate outcomes of these disputes to a greater extent than decisions of their central governments. Caught between the general principle of rule of law and territorial sovereignty and the peculiar desire for extraterritorial immunity from Chinese law, Euro-American agents had to tread a thin line between protecting their lives and liberty and risking the important China trade. The resulting sense of insult and precariousness became a driving force behind the increasingly disparaging portrayal of Chinese law and government in the eighteenth and nineteenth centuries. This chapter shows the techniques and processes by which the preferred narratives or authorized "primary discourses" about these past events became part of the imperial archives, and thus "primary sources" for students of the early modern Sino-Western encounter.

In chapter 2, I trace the politics and colonial origins of the emergence of modern comparative study of Chinese law by investigating the creation of authoritative knowledge and categories of Chinese law as a result of Sino-Western legal disputes. I focus on the historical context, process, and legacy of Sir George Thomas Staunton's translation of the Qing Code in 1800–1810. As the first direct English translation from any Chinese text, Staunton's work was retranslated into French, Italian, and Spanish and featured in numerous journals, influencing Western perception of Chinese law and culture for nearly two centuries. As a result of the translation, late imperial Chinese law, through the lens of Western categories and in the process of translingual practice, was represented as exclusively penal and fundamentally unchanging. This was how Chinese law was then classified by Sir Henry Maine when he pioneered the modern discipline of comparative law in the 1860s. These constructs would also influence Chinese legal reformers beginning in the late nineteenth century.

Frequently compared to Sir William Jones's Indological projects, this influential but underexamined translation became an epistemological breakthrough that supposedly deciphered the inscrutable China by reducing its dazzling complexities to a docile text. It also gave rise to modern British Sinology and comparative study of Chinese law. As an EIC employee in southern China, Staunton tried to mediate the widely assumed cultural dichotomy in order to produce authentic and useful knowledge to advance British commercial and political interests in the East. As the first modern British Sinologist, Staunton targeted his translation also at the Western metropolitan intellectuals, and his overall portrayal of China was influenced by contemporary Orientalism (especially Indology), earlier missionaries and Enlightenment thinkers, and his own political ambitions. The translator's multiple subject positions thus resulted in an ambivalent and multivocal text of Chinese law and culture, from which different readers could draw different conclusions even though they might be influenced more or less by the Orientalist discourse.

It is well known that Western institutions and ideas, often through Japan, have heavily influenced Chinese legal and political "modernization" since the late nineteenth century. Few scholars, however, have studied the role of Chinese law and government in shaping the Western discourse of modernity in the preceding century. This is the subject of chapter 3. Montesquieu and various other Enlightenment thinkers viewed China as a quintessential example of Oriental despotism ruled not by law, honor, or virtue but by fear. However, they considered various aspects of Chinese law as rational or humane, and thus an exception to their overall portrayal of Chinese polity and society. By separating the merits of Chinese law and other institutions from that despised Oriental civilization, these commentators and reformers could appropriate the former while maintaining their sense of cultural identity and boundary. This conflictual representation also reflected the tensions between the growing demand for reform of the much-maligned ancien régime institutions at home and the continuing need to defend imperial expansion as a civilizing mission by a "modern" empire. The strategic appropriation of Chinese ideas or experiences in Europe presented an interesting instance of metropolitan transculturation that was very different from that in many colonial contact zones, where the local people absorbed or appropriated European culture.

Although some British reformers cited Chinese law as a model for improving or "modernizing" their legal system in the early 1800s, their opponents attacked the proposed legal reforms for being inspired by despotic Chinese law. Codification was eventually rejected as being inconsistent with the British tradition of liberty and justice but was carried out in India and other colonies under the guise of the blessings of colonial modernity. The spread of these colonial legal codes later enabled Max Weber and his followers to include the uncodified British law as part of the world's modern legal systems, in contrast with the "primitive" laws in China and other Oriental countries. Chapter 3 examines these instances to historicize the internal ambiguities and contradictions of the Euro-Americentric grand narrative of legal modernity.

In chapter 4, I shift focus from the archival and intellectual terrains to the popular, sentimental aspects of the Sino-Western encounter. I analyze how Chinese law and subjectivity were redefined by the widespread visual and textual documentation of Chinese punishments and torture across Euro-America from the 1740s through the 1890s. The terrifying but fascinating spectacle of Chinese judicial violence has had a profound impact on the modern image of the Chinese people and civilization. This chapter argues that, among other things, this body of sentimental literature helped create an "emotional community" whose norms often served to train or discipline a viewer's reaction to, or representation of, Chinese judicial violence. Sentimental liberalism became an innovative technology of empire and subject formation as it helped redefine cultural boundaries and hierarchy.

The Enlightenment notion of sympathy as a defining marker of modern sensibility and humanity empowered foreign spectators to claim the mental capacity and moral authority to feel, articulate, and define the pain of Chinese sufferers despite long-avowed cultural and racial incommensurability. The graphic visuals seldom led to genuine empathy with the sufferers but often resulted in differential valuation of human lives to rationalize colonial violence and wars. The contradiction between the universalistic humanitarian ethos and the ethnocentric notion of a modern subject and civilization also came back to scandalize the foreign empire builders when they resorted to similar forms of punishment to terrorize the local people in China and elsewhere later in the century. By analyzing visual materials, mass media, travel accounts, and diplomatic correspondence, chapter 4 explores the sentimental modality of imperialism, showing how Chinese law, people, and sovereignty were reclassified by the sensational literature of Chinese punishments and cruelty.

Chapter 5 then revisits the First Opium War as a revealing example of how the earlier archival, intellectual, and popular representations of Chinese law and civilization came to influence official decision making in this landmark event that had global repercussions. Many historians have studied this war from the perspectives of opium economics, free-trade imperialism, or clash of cultures. Few, however, have paid serious attention to its legal dimension even though the issue of legality was often the first and foremost factor used by the Qing and British governments to rationalize their reactions to the opium trade or its destruction, respectively. Besides voluminous records of parliamentary debates and the mass media, I also examined the behind-the-scenes decision making of the British superintendent in China, leading British opium merchants and lobbyists, the Foreign Office, the cabinet, and both Liberal and Conservative parliamentarians. Although economic considerations were crucial to the decision making, a long-term goal of the British authorities was to protect British nationals and interests through a treaty-based relationship with China.

The public debates in Britain showed that the entire nation and empire had been responsible for encouraging, or benefiting from, this admittedly illegal and immoral drug. This made it imperative for opium merchants, free traders, and their allies in Parliament and in the government to maintain that the despotic, irrational, corrupt, and cruel nature of the Chinese legal system and government effectively made their law enforcement against opium smuggling illegitimate under international law. At the same time, my analysis of the intense British domestic debates also draws attention to the widespread criticism of the opium trade and the First Opium War among people of all walks of life in Britain. The century-old discourse of Sino-Western incommensurability was not as hegemonic as it would become after the two Opium Wars. Britain's military victory and the subsequent treaties established *by force* extraterritoriality and the credibility of earlier narratives of Chinese law and society as premodern or uncivilized. Contrary to what Samuel Huntington and others have argued, therefore, this book shows that it was the "battle lines" of empires that produced the "fault lines between civilizations," not the other way around.[80]

1

IMPERIAL ARCHIVES AND HISTORIOGRAPHY OF WESTERN EXTRATERRITORIALITY IN CHINA

November 24, 1784, looked like another busy day of the trading season at Guangzhou. In the late eighteenth century, thirty or so large ships under British, French, Danish, Dutch, Spanish, Portuguese, or Swedish flags sailed off every year with Chinese goods for eager buyers in places like India, Europe, and America. Besides tea, silk, and porcelain, other popular Chinese exports included lacquered furniture, wallpapers, handkerchiefs, and sweetmeats in jars. Not only had this trade stimulated a chinoiserie culture in Europe from the seventeenth century on but its revenue affected the fortunes of multiple empires, including Britain, which by now had taken the lion's share of the China trade among the Western nations.[1] Just as local Chinese officials were reluctant to antagonize the foreign community when enforcing Chinese law, the importance of the China trade also made it increasingly difficult and costly for the foreign officials to upset the status quo of Sino-Western relations as structured by the Canton System. A kind of "good understanding" had thus developed between the Chinese and foreigners in Guangzhou, but this precarious equilibrium was interrupted by an "extraordinary" event on this day.[2] A gunner from a British ship named the *Lady Hughes* fired a salute for a departing Danish ship at the anchorage of Huangpu, about twelve miles downriver from the city of Guangzhou, and killed two Chinese men in a nearby boat. Five days later, officials of the British EIC in China reluctantly handed over the gunner after Chinese officials suspended trade and detained the *Lady Hughes*'s supercargo. A month later, the gunner was executed by strangulation. Scandalized by the outcome, the British and their sympathizers complained that China's criminal justice was based on the primitive notion of blood for blood regardless of the circumstances of a homicide case, that the entire Western community in China was held liable for an individual's fault under the irrational notion of "collective responsibility," and that the gunner had never been properly tried before being summarily executed.

In the history of the Sino-British encounter—which officially began in 1637 with the arrival of the first British expedition in southern China—this was the first and last time that British officials delivered one of their people to the Chinese government to be tried for homicide according to Chinese law.[3] Despite or rather because of its singularity, this case was frequently cited in newspapers, diplomatic correspondence, parliamentary hearings, and Sinological publications in the next two centuries as undisputable evidence of the incommensurability and thus inevitable clash of Sino-Western civilizations, which supposedly then led to the First Opium War and foreign extraterritoriality in China.[4] Jonathan Spence, a leading American historian of China, has recently described the *Lady Hughes* case as an event that forced the British to fundamentally reconsider "how to deal with the Qing at the international diplomatic level."[5]

The Anglo-American and French acquisition of extraterritoriality in 1843–1844 through unequal treaties with China in consequence of the First Opium War soon became a new model for Western powers' dealing with other Asian countries. Exempting foreigners from local jurisdictions, extraterritoriality provided a vital institutional infrastructure and legal foundation for Western expansion in the Asia-Pacific until World War II. By the turn of the twentieth century, abolishing extraterritoriality had become a powerful rallying call among the Chinese, who were led to believe it imperative to reform their legal and political systems in order to regain national sovereignty and international recognition. The fact that China could not abolish extraterritoriality until 1943 and that by then it had become the only country still "subject to this nineteenth-century bondage" has since left a painful scar on the national psyche of modern China.[6] For many Chinese and Euro-Americans alike, extraterritoriality itself helped perpetuate the discourse of Sino-Western difference and clash in the nineteenth and twentieth centuries.

Given the pivotal role of the *Lady Hughes* controversy in shaping the historiography of extraterritoriality and early modern Sino-Western conflicts, a critical reexamination of this case in conjunction with other, similar disputes before 1840 offer new clues on how we might go about rethinking the received wisdom about the nature and history of Sino-Western relations during this period. For instance, as explained in the introductory chapter, the European quest for extraterritoriality in China long predated the *Lady Hughes* and other eighteenth-century Sino-Western legal disputes, or, in fact, European acquisition of any substantial knowledge of Chinese law and government. It is therefore ahistorical to attribute extraterritoriality to this or other such cases or what they supposedly stand for. However, this study is not intended to valorize Chinese law and justice; rather, its focus here is on a different question: by what forces and representational politics was the *Lady Hughes* case transformed into the *originary* moment in the archives and historiography of British or Western extraterritoriality in China? First, I reexamine this controversy by tackling the still-dominant assumptions about the causes and nature of the *Lady Hughes* case in present-day scholarship. Traditional historiography has generally taken for granted that the deaths caused by the gunner of the *Lady Hughes* constituted only an accidental homicide.[7] This presumption, central to the popular perception of the gunner as innocent and Chinese law as antithetical to Western notions of law and justice, is based on a highly problematic conflation of accidental homicide and homicide committed without an express intent to kill—an equivalence that was untenable under either Chinese or English law. Second, my other main purpose for revisiting this incident is to explore the nexus between the *Lady Hughes* controversy and the competing imperial interests that were at work in southern China and in the larger global context in the eighteenth and early nineteenth centuries. By tracing the genealogy of the *Lady Hughes* case in relation to earlier and later legal and political disputes, I analyze the discursive patterns and archival regimes that shaped the dominant interpretations of Western extraterritoriality and early modern Sino-Western conflicts.

Main sources consulted for this chapter include (1) the official report on the *Lady Hughes* case submitted by the EIC agents to the London-based EIC Court of Directors ("the *Narrative*"), the Court of Directors' reply to the *Narrative*, contemporary newspaper reports, multiple witness accounts, and correspondence between local Chinese officials in Guangdong and the Qing emperor; (2) records of other Sino-Western legal disputes from the 1680s to the 1840s in Chinese and English archives and, to a lesser extent, from Portuguese, French, Dutch, and American sources; and (3) re-presentations of these legal disputes in subsequent diplomatic dispatches, foreign policy deliberations, and scholarly works by Sinologists and professional historians in the nineteenth and twentieth centuries.[8] Although it is useful to interrogate the discrepancies and manufactured stories in the sources about these events, dismissing the imperial archives or colonial narratives "as biased limits the possibilities of understanding the interior logic and effects of domination and unnecessarily suggests the possibility of an objective history of the event" just because of the type of historical sources one comes across.[9] In this book, I draw upon recent critical scholarship to read these archival materials not simply as a repository of facts or "primary sources" that promise to lead us to the historical "truth." As Ann Stoler, Nicholas Dirks, and other postcolonial scholars have shown, to read *against the archival grain* may make us more sensitive to the meanings and voices that were hidden between the lines or suppressed by the official interpretations or records; to read *along the archival grain* may encourage us to take more seriously the emotions and dispositions of individuals and communities in order to recover different historical narratives from the dominant ones.[10] I strategically employ both techniques, reading along and against the archival grain, in an attempt to decipher the textualized common sense and sensibilities of the Chinese and Western actors involved in these encounters, and to analyze the practices by which certain *primary discourses* acquired evidentiary and epistemic authority as *primary sources* in displacing alternative perspectives and stories in the prevailing historiography. On the one hand, as we shall see, the *Lady Hughes* case became a powerful filter for reinterpreting the records of other events and conflicts into a seemingly coherent narrative of British or Western anxieties and desires for justice and security in a presumably hostile and despotic Oriental country. On the other hand, the traditional historiography has concealed much of the complex and unfolding processes of the formation of a judicial subculture in the contact zone, where orthodox notions of legality and justice from either the Chinese or Euro-American perspective could not be fully operative, and where everyday negotiations over law and jurisdiction came to transform the understanding of sovereignty and cultural boundary of both sides of the encounter.

THE *NARRATIVE*: BRITISH OFFICIAL REPRESENTATION OF THE CASE

On the evening of November 24, 1784, at the British Factory located near the city wall of Guangzhou, the Council of Supercargoes, in charge of EIC and British interests in China, received word of a troubling incident. A Chinese boat at Huangpu, "lying alongside the *Lady Hughes* country ship [a private British ship from Bombay], being unfortunately in the way of one of the guns while fired in saluting, received very considerable damage, that three Chinese belonging to her were so much hurt that their lives were in danger, & one in particular despaired of." The latter—Wu Yake by name—was confirmed dead the next day. The council, headed by President William Henry Pigou (1751?–1837), further noted, "The Gunner, tho' innocent of any criminal intention, had, from apprehension of the undiscriminating severity of the Chinese Government, absconded." The following day, Muteng'e, the customs superintendent (*yue haiguan jiandu*) who managed the foreign trade together with the provincial governor of Guangdong, sent two deputies and the Chinese Hong merchants to get the gunner for judicial investigation within the city of Guangzhou. The council refused to comply, citing fear for the gunner's safety.[11] Thus commenced the long *Narrative* or report sent by the council to the EIC Court of Directors in London on December 4, 1784.[12]

When the Chinese officials returned with the same order the following day (November 26), the council stood firm, maintaining that it had no authority over private British ships and that George Smith, supercargo of the *Lady Hughes*, was more qualified to address the issue. The council did add, however, that if the Chinese would agree to conduct a trial in the British Factory for the sake of formality, it would be happy to persuade Smith to arrange for someone to stand in for the gunner.[13] The council members insisted on having the trial in the British Factory because they and other Europeans often treated their so-called factories (where they lived and stored goods under guard by armed sailors) as sovereign sanctuaries to shield their lives, property, and liberty from the local authorities in those Asian countries where they did not yet have fortified settlements. The origin of British colonization of India can be traced back to the first few factories and fortresses built by the EIC, first in Surat in 1612 and then Madras and Balasor in the 1630s and 1640s.[14] The Qing government never formally recognized the inviolability of the foreign factories on its soil, although local officials had generally refrained from making forced entries into these factories. Unconvinced that the council lacked influence over private British traders—who were actually subject to the "arbitrary and absolute" power of the EIC officials because they could not even come to China without the latter's license—and that the gunner had absconded, the Chinese officials threatened to send soldiers to seize the gunner from the British Factory if he did not appear before the provincial tribunal.[15] On November 27, the second Chinese victim, Wang Yunfa, died of his wound. George Smith was "decoyed" from the British Factory by a "pretended" message from the Chinese Hong merchant Pan Qiguan and then hauled to the provincial government office, apparently in the hope of pressuring the Britons to be more cooperative in delivering the gunner. Although the Guangdong officials might have thought this tactic less confrontational than forcing their way into the factory, it reinforced the image of the Chinese as being untrustworthy. The council called Smith's detention an "act of violence towards a European unconvicted & uncharged with any crimes contrary to every idea of reason & justice."[16]

In the meantime, the Chinese barricaded the streets leading to the Guangzhou quay, and Chinese compradors, interpreters, and servants fled from the foreign factories and ships. The seizure of supercargo Smith sparked general alarm among the Euro-American sojourners and caused concern for their safety. In protest, the French, Dutch, Danish, and Americans ordered up armed boats; so did the EIC Council of Supercargoes, despite having been assured by Guangdong governor Sun Shiyi (1720–1796) that Smith would be sent back after brief questioning. Thus some fifteen boats with 400 to 500 armed men reached the foreign factories outside the Guangzhou city wall on the night of the twenty-seventh.[17] According to Supercargo Samuel Shaw (1754–1794) of *the Empress of China*, which had just arrived as the first ship from the newly founded United States to commence trade with the Chinese empire, "everything wore the appearance of war." Unwilling to jeopardize the highly lucrative China trade, the council warned its people to exercise restraint and not open fire.[18] That same night, Sun Shiyi issued a proclamation to clarify his stance in the capacity of governor, an English translation of which was preserved:

> A Native of this Country having been killed by a Gun fired from the Ship of Captain Williams, whether by accident or design it is necessary that this Man should appear before me for examination that he may be tried conformably to our Laws: Three days are now elapsed, & you have not sent me this Gunner which denotes on your part a resistance to our Laws; nevertheless, Mr. Smith who is detained in the City is very prudent & discreet, he has consented to write to Whampoa to demand this Gunner that he may appear before our Tribunal & I can return Mr. Smith to you as soon as this Gunner shall arrive; I exhort you therefore to remain quiet & conform yourselves to my Mandate, & shew no token of resistance . . . [and] if you dare in our Country to disobey & infringe our Laws, consider well that you may not repent when it is too late.[19]

The next morning, the foreign chiefs sent a joint protest to the governor, accusing him of wrongfully holding Smith liable for the homicide.[20] As we shall see, Sun actually adopted a very conciliatory approach to the Westerners in this case. Rather than holding the supercargo personally responsible for the homicide, Sun detained him in order to make the British hand over the gunner to complete the judicial investigation according to Chinese law, but Sun planned to eventually let the gunner off the hook by sending him back to England for punishment. His plan was aborted only because of the Qianlong emperor's intervention.

The foreign agents' united hostility alarmed the Chinese authorities. In response, they posted troops near the foreign factories on November 28 and cut off communications between the factories and their ships downstream. The foreigners who remained behind at Huangpu became anxious about their provisions and the safety of all the Europeans at Guangzhou.[21] On the same day, however, Governor Sun resumed supplying provisions to the foreign factories in order to cool things down and invited representatives of all the Western nations except Britain to meet with him at a local temple, the Pagoda, that evening. After expressing dismay about their active involvement, Sun said that he meant them no harm and that all he wanted was to have the British deliver the gunner. He asked his guests to persuade the British to comply; in return, he would drop the issue of the armed ships' illegally coming to Guangzhou and resume the trade. Sun promised that Smith would be sent back if the gunner was delivered within three days. In the end, he gave each gentleman two pieces of silk as a token of amity. Samuel Shaw, who would be appointed the first American consul to China by President George Washington in 1786, later sent the silk to U.S. Secretary of State John Jay as a testimony of Chinese friendship toward the American nation.[22]

The French, Dutch, and Danish accepted Sun's offer later that day and sent their boats back to Huangpu under the protection of a Chinese pilot with a red flag and resumed their trade. Samuel Shaw lamented that the lack of determination and solidarity among the Western nations allowed the Chinese to skillfully end this affair by pitting other nations against the British. In fact, the French consul, Monsieur Vieillard, had already reached the compromise with Governor Sun hours before the general meeting. Since the other Europeans did not want to risk war with China for the British, Vieillard advised Shaw to withdraw as well. Eager to impress the Europeans and Chinese with an honorable image of his new nation, however, Shaw and his American crew stood by their British brethren till the very end, reportedly for "the rights of humanity." But the loss of other nations' support and the trade embargo soon wore down the resolution of the British supercargoes.[23] They were now jeopardizing the China trade, which was crucial to the EIC, British India, and the British Empire itself. In the 1785 season alone, for instance, nineteen EIC ships realized a total of approximately 700,000 taels (or about 840,000 Spanish dollars) in cash proceeds from selling woolens, lead, cotton, and pepper to China and carried home a total of about three million taels (or 3.6 million Spanish dollars) of Chinese exports at invoice cost.[24]

In the meantime, on the twenty-eighth, the council received a message from Smith addressed to Captain Williams of the *Lady Hughes*. Smith stated that he could not leave until the gunner or a substitute for the gunner was sent up to answer the Chinese inquiry. He urged Williams not to leave Guangzhou before the matter was settled, and concluded with the observation that "there must have been gross misconduct on board the *Lady Hughes*." The next morning, the council members informed the Chinese that they had ordered Captain Mackintosh of the *Contractor*, an EIC ship, to take the accused gunner, by force if necessary, when delivering Smith's message to Captain Williams, who was expected to comply immediately.[25]

Thus, five days after the fatal incident, the council finally agreed to search for the gunner. The council made such a gesture of compliance in order to secure supercargo Smith's release and reopen trade, but this show of effective power over the British private ships reinforced the Chinese belief that the council's earlier noncompliance was unjustified. It turned out that the council had no intention to actually deliver the British suspect. On the morning of November 30, some council members privately told Shaw that "as the Gunner was not to be found, Captain Mackintosh would necessarily return without him."[26] Accordingly, just as the Chinese officials became hopeful of the gunner's delivery, the council told them that same day that the gunner might have already left with the *Neckar* on November 28 (though in fact that ship did not leave China until December 1). As the council later explained to the Court of Directors, Mackintosh had indeed planned to return to Guangzhou empty-handed, by echoing the rumor spread by officers of the *Lady Hughes* that the gunner "was not on board" and was believed to have "gone in the *Neckar*," until Captain Williams of the *Lady Hughes* unexpectedly delivered the suspect to him on the evening of November 30. Williams might have been persuaded by Smith's entreaty or pressured by the Chinese threat to stop the British trade indefinitely and keep British ships from leaving unless the gunner was handed over within two days.[27]

The suspect was taken to the British Factory and delivered to the Chinese at the Pagoda, where a Chinese government deputy reportedly asked the Britons not to worry because nothing would happen to the gunner before the emperor had reviewed the case. Despite its earlier efforts to prevent this outcome, the council now hoped that the delivery of the suspect would instill in the Chinese a just opinion of British honesty and intention. The foreign representatives sent a joint plea to the governor for clemency under Chinese law since, they claimed, the disaster occurred by misfortune. Smith returned an hour later and gave a "satisfactory" account of his treatment by the Chinese officials. The embargo ended on December 6, and the *Lady Hughes* sailed for Bombay the following day.[28]

Although the EIC council members had worked hard to avoid exposing any British subject to Chinese law and punishment, they assumed that the Chinese trial was just a formality and that the prisoner would soon be freed. Now that the supercargo was released and trade had resumed, they were relieved by the end of this troublesome affair. They attributed the positive result to the ordering up of the armed boats in concert with all the other foreigners. Conscious of their superiors' dislike of such unauthorized, dangerous confrontation, they added that this measure was adopted chiefly at the instigation of other nations. On December 4, they wrote a complimentary letter to the Chinese governor and customs superintendent asking for continued protection and favor, and sent a lengthy *Narrative* about the case to the Court of Directors.[29] Unless otherwise indicated, the foregoing reconstruction of events has been based on this official dispatch, supplemented by a few contemporary Western accounts.

About five weeks later, on January 8, 1785, representatives of the Western nations were summoned, together with the Hong merchants, to the office of the provincial judge (*anchashi*). With Hong merchant Pan Qiguan as the interpreter, they were told that the emperor was very displeased that they had delayed for five days before turning in the gunner, and that they must respect the emperor's judgment once it was announced, and more readily follow the commands of Chinese officials in the future. The council got the impression that the emperor's decision was not yet known but later learned that the gunner had been executed by strangulation around the same time the foreign representatives were receiving the foregoing admonition.[30] Having just reported a satisfactory resolution of this dispute, the council members now found the execution devastating to their image in the eyes of their superiors in London and their peers in Guangzhou. They denounced the Chinese for executing the gunner because of an accident and for their trickery in not giving the gunner the fair trial and leniency they had promised. For the supercargoes, the entire Chinese legal system was barbaric and sanguinary—a view that would soon become the dominant representation of this dispute for the next two centuries.[31]

Based on the close reading so far, the council's *Narrative* itself has registered a few serious transgressions of law by the British in this case, even though modern historians have seldom noticed this: the killing of the two Chinese by the *Lady Hughes*'s gunner, the council's obstruction of a homicide judicial investigation, and the sending of armed boats to Guangzhou against Chinese law. However, representing the Chinese deaths as accidental homicide implied that the gunner and those who assisted him were not legally culpable, which then changed the whole controversy from an issue of how to punish the gunner for killing two Chinese to one of how to protect an innocent British subject from despotic Chinese law and officials. This in turn would morally, if not legally, justify the council's refusal to let the Chinese government search the British Factory and ships for the suspect and excuse the council's decision to send hundreds of armed sailors up to the foreign factories. Since the assumption that this was a case of accidental homicide has been the point of departure of virtually all subsequent commentators, I shall now examine the legal nature of the case.

ACCIDENTAL HOMICIDE? REVISITING LAW AND FACTS OF THE CASE IN A LARGER CONTEXT

The idea that a homicide committed without a plan or an express intention to kill must necessarily be an accidental homicide and thus legally excusable was not based on either Chinese or English law. With more similarities than differences in their statutory definitions of criminal intent and accidental homicide, both the English and Chinese legal systems then punished various acts that, although unintentional, evidenced negligence, recklessness, or willfulness. Under English law, criminal intent, including a murderous one (or *malice aforethought*), could be implied by or inferred from the circumstances, whereas Chinese law made more elaborate distinctions among shades of mental culpability in punishing intentional and unintentional acts. Sir William Blackstone (1723–1780), a leading authority on English law, stated that a homicide was excusable only if the offender was then performing a lawful act with no intention to hurt. Anyone who killed another in the course of a felony was guilty of murder even though the death might have resulted from a pure accident.[32] Under the Chinese statute on *guoshisha*, or killing by misadventure, the deadly outcome must be what the eyes, ears, and intelligence did not detect or foresee, and the actor meant no harm in the first place (*chu wu hairen zhiyi*). In other words, an accidental homicide could be established under Chinese or English law

FIGURE 1.1 View of Whampoa anchorage, ca. 1810 (part of a set of four), 1785–1835. Oil paint, copper, metal; frame 8 × 9 × ½ in. (20.32 × 22.86 × 1.27 cm), Chinese artist.

Courtesy of Peabody Essex Museum, M20531.

only if it were proven—by the accused under English law—to be an *unfore-seeable* result of a *lawful* act properly executed.[33]

Europeans had long been prohibited from possessing or firing guns at Huangpu or Guangzhou, so the saluting of the departing ship itself could constitute an illegal act that disqualified this case as an accidental homicide even under English law.[34] More important, under the Chinese statute of *guoshisha*, the concept that "contemplation should not have anticipated the death" in order for it to be considered accidental homicide meant that the incident should have occurred in a secluded place where there ought to be no people. The British gunner fired when a boat was admittedly lying alongside and where numerous Chinese and foreign ships would have filled the water at Huangpu at the time.[35] By itself, lack of intent to kill would not be sufficient to acquit an offender of homicide. Under the Waltham Black Act of England, it was a capital offense to shoot at any dwelling house, regardless of intention or injury.[36] The totality of the circumstances was

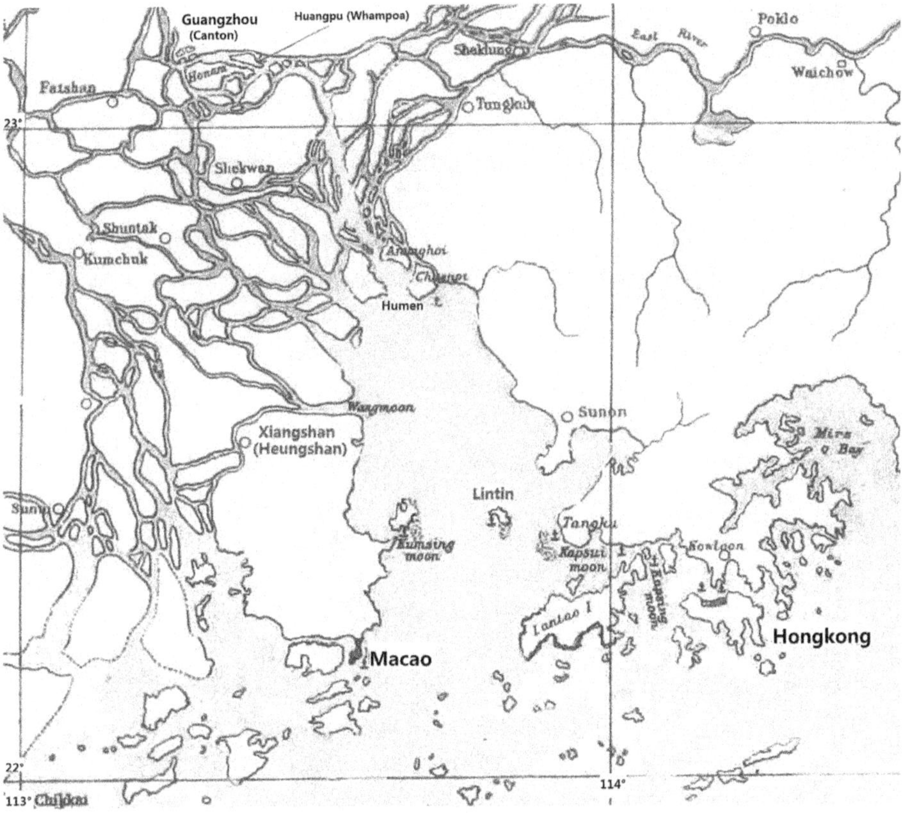

FIGURE 1.2 Estuary of the Canton River (adapted from Hosea Morse, *The International Relations of the Chinese Empire*, 3 vols. [New York: Longmans, 1910], vol. 1, facing p. 1).

therefore likely to lead a Chinese court or English-style jury to conclude that the gunner was criminally punishable for the deaths. The use of a dangerous weapon, the loss of multiple lives, and the refusal to appear in a court of law (which alone could make a homicide suspect guilty of murder under English law) might all constitute aggravating factors that would make the accused liable to capital punishment under English and Chinese law.

Why did the foreign community insist on calling this case an "accident" before any judicial investigation by either side? Examination of the relevant archives shows that by 1784 it had become an established pattern for the Europeans to label as "accidental" any Chinese deaths or injuries caused by foreigners.[37] In 1722, for instance, it was reported as an accident that a gunner's mate from the British ship *King George* came to Guangzhou for bird hunting and killed a Chinese boy working in the paddy field. In the Mo Lunzhi case of 1736, a Chinese "was accidentally killed" by French sailors who went shooting at a village near Huangpu. In the same year, the British sailors aboard the *Richmond* fired into a Chinese customs boat and seriously injured a woman on it when the latter boat came to seek shelter from the stormy weather near the British anchorage at Huangpu. The British archive called it an unlucky accident. Another shooting took place in 1800 under almost identical circumstances, resulting in two "accidental" Chinese deaths.[38] Euro-American offenders would thus generally be deemed "innocent" so long as they were not tried *and* convicted by their authorities according to their own law. Chinese law, procedure, and witnesses were considered unqualified to convict a Westerner.[39] As noted earlier, all these offenders might well have been guilty of causing death or bodily injury through unlawful acts or criminal negligence in discharging guns or hunting where they were not supposed to, but none was ever punished or delivered to the Chinese for trial. Other cases involving Chinese victims over the next few decades were similarly represented in the foreign archives and popular accounts.[40] At the same time, nearly all Chinese who caused the death of foreigners were considered malicious "murderers." For example, EIC officials declared in 1785 that a Chinese who killed a British sailor in an affray was guilty of murder and deserved death, even though killing in a common affray would be manslaughter under contemporary English law.[41] Portuguese, Dutch, French, and American officials adopted a similar strategy in representing homicide cases in China.[42]

Deciphering the discursive density around the trope of accidental homicide involving Euro-American perpetrators and local victims helps reveal the genealogy of foreign extraterritoriality and the logic of colonial legality and justice. The virtually complete silence about the native victims and the representation of Euro-American offenders as almost always innocent suggest a common practice of hierarchical valuation of human lives based on cultural, racial, or national boundaries. Moreover, the trope of accidental homicide was a product of the ideological contradictions that the British and other Western empire builders were struggling with during the eighteenth and early nineteenth centuries. As explained in the introduction, many of the European empire builders simultaneously sought to prove that they were law-abiding, just, and civilized people and to maintain their cultural identity and extraterritorial legal immunity in non-Western countries. The strong attachment to their own legal systems was evident especially among British visitors to China. Historians have shown that liberty was considered the most important marker of the British imperial identity in this period, and that even the two other defining features of that identity, Protestantism and the cult of commerce, were also built on liberty. British political and legal institutions, including the common law, were deemed essential to securing their rights to law, liberty, and property. By the early seventeenth century, these notions of law and liberty had come to define what Englishness or Britishness meant for many empire builders in the next few centuries.[43] This desire for maximum security of life, liberty, property, and identity led British sojourners to generally refuse to submit to any non-Western legal system. The demand for legal immunity was in tension with the still prevalent legal principle that a sovereign state like China had exclusive jurisdiction over foreigners who voluntarily entered its territory. As late as 1839, Lord Palmerston, the British foreign secretary, informed the British superintendent of trade in China that the superintendent's attempt to establish a police force to regulate Britons within the dominions of China would constitute "an interference with the absolute right of sovereignty enjoyed by independent states, which can be justified [only] by positive treaty or implied permission from usage."[44]

The tensions between the general recognition of territorial sovereignty and the particular desire for exemption from Chinese law and jurisdiction led the British and other Europeans to seek extraterritoriality by bilateral agreements from early on. In other words, the original reason for Western extraterritoriality in China had hardly anything to do with the actual nature or operation of Chinese law except that it was an "Oriental" legal system. For instance, the first Portuguese (and European) embassy to Beijing, led by Ambassador Tomé Pires in 1521, was instructed to obtain consent to build a fort in Guangzhou and *a nearby island under Portuguese jurisdiction*, even though the Portuguese soon learned that the Chinese were "very jealous" of their territory and prohibited any foreign-owned settlement.[45] The embassy ended up being a disaster, with its members either imprisoned or executed, after the Chinese government became seriously alarmed by the Portuguese conduct and defiance of its foreign policies and sovereignty.[46] The Portuguese claim that by 1585 their settlement in Macao was no longer subject to Chinese law and jurisdiction was disproved by the continued Chinese control and sovereignty over that settlement, but it at least reflected their strong desire for that ideal scenario. That the European demand for extraterritoriality in China had little to do with Chinese law or culture is also corroborated by the fact that the early modern Europeans made similar demands in other Asian countries. After reaching Japan in 1613, British EIC agents immediately requested the rights to perpetual free trade and extraterritorial jurisdiction over British subjects. The Japonian Charter that they reportedly obtained reads in part: "For any offence committed by [the English in Japan], the justice of this land take[s] no hold either of their persons or goods, but [the case is] to be referred to the said [English chief] merchant's discretion."[47] They asked for similar privileges from Annam (Vietnam) in 1696, stipulating that no local officials should be allowed into their factories to seize anyone without their permission.[48] In 1670, British EIC officials also tried to secure free trade and extraterritoriality in Taiwan before its reintegration into the newly established Qing empire (1644–1911).[49] After direct trade with mainland China was approved in the 1680s, they soon tried, to no avail, to obtain similar immunity from Chinese law and punishments in 1715 and 1729, insisting that British supercargoes should mete out due punishment according to their own laws if British subjects were the aggressors in any affrays with the Chinese.[50]

When that privilege was not granted, the discourse of accidental homicide acquired wide purchase to justify resisting local law and jurisdiction. EIC representatives reported in 1721 that some of the *Bonitta* people had "shot a Chinaman" near Huangpu and that supercargo Scattergood had withdrawn himself to the factory "to escape, though entirely innocent, from falling into the hands of these Barbarians, who are glad of the least handle to plague people." Describing the shooting as accidental, the British officials refused to surrender the suspects, but the offender's captain revealed elsewhere that the accused had killed the Chinese officer to avoid customs inspection, making this a murder case and those who harbored him criminals as well. The Chinese attempt to press for delivery of the suspects (without forcing into the factory) led the British to condemn Chinese law as arbitrary and contrary to all reason and justice. They threatened to abandon the trade and send in British warships to protect their people.[51]

More tellingly, trying to prove that Europeans could punish their own offenders rather than turn them over to the Chinese, the EIC supercargoes wrote in 1780 that "the last accident [like that] which has happened here was the murder of a Dutch Seaman by one of his own countrymen."[52] In the imperial archives, *murder* was thus rendered interchangeable with *accident*. This oxymoronic term of *accidental murder* captured a practical predicament in the Sino-Western contact zone. In the absence of extraterritoriality, representing foreign killings of local people as *accidental* served to cope with the conflict between the formal obligation to respect others' law and sovereignty and the desire for extraterritoriality based on presumed cultural or racial superiority.

Likewise, the French, Dutch, Danish, Swedish, Portuguese, and Prussian representatives also took pains to deny the application of Chinese law to their people, as if the latter were floating embodiments of imperial sovereignty in the East Indies. For instance, in 1783, after having exhausted all means to save one soldier who had killed a Chinese, the Portuguese officials executed the culprit by shooting in the presence of Chinese officials and absolutely refused to let the Chinese strangle him according to Chinese law.[53] Dutch and French officials followed suit, trying to keep Chinese hands off their capital offenders by carrying out the punishment themselves.[54] The main concern of the foreign officials in these cases was no longer so much about the rule of law, universal justice, or even their compatriots' lives as about performing the strenuously asserted right of extraterritoriality in the Orient.

Such impunity from Chinese law and jurisdiction, as the French consul argued in the 1754 *Lord Anson* case, was essential for protecting the European nations' reputation, commerce, and liberty in China.[55] While refuting the French argument in the 1754 case since a British sailor was killed by a French officer, the British EIC officials in 1781 claimed such legal impunity as "a small consolation for the many deprivations" they had suffered in China, without which they would be worse off than the native subjects of that "tyrannical" government. They avowed that it would be better to let a British killer escape than deliver him to the Chinese even in a murder case since it was "little probable that there would be sufficient proof to condemn the guilty person." From 1637 through 1834, the British judicial authorities indeed never convicted or punished any British subject for killing or murdering a Chinese in China.[56]

JURISDICTIONAL POLITICS AND CREATION
OF LEGAL LIMBO IN THE CONTACT ZONE

A highly complex dispute like the *Lady Hughes* case cannot be reduced to a classic example of the inevitable clash between a justice-seeking Western sojourning community and a lawless Oriental regime. Such a dichotomy is seriously problematic not because Chinese law and officials were free from blame, corruption, or injustice but because the British and other Euro-Americans themselves played an essential role in creating a *subculture of judicial administration* concerning the Western community in Guangzhou that they decried as unjust, corrupt, and arbitrary.

The *Lady Hughes* case reveals much less about Chinese law and diplomacy than about how British, Chinese, and other actors from multiple imperial formations actively participated in the making and remaking of a hybrid judicial order in their contact zone. It indicated the complexities of what Lauren Benton has called "jurisdictional politics" in the Sino-Western encounter.[57] The contestation and compromise in this case helped maintain the sovereign status of the Qing empire in the short term but ended up further eroding or fracturing Qing sovereignty in the long run. This case would become the last instance of British surrender of their subjects for Chinese punishment as well as the raison d'être for extraterritoriality. Because of their evasion or resistance, the British and other Westerners who committed crimes in China after the *Lady Hughes* incident were *in practice* often left in legal limbo, a juridically unrecognized or undefined borderland between different legal systems or sovereign states, where the offenders were neither held responsible under the law of their own country nor made amenable to the law of the host country. As I discuss at the end of this chapter, some observers in the early nineteenth century even compared the situation of Westerners in southern China to "the state of nature," in which the foreign residents presumably had all the natural rights but no legal obligation and thus were exposed to all the unregulated vices and dangers. In the present section, I focus on how the EIC Council of Supercargoes contributed to the emergence of this legal limbo and examine the impact of the practical considerations and different interests of the Qing central and local authorities on the outcome of the *Lady Hughes* case and the long-term jurisdictional politics in the Western community in southern China.

As we have seen from the *Narrative*, the EIC Council of Supercargoes was deeply involved in the *Lady Hughes* controversy throughout. It should be reiterated that the British regarded their boats and factories as sovereign spaces. What this meant was that uninvited Chinese officials could not board or enter these armed places without causing furious protests and violent reactions. If British suspects hid themselves in these places, the Chinese authorities could not get them peacefully without the council's cooperation. Initially, the council steadfastly refused to provide any assistance to the Chinese officials who were searching for the gunner. As the Chinese officials pressed on, the council proposed that the Chinese stage a fake trial using a substitute for the gunner, to put on an appearance of due diligence. Hoping to quash this case by intimidating the local officials into submission or manipulating loopholes of the Chinese bureaucratic and judicial systems, the council obstructed the Chinese process of judicial investigation. In response, the Chinese detained the supercargo of the *Lady Hughes*, George Smith, partly to pressure the British to take action and partly to enforce the long-standing Chinese regulation that held foreign supercargoes and captains "culpable for not governing their people properly."[58] Taken aback by the Chinese move, which they considered dangerous to the lives and liberty of all foreigners, the British and other Westerners summoned armed boats to the gate of Guangzhou in protest, turning a legal dispute into a military showdown and diplomatic crisis. After a mutual display of force and relative bargaining power, the British yielded to Chinese pressure and economic considerations and surrendered the gunner. Although the final outcome might have been the same had the gunner been turned over at the outset, the council's intervention and later representation of this homicide case turned it into an event of disproportionate significance in the history of Sino-Western relations.

The council's account of this dispute influenced nearly all subsequent writings about the case, including the widely circulated version in the mass media, British diplomatic or parliamentary papers, and scholarly publications. The lasting effects of such accounts centered on two aspects. First, as detailed earlier, representing the gunner's offense as an accident or accidental homicide was central to the construction of the barbarous image of Chinese law, and yet such representation confused accidental homicide with homicide without express intention to kill. Whereas the former was not capitally punishable, the latter was, under both Chinese and British law at the time of the incident. Second, the council's interpretation of the controversy promoted and perpetuated the myth of collective responsibility. After the Chinese detained supercargo Smith, the council accused the Chinese government of holding Smith liable for the homicide.[59] Whether this charge was based on miscommunication or misinterpretation of the Chinese motive, it outraged the Westerners and reinforced an enduring myth about Chinese treatment of foreigners—making the whole Western community answerable for the crime of a Western individual—a myth that was later dubbed "collective responsibility." How much impact the council's representation had on the traditional understanding of this case becomes obvious if we consider some of the alternative narratives about the event by other Westerners.

Regarding what actually happened on the *Lady Hughes*, two newly discovered witness reports suggest that the offense was a far cry from accidental homicide. Recall that Captain Mackintosh of the *Contractor* delivered the *Lady Hughes* gunner to the Chinese. The *Contractor* lay at some distance from the latter when the shooting occurred. One of its crew members left an account that was published anonymously in the 1830s. According to this account, he had observed from the *Contractor* only that something had gone wrong with the *Lady Hughes*'s return of the salute to some departing ships. Later that evening, he learned what had happened: the gunner had warned his officer that the Chinese in the nearby boat would be endangered, but the commanding officer had given a peremptory order to fire as the *Lady Hughes* was rather late in returning the salute—leading to one death and one injury.[60]

In 1808, Chrétien-Louis-Joseph de Guignes (1759–1845), a French diplomat in Guangzhou from 1783 to 1796, published a similar account of what he had "witnessed." According to him, the *Lady Hughes*'s gunner warned a Chinese boat, which was busy loading goods alongside, to move away before he fired two shots in salute on the opposite side of the *Lady Hughes*. The gunner then paused as the Chinese boat had not yet moved back far enough. After being told why the gunner suspended the salute, an officer "forced him, by threats, to shoot without delay." The third shot killed one Chinese and injured another, who later died despite medical treatment. On the boat were also two Chinese women with children, who screamed loudly after the third shot hit the boat. This is the most detailed account of this incident I have found. Apparently, de Guignes obtained these details from Captain Williams of the *Lady Hughes*, who sought advice from Captain Dordelin of the French vessel *Triton* right after the shooting. He published the "fact" to correct a misinformed account in a recent French book while many other witnesses were still alive.[61]

Contrary to the council's reports, therefore, these two accounts show this to be a case of murder under English law and likely a case of intentional killing (*gusha*) under Chinese law.[62] A similar version appeared to have circulated orally in the local foreign community. Robert Forbes (1804–1889), an American merchant who first visited China in 1818, learned that the gunner "had notified his officer that a Chinese boat was just in range but was imperiously directed to fire."[63] John Francis Davis (1795–1890), who joined the EIC business in Guangzhou as a writer in 1813, also held that the gunner acted in obedience to orders.[64] Acting in obedience to one's superior did not necessarily make the actor innocent, however, and would not constitute a legal defense to a charge of murder under English law either. Both the officer and the gunner could have been punished by death for the murder under English law, while Chinese law would have punished the principal more severely than the accessory.[65]

Despite all the expressed indignation about his death, the EIC official records never mentioned the name or age of the gunner or the strangled prisoner. The above-mentioned witness from the *Contractor* saw the prisoner right before the surrender and described him as "an elderly man, of low stature, and of that darkness of colour which is usual among the descendants of the old Portuguese colonists of Hindoostan, and particularly among those who had commingled their blood with that of the native." De Guignes described him as a Filipino (*Manillois*).[66] Two other contemporary accounts published in a major English newspaper based in India even explicitly claimed that this prisoner was a substitute for the British gunner.[67] It is not surprising to find such information excluded from the official archives given the "allusive, incomplete nature of colonial knowledge."[68] The fact that the executed prisoner either was ordered by his officer to fire or was a scapegoat for the real gunner might explain why many British commentators, including Davis, were so certain of the prisoner's innocence. The witness from the *Contractor*, who even went to the execution ground but left before the prisoner was strangled about 4:00 p.m. on January 8, 1785, lamented that the prisoner must be considered an innocent man since he was "compelled" by his superior officer to follow orders, and that the officer was the one to blame.[69]

So much attention has been paid to the injury caused by Chinese law to the foreigners that the latter's role in the outcome of the *Lady Hughes* and similar cases, and more generally in the shaping of Chinese judicial administration and its representation, has been largely erased in modern historiography. The local Chinese officials and the Hong merchants (who as the translators or mediators between the foreign and Chinese sides often manipulated the circumstances and communications to minimize risks to their own interests) were certainly not free from fault, but the corrupted legal culture that the *Lady Hughes* case supposedly exemplified was coproduced by the British and other Westerners in China. The consequent portrayal of Chinese law as the negative other of Western law was a result of this ongoing process of negotiation and contestation. If legal Orientalism is thus understood as an unfolding transcultural relationship, the Chinese side was far from being a passive victim of Western domination during this period. In the next section, I analyze the extent to which the *Lady Hughes* case was shaped by the agendas and strategic decisions of the Qing authorities in Guangzhou and Beijing, respectively. The analysis again illustrates why it is problematic to treat the controversy as a clash of two incommensurable legal cultures.

AGENDAS OF THE QING AUTHORITIES IN BEIJING AND GUANGDONG IN HANDLING SUCH DISPUTES

As recounted in the *Narrative*, the British EIC officials were informed of the Chinese emperor's displeasure at their delay in handing over the gunner, and the next thing they knew was that the gunner had been strangled. Chinese records of the *Lady Hughes* case were typically meager, but some newly discovered Qing official documents shed fresh light on the decision-making process behind the scenes. Like their Western counterparts, the Chinese imperial archives had their own contradictions, discrepancies, and representational politics that must also be critically scrutinized. These extant Chinese sources do suggest that the frequently conflicting agendas and priorities of the Qing central and local governments exerted considerable influence on their actual decisions regarding foreigners during this period.

On December 22, 1784, the Qianlong emperor reviewed and replied to two secret memorials from Guangdong governor Sun Shiyi and one from Customs Superintendent Muteng'e, all dated December 1, one day after the gunner's surrender.[70] One of Sun's memorials suggested that to minimize future troubles, Western missionaries should no longer be allowed to live in the city of Guangzhou for purposes of managing correspondence with missionaries in Beijing. Sun's other memorial, which took me almost a decade to track down and is still not publicly available, is probably the most essential document about the *Lady Hughes* case as it contained key details that formed the grounds of the emperor's final judgment. According to Sun, a Qing commander in charge of the foreign ships at Huangpu reported that a British ship under (Captain) Williams, when saluting a departing Danish ship around noon of November 24, "did not notify people" on other ships and caused the injury or death of three Chinese seamen, who could not avoid the shooting. Claiming that the victims were "injured accidentally and unintentionally" (*wuxin wushang*), the foreigners (*yangren*) procrastinated in delivering the gunner—spelled "Dixiehua" in Chinese—until after Sun had dispatched local officials and soldiers to bring supercargo Smith in chains from the foreign factory into the walled city of Guangzhou. Citing the precedential substatute enacted in 1744 as a result of the Chen Huiqian case (explained below), Sun inquired whether the gunner, who caused the deaths without the intent to kill (*chuzi wuxin*), should be sentenced, by analogy, under the Qing statute of *guoshi sharen* and then sent back to England for punishment to "demonstrate [His Imperial Majesty's policy of] cherishing those from afar" (*yishi rouyuan zhichu*). As this was a serious case involving two deaths, Sun understood that it was ultimately the emperor's prerogative to decide whether imperial mercy was due to the British offender or not in this case.[71] Qianlong's reaction and final judgment showcased the different practical considerations on the part of the central government in Beijing and the local officials in Guangdong.

Local Officials' Struggles to Balance Duties
and Challenges in the Contact Zone

The logical tensions within Sun's first memorial about the *Lady Hughes* case are evident. On the one hand, he acknowledged that the Britons aboard that ship were criminally liable for their failure to warn the Chinese victims or to avoid the fatal incident. He probably had no choice since the secret memorial of Superintendent Muteng'e informed the emperor on the same day that the Britons "did not exercise due care to warn [*bu xiaoxin zhihui*] the nearby ship(s) and caused two deaths by gunfire, [which] should be investigated and punished."[72] On the other hand, Sun relied upon the foreigners' assertions to downplay the severity of the offense while ignoring the fact that the absence of intent to kill would not in itself turn a homicide into killing by accident. For instance, in the Chen Huiqian case of 1743, Governor-General Celeng (d. 1756) noted that the Portuguese offender killed the victim in an affray "without the intent to kill" (*shafei youxin*) and should be punished by strangulation.[73] In addition, Sun made no mention of the foreign nations' joint defiance of Qing laws in sending hundreds of armed sailors to Guangzhou to demand Smith's release. Instead, he stressed that all the foreign supercargoes came to his office to beg mercy for Smith and "volunteered" to find out and deliver the offender within two days, which manifested their "sense of fear and respect" (*zhisuo jingwei*). By taking at face value the interested Britons' statements while overlooking the aggravating circumstances, Sun tried to minimize the consequences of this dispute without totally neglecting his duty to enforce the law. He concluded the report by appealing to the emperor's pretension to universal benevolence under the *huairou* doctrine in granting extralegal leniency to foreigners.[74]

Emerging from this account is Sun Shiyi's role as a mediator seeking to balance a set of competing interests and priorities. As governor of Guangdong, he was responsible for administering a province that had a reported population of 15,413,467 in 1784, a figure nearly twice that of contemporary England and exceeding the combined total of 14,133,000 for Great Britain in 1790. Yet he had only a modicum of the British government's personnel and resources with which to carry out his duties.[75] In addition to the domestic affairs in the province, Sun was the emperor's representative in managing the Westerners in southern China. However, his loyalty and obligation to the emperor were complicated by the need to accommodate the Westerners.

Although the Qing authorities were still in control of the China trade, the burgeoning size of the European community and the growing militancy of the British had already come to influence the mentality of local Qing officials. The Portuguese, French, and Dutch also complained about the Canton System and China's restrictions on foreign trade, but the British were particularly vocal and bellicose from the mid-eighteenth century onward as they became increasingly confident in their cultural and material superiority. After the Seven Years' War with France (1756–1763), the Battle of Plassey in 1757, and other victories in India, the British EIC had evolved from a privately owned joint-stock company into a sovereign power ruling a large chunk of the Indian Subcontinent. Britain also replaced the Iberians and the Dutch as the dominant European power in the East Indies and was headed toward global maritime supremacy, a status that would be sealed by the decisive defeat of Napoléon's France at Waterloo in 1815. Its advances in science and technology, the Industrial Revolution, and global commerce during the same period further strengthened the empire and in turn affected how even ordinary Britons understood what Britishness meant.[76] The loss of American colonies only intensified its interest in Asia and the China trade. Britain colonized Penang in Southeast Asia in 1786 and embarked on a similar project in Australia in the same period. Forty years before the First Opium War, it sent two military expeditions, in 1802 and 1808, in an attempt to seize Macao as a colonial outpost in China.[77]

Under such circumstances, the local officials were naturally alarmed by the foreigners' decision to send a few hundred armed men to Guangzhou in disregard of the legal prohibition and the gunfire from the military forts along the river. At his meeting with the foreign supercargoes on November 28, Governor Sun appeared agitated and eager to end this dispute.[78] Samuel Shaw even stated that this dispute "gave rise to what was commonly called the *Canton war*." An English newspaper, to be renamed the London *Times* several years later, called this a "Riot at China."[79] Sun stood firm, as required by law, in demanding to try the offender, but it was also in his interest to explore circumstances and legal arguments to close the case soon without escalating the tensions.

In this regard, Sun was following an old practice among Guangdong officials. In attempting to cope with the difficulties of managing the frequently defiant foreign community and with a variety of other administrative duties, Qing officials in Guangdong, ranging from the provincial governor to the vice-magistrate in Macao, had a common interest in convincing their superiors that they were doing their job diligently. The degree of diligence in actually enforcing Qing laws and policies concerning foreign trade varied considerably from official to official, or even from case to case. Some officials were more determined or persistent in claiming Qing jurisdiction, even in cases involving only foreigners,[80] but most were averse to violent confrontation with the well-armed foreigners. They might make initial attempts to enforce Qing law when serious crimes occurred, but they often ended up dropping the matter when they encountered the foreigners' strong protests, artful procrastination, or threats of trade stoppage or violence. As a result, some local officials acquiesced in using false testimonies in several cases to get closure and avoid administrative complications.[81] The official archives in Chinese and European languages documented such negligence or Sino-foreign complicity on a number of occasions, although it should be noted that in most such cases, the foreigners' reluctance to submit to Chinese jurisdiction was a major cause of local officials' inconsistency in enforcing the law.[82] Naturally, all the actors involved would rarely volunteer such unflattering details or incriminate their collaborators when briefing their superiors; even the remarkable Qing imperial communications system of "secret palace memorials" (zouzhe), which was refined in the early eighteenth century to enable officials to report on their colleagues confidentially, could do relatively little to halt such entrenched bureaucratic practices.[83]

The Qing Central Government's Policies: The Legal Framework for Westerners

Besides the influence of perceived Western bellicosity and danger, the actions of Qing local officials should also be understood in the context of local-central tensions within the Qing political system. The Manchu ruling house governed the Han Chinese majority and other ethnic groups in a vast empire with a complex power structure. After subduing the Dzungar Khanate of the Uighur "rebels" and renaming that region as the

"New Territories" (Xinjiang) in the 1750s, the Qianlong emperor had pushed China's territorial reach to a new peak. Yet military victories, economic prosperity, and displays of imperial grandeur and legitimacy (for instance, by giving thanks to heaven atop Mount Tai or embarking on the southern tours) were at times eclipsed by continued social and ethnic inequalities, literary inquisitions, military uprisings, and bureaucratic corruption and entrenchment.[84] Even an unusually active and domineering monarch like Qianlong repeatedly experienced frustration over the limitation of his supposedly limitless power. In a masterful study of the Qing prosecution of "soul-stealing" or sorcery cases in the 1760s, Philip Kuhn has revealed the tensions as well as compatibility between absolutist imperial power and routinized bureaucracy within the Qing "bureaucratic monarchy."[85]

The Qianlong emperor and his predecessors knew too many examples of bureaucratic inertia and malfeasance to trust even their most senior officials. In relation to the case of Chen Huiqian, Qianlong was informed that Guangdong officials had generally failed to prosecute homicide by Europeans or had often downgraded killings in an affray (*dousha*) to killings by accident (*guoshisha*) after the Europeans refused to surrender the offenders.[86] This then led to the Qing government's attempts to enforce Qing law and sovereignty more effectively.

Chen Huiqian, a local Chinese man, was killed by a Portuguese in Macao in December 1743. As they had done over the previous century, Portuguese officials refused to hand over the accused to the Chinese, claiming that they would otherwise be severely punished by the Portuguese government. In February 1744, at the suggestion of Acting Governor-General Celeng (Dzereng), the Ministry of Justice (Xingbu) and the Qianlong emperor enacted a new substatute (*tiaoli*) that simplified the complicated normal procedures for serious cases involving foreign offenders in Macao. According to the new substatute, if a foreigner was found guilty of killing a Chinese with premeditation or intent or in an affray and was punishable by decapitation or strangulation, Guangdong provincial officials would review the judgment of the lower Chinese courts. If they affirmed it as just and accurate, they would forward the case record to Beijing while sending lower officials, together with the foreign chief, to carry out the execution. Before this, the offender would be in the foreign chief's custody and spared from the Chinese detention, judicial interrogation, and long process of multiple-level judicial reviews involved in homicide cases. This substatute was designed to facilitate the "enforcement of the law of the country" (*shangshen guofa*) while "accommodating the foreigners' sentiment" (*xiashun yiqing*). As the Ministry of Justice reasoned, although foreigners were subject to the Qing Code the same way as Chinese subjects were, the ultimate goal was to duly punish all wrongdoers, and certain procedural aspects could be modified if they had prevented effective law enforcement. A similar simplified procedure had been applied to certain domestic cases of violent crimes, rebellions, or explosive frontier situations. In this sense, the Qing authorities were flexible enough to adapt its normal legal procedure to the peculiar circumstances in the contact zone, to counter the European efforts to evade China's territorial sovereignty. For such purposes, they also made the foreign representatives (and their Chinese trading partners and compradors) agents for enforcing Chinese law and order among the foreigners.[87]

The foreign community continued to resist Chinese jurisdiction, however, and many local officials prioritized their own interests over strict enforcement of the law or Qing sovereignty. Barely four years after the promulgation of the new substatute, the Qianlong emperor learned of a new instance of gross negligence on the part of his senior officials in Guangdong. In 1748, two Chinese, Li Tingfu and Jian Ya'er, were beaten to death by Portuguese patrollers in Macao after being detained for allegedly breaking into a house at night. Governor Yue Jun initially reported that the foreign offenders were to be punished by exile to a distance of 3,000 *li* (just under 1,000 miles) for throwing the corpses into the ocean. Unable to convince the Portuguese to give up the offenders, the governor reluctantly accepted their proposal to send the latter to the Portuguese colony at Timor to "suffer for a lifetime." He explained to the emperor that this compromise was necessary to pacify the foreigners while allowing Qing law to be technically honored. The emperor fumed in November 1748,

> The victims were dead and could not testify; [you] relied on only the foreigners' story. Given their initial denial [of the killings], the actual cause of the deaths must be different [from what they said]. Foreigners who enter the Interior must be careful and obedient and respect the Law. Killing multiple people showed [their] arrogance and brutality, and throwing the corpses into the sea for cover-up further proved them to be

unusually cruel and treacherous. They each should be punished for taking others' life. If [we were to] apply the Law Code of the Interior to only sentence [them] to beating and exile [as the governor proposed], there would be no end to the foreigners' unruliness and malice. The proposed punishment is seriously wrong. . . . How can [we] know whether or not they will be actually [punished once they are sent away]? If that government does nothing, will the lives of Li Tingfu and Jian Ya'er not have been lost for nothing? . . . [Future Sino-foreign cases] must be decided according to the Law Code so that all foreigners [*yiren*] will learn to fear and respect [the Law]. Local peace will resume.[88]

This case was remanded for a new trial, although the emperor learned four months later that the two Portuguese offenders had left in January 1749. While reluctantly approving the local officials' suggestion to drop the matter to avoid further agitation among the Portuguese, who were described by the officials as having been loyal and obedient for the past two centuries, the emperor stressed again that the best way to govern them was to artfully apply mercy and discipline (*enwei bingji*): the foreigners should not be treated harshly without serious cause, but if they had "violated the Fundamental Law of the Empire," they should not be spared punishment simply to avoid trouble; otherwise, they would "never learn how to behave properly and lawfully" and would become arrogant and commit more transgressions of law.[89] This was a succinct restatement of the guiding principle of Qing policies regarding the Euro-Americans in China, although it was the 1744 substatute and the derivative provincial regulations promulgated in 1749 that provided the legal framework governing Westerners in southern China until the First Opium War in 1840.

Since there has been some debate or confusion about this legal framework, some further clarifications are necessary here. The provincial regulations of 1749 extended the modified procedure under the 1744 substatute to noncapital cases in which foreigners were punishable by exile or labor servitude. Just as in capital cases under the 1744 substatute, the Chinese judge or magistrate would conduct the investigation and trial, and if his judgment was affirmed by the provincial authorities, he was to punish the foreign offender. The foreign chief's role was limited to *assisting* the Chinese officials in taking custody of the offender and then in carrying out the execution or other, less-serious penalties under the Chinese officials' supervision (*dutong*). The Portuguese chief was given the power to inter-rogate Portuguese offenders in minor cases that merited the punishment of beating by heavy or light bamboo; his decisions were then submitted to the Chinese authorities (most likely the *Aomen tongzhi*, or vice-prefect of Macao), who would review and determine (*heming*) the nature of the offense and penalty before ordering (*chiling*) the Portuguese chief to carry out the punishment accordingly. Some of the regulations were applied to Westerners outside Macao as well.[90]

In a recent study, Pär Cassel has fruitfully analyzed the operation of foreign extraterritoriality in post-1860 China (as well as Japan) by placing Qing responses to the European quest for extraterritoriality within what he calls a "pluralistic Qing legal order" that allowed the Manchu rulers to apply different laws to different ethnic groups within the empire.[91] This pluralistic legal order appears true to a limited degree with regard to the pre-1840 Sino-Western relationship in southern China. The extant records indi-cate that Guangdong officials understood that the Qing government had jurisdictional power over Westerners within its territory, and that most of them attempted to claim jurisdiction or enforce Qing law even though they might eventually accept a compromise when faced with resistance from the foreign community.[92] As noted above, the 1744 substatute and the 1749 regulations also made it clear that the Qing authorities retained ultimate jurisdiction over the foreign community within its territory, even though it might tactically let the foreign officials help maintain law and order among their own people or carry out certain punishments deemed appropriate by the Chinese government.

In 1754, the Qianlong emperor, influenced by the *huairou* doctrine and possibly a recent suggestion of the Dutch officials, did order the Guang-dong officials to repatriate a French offender, who had killed a British sailor from the ship *Lord Anson* at Huangpu earlier that year, to be "handled" (*chuli*) by the leader of France (*yiqiu*), who should be apprised of the appro-priate penalty under Qing law.[93] The long-term legal standing of this con-fidential court letter (*tingji*) was not comparable to the 1744 substatute, and its actual effect appears insufficient to support a firm conclusion that "by the Qianlong period the emperor had established that the Qing government would only claim jurisdiction in cases where the Chinese had been killed by the foreigners."[94] Qing officials continued to claim jurisdiction over the foreign community (including Macao) in a wide variety of legal matters up to the First Opium War.[95] In 1780, for instance, Guangdong officials insisted on and succeeded in prosecuting and executing a Frenchman for killing a Portuguese sailor, despite foreign protestation.[96] Although the lack of consistency in law-enforcement efforts created room for the Qing officials and foreigners alike to manipulate the system or negotiate with each other for a more favorable outcome, all the foreigners in China, including the Portuguese in Macao, remained ultimately subject to "the Laws of the Heavenly Dynasty" (*tianchao guofa* or *fadu*).[97] Since Chinese law and government had been widely portrayed in Europe by Montesquieu and others as despotic and cruel, the fact that the Chinese authorities in principle could always enforce their law against foreign offenders remained a major source of the insecurity and indignation felt by the Western community until extraterritoriality was obtained.[98]

Qianlong's insistence upon punishing the *Lady Hughes*' gunner strictly according to the Qing law on double homicide by firearm also had something to do with the internal tensions of the Qing empire itself. After all, he had extended extralegal leniency (*fawai shi'en*) to foreign offenders (including missionaries) on various other occasions.[99] Not this time, the emperor ruled. Given the recent Muslim uprising in northwestern China and its suspected religious connection with the outlawed Christian missionaries, Qianlong apparently considered it a good time to hammer home his message among the local officials in Guangdong and beyond. He had just reprimanded Governor Sun Shiyi and Governor-General Shuchang (d. 1798) for their failure to detect or prevent the foreign missionaries from sneaking through their jurisdiction into the inland provinces. The emperor became more upset when these officials could not capture the few missionaries reportedly hiding in Guangdong even as they continued to find excuses or make empty promises as usual. Even worse, Guangdong was by no means an exception.[100] In this sense, the *Lady Hughes* case might also be viewed as one of the "concrete events" that the frustrated monarch utilized to counter such "routinization and assimilation" of the local officials and "whip his bureaucracy into line."[101]

The confidential court letter of December 22 showed that the Qianlong emperor was not convinced by Governor Sun's story. He suspected that

Smith had not been taken into the city "in chains" and that Dixiehua (the gunner) might not be the actual principal offender. He doubted that the culprit would be punished at all in Britain. Since Smith had already identified the gunner as the actual killer, Governor Sun should have immediately executed the offender by strangulation in the foreigners' presence to teach the latter a lesson. The emperor wondered aloud, "How could [Sun] still propose to send the culprit back? Let's imagine how Sun Shiyi could know whether or not that country carried out [the penalty for] that culprit after he was sent back?"[102] Interestingly, the emperor's concern actually echoed that expressed by the British EIC officials in the 1754 *Lord Anson* case. In that case, French officials characterized the British death in an affray as killing in self-defense or accidental homicide and offered to punish the French offender back in France. They also warned the British that it would do injury to the British and other Western nations if they started to acknowledge Chinese jurisdiction over a dispute between Europeans. The French also described the exemption from Chinese law as crucial for the foreigners' interest and dignity in China, and their sentiment was shared by many other Western representatives in China. The British officials, however, did not think it even possible to prosecute someone in a European country for committing a homicide in China, so they insisted that the Chinese take jurisdiction over this Anglo-French dispute and punish the French culprit according to Chinese law. Otherwise, as they told the EIC Court of Directors and the Chinese government, any European would "think himself at liberty to cut the throat of another person [in China] with impunity."[103]

This rationale, offered by the British in 1754, for prosecuting the French offender promptly was similar to that offered by the Chinese officials and the Qianlong emperor in the *Lady Hughes* case. The emperor rebuked Governor Sun for his "error and cowardice" (*miuqie*). The governor, who was on his way to Beijing as one of the honored guests at an imperial banquet in the spring of 1785, was ordered to return to Guangzhou and to gather all the Britons to witness the execution of the offender while continuing to search for the foreign missionaries hiding there.[104] It should be emphasized that this case was not treated exactly the same as one of the "political crimes," such as prosecution of corrupt officials or the soul-stealing cases discussed by Philip Kuhn.[105] The emperor's decision to reject the Guangdong officials' proposal did have some substantial legal basis, and it was meant to strictly enforce Qing law and deter Westerners from challenging Qing power and sovereignty, rather than simply demanding life for life, as often assumed in subsequent historiography. Regarding the legal basis of Qianlong's decision, as Thomas Buoye has noted elsewhere, it was "extremely difficult, although not impossible, to escape a sentence of intentional killing in shooting" by firearms in eighteenth-century China because using such dangerous weapons at close range generally implied the intent to kill.[106] The circumstances of the *Lady Hughes* case, especially the loss of two lives by shooting without adequate warning at a busy place like Huangpu, would make it very hard not to treat this as a case of intentional killing under the applicable law of Qing China. The British gunner was executed by strangulation, a punishment technically imposed for killing in an affray and less severe than the punishment of decapitation for intentional killing or murder.[107] Such a mitigated punishment was, in the mind-set of the Qing emperor, supposed to demonstrate both the inviolable sovereignty and the universal benevolence of the Qing government.

After receiving the aforementioned court letter about a week later, Governor Sun thanked the emperor for allowing him to remedy his serious mistakes and promised strict compliance with the injunctions while explaining away the emperor's queries noted earlier. According to his memorial of January 28, 1785, Sun and other provincial officials held a retrial of the foreign prisoner and then sent Provincial Judge Yao Fen to remind the Euro-Americans of all the imperial favors, adding,

> When saluting to a departing ship, [Captain] Williams's ship did not take care to notify the neighboring ship [*bing bu xiaoxin zhihui linchuan*] and caused two deaths. The punishment for this offense was serious. By the Law of the Empire, not only would the culprit be executed, but the ship's chief was severely punishable for negligence in supervising the crew. Considering that you came from the outer ocean [*waiyang*] and are ignorant about [our] laws, we now only put Gunner Dixiehua to death. This is truly the emperor's extra grace.

This report finally converged with the earliest characterization of the gunner's offense in Superintendent Muteng'e's secret memorial. Sun and

Shuchang also told the emperor that they and other officials came out of the city to prevent any potential disturbance among the foreigners when the gunner was being put to death. Between those lines, the emperor noted in vermillion, "Unnecessary! This clearly betrayed your timidity and cowardice [*qienuo*]. Should unexpected things indeed happen, you would absolutely be unable to handle it properly!"[108] Qianlong showed no confidence in the Guangdong officials' ability to balance diplomacy and coercion in dealing with the Westerners in the future. The British authorities in London had similar concerns regarding their own agents in China.

PERSPECTIVES OF THE BRITISH AUTHORITIES IN LONDON AND BRITISH POLICY RESPONSES

If the *Lady Hughes* incident served as a concrete, exemplary event through which the Qing court sought to goad local officials to better safeguard Qing law and sovereignty, it afforded the British and many other Westerners an outlet to express and act out the frustrations, indignities, and precariousness that they had felt in China.[109] The EIC officials and other British traders urged their superiors in London to allow them to take more aggressive measures, if necessary, to resist Chinese arbitrary power or to obtain de facto extraterritoriality. Right after the *Lady Hughes* case, the Council of Supercargoes suggested to the EIC Court of Directors that from now on they should deliver any British suspect to the Chinese authorities only after they themselves had tried and conclusively found the suspect guilty of "willful murder" according to English law and judicial procedures. In all other cases, they should be authorized to resist the Chinese demand for the British suspects "by every means" in their power, even if it meant retreating to their ships or hazarding the China trade that had become enormously important to their company and nation. By way of illustration, the council members mentioned the homicide case in 1780 in which a French seaman was convicted and executed by the Chinese court for killing a Portuguese crewmate. The council inferred that the hapless man must have acted in self-defense, might be substituted (by the French consul) for the real killer, and was strangled "without form of trial or any circumstance that would distinguish this act of their [Chinese] justice from the summary execution of the Malays, or other barbarous nations." As the Chinese practice was thus seen "so contrary to what Europeans deem humanity or justice," they told the Court of Directors, their voluntary submission to it "must appear to all that [they] gave up every moral and manly principle to [their] interest."[110] These emotionally charged arguments for extraterritoriality became dominant over the next two centuries.[111]

Nevertheless, a confidential reply from the Court of Directors, which has not yet been noticed or analyzed in prior scholarship, shows us how the official representation of the *Lady Hughes* case and other Sino-Western disputes can be better decoded and reinterpreted. Like the Qing court's trying to monitor the Guangdong officials, the EIC Court of Directors required their supercargoes to send back to London the most recent diary and consultation books up to the very day when the messenger left China.[112] They knew the tendency of their overseas agents to often tell a partial or distorted story out of self-interest. Given what was at stake in the China trade, they apparently deemed it more essential to protect the economic interest of the company and its shareholders than to avenge the inconvenience and sentiment of their subordinates in China. After finally receiving the council's *Narrative*, the directors wrote in February 1786 that they had found "sufficient cause" from the council's own account for censuring the latter's conduct, "which began by an injudicious and unjustifiable opposition, and ended with a humiliating though necessary submission."[113] As far as they could tell, the *Narrative* was "erroneous, contradictory and imperfect," the council's blunt refusal to surrender the gunner was unwise, and the council was self-contradictory in first refusing to deliver the gunner for distrusting Chinese justice and then writing to request the clemency of Chinese laws. The *Narrative* stated that on November 27, 1784, an official with Governor Sun's message "was civilly desired" to enter and remained in the factory for the night. The directors had "grounds to suspect that instead of a desire, it was an absolute detention."[114] Nor were the directors convinced that the council had good or sufficient justification for sending up armed boats to protect their persons, which they considered an "ill-judged" attempt to challenge the laws of the country where the British traders resided. The directors wrote, "Such an act would have been passed nowhere—in China, a kingdom which has no political connections with this country, it was most likely to bring on the consequences it did—a resolved perseverance on their side, and an entire submission on yours." They believed that the council's action had hastened the death of the gunner, whom they had no doubt the council meant to shield from Chinese punishment. The directors were particularly unhappy that the foreign nations had thus betrayed their inability to resist the oppressions they complained of: "Your conduct has made the Europeans appear to be, what you presumed the Chinese were, 'a people weak enough to threaten without the power to execute.'"[115] This embarrassing and unsuccessful experiment would only make their situation in China worse.

Some directors privately did share some of their subordinates' sentiment. In the margins of an earlier report of the strangulation of the gunner, they noted, "A deplorable transaction, & disgraceful to those [involved]."[116] But they were more concerned about the magnitude of the economic interests endangered by their servants' rash conduct. They reminded the council that rather than force or intimidation—which was an ineffective strategy when dealing with officials of a peculiar and despotic government like the Chinese one—it was the Chinese officials' corruption and the Hong merchants' complicity that had protected foreigners in the past. In all future cases, the council should immediately use every means in its power, through the Hong merchants, to make such a representation to the Guangdong officials as might save the offender's life. The directors approved the council's idea of delivering only a *proven* willful murderer to the Chinese, which was after all only a hypothetic scenario to placate the Chinese.[117] Indeed, the court wrote the word "Never" next to the sentence containing the council's original proposal to deliver up a convicted murderer.[118] What the directors disliked were not the council's efforts to evade Chinese law and jurisdiction but the risky and ineffective strategies used for this purpose.

On both sides, the official agents on the ground were subject to some seriously flawed or hard-to-enforce systems of monitoring and accountability. For the Qing officials in Guangdong, the consequences of failing to prevent a major disturbance or failing to close a homicide case because an accused foreigner was protected by his countrymen were serious enough to make many officials willing to risk administrative penalties by hiding key information from their superiors in Beijing, as they did in the *Neptune* case of 1807, discussed in chapter 2. Qianlong's remonstrations in 1784 brought little change to this practice in the long run, and both the inconsistencies or negligence of local officials and the sporadic ironhanded intervention by the Qing court in Beijing as in the *Lady Hughes* case fed into the already widespread perception of Qing law as arbitrary and unjust. The British representatives, on the other hand, were carried away on various occasions by emotions and peer pressure from the foreign community in Guangzhou to take actions that sometimes jeopardized the interests of their employers or country. In cases such as the *Lady Hughes* that were supposedly bound up with the issues of natural justice, liberty, and national identity and honor, all the senior officials (including the council members in this case) in China were expected to support the aggressive response. It took six months for London to receive the council's dispatches about the *Lady Hughes* case, but Chinese express couriers made round trips between Guangzhou and Beijing in four to six weeks through the secret memorial system.[119] The Qing court thus had an informational advantage in promptly intervening and instructing the local officials, whereas the British authorities often had to rely on their agents in China to improvise. When it took one year or so to get any feedback from London about their decisions, the British representatives in China (like many of their counterparts from other European empires) effectively took most matters into their own hands. Even when they made mistakes, the home government's response was generally too little too late to prevent future rashness. Once the representatives had acted in the name of their government to commence serious hostilities with another government, it could become very difficult for those in London not to bail out their agents and their nation's reputation. The two Opium Wars were both *directly* triggered by such actions of British officials in southern China.[120]

In the aftermath of the *Lady Hughes* affair, the EIC council, along with other foreign representatives, prohibited saluting within the Pearl River. The British Parliament confirmed the council's power to arrest British subjects and send them back to London for illegal conduct in China.[121] The agents, captains, and supercargoes of British ships were also made "personally" responsible for compensating any financial damages caused by the misconduct of their ships' crew within Chinese waters and territory,[122] a strategy of deterrence similar in rationale to what some scholars have dubbed "collective responsibility" when discussing Chinese policies on foreigners in this period.

In the meantime, sensational reports of this case spread far beyond southern China. It was recounted in detail by Major Samuel Shaw in May 1785 in the official report of the first U.S. attempt to establish direct trade with China, which was then presented to Congress by Secretary of State John Jay. A passage from Shaw's letter captured the prevailing sentiment among the Western sojourners regarding Chinese law and justice even before the fate of the British gunner was known: "It is a maxim of the Chinese law that blood must answer for blood; in pursuance of which they demanded the unfortunate gunner. To give up this poor man was to consign him to certain death. Humanity pleaded powerfully against the measure."[123] Such was the first American official portrayal of Chinese law. The first British report of the dispute in the *Universal Register* (predecessor of the London *Times*) in June 1785 excited so much curiosity and alarm that the same newspaper published a more detailed "authentic" account the following month, which turned out to be just a condensed version of the council's *Narrative*.[124] All the attention attracted by the incident in Guangzhou, Calcutta, and London prompted a British embassy to China in 1788, sponsored by the EIC. The ambassador, Lieutenant Colonel Cathcart, was instructed to negotiate the best terms for British trade and the cession to the British Crown of a depot where Britons would be governed by their own laws. The embassy fell through when Cathcart died before reaching China.[125]

In December 1791, when the EIC submitted reports to Parliament in connection with the renewal of its charter, the *Lady Hughes* case again became a major concern. It was reiterated that the Chinese government was not only absolutist but also inflexible in holding every European responsible for the accident and for executing the gunner for the misadventure without proper trial.[126] This was followed in 1793 by the world-famous but ill-fated Macartney Embassy, which failed to achieve its goals not so much because Macartney refused to kowtow to the emperor—even though the Qing imperial ritual did play a crucial role in structuring the political relationship between Qing emperors and other rulers—but because the British alarmed the Qing court when they demanded permission to establish a permanent embassy and a factory in Beijing, open ports in eastern and northern China, and obtain the cession of one or two islands near Zhoushan (Chusan). It reminded the Qing authorities of the story of Macao and of British attempts to create another Macao in Zhejiang in the 1750s, which was mainly why the foreign trade had been restricted to Guangzhou in the first place. King George III might claim these concessions as proof of "brotherly affection," but the Qianlong emperor apparently saw the iron fist more than the velvet glove.[127]

The Cathcart and Macartney embassies were both designed to help place the British in China at least on the same footing as the Portuguese through treaties, but ideally with greater autonomy and immunity from Chinese law. To obtain an island in eastern China or establish a factory in or near Beijing would be a promising start. That was how British India and many other colonies were started. As the EIC officials stated in 1781, should an islet like Macao (or Zhoushan) ever fall into the hands of an "enterprising" people like the British, who knew how to extend all its advantages, it would "rise to a state of splendor, never yet equaled by any port in the East." That splendid prospect was precisely what the Qing authorities dreaded.[128] Qianlong thus warned George III in 1793, "Every inch of the territory of our Empire is marked on the map and the strictest vigilance is exercised over it all: even tiny islets and far-lying sandbanks are clearly defined as part of the provinces to which they belong."[129] The requests made by the British ambassador in 1793 were not fulfilled until after the First Opium War.

LEGACY IN MODERN HISTORIOGRAPHY: CULTURAL CLASHES AND ORIGINS OF EXTRATERRITORIALITY

Hosea Morse (1855–1934), an influential Anglo-American historian of Qing China's international relations, stated in 1910 that "the last Englishman surrendered for trial and execution was the Gunner of the *Lady Hughes* in 1784" and that "it had been a settled point in English policy that men accused of homicide should not be given up to trial by Chinese procedures" since then.[130] In this section, I briefly survey the intellectual genealogy of this origin myth of extraterritoriality in China and trace how it took root in the modern historiography of the past century. In his influential history of China in 1836, John Davis, by now a leading British Sinologist and a future governor of Hong Kong (1844–1848), maintained that it was a great mistake to think that Chinese law lacked the notions of justice and humanity or mental culpability. Rather, the Chinese clearly understood the differences between malicious, excusable, and justifiable homicide and shared the same principle as the British that it was "better [to] let the guilty escape than put the innocent to death." Nonetheless, he argued that every legal safeguard provided for the natives was unavailable to foreigners accused of homicide and that the Chinese treatment of the latter was "so perfectly unjustifiable" that it was "not only *excusable but imperative* in Europeans to resist the execution, *not of law, but of illegality*" (emphasis added). The *Lady Hughes* case was his most remarkable example.[131]

Davis was influenced by his Chinese language teacher, Robert Morrison (1782–1834), who went to China in 1807 as the first Protestant missionary and later became Chinese secretary and translator to the EIC factory and, in 1834, to the first British superintendent of trade, Lord Napier. In an anonymous essay in the *Chinese Repository* in 1834, Morrison maintained that the Chinese had a prejudice against all foreigners and required the life of a foreigner whenever he somehow caused the death of a Chinese. That practice was against the law of reason, of nature, and of nations. In his view, the Chinese considered homicide a debt that must be repaid in kind, and there were few exceptions in Chinese law to the general rule of blood for blood. The *Lady Hughes* case again served as the linchpin of his argument.[132]

Morrison, Davis, and many of their readers were fully aware that since their first arrival in southern China, the British and other Westerners had fought hard to prevent the Chinese government from applying Chinese law and procedure to the foreigners the same way as it did to the Chinese. They now argued that the Chinese government's "unequal" legal treatment of foreigners justified or even obliged Western defiance of Chinese law and sovereignty. More knowledge of Chinese language and law, especially after Sir George Thomas Staunton (1781–1859) published an English translation of the Qing Code in 1810, had cast doubt on the other, popular argument for extraterritoriality that had dismissed Chinese law as primitive and barbaric and thus inapplicable to Euro-Americans. Such knowledge prompted these founders of modern Sinology, including Staunton, to develop this new line of reasoning to legitimate extraterritoriality.[133]

Both Morrison and Davis contended that the Chinese application of different legal procedure to foreign homicides (according to the 1744 substatute) justified denial of Chinese jurisdiction. Morrison reasoned that since the laws of the host country failed to protect foreigners, the latter's obligation to obey those laws was canceled.[134] In Davis's view, it would have been difficult for foreigners to "make out a right" to oppose the laws of the country where they sojourned if they had been treated the same as the natives according to the Chinese law code. He insisted that a just and equal administration of the laws over foreigners and natives alike should be the precondition of the former's submission to those laws, a seemingly fair principle that would be conveniently ignored by the Western nations busy passing Chinese-exclusion laws later in the century.[135] This proposition then served to explain away the rampant foreign criminality that they now admitted with alarming honesty: "It is *in consequence of this* that *acts of atrocious violence,* on the part of foreigners, committed by them under the plea of doing themselves right, have been *attempted* to be justified, though coming *strictly under the definition of piracy, murder, or arson, which,* under a more vigorous Government, would have rendered them the property of the public executioner" (emphasis added). The British authorities felt compelled to systematically shield even known criminals from Chinese law.[136]

Extraterritoriality was proposed as an inevitable and benevolent solution to the problems of China's maladministration and unchecked foreign illegality. Davis thus noted, "This is a very barbarous and shocking state of things, little better on our side than on theirs, and it seems the duty of a great and civilized state, like England, to provide a remedy."[137] The alleged anomaly and disorder of the Indian legal system enabled the British colonial authorities to centralize power through codification in the same period, and a similar discourse of Oriental despotism and legal chaos now served to extend British law and jurisdiction to Chinese territory.[138] In June through August 1833, representing Chinese laws on homicide as unjust and unacceptable, Sir George Thomas Staunton twice introduced a motion in Parliament to set up an extraterritorial court in China to "end this anomalous state of the law." This British court of justice in China, first authorized by the China Trade Act of Parliament in August 1838 and then by an Order in Council on December 9, 1838, hardly functioned in the next decade, but Britain's victory in the First Opium War made it a treaty-based institution from 1843 to 1943 and *retrospectively* validated the century-long discourse of Chinese legal barbarity.[139]

These characterizations of Chinese law and justifications of extraterritoriality informed historians of China in the nineteenth and twentieth centuries. In his extremely popular book *The Middle Kingdom* (1848), Samuel Williams (1812–1884), an American missionary turned diplomat and Sinologist, defended extraterritoriality as a means of bringing law and order to a "state of nature" in the Sino-foreign contact zone.[140] In 1910, Morse's acclaimed study of China's foreign relations attributed earlier Sino-Western conflicts to the clash of cultures. Under this theory, as summarized by Peter Fay, the British "went to war with China over the strangled Gunner of the *Lady Hughes*, the kowtow, cottons—and nothing more!"[141] For Morse, the English laws on homicide were harsher than the Chinese laws but at least offered a fair trial for the accused; not so in China, however, and "the divergence in the views remained one of the questions to be settled by the arbitrament of war." Regardless of whether they used the British official archives, this preconception led scholars such as Morse, Earl Pritchard, Hsin-pao Chang, and Fay to reinforce the earlier narrative.[142]

Thanks to the work of various leading modern historians of China, the traditional narrative continued to enjoy wide purchase in the late twentieth century. John King Fairbank, a founder of modern Chinese studies in the West and one of Morse's disciples, helped turn the earlier discourse of cultural incommensurability into a scientific theory to account for Sino-Western conflicts and Western domination. He noted that the old China made no legal distinction between willful murder and accidental homicide, and that the lack of intent was not a mitigating factor in judging a crime there. From his perspective, the "right of extraterritoriality that the British and the rest of us claimed in China in the age of imperialism" was "a concrete expression of what we now call human rights."[143] When discussing the Lin Weixi case, which partly triggered the First Opium War in 1839, Frederic Wakeman Jr. (1937–2006) also saw this murder case as just another instance of the continued Sino-Western conflict over law and jurisdiction. After noting the comparative merits of Chinese justice, he then characterized extraterritoriality as the result of the incommensurability between Chinese and Western legal cultures. He explained the British refusal to turn over the homicide suspects in 1839 thus:

> In 1784, for example, a salute fired by the Country ship, *Lady Hughes*, accidentally killed a Chinese bystander. It was impossible to tell which gunner had delivered the fatal charge, but the Chinese had to have a

culprit so that the crime would not go unpunished. To them, the act was far more important than the motive, just as redressing a wrong was more important than punishing the perpetrator. What sounded like *lex talionis* in the 'life for a life' doctrine, was the desire to restore the ethical balance of a just reign by exchanging the victim's injured spirit for the culprit's life. Consequently, when the supercargo of the *Lady Hughes* could not produce the guilty gunner, he was seized as 'forfeit' instead. Eventually a hapless gunner was turned over to the Chinese and executed. The same kind of thing happened again in 1821, so that by the 1830s, Westerners were determined not to surrender a man to the local authorities unless he had already been tried by his own people and clearly proved guilty of homicide.[144]

This shows how the dominant discourse led an accomplished historian like Wakeman to adopt its discursive tropes as primary sources. Even the EIC officials had never claimed the identity of the gunner as an issue but only spread or repeated the rumor that the gunner himself was supposed to have absconded. Influenced by EIC secretary Peter Auber's misleading paraphrase in 1834, Morse stated in 1910 that the Chinese "were informed that it could not be definitely ascertained who the man was." Wakeman then emphatically asserted that "it was impossible to tell which gunner had delivered the fatal charge" before venturing a nuanced explanation of Chinese legal tradition.[145]

Wakeman held that Chinese justice was concerned more about punishment and the restoration of an ethical balance than about the actual identity and guilt of the offenders, and that the primary Chinese concern was to exchange the victim's "injured spirit for the culprit's life." He may have been influenced by Derk Bodde and Clarence Morris's widely read *Law in Imperial China* (1967), which argued that the Chinese legal system was obsessed with the cosmic order, which, when disrupted by a human crime, could be repaired only by adequate requital, demanding blood for blood. Chinese criminal justice was designed more to achieve the requital per se than to punish the real offenders or serve justice.[146] Through such influential works, the discourse that dated back at least to the *Lady Hughes* case gained renewed momentum two centuries later. Echoing Morrison's assertion that the Chinese considered homicide a debt, Wakeman's discussion appeared to rationalize the Chinese by design but was likely to perpetuate the origin myths of extraterritoriality. Historians writing before and after his work have challenged that argument, but to varying degrees, the traditional narrative has continued to influence the most recent scholarship and popular textbooks.[147]

In light of their scholarly achievements, the treatment of the *Lady Hughes* case and other disputes by these most renowned historians demonstrates the unusual difficulty of studying early modern Sino-Western relations under the shadow of traditional historiography. Over the course of two centuries, numerous commentators have updated and reinforced the earlier dominant representation of such landmark events. The passage of time and the accumulated weight of intellectual authority have made it seem both unnecessary and impossible to read these events from alternative perspectives or question the evidentiary basis of the dominant narratives. The resultant discourse of Chinese law and government has profoundly shaped our understanding of the Sino-Western encounter. The complex unfolding processes of negotiation, accommodation, and jurisdictional politics in the contact zone were blotted out in the discursive construction of cultural and racial boundaries. The next chapter explores how the dominant narratives about such disputes stimulated intellectual interest in studying Chinese law and imperial institutions and contributed to the rise of modern Sinology.

2

TRANSLATION OF THE QING CODE AND COLONIAL ORIGINS OF COMPARATIVE CHINESE LAW

After Sir George Thomas Staunton (1781–1859) published the first English translation of the Qing Code in 1810, known as *Ta Tsing Leu Lee* (hereafter *TTLL*), his work or its Italian, French, and Spanish retranslations became an indispensable text for serious discussions of late imperial Chinese law in Euro-America until the late twentieth century.[1] Presumably providing more accurate information of Chinese law and society than all prior publications in the West, *TTLL* was widely lauded as an epoch-making breakthrough in Western knowledge of not just Chinese law but also Chinese civilization, contributed to the rise of modern comparative study of law, and facilitated Western expansion in China and the Asia-Pacific.

This chapter addresses two sets of interrelated questions regarding Staunton's translation project. First, what gave rise to Staunton's interest in Chinese law? What was his role in the Sino-British encounters in the first half of the nineteenth century? Second, how did Staunton's transcultural experience shape the strategies he adopted in translating the Qing Code and trying to establish the authority of his translation? How did he resolve the discrepancies between legal categories rooted in two different legal traditions, and, in the process, how was Chinese law redefined and reclassified? As we shall see, Staunton was deeply involved in a number of legal disputes involving Britons in China. His linguistic fluency and knowledge of Chinese law and government helped the British extricate themselves from various difficult situations in China. After he became a member of

Parliament upon returning to Britain, Staunton actively participated in the policy debates concerning Britain's political and economic relations with China over three decades. His insistence that British diplomats should not perform the ceremony of *koutou* to the Jiaqing emperor was a direct cause of the failure of the Amherst Embassy of 1816 to get an imperial audience, let alone achieve the embassy's goals. He was a leading advocate of extraterritoriality in China and vocally defended the British government's decision to wage the First Opium War. *TTLL* also became a crucial instrument of colonial administration: after Britain colonized Hong Kong, Governor John Davis found "no better way of governing the Chinese population (by far the majority) than by the Penal Code" translated by Staunton, and British judges in Hong Kong and other colonies reportedly always had a copy of *TTLL* before them in cases involving Chinese.[2] Addressing the foregoing questions will illuminate the interplay between cultural and political practices of empire, which has important implications for modern knowledge of Chinese law and for the history of the Western quest for extraterritoriality and epistemological conquest in China.

In studying Staunton's translation and its broader context at the early stage of modern Sinological Orientalism, this chapter seeks to chart the complex, dynamic web of competing knowledge regimes, imperial formations, and cultural assumptions that informed the production and reception of *TTLL*. It does so by focusing on the translator and his multiple subject positions as a senior EIC official and expectant diplomat and politician representing British interests, an ambitious Orientalist challenging prior China knowledge, a cultural mediator seeking transcultural engagement, and an heir of the Enlightenment ideas of objective knowledge. These subject positions produced what is called an "ambiguated" attitude of the translator toward Chinese law and civilization, an attitude characteristic of a number of nineteenth-century British Sinologists such as John Davis (1795–1890) and James Legge (1815–1897).[3] This attitude impacted how Chinese law was represented and, as we shall see, also resulted in a certain kind of multivocality in the text of *TTLL*—an openness to different interpretations, albeit not in an unlimited way, by differently positioned readers. Tracing the origins of this translation project also reveals how local Chinese officials participated in the Western representation of Chinese laws. In this process of translingual practice, Chinese law was reconceptualized through familiar

Western categories and terminology. As *TTLL* was regarded as the most authoritative document for deciphering the essence of Chinese civilization and tradition, Staunton's project allowed Western intellectuals to claim that China and its culture and institutions were finally made intelligible and classifiable as part of Western comparative literature. Far from simply an apolitical transfer of knowledge, *TTLL* should be seen as an instance of the British seeking to gain epistemic control over the "inscrutable" Chinese empire. It was indeed celebrated as such by Staunton's contemporaries in Britain and other European countries and was retranslated and widely cited in other major European languages.

The chapter begins with an overview of imperial knowledge production and the Sino-European struggles for the control over language, translation, and official communications. This is followed by an analysis of Staunton's efforts to produce *TTLL* out of two presumably incommensurable legal, linguistic, cultural, and epistemological traditions. The third section focuses on Staunton's translation strategies and his motivations for undertaking this project. The last section discusses the enduring impact of Staunton's endeavor on the Western knowledge of Chinese law and culture.

LANGUAGE, REPRESENTATION, AND KNOWLEDGE PRODUCTION IN THE PRE-1810 ENCOUNTER

Staunton's translation of the Qing Code can be seen as a key node in the transnational network of knowledge production in the age of empire. It occurred at a time when "the cultural riches of India, China, Japan, Persia and Islam were [being] firmly deposited at the heart of European culture."[4] While preaching their religion or conducting trade, European religious or mercantile explorers generated travel writings, surveys, maps, scientific specimens, reports, pictures, and statistics regarding foreign peoples and lands. These filled the imperial archives as intelligence for improving the administration and defense of the far-flung colonial empire, and also paved the way for modern sciences and disciplines such as botany, zoology, geography, anthropology, political economy, and comparative studies.[5] For Britain, the pursuit of scientific knowledge had been "tightly bound" with the promotion of commerce, colonialism, Christianity, and emergent patriotism. By the mid-nineteenth century, "a formal empire of professional knowledge"[6] had been created alongside the expansion of Britain, and the ascendancy of British power in India had also "induced a desire for further knowledge about the Empire of China."[7]

However, there was a key difference between Western acquisition of knowledge in China and elsewhere, since China retained control over the terms of its contact with the Western states until the early 1800s. To win the Chinese elites' approval of their evangelical mission, many early European missionaries followed the tactic of "accommodation" of Matteo Ricci (1552–1610) and Michele Ruggiero (1543–1607), who entered late-Ming China in the 1580s. They took pains to learn Chinese languages and culture, worked as court astronomers or artists, made cannons or maps, or helped negotiate the Sino-Russian Treaty of Nerchinsk for Qing China in 1689 on the basis of the European law of nations.[8] But even such efforts could not secure a "stable foundation" for their mission, which was officially banned in the early 1700s after the Rites Controversy with the Vatican papacy.[9] The fact that they could not simply impose their will upon the Chinese influenced the way the Europeans interacted with and wrote about the latter. Roger Hart and others have shown that the conceptual ambiguities in seventeenth-century Chinese translation of European texts were not produced by the presumed Sino-Western linguistic or cultural "incommensurability" but introduced by Jesuit missionaries and their Chinese patrons trying to operate in a China-dominated political milieu.[10] When trying hard to speak, think, and act like Chinese literati, Ricci and other missionaries, as Willard Peterson has noted, "were indoctrinating themselves" even as they sought to disseminate Western learning and religion. How to maintain the increasingly blurred epistemological or cultural boundaries was "at the core of the debates among missionaries as well as among Catholics back in Europe over the policy of accommodation" and over the translation of such key words as "God" during the Rites Controversy.[11] To maintain the assumption of Christian or Western superiority while claiming the Chinese as "civilized" enough to deserve evangelical or diplomatic missions persisted in causing tensions and ambivalence in the resultant Western writings about China. As Sir William Jones (1746–1794), a leading Orientalist of the century, noted in 1792, China was extolled by some Europeans as the oldest and wisest and the most ingenious of all nations but denied by others in its claim to antiquity or any original achievement in culture, science, government, or the arts.[12]

The political and legal conditions of pre-1810 Sino-Western contact also influenced the issue of language and bilateral communication. Early modern transcultural encounters often involved different languages and peoples characterized by asymmetrical power relations. Language, as the medium of communication and a marker of cultural or ethnic identity, was crucial to imperial administration at home and to international relations among jostling empires.[13] Hence, many sixteenth- or seventh-century European colonial explorers considered it a priority to not just master the local languages they came across—by studying, publishing, and classifying their alphabet, vocabulary, and grammar—but also to *displace* them whenever possible.[14] Keeping the natives' language and culture intact, in spite of foreign military or political domination, could threaten the conquest regime's legitimacy and long-term legacy. Students of South Asian history know well the famous policy advocated by Sir Thomas Babington Macaulay (1800–1859), a British Liberal politician and senior colonial administrator, to Anglicize Indian education in order to produce "a class of persons, Indian in blood and colour, but English in taste, in opinions, in morals, and intellect."[15] Besides improving colonial governance, this would assure an "imperishable empire" by naturalizing Britain's language, literature, law, and values among the colonized.[16] China and India were different in their formal political relationship to the European empires at least until the mid-nineteenth century. But the epistemological and political value of controlling language and education was not lost on early European explorers in China. This was rather dramatically illustrated by Father Alonso Sánchez, a Jesuit leader in the East Indies, who echoed others in urging King Philip II of Spain in 1587 to conquer China to revenge its restrictive foreign policies and liberate its people from tyranny and depravity. For eternal glory to God and the king and all Christians, Sánchez also envisioned a "hispanized and christianized" Chinese empire by educating the Chinese in Western languages, culture, and sciences at Spanish schools; he believed that the Chinese and Spanish-Chinese creoles, thus educated, would fight for the Spanish global empire as if it were their own.[17] Several Spanish scholars have discussed this proposal, but few have noticed its call for colonizing the Chinese language and education and the similarity of its rationale with other, later colonial projects such as Macaulay's.

As this ambitious proposal to send a military expedition to turn China into a "tributary" state fell through after the Spanish Armada was defeated by the English navy in 1588, Western missionaries, traders, and diplomats entered China under far less favorable conditions than Sánchez and others had envisioned for the next 250 years.[18] But the Europeans recognized the importance of mastering the Chinese language from the outset. A factor that reportedly contributed to the disastrous fate of the first Portuguese (and European) embassy to China in 1521 was that the Portuguese letter of state was found different in form and content from its supposed Chinese translation received by the Ming court.[19] As early as the 1550s, Jesuit missionaries in Macao urged their patrons in Europe to have people study Chinese language and law.[20] Improved Chinese proficiency partly helped save a Portuguese mission in 1667–1670. The missionaries in Macao and Beijing secretly collaborated in translating the Portuguese letter of state by deleting the sensitive issue of Macao and by calling the embassy a "congratulatory mission" (*jinhe*) instead of a "tributary mission" (*jingong*) to avoid offending the Qing government or undermining Portugal's national honor.[21]

From their experience of dealing with the contentious issue of Manchu and Chinese languages in their conquest regime, the Qing rulers were aware of the practical and symbolic significance of language control in imperial governance.[22] Although European missionaries were permitted to study and use Manchu (until 1805) and Chinese in order to better serve the Qing court, Western traders and official agents were subjected to a different set of rules. Under the so-called Canton System, all Westerners in southern China were required to submit any written correspondence, known as *bing*, or "petition," in their own language, which would then be translated into Chinese by licensed linguists and forwarded by the Hong merchants to the local Chinese officials. In addition, the Chinese linguists and merchants were to explain Chinese laws and customs to the foreigners and monitor their compliance. From 1744 onward, a foreign petition normally had to go through the different levels of local government before it was allowed, if at all, to reach the Qing provincial or central authorities.[23] To be sure, these regulations were partly based on practical considerations and were intended to minimize potential trouble by tightly controlling the Westerners, who were far from being considered peaceful and trustworthy in the Chinese official discourse since the early seventeenth century. But this language policy also reflected a desire to maintain the Sino-Western distinction or hierarchy despite the Qing official ideology of universal rulership, which the Guangdong officials admitted would suggest "the same language by all in a prosperous era" (*shengshi tongwen*).[24] In a memorial approved by the Qianlong emperor in 1760, Liangguang governor-general Li Shiyao justified the codification of such regulations (*dingli*) as necessary for controlling foreigners, particularly the "arrogant and troublesome British," and for preventing their conspiracy with "treacherous Chinese" (*hanjian*). To these Qing officials, the regulations struck a fine balance between taking precautions at early signs of danger (*fangwei dujian*) and cherishing those from afar and encouraging commerce (*rouyuan xushang*).[25]

Until the First Opium War, Qing officials generally viewed the authorized Chinese version of foreign correspondence as the only binding one. When the Portuguese Senate in Macao resolved in 1803 that future petitions would include the Portuguese original and a Chinese translation, the Xiangshan county magistrate rejected this as a transgression of both the established rules and Sino-foreign boundaries. Likewise, in 1810 the Liangguang governor-general refused to accept British communications written in Chinese.[26] These two examples indicate that the Europeans were not unaware of the actual and symbolic significance of these linguistic policies. As in the notorious controversies over *koutou* in the Macartney Embassy and then in the Amherst Embassy of 1816, Lydia Liu's recent study of the "supersign" of *yi*/barbarian once again demonstrates the considerable imperial interests at stake underlying such seemingly trivial quarrels over words and rhetorical etiquette.[27] It took the First Opium War and the Treaty of Nanjing in 1842 to replace the term *bing* (petition) (which came to upset and haunt Foreign Secretary Lord Palmerston throughout the late 1830s) with "communication" or "statement," and the Second Opium War and the Treaty of Tianjin in 1858 to establish the English version as binding in all British official communications with the Chinese.[28]

In the meantime, the Qing government officially prohibited the teaching of Chinese among Westerners in China in 1760, after the British made several attempts to challenge the Canton System by sending trading ships to eastern and northern China with the assistance of James Flint. Flint became the first British to speak Chinese with some fluency after several years of language study starting in 1736 and was later appointed Chinese translator for the EIC officials in China.[29] Having sailed to Tianjin to file a complaint against the Guangdong officials in 1759, Flint was eventually sentenced by the Qing authorities to three years of confinement near Macao for his "cunning and deceitful" (*qiaoza*) conduct, while his Chinese collaborator, Liu Yabian, was executed for drafting the British complaint in Chinese and "instigating" the British violation of the law.[30] After the departure of Thomas Bevan (who succeeded Flint) in 1780, the British had no trusted Chinese interpreter for two decades. In the *Lady Hughes* dispute, they often relied on the French consul's Chinese interpreter, a Mr. Galbert, who was later appointed to the aborted Cathcart Embassy in 1788.[31] As both Flint and Galbert had passed away by the time of the Macartney Embassy, it hired two Chinese priests in Naples. The embassy's important letters were translated from English into Latin by John Hüttner, a German doctor, and the Chinese interpreter, Li Zibiao, who understood no English, explained the meaning of the Latin version orally to the Chinese scribe; the scribe then organized the letter in the appropriate style before Staunton copied it out. The British found this process of multiple translations hopeless for faithful communication of their sentiment and demands, especially given the participation of Chinese natives.[32]

Of course, despite all the government restrictions, transcultural adaptation and accommodation in southern China had existed at the societal level, and the contact and collaboration between foreigners and local Chinese had continued to grow far beyond the authorized extent and scope since the late Ming. Besides the large number of Chinese living within the walled Portuguese settlement in the Macao Peninsula, Chinese compradors, pilots, and domestic servants, as well as thousands of laborers, were hired by the Euro-Americans each trading season. Many other local people made a living by selling goods and services to the foreigners. All this interaction and mingling necessitated communication through a commonly understood language. The Europeans had turned to Chinese linguists for help since their arrival in the sixteenth century. These linguists were later licensed by the local government to provide foreigners with a variety of services, including all Chinese paperwork, for handsome fees.[33] By the early 1700s, the common dialect used by the three or four licensed linguists and other Chinese to communicate with the Europeans was so-called pidgin English, a mixture of European (mostly English and Portuguese) and Chinese words. In the same period, Yin Guangren (1691–1758) and Zhang Rulin, the first two Macao vice-prefects, recorded the increased popularity of that hybrid dialect and included a vocabulary of about 400 foreign words, transliterated with Chinese characters, in their famous chronicle of Macao.[34]

The Europeans' insistence upon their own dialects and linguists as the only trustworthy means of representation and communication was related to their concern about imperial identity and interests in the contact zones. The Qing authorities found pidgin English and native linguists adequate for their purposes. Because these foreigners presumably came only for trade, as Governor-General Li Shiyao explained in 1759, there was no need for them to interact with the local people beyond selling and buying goods.[35] Like many other Europeans, however, the British came to China not just as ordinary traders but also as subjects of an ambitious colonial empire who expected the same dignity and privileges that they had enjoyed elsewhere in the Indies. This strong sense of imperial subjectivity required faithful representation of British power and entitlements. The British in China complained that the failure of Chinese linguists and merchants to communicate their rights and feelings contributed to the insults and injuries they suffered. They observed in 1728 that the Chinese linguists feared their government officials so much that they dared not communicate foreigners' true sentiment to the latter. A century later, the British still pointed to inability of Chinese linguists to translate the full force of their arguments as a cause of their unsatisfactory status in China.[36]

Chinese policies on language and information made attempts to acquire knowledge of China a difficult task. It was lamented that China remained a geopolitical terra incognita to the West as late as the 1830s. The rapidly proliferating information about other parts of the world made the opaqueness of China and East Asia in general all the more striking and frustrating.[37] To a great extent, the Macartney Embassy constituted "a sort of first enabling experience" for modern Sinology, as Edward Said has characterized Napoléon's Egyptian expeditions in 1798–1801 in relation to modern Orientalism.[38] In 1797, Sir George Leonard Staunton (1737–1801), Thomas

Staunton's father and a longtime associate of Lord Macartney's in the Indies before becoming deputy ambassador of the embassy, published the embassy's official account. John Barrow (1764–1848), Thomas Staunton's math tutor and the ambassador's comptroller, published his *Travels in China* in 1804 and an abridged version of Macartney's *China Journal* three years later. In these influential publications, which claimed to update European knowledge, China was no longer regarded as a powerful and highly cultured nation awaiting the Gospel, but it was seen as an ancient and stagnant society under a despotic government that was unable or unwilling to appreciate modern diplomacy, science, free trade, bourgeois values, and British superiority.[39]

What fueled the optimism of Macartney, Barrow, and other Britons about future relations with China was not just British domination over the maritime world, and over the China trade among Western nations, but also its anticipated mastery of the Chinese language, the "universal" written script in East and Southeast Asia, which would greatly facilitate British ambitions in the Asia-Pacific.[40] Anticipating an English translation of the Qing Code soon, Barrow and his readers were eager to see how this largest Asian empire had been governed.[41] The translator Barrow had in mind was the young Thomas Staunton, whom Macartney and others had expected to master the Chinese language a few years earlier. In 1792–1794, Staunton had accompanied his father to China as Macartney's page boy. For some time before and during the yearlong voyage, he had studied with the two Chinese interpreters and become fluent enough to "copy all [Macartney's] diplomatic papers for the Chinese government" (which the Chinese interpreters had declined to do for fear of offending their government) and to speak with the Qianlong emperor in the audience of September 14, 1793. Already well versed in English, Latin, Greek, French, and Chinese, this twelve-year-old boy seemed to Macartney and others to be destined for a prominent career as another "Oriental Jones."[42] Staunton did not disappoint them. If, as Macartney and others claimed, linguistic deficiency was indeed an important reason why the embassy failed to obtain formal diplomatic recognition and other legal and economic privileges from China, Staunton's China knowledge and translation of the Qing Code would become not just a cultural event but also an epistemological and political event that had the potential to reconfigure Sino-British relations.

STAUNTON'S ROLE IN MEDIATING LEGAL
DISPUTES IN SOUTHERN CHINA

After a six-month voyage from England, Staunton arrived at Guangzhou on January 22, 1800, as a writer (i.e., clerk) for the British Factory. Such an appointment, usually reserved for sons of EIC directors, was considered a sure and rapid path to fortune or power.[43] His father's network helped, but the young Staunton maintained that he was appointed because of his proficiency in Chinese.[44] He scarcely enjoyed his time in a strange place so far away from his parents, but he soon found more than a little gratification in his value to the enormous British interests in China.

Within three weeks of his arrival, the British were involved in another troublesome homicide case. Although reminiscent of the tensions and compromises between the Chinese and Europeans in southern China as analyzed in chapter 1, this case is worth mentioning because it was another important step in the British quest for extraterritoriality in China. It provided EIC officials with further proof of the vital importance of having a China expert as an employee, and of deciphering not just Chinese law but also its administration. I highlight here only some of the relevant facts of this meticulously documented case.

On February 11, a British officer aboard His Majesty's schooner *Providence* opened fire at a suspicious Chinese boat nearby, killing two and injuring a third Chinese person at Huangpu. The EIC Select Committee tried to "hush up the matter" by offering several hundred dollars to relatives of the victims while denying any influence over the British naval officers. Captain John Dilkes, commander of the Royal Navy in China, found the EIC officials' tactic cowardly and humiliating, however, and he declared that he would rather settle "the disputes between the King of England and the Emperor of China." Refusing to surrender the suspect, he insisted that the Chinese authorities should first hear his countercharge against the victims as thieves who were attempting to cut the anchoring cable of the *Providence*, an accusation denied by the surviving Chinese witnesses. Staunton's linguistic skills were crucial to all communications and negotiations with the Chinese. With his help, Dilkes and the Select Committee pressured the Hong merchants and then the local officials to agree to conduct the trial in the presence of British officials for the first time in the history of

FIGURE 2.1 Sir George Thomas Staunton (1781–1859), politician, writer, and Sinologist. Oil on canvas, 127 × 100 cm; Sir Martin Archer Shee (1769–1850).

Presented by Squadron Leader Lynch-Staunton, 1951.
Courtesy of UK Government Art Collection, No. 1240.

Sino-British relations. During the trial, when the provincial judge refused to accept as conclusive evidence statements obtained by Dilkes from British sailors, Dilkes protested loudly and began interrogating the witnesses through Staunton. Apparently never expecting such contempt of his authority, the provincial judge angrily ordered the Britons removed, but he also had to stop the trial. Unwilling to confront hundreds of armed British sailors in order to arrest the suspect, some local officials eventually manipulated the statutory language of the Qing Code to conclude that the injured Chinese had survived the forty-day statute of limitations (*baogu xianqi*) for homicide. Although the accused was still punishable under Chinese law for causing two deaths, the British were told that Governor-General Jiqing's benevolent disposition had induced him to dispense with the strict execution of the law and that, in the future, they must report any alleged theft to the Chinese authorities first instead of shooting people.[45]

The Qing officials' pretension to universal benevolence proved less objectionable this time than on other occasions. Staunton and the EIC Select Committee praised their humaneness and justice, while the British vice admiral in the East Indies believed that the accused probably would not have been acquitted by an English jury under English law.[46] Reflecting upon the *Providence* case, Staunton observed in a note to *TTLL* that knowledge of the legal technicality regarding the statute of limitations in homicide cases "contributed to extricate the East India Company's representatives in China, from very serious difficulties, and from the distressing alternative, of either ignominiously sacrificing the life of a British subject, or totally abandoning the important commercial interests under their management."[47]

The *Providence* case led to a rethinking of Qing law and justice in the foreign community. The British attempt at a "joint trial" in their own style provided an example for the British officials in the 1807 *Neptune* case, explained below, and for the Americans in the *Emily* case of 1821. It was later cited as a precedent for the Mixed Court that handled Sino-Western cases in the treaty ports after the Second Opium War of 1860. "Nothing could have been handsomer," Morse declared a century later, "than this settlement of what might have become a second *Lady Hughes* case."[48]

According to Staunton and his superiors, having a trusted British interpreter instead of a "corrupted or intimidated" native linguist made all the difference in the *Providence* case.[49] While Staunton might have exaggerated his personal role, there is no doubt that without his linguistic ability, a Mixed Court would have been unimaginable, and the result of this case might have been very different. Staunton provided the interpretation and translation at critical moments of the dispute, including meetings with Chinese officials in April 1800. His accounts became the official records of the British, and thus modern historians' only primary sources for the negotiations and trial since no such Chinese reports have survived.[50] His Chinese proficiency, although reportedly limited, presumably made the Qing officials fully cognizant of the justice of the British position.[51] For the first time, the British could count on one of their own to write letters *in Chinese* to the Qing government, thereby controlling how they were represented by avoiding, among other things, Chinese expressions injurious to their interests and national honor.[52] As shown in the case of James Flint, who used his Chinese proficiency to help the British in China challenge the Canton System in the 1740s and 1750s, this new linguistic power began to loosen Qing China's long and firm control over the Sino-Western encounter. When briefing the Court of Directors three months after the *Providence* case, the Select Committee made some prophetic remarks that also revealed the motives for Staunton's translation of the Qing Code:

> We cannot dismiss this subject without conveying our testimony & Satisfaction at the attention Mr. Staunton pays to his improvement in the language of the Country, nor contemplate but with pleasure the use he has, and may hereafter be of in any negotiations with the Chinese Government; in proof of which we need only observe that, at the last conference, on the 9th of April, the Mandarine was not desirous that any Hong Merchant should attend. We understand likewise that he has some prospect of obtaining a Copy of the famous Chinese Code, so highly extolled in the French work, 'Mémoires sur les Chinois,' in which case, perhaps the honour is reserved for him supplying in time several desiderata in literature.[53]

At the end of this dispute, Richard Hall, president of the Select Committee, asked the Guangdong officials for permission to hire language teachers and obtain a copy of the printed Chinese laws for their information and obedience, as the British were "continually liable to involuntary infringements of them." Governor-General Jiqing appreciated their proclaimed intent but declined the request, noting that Chinese literati were not among those allowed to provide services to foreigners and that a copy of the Qing Code was too voluminous and complicated to be useful to foreigners. Those reasons were not totally groundless, but the more serious concern was, as Jiqing added, that because of the Qing Code's official nature, it could not be given to foreigners without the emperor's approval. Hall denied any inappropriate design to spy on China's political institutions, but the local officials agreed only to provide extracts of relevant statutes from the code.[54] EIC representatives had made similar requests in 1795, also to no avail.[55]

In fact, however, these Chinese restrictions had become a dead letter when Staunton privately purchased a copy of the Qing Code prior to Hall's formal request.[56] During the next sixteen years, until he permanently returned home in 1817, Staunton used his knowledge of the Chinese language, law, and government to play a key role in helping improve the British status in China, including a hard-won temporary consent from the Guangdong officials in 1814 to permit the EIC Select Committee to submit petitions *in Chinese* if written by themselves or their designates as long as the subject matter of the petitions did not require the emperor's attention.[57] In light of his success in mastering the Chinese language, the EIC devoted far greater resources to Chinese study among its agents in the next few decades. The Amherst Embassy in 1816 boasted five British-born Chinese interpreters, besides Staunton as a royal commissioner.[58] From 1816 to 1834, eleven EIC writers studied Chinese with Robert Morrison in Guangzhou.[59] Staunton's example in breaking down the linguistic walls of the Chinese empire was soon followed by other Euro-American Sinologists such as Morrison, William Milne (1785–1822), John Davis, Karl (Charles) Gutzlaff (1803–1851), and Samuel Williams (1812–1884). Before Britain and other Western powers were able to make their language the binding language for official communications with the Chinese government after the Opium Wars, the ability to decode and manipulate Chinese had enabled them to gradually but steadily undermine the Canton System and thus Qing China's sovereignty and control over the Sino-Western encounter.

If the *Providence* case highlighted the importance of understanding Chinese law, the *Neptune* case in 1807 reinforced the belief that knowledge of Chinese law and governing logic could actually make Chinese institutions and bureaucrats serve British interests. In Staunton's words, mastery of Chinese laws would enable the British to "submit to the forms of Chinese justice . . . without risking unwarrantably the sacrifice of the life of a British subject."[60] Although the sale of Chinese books and state papers to foreigners was strictly forbidden by law, Staunton had amassed a considerable personal library by the end of 1800, with nearly a thousand volumes of Chinese books, including large collections of Qing law and cases and the *Peking Gazette*, which published official memorials and edicts every other day. From the latter, he translated those documents most relevant to British concerns for the EIC management and Governor-General Lord Wellesley in British India. Access to Chinese language and law gave Staunton and his countrymen the ability to navigate the labyrinth of the Chinese legal system. Indeed, he and his superiors might have drawn directly from the time-honored practice of Chinese pettifoggers by perusing their "secret handbooks" (*songshi miben*) in his collection, such as *Jingtian lei* (*Advice for Thunderous [Victories]*) and *Fajia toudan han* (*Legal Specialists' Scary Strategies*).[61] Besides explicating the statutes in simple language, these handbooks, outlawed since 1742, provided specific strategies and models for drafting accusations and defenses in all kinds of legal disputes, including homicides.[62]

One thing we know for sure is that Staunton's knowledge of Qing law on "purely accidental homicide" enabled the British to pressure Chinese officials to fit the *Neptune* case into that law in order to avoid punishment of the British offenders.[63] The basic facts of the case were similar to those of the *Lady Hughes* and *Providence* cases. Fifty-two British sailors from an EIC ship, the *Neptune*, engaged in a series of violent riots and affrays with local residents at Guangzhou and killed one of them, Liao Yadeng, on February 24, 1807. After a month of delay and trade stoppage, the British finally agreed to send the sailors for trial at their old factory, guarded by two British Royal Marines with fixed bayonets (see figure 2.2). Under contemporary English law, all rioters would have been presumed guilty of the killing unless they proved otherwise, but Chinese law required the judge to identify the principal offender who either instigated the riot or dealt the fatal blow. Thanks to Staunton's knowledge of Chinese law, all the suspects denied responsibility and refused to testify against one another; the British officials conceded only that eleven sailors were *equally* responsible for the "disorderly" conduct but not for the homicide. As Staunton noted, the Chinese judges did not know what to do in the three hearings conducted under the unusual restrictions by the British.[64]

Unable to obtain the evidence or suspects and anxious to avoid administrative liabilities for failure to close such cases before the strict deadline, the Chinese officials eventually submitted a fabricated story to the emperor, stating that a sailor named Edward Sheen (who admitted only holding a tobacco pipe near the crime scene) accidentally dropped a stick from an upper-floor street-side window and killed the victim, who was passing below. That made it unnecessary to arrest or punish Sheen or any other Britons, except for imposing a fine of 12.42 taels (about four pounds, four shillings sterling) under the Qing statute of accidental homicide (*guoshisha*),

FIGURE 2.2 Trial of the sailors of the ship *Neptune*, ca. 1807. Oil paint, canvas, 32 × 43½ in. (81.28 × 110.49 cm), attributed to Spoilum (ca. 1770–1805), Lamqua (ca. 1825–1860).

Museum purchase, 1970. Courtesy of Peabody Essex Museum, M14311.

even though the death was at least a case of intentional killing (*gusha*) or killing in an affray (*dousha*).[65] Manipulating the legal system at the expense of the victim and the Qing central government, the local officials again extricated themselves as well as the British from the practical predicament.

Staunton appended his translation of the Chinese official report of this case, as approved by the Jiaqing emperor (r. 1796–1820), to the end of *TTLL* in 1810. There a reader would see only the corruption or dishonesty of the Qing officials without knowing the role of the British. More important, the century-old representation of the killing of local Chinese by Europeans as accidental homicides, as analyzed in chapter 1, now became self-perpetuating with the complicity of Guangdong merchants and officials, who prioritized personal interests over those of their superiors or the dead Chinese victims. In this sense, these Chinese actors actively participated in the Orientalist construct of Chinese law and justice that would prevail among Euro-Americans in this period. Just as the British EIC agents often faced the dilemma of either knowingly obstructing or scandalously submitting to Chinese law and justice, local Chinese officials faced a tough situation. According to contemporary witnesses, if they had tried to take the suspects by force in the *Neptune* case, they would "get a sound drubbing," as the British had a force of 2,000 men near Guangzhou eager to attack.[66] To the Guangdong officials and merchants, that danger outweighed the danger of being detected by the Ministry of Justice or the emperor in Beijing. Staunton also saw that, but he preferred to interpret the outcome as proof that the Chinese had come to develop "a distinct perception of the very great additional weight and respectability" carried by the English name since the *Lady Hughes* case of 1784.[67] When a local official implied that the Select Committee and Staunton might suffer inconveniences if the offenders were not handed over, Staunton warned the Chinese to abstain from such menacing remarks in the future because the Britons could not be intimidated but had a keen sense of insult. This portrayal of the British as a fearless but sensitive people, which reportedly lowered the Chinese officials' tone and made them more conciliatory throughout this dispute, was frequently used in the Sino-British encounter.[68] The Select Committee reported that the value of Staunton's assistance on this trying occasion could not be overestimated. Echoing this in April 1808, the EIC directors noted that Staunton's Chinese proficiency enabled him to give "a faithful interpretation" of British sentiment to the Chinese even though it might be displeasing and would not have been conveyed by the native linguists or merchants. They appointed Staunton Chinese interpreter to the British Factory with an additional annual salary of 500 pounds as a token of appreciation and an incentive for other junior employees to follow suit.[69] Staunton and his superiors were further convinced that deciphering the local language and law could help them make the Chinese authorities, however corrupt and despotic, work for British interests. Translation of the Qing Code became a priority.

THE POLITICS OF CULTURAL TRANSLATION OF CHINESE LAW

The traditional understanding of translation hinges on the prevalent notions of knowledge and representation grounded in Western philosophy, which often assume the neutrality of translators and the transparency of the translation process itself.[70] Recent critical studies have challenged these assumptions. Translation is no longer understood as simply a project to find equivalents between two seemingly incommensurable linguistic or cultural systems. Instead, as Lydia Liu has pointed out, what the translator actually does is to "create tropes of equivalence in the middle zone of translation" between the two languages. This zone of hypothetical equivalence becomes a site where new vocabulary, meanings, or discourses are invented, contested, or normalized, and where possibilities of change are enabled.[71] Many such features of translingual politics can be seen in Staunton's *TTLL*. In this project, he not only created a whole body of information about nearly every aspect of the formal Chinese legal system but also introduced numerous new definitions, phrases, and conceptual categories that are still used to characterize or compare Chinese legal tradition.

In this section, I am particularly interested in how *TTLL* was conditioned by the multiple subject positions of the translator, George Thomas Staunton, in light of his role as would-be diplomat and politician, Sinologist, intellectual, and EIC official. Its direct linkage to the political-economic interests and epistemological agenda of the British imperial project has been discussed in the previous sections, but the imperial orientation did not entirely *determine* the translation and representational processes. Modern scholars have offered divergent assessments of Staunton's translation. Publishing a new English translation of the statutes of the Qing Code in 1994, William C. Jones (1926–2005), an American specialist in Qing legal history, suggested that Staunton's translation, with the numerous substantial changes and omissions noted below, was "so free as to be inaccurate" and almost useless.[72] Translation scholar James St. André argued ten years later that Staunton's "free translation" was designed to valorize Chinese law and culture in the West by making them appear more logical and just than they actually were.[73] The translation's "accuracy" and the question of whether the translator intended to valorize Chinese law are not my main concern here, as focusing on them would risk oversimplifying the nature and implications of this transcultural text.

In explicating the characteristics and cultural-political effects of *TTLL*, I draw upon French literary theorist Gérard Genette's influential analysis of "paratexts." Staunton's *TTLL* begins with a preface, followed by a table of contents, the main text of the translation, and an appendix consisting of miscellaneous notes and translations of Chinese official documents. Except for the main text, all the information in the book—title, dedication, preface, table of contents, page format, notes, appendix, and the relevant advertising, diaries, correspondence, and translator's subsequent commentaries—constitute what Genette has called paratexts. They form a "zone" of information at the "fringe" of the main text but crucially mediate or even "control" a reader's experience with the text.[74] As will become clear, some of *TTLL*'s paratexts took on a life of their own or overshadowed the main text in reshaping the image of Chinese law. Thus, this analysis may suggest a potential antidote to the totalizing theories of empire, knowledge, power, or Orientalism.

Reducing the Foreignness of the Chinese Text

Staunton's private ambition was to firmly establish his credentials as a leading Sinologist by undertaking this translation project. This would require him to deeply engage with Chinese texts and informants to mediate the difference between the two cultures and peoples. It was a daunting task since he had to overcome the prevailing British view, which he shared to a certain extent, of the Chinese as inherently dishonest and timid, and thus untrustworthy as sources of reliable knowledge.[75] Given the presumed cultural, linguistic, or ethnic incommensurability, how was it possible then to produce accurate and valuable knowledge from a Chinese text? What strategies did Staunton adopt to prove himself to be an objective and transparent translator, and his translation an authoritative representation of the Chinese original? What impact did these strategies have on his work?

By comparing the translation with contemporary editions of the Qing Code, one sees Staunton's specific tactics and struggles in trying to create a zone of hypothetical equivalence between the two supposedly incompatible systems. While these tactics enabled him to suspend the cultural difference in order to assert the authenticity and authority of his translation, they also resulted in new information that reinforced Sino-Western cultural boundaries for some of his readers while allowing other readers to find evidence of greater commonalities than had been recognized before. One of Staunton's first tasks was to make *TTLL*, the translated text, conform to the European or British visual sensibility by changing the organizational structure of the Chinese source text. Although he admitted that the original structure of the Qing Code might be very clear to Chinese readers, Staunton found it most perplexing to Western foreigners.[76] To tame the alienating visual difference, Staunton adopted a multilayered system to divide the code into *Divisions*, and further into *Books* and distinctively numbered *Sections* (totaling 436). He also made significant alterations to the important tables at the beginning of the code concerning the scale of punishments, monetary redemption, instruments for interrogation, and degrees of familial relationship.[77] Sometimes he omitted tables or converted them into text, and text into numerical scales, leaving out much relevant information.[78] For instance, he reduced the highly nuanced definitions of Chinese familial relationship and mourning obligation (*shangfutu*) in eight tables to a half-page textual summary based on the European idea of kinship of four degrees, even though the original Chinese distinctions were essential for interpreting many statutes, such as when determining offenses committed against relatives.[79]

Visual differences were easier to handle than linguistic and conceptual differences. Staunton informed his readers that the major obstacle to Western inquiry into Chinese law and culture was the language, which was "by far the least accessible to a foreign student of any that was ever invented by man." What distinguished Chinese from all the other languages of the world, he added, was its use of the nonalphabetical script of characters, of which "the practice is no less convenient and perplexing than the theory is beautiful and ingenious."[80] The larger implications of linguistic difference were stated more bluntly by the Shanghai-based *North China Herald* in 1889: "As a medium of thought English (and indeed any foreign language) is immensurably superior to Chinese in precision and clearness. The English speaking student has a vast field of collateral thought open to him which does not exist, and never will exist; in Chinese. . . . It seems to us as easy for a man born blind to apprehend colours as for a Chinaman who knows none but his own language to reach any proficiency in modern science."[81] These writers were echoing a long-standing view of China's linguistic "singularity." In the late sixteenth century, the ideographic script of Chinese led Europeans to consider it a "sacred language" that could be used to help recover the "universal cipher" or language. By the late eighteenth century, however, comparative philologists had begun to regard its distinct sound, syllables, grammar, and script as signifiers of and reasons for China's "lack" of modern science and progress.[82]

Strictly speaking, Staunton averred, the Chinese text was almost "untranslatable" into English because Chinese idioms and style were hardly conformable to the European notions of linguistic propriety or grammatical rules. A further complication was that the Chinese way of thinking and acting could not be made "agreeable to the taste of European readers," no matter how the translation was done.[83] Staunton's emphasis on linguistic alterity here appears to have been at least partly motivated by a desire to stress his unique contribution to European Orientalism by mastering that peculiar language. At the same time, he had to assure readers that he did manage to penetrate the Oriental linguistic barriers. He explained that despite its technical nature, the Qing Code was remarkable for its simple and concise language, in contrast with other unfathomable Chinese literary texts of poetic or embellished style.[84] Moreover, the vital importance of the subject matter and the authenticity of the Chinese text should override concerns over the "imperfections" of the translation.[85] Fascination with the exotic thus operated to suspend the recognition of fundamental difference, making the allegedly incommensurable now translatable through the universalized English language, grammar, and categories while glossing over the unavoidable loss or invention in the process. For terms peculiar to the Chinese, Staunton decided against the easier approach of keeping the Chinese expressions because "the very sounds of the language are strange and unpleasant to European ears" and difficult to represent with any European alphabet.[86]

At one point, Staunton conceded that adopting the "more pleasing" arrangement, style, and phraseology, as he did, would have proportionally impaired the translation's two essential qualities: authenticity and originality. For that reason, William C. Jones in 1994 opted for an ungraceful but more literal translation that reflects the content and sentence structure of the original text.[87] Staunton felt, however, that he had drawn "the middle line" between a free but unfaithful translation and a close but ungraceful translation. With this disclaimer, he readily restructured words and sentences and often left out certain words "integral" to the original text or supplied a definition for lack of an equivalent expression.[88] All such labor was deemed necessary because the Chinese text was too concise and brief in some places, tedious and prolix in others, and "generally unsuitable" for translation into English idioms.[89] Despite all his changes and omissions, Staunton believed that he provided a faithful version of the Qing Code, and many of his readers concurred.[90] The *Edinburgh Review* in 1810 recommended the translation, with its "fidelity to the sense, though not to the idiom" of the Chinese text, as a judicious model for all translators of important Eastern works.[91]

Redefining the Qing Code as a Penal Code

Given that we are all prone to see a different society or culture through the lens of our own tradition or preconceptions, as Teemu Ruskola has rightly reminded us, it is not surprising that Staunton frequently took for granted the universality of English or European concepts or categories when translating the Qing Code.[92] More worthy of study is how those presumably universal categories served to *translate and transform* the meaning of late imperial Chinese legal institutions and social practices.

Staunton translated the seven parts of the Qing Code as follows: Division I—The General Laws [*minglilü*], Division II—The Civil Laws [*lilü*], Division III—The Fiscal Laws [*hulü*], Division IV—The Ritual Laws [*lilü*], Division V—The Military Laws [*binglü*], Division VI—The Criminal Laws [*xinglü*], and Division VII—The Laws Relative to Public Works [*gonglü*]. However, to impose Western legal concepts upon an admittedly very different legal system raised more problems than it solved for Staunton and his readers. Staunton was not unaware of this. For instance, division II actually regulated government employees and had little to do with what "civil law" implied in nineteenth-century Euro-America. Division VI dealt with many legal issues (such as homicide and robbery) belonging to the area of substantive criminal law in Western legal parlance, but it also had other statutes concerning evidence, trial procedure, sentencing, appeals, and so on. Division III was far broader than fiscal matters, as it covered household registration, taxation, markets, marriage, and land.

As seen in figures 2.3 and 2.4, the four-word title, *Ta Tsing Leu Lee*, was a transliteration of *Da Qing lüli*, but Staunton invented the rest of the

FIGURE 2.3 Title page of the original Qing Code (1805).

Courtesy of Columbia University Law Library.

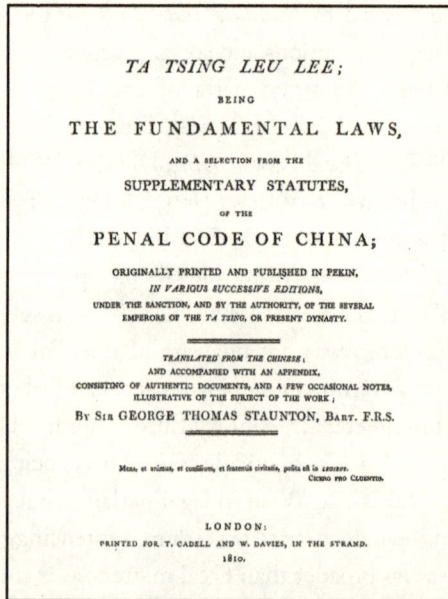

FIGURE 2.4 Title page of Staunton's translation, *Ta Tsing Leu Lee*.

Courtesy of Columbia University Law Library.

subtitle. The strange-sounding transliterated title served to remind the public (not just the actual readers) of the exotic authenticity of the original text, but its importance was eclipsed by the English subtitle—with "The Fundamental Laws" and "Penal Code of China" in a larger font and on separate lines—which effectively took center stage. Only after perusing fifty-six pages would a careful reader find Staunton's more literal rendering of the title of two different editions of the Qing Code, as *Ta Tsing Leu Lee; or The Laws and Statutes of the Dynasty of Tsing*.[93] This literal translation, a British reviewer noted in 1811, better captured the nature of the contents of the translation. The reviewer added that the epithet "penal" was applied to the laws of China in this translation because the translator desired the "convenience of this distinction."[94]

It is clear, however, that Staunton did not choose the English subtitle on the title page casually, as he also added enticing information beyond that found in the Chinese original to stress that the source text was "originally printed and published in Pekin" and sanctioned "by the authority of the several emperors" of the present dynasty. In contrast with all his emphasis on the authority of the original text, the copies of the Qing Code he relied on were actually compiled by *private* legal specialists, printed by commercial publishers, and obtained by illegal means, which reminds us of the Westerners' embarrassing legal status in China then. Nevertheless, Staunton's title page performed its paratextual functions well; besides identifying and describing the contents of the entire work in a very "tempting" way, the title and subtitle also served as the "key to interpretation" of this work, as I discuss below.[95]

Despite substantial changes in its contents and implementation, the Qing Code inherited the basic structure of the Ming Code of 1397, with the statutes organized around the six boards or ministries of the central government based on their division of labor.[96] Legal historians have shown that what may be called civil matters today constituted a large portion of the local judicial docket in late imperial China and were handled according to a combination of codified laws and customs. According to Philip Huang, the Qing legal system "embodied the practical reality of civil law and property rights without representational realities" in the Qing Code.[97] The *modern-day* categorical distinction between civil and criminal or penal laws, or between substantive and procedural laws, was not used to define or structure the *entire* Qing Code or imperial Chinese legal system until the late Qing legal reformers imported some of those categories in the first decade of the twentieth century. For students of Western law who take those distinctions of relatively recent origin for granted, it is naturally frustrating to try to understand the Chinese legal system as represented by Staunton. A reviewer stated in 1810 that his first general impression of *TTLL* was that in China the *penal* code covered almost every possible subject of law and equity, with no distinction between criminal and civil law or between public and private wrongs.[98] About two centuries later, William C. Jones aptly explained how privileging one's own perspective might make another's seem irrational and bewildering:

> One consequence of the difference in points of view is that the categories of Western law are meaningless within the Chinese system of formal law, that is, the Code. One cannot speak of the Code as being a body of civil or criminal law nor of its being a combination of the two. . . . The Code has often been described as a penal code. If by that it is meant that each article imposes a penalty, the statement is correct. But does the term "penal code" connote a body of law that deals with such matters as breach of promise of marriage and the quality of goods produced in the imperial manufactures? So also for the administrative law or the public-private law distinction. . . . So far as the Chinese were concerned, there seems to have been one body of law. The only categorization was the grouping of articles under the name of the board or ministry of the central government to whose work they seemed most closely connected.

Jones did not inquire into the historical genealogy of this issue and the underlying asymmetrical relationship between languages and cultures. Ironically, he himself later applied a modern Western legal concept to the Qing Code when he described it as a body of "entirely administrative law."[99] Regarding Staunton's translation, the source of confusion was not the Chinese legal system itself but a nineteenth-century impulse to subject it to a universalized British or European legal framework.

Contemporary historians of Chinese law are still debating whether there was any distinction between criminal and civil law jurisprudence in late imperial China.[100] But few of them have noticed that it was Staunton's translation that for the first time defined imperial China's comprehensive law code *authoritatively* as a "penal" code, displacing earlier European writings that presumed the existence of both "civil laws" and "criminal laws" in China.[101] Staunton explicitly stated, "[I]ndeed there are no traces of any such distinction, as that of civil and criminal, in the jurisprudence of the Chinese."[102] This is not to belabor a trivial technical distinction or quibble over the translator's choice of word. At stake here is not just "how we categorize the Chinese legal system, but also how we define the very categories of modern and pre-modern law."[103] Scholars of Chinese law know well that calling the entire formal legal system of (late) imperial China a penal or criminal system effectively reduced it to a punitive tool of tyrannical power or, in William Alford's words, at best "an instrument of state control little concerned with the attainment of individual justice," in contrast with the presumably rights-conscious legal systems in Euro-America.[104] Staunton's choice of the word "penal" reflected a common tendency among Orientalists then to universalize their own cultural experience, but Guangdong officials' attempt to assert Qing judicial sovereignty by emphasizing the punitive power of their law also played a part. In this sense, the Chinese officials participated in the genesis of the Orientalist portrayal of Chinese law. Some otherwise banal transactions in the contact zone of empire came to exert an enduring influence on imperial identities and legal subjectivities, far beyond what the individual actors anticipated.

Recall that the EIC Select Committee requested through Staunton a copy of the Qing Code for their information right after the *Providence* case in early 1800. The Guangdong provincial authorities declined but did send over, on April 7, 1800, a hundred copies of extracts from what they called the "Chinese Code of Law." Staunton did the English translation (quoted below) with help from some educated Chinese. It is clear that the Guangdong officials intended the extracts to scare foreigners away from serious crimes by warning them that they could expect no mercy. Most of them involved homicide, all relevant to earlier Sino-European legal cases, including the *Neptune* and *Lady Hughes*. But these extracts, which were reissued a few times and widely circulated through Staunton's translation in India, Britain, and the United States, did less to enhance Qing law's deterrence than to reinforce its harsh and despotic image among the foreign communities.[105]

Extracts from the Chinese Code of Laws.

1st Article. A Man who kills another on the suspicion of Theft shall be strangled according to the Law against Homicide committed in an Affray.

2. A Man who fires at another with a Musket and kills him thereby shall be beheaded as in cases of willful Murder [*sic.*, which should be translated as intentional killing, or *gusha*]; if the sufferer is wounded (but not mortally) the Offender shall be sent into Exile.

3. A Man who puts to death a Criminal who had been apprehended and made no resistance, shall be strangled according to the Law against Homicide committed in an Affray.

4. A Man who falsely accuses another innocent person of Theft (in cases of greatest criminality) is guilty of a capital Offence; in all other cases the Offenders whether principals or accessories shall be sent into Exile.

5. A Man who wounds another unintentionally shall be tried according to the Law respecting Blows given in an Affray, and the Punishment rendered more or less severe according to the degree of Injury sustained.

6. A Man who intoxicated with Liquor commits outrages against the Laws, shall be exiled to a desert Country, there to remain in a state of Servitude.

The foregoing are Articles of the Laws of the Empire of China according to which Judgment is passed on persons offending against them, without allowing of any Compromise or Extenuation.[106]

The most important thing about these extracts is that they provide clues for understanding why Staunton called the Qing Code a "penal" code. Probably influenced by his Chinese collaborator (likely his underground language tutor), Staunton's translation, the first English translation of any passage from the Qing Code, was originally titled "Extracts from the Chinese Code of Laws." But when introducing it in the EIC official record in

1800 and on later occasions, he and other Euro-Americans described it as "Translation of Extracts from the Chinese *Criminal* Code of Law" (emphasis added).[107] Apparently Staunton changed the title because he assumed that a law code that dealt with homicide must necessarily be a *criminal or penal code*. After he had obtained copies of the entire Qing Code, however, he did not call it a criminal or penal code until almost ten years later. In 1804, Barrow, clearly quoting Staunton's letters, referred to the Qing Code as "Ta-tchin Leu-Lee, the laws and institutes under the dynasty Ta-tchin [Great Qing]." The word "institutes" would remind a European reader of the revered *Institutes of Justinian* (issued in 533) of the Eastern Roman Empire, the *Institutes of the Laws of England* (1628–1641) by the famous British jurist Edward Coke, or Sir William Jones's *Institutes of Hindu Law* (1794).[108] In 1807, Staunton and his correspondents still referred to the Qing Code as simply "Chinese laws."[109] The term "penal code" was formally attached to his translation of the code around January 1809, when its publication was advertised in British magazines.[110]

The *Monthly Review* immediately questioned whether it was appropriate to add the word "penal" to the title of the English translation, suggesting that it be changed to "general" if any epithet was necessary, because a reader would be surprised to find in a penal code all the civil legislation contained in *TTLL*. For the *Critical Review*, that was like squeezing the contents of all four books of Sir William Blackstone's famous *Commentaries on the Laws of England* into just his fourth book, on criminal justice. Amid these doubts and ambivalence, however, a new discourse and a new mode of interpreting Chinese law came into being through cultural translation, and would take root in the next century and beyond. The same *Critical Review* remarked tellingly, "This odd assemblage of discordant subjects [in *TTLL*] serves well enough, however, for a specimen of what, in China, is included under the denomination of Penal Law."[111] For many Western readers, the conceptual confusion, to a large extent actually due to the translation, became evidence of the irrationality of Chinese law and culture. This spread far and wide as Anglo-American, French, Italian, and Spanish translators or reviewers of Staunton's *TTLL* referred to the Qing Code simply as the penal code, code pénal, codice penal, or código penal of China.[112]

Almost a century later, Ernest Alabaster, a British barrister who studied Chinese law, still found the title of Staunton's translation troubling. He noted that the Chinese term *xing* had a more comprehensive import than what criminal or penal law meant in the West. However, he felt obliged to title his volume *Notes and Commentaries on Chinese Criminal Law* in deference to the conventional usage (started by Staunton) among Western readers. That he added the subtitle *Brief Excursus on the Law of Property* did not seem to have changed his readers' preconception of the penal nature of the Chinese legal system.[113] Scholars at the turn of the twenty-first century are still urging that Chinese law be examined on its own terms.[114]

The significance of Staunton's "penalizing" of Chinese law, regardless of his intention, was not limited to one's assessment of Chinese legal tradition. In his famous *Ancient Law* (1861), Sir Henry Sumner Maine (1822–1888), a prominent British comparative jurist, historian, and colonial legislator in India and a founder of modern anthropology and comparative legal study, construed Roman law and its offshoots in Europe as the yardstick in tracing a universal trajectory of evolution from primitive status-based societies to modern societies based on contractual relations and individual agency. For him, a key distinction between traditional jurisprudence and modern legal systems was the former's emphasis on criminal law over civil law. As a general principle, he insisted, "the more archaic the code, the fuller and the minuter is its penal legislation." In light of the translated collections of Asian law, he concluded that India was still at a stage where a rule of law was indistinguishable from a rule of religion. China had passed that stage, but its progress had been arrested because of its deficiencies in civil law, indicative of the deficiency of that race or culture. Echoing reviewers of *TTLL*, Maine further noted that although civilization might have expanded law in other countries, law had actually handicapped civilization in China.[115] Hugh Scogin observed in 1994 that taking the nineteenth-century British or European perspective as the norm, one would naturally find other societies lacking in many aspects.[116]

Maine's ideas of sociolegal evolutionism also influenced a number of twentieth-century sociologists and anthropologists, including Émile Durkheim (1858–1917) and Max Gluckman (1911–1975). Maine's arguments did not go unchallenged. Prominent anthropologists Bronisław Malinowski (1884–1942) and Adamson Hoebel (1906–1993) later stood Maine's theory about the teleological progress from status to contracts and his categorizations of public or criminal law vis-à-vis civil or private law on their heads.

They countered that the prevalence of private or civil law preceded that of criminal law in the evolution of human societies. In Hoebel's words, "private law dominates the primitive scene."[117] Sally Moore, a leading American legal anthropologist, has also found it very confusing to use the civil-criminal or private-public dichotomy to classify or distinguish an entire legal system as Maine and others did. For her, "the foundational analogues" of some aspects of Western civil and criminal (or public and private) law exist in all societies because the social problems they are designed to cope with can exist everywhere.[118] Valerie Hansen's recent study of the pervasive use of "contracts" (*qiyue*) in imperial China from 600 to 1400 C.E. has further undermined Maine's thesis about the shift from status to contract in all human societies. As contracts were mentioned even in the earliest Chinese written records, Hansen writes, it is doubtful whether a status-based society ever existed in China.[119]

An Enlightened Comparativist and Empire Builder in a Transnational Community

Staunton was not simply a pioneering Sinologist. He was also a man of his own time, informed by Enlightenment ideas of scientific knowledge and by ambitions for a successful career in the service of a global empire. This section discusses how Staunton's multiple and sometimes conflicting roles as "enlightened" intellectual and empire builder shaped some of the characteristics of *TTLL*. This work will be examined along with some of Staunton's later, privately circulated publications and manuscripts. These texts constitute a site where competing views about cultural difference and identity were fleshed out, perceived national boundaries were renegotiated in some aspects and reinforced in others, and different imaginations about Chinese law and government were mediated. By examining these texts, I hope to show how Staunton's representation of Chinese law, society, and civilization was informed by and also contributed to the contact-zone cultural production of empire.

First, Staunton claimed for himself and his nation a unique contribution to European knowledge of China by implying that *enlightened* intellectuals (like him) would produce more authentic, impartial, and accurate representations of the Oriental societies than earlier Jesuit missionaries.

He echoed the suggestion of others that the Continental European missionaries were "incapacitated" from producing objective knowledge by their evangelical agendas, long attachment to the Chinese, and dependence upon the Chinese government for protection.[120] This Enlightenment notion of Orientalist epistemology had also been articulated by Sir William Jones, who declared in 1785 that the goal of the newly founded Asiatick Society in Bengal was to "seek nothing but truth unadorned by rhetorick" or by self-flattery. Lord Macartney maintained that the only purpose of his *China Journal* was to represent Chinese things exactly as they impressed him because the pursuit of truth required one not to judge China by European standards.[121]

This image of enlightened Orientalism was essential to these authors' credibility but also obligated them to disabuse their readers of the misconceptions of Oriental societies directly contradicted by their writings or translations. Thus, in the preface to the *Code of Gentoo Laws*, Nathaniel Halhed (1751–1830) questioned popular but ill-grounded opinions about Indian literature, religion, history, and law while excusing several otherwise objectionable native religious or legal practices by analogizing them to *ancient* Roman, Greek, or Jewish ones.[122] Besides the missionaries and Indologists, Staunton's real or imagined interlocutors also included earlier popular British authors like Daniel Defoe and Lord Anson, Enlightenment thinkers like Montesquieu and De Pauw, and contemporary British writers like John Barrow and Francis Jeffrey. These authors generally regarded the Chinese as a people without law, justice, honor, and virtue,[123] but both Staunton's personal experience and the Qing Code that he translated made it necessary for him to qualify these influential stereotypes, even though he agreed that the Chinese were undoubtedly "inferior" to Christian Europeans in those respects as well as in political liberty and modern science.[124] He also corrected some obvious misconceptions and criticized the popular tendency to exaggerate the ubiquity of "cruelties" and "barbarous executions" in the Chinese "ordinary course of justice."[125] He toned down the sweeping condemnation by his former tutor and friend, John Barrow, of Chinese inhumanity for the alleged official authorization of infanticide, by pointing to contrary evidence in *TTLL* and contrasting it with the "legalized cruelty and unnatural indifferences" in the Roman Empire.[126] In the late 1820s, Staunton again sought a middle ground between the missionaries' "flattering picture" and modern travelers' "vituperative sketches" of China in his attempt to refute his reviewers' criticism of the Chinese legal system as good only in theory but corrupt and oppressive in practice. For him, this admitted discrepancy was true of institutions everywhere, and the difference was only a matter of degree.[127]

Second, underlying Staunton's representation were also other, more practical considerations. It may be true that he stated only what he knew about the Qing Code or judicial administration in China, but his decision not to recycle some of the popular stereotypes (even when he recycled others) was partly attributable to his desire to make China worth studying and dealing with diplomatically, and to his relatively conservative view toward social changes and toward the interventionist policies of liberal imperialism in India.[128] Since 1637, the British had tried various means of improving their status and treatment in China, but most efforts had proved fruitless. Before leaving Guangzhou for London in January 1794, Lord Macartney did a careful cost-benefit analysis of whether Britain should break up China, snap Taiwan and Korea asunder, and make Tibet a headache for China. Even though all these scenarios came to pass in the next century or so, with or without British initiatives, Macartney considered these "offensive measures" injudicious (for damaging Britain's immediate interests) and unjustified as long as "a ray of hope remain[ed] for succeeding by gentle ones [i.e., by less costly and violent means]."[129] The Amherst Embassy in 1816 testified to the continued adherence of the British government to this policy.[130] To bring the Qing authorities to recognize Britain's rightful status and interests in China through diplomacy and a display of British superiority remained a preferred strategy for many Britons until the early 1830s.

Staunton also supported this strategy at least until that time. From the moment he landed in Guangzhou in 1800, he frequently discussed the prospect of leading another embassy to China in his correspondence with his father (who would have been the first British resident minister in Beijing if the Qianlong emperor had given his approval in 1793), Barrow, and Macartney. Besides helping the British outwit the Chinese in legal disputes or other transactions, his main incentive for studying the Chinese language was to establish himself as a leading Orientalist and successful public officer.[131] Thus, he had to strike a subtle balance between maintaining the British claims to superiority and extraterritorial privileges and representing the Chinese as civilized enough to deserve his Sinological labor and another British embassy. He was more appreciative of the merits of Chinese legal and political institutions than many of his contemporaries, including Robert Morrison, who tended to depict Chinese culture and institutions negatively as the results of idolatry and pagan sins.[132] For instance, Staunton noted that the Chinese educational system and diffusion of knowledge made that people competitive with at least some European nations in all the essential aspects of civilization.[133] To add to the British stock of knowledge in natural philosophy, he also urged attention to the little-studied Chinese practical science and belles lettres, the latter of which would soon be taken on by John Davis, who later published a series of influential translations of Chinese literature.[134]

Third, *TTLL* was influenced by earlier European writers' attitude toward China or the Orient. While some modern scholars have tended to interpret Staunton's relatively more balanced portrayal of Chinese law and institutions as evidence that he was another Sinophile, Staunton himself made it clear that he was informed by the culturalist argument of both Montesquieu and Sir William Jones that laws must be suited to the disposition, prejudice, and level of liberty or development of the (Oriental) people.[135] This logic of culturalism allowed Staunton to rationalize certain Chinese institutions and practices as most effective or appropriate for the Chinese given their cultural tradition or peculiarities. This kind of "sympathetic identification" enabled him to mediate the cultural difference and make China a useful reference point for Europeans even though he did not break down, and in some ways even reinforced, the cultural boundaries.[136] From this perspective, the time-honored Chinese "government and constitution," as the "most conformable to the genius and character" of that people, had the benefit of "being directly sanctioned by the immutable and ever-operating laws of Nature."[137] By the same token, he even implicitly questioned Montesquieu's portrayal of China as an Oriental despotism (which I discuss in the next chapter) by suggesting that the seemingly excessive reach of Chinese laws in regulating human conduct and feelings was necessary precisely because those laws did not originate in honor or religion.[138]

In the meantime, as declared in the mission statements of the Asiatic societies founded in Bengal by Jones in 1784 and then by Staunton and others in London in 1823, valuable knowledge could be obtained from Asian sciences, arts, and inventions for the improvement of Western nations.[139] "Every accumulation of such knowledge," according to Governor-General of India Warren Hastings, "and especially such as is obtained by social communication with people over whom we exercise a dominion founded on the right of conquest, is useful to the state."[140] China's political independence from the Western empires made its civilizational maturity and remarkable stability as the largest empire even more impressive to Staunton. This suggested to him that the Chinese possess "considerable and positive moral and political advantages," thanks to their legal system, which might be worth imitating even by "the fortunate and enlightened nations of the West."[141] *TTLL* would indeed inspire debates on British legal reform and codification that had just begun at the time of its publication.[142]

Fourth, it is also important to emphasize that the different legal status of Britons (as well as Europeans) in China and India affected the production and reception of the Oriental projects of Staunton and contemporary Indologists. The legal collections translated by the Indologists, or even the later French translation from Chinese of the Gia Long Code of Annam by Paul-Louis-Félix Philastre in 1876, were all designed to provide an authoritative legal text for colonial administration. As Bernard Cohn has noted, in response to the popular view of India as a *lawless* Oriental despotism, early Indologists formulated a "countermodel of India as a theocratic state" with a large body of ancient legal texts and customary practices respected by the natives. To increase stability and decrease administrative cost, the colonized would then be ruled by Indian laws that would cater to their religious or cultural prejudices, rather than by the supposedly complicated British laws and procedures.[143] These colonial translators valued accuracy more than elegance because a literal, ungraceful translation would enable the colonial administrators to know the natives' customs and manners precisely, or use them to administer justice in the colony.[144] *Le Code annamite*, Philastre's French translation of the Gia Long Code (which was in turn based on the Qing Code), cites Staunton's *TTLL* but is considered by modern scholars to be far more accurate, complete, and faithful than the latter.[145] In contrast, Staunton had no intention or capacity to offer such a translation of the Qing Code, for two reasons: circumstances would not permit it, and the colonization of China still appeared unrealistic.[146] Whereas the Indologists readily got Indian elites or Brahmans to teach them the languages and help obtain and translate the rarest native texts, Staunton and his superiors at Guangzhou could not even obtain Chinese language instructors or a copy of the Qing Code except by illegal means.[147] Furthermore, Staunton did not think it necessary to translate the entire Qing Code anyway, for his objective was partly to decode Chinese culture, not create a reliable means of governance. According to him, the statutes as the "fundamental laws" were the most authoritative means of decoding Chinese law and culture, even though he noted that the substatutes were revised regularly to adapt to judicial practice.[148] The underlying assumption was that the national spirit had been reified into the allegedly fixed and original fundamental laws of that vast and ancient empire.[149] To reduce a foreign culture as enigmatic and complex as that of China to "a fixed, originary source" to make it legible to European observers was, as David Porter has shown, a popular interpretative framework for other European representations of Chinese culture during the seventeenth and eighteenth centuries.[150] In the end, Staunton translated only the 436 statutes (*lü*) in the Qing Code, leaving out most of its 1,000 or so substatutes (*li*), which, in judicial practice, would actually prevail if they came in conflict with the former. The statutes remained unchanged after 1740, but their substatutes, resulting from periodic revisions and codification of cases, increased rapidly from 1,049 in 1740 to 1,892 in 1870, to adapt to changing socioeconomic realities.[151] In 1917, Edward Parker, a former British consul and professor of Chinese studies, noticed that Staunton had left untranslated the most important part of the code, the judge-made law or case law, even though Staunton's translation had since become a major source of Western knowledge of Chinese law. In this sense, as Alabaster noted in 1899, Staunton's laborious work was already outdated even in 1810.[152]

The most significant consequence of Staunton's selective translation was the creation of an ossified image of China or Chinese law by fixing it with a single text. Indeed, Staunton's project helped rekindle the already popular idea of a stationary or regressive China. China was known as having become somewhat civilized before most European nations, and even enjoying advantages over the latter in living standards, arts and manufacturing, and religious freedom until the late 1500s, but then stagnating as a semi-civilized or barbarous country in contrast with progressive Europe.[153] The problem, according to Macartney, was that a "nation that does not advance must retrograde, and finally fall back to barbarism and misery."[154] This view of social evolutionism thus recast the Chinese into an "anachronistic space" of history, from which their "premodern" contributions to world civilization could be appropriated or appreciated without threatening the imagined cultural hierarchy *in the present* because they lacked Europe's modern learning and science. This ambivalent attitude, as Michael Adas has noted, characterized many Western writings on Oriental societies like China and India in the eighteenth and early nineteenth centuries.[155] The *Edinburgh Review* thus held that the Chinese were an unchanging people whose respect for antiquity and tradition obstructed their improvement. The reviewer was inclined to consider the Chinese "a much more unimprovable race than any of the South-Sea savages," with a "fatal absence of energy."[156] In the previous century, China had been admired for its antiquity and stability in contrast with a conflict-ridden Europe, but these attributes now became grounds for contempt. Even as he was trying to mediate the cultural difference in order to introduce and compare Chinese law and culture, Staunton was also partly responsible for reconfirming the cultural boundary, now defined more by individual liberty, commercial aggression, and scientific discoveries since Isaac Newton became a symbol of national pride for Britain in the late seventeenth century.[157]

Epistemological Implications of TTLL
in Reducing China to an Intelligible Text

By so representing his project, Staunton, like many contemporary Orientalists, claimed to have achieved an epistemological feat by which an otherwise incommensurable and inscrutable Asian legal system and civilization was made translatable, decipherable, and classifiable for Western readers. As South Asian historians have shown, the legal collections translated by Indologists such as Halhed, Jones, and Henry Colebrooke were crucial for demystifying India and establishing Indian studies in Europe. Thanks in part to these, Sir William Jones, popularly known as Oriental Jones, became the most renowned Western scholar on Arabic-Persian-Indian languages and studies. If these projects defined the European conception of the nature of Hindu law and culture, which then shaped the relevant Indo-British policies and institutions in the following century, as Cohn has argued, it is not a stretch to suggest that Staunton also exerted an enduring influence on Western views of Chinese law.[158]

In this section, I would like to briefly reflect on the intellectual and political impact of *TTLL*. Edward Said and other scholars have identified a "textual attitude" that is popular in modern Orientalism and colonial representation. The attitude indicates "a common human failing to prefer the schematic authority of a text to the disorientation of direct encounters with the human" when such encounters appear strange or threatening. The resulting texts "can create not only knowledge but also the very reality they appear to describe."[159] One may find many such examples in the Sino-Western encounter, but what is peculiar about Staunton's and similar translation projects is the fact that the authority of these textual representations of Oriental societies hinged on the authority of the original *Oriental texts*. Unlike the Indologists, who had to take pains to prove that their original texts were of ancient and authoritative origins, Staunton simply pointed to the undisputable official status of the Qing Code for that purpose. Even nineteenth-century British naturalists, in what Fa-ti Fan has called a "textual practice," did not have the same advantage of being assured of the authority of the Chinese texts from which they were trying to glean botanical knowledge.[160] To emphasize the intrinsic value of law for deciphering a civilization, Staunton quoted Cicero on the title page, and then quoted famous historian Edward Gibbon in the preface, to the effect that "the laws of a nation form the most instructive portion of its history."[161] With this combination, he convinced contemporary readers that the importance of the subject matter and the "authenticity and originality" of the Chinese text more than compensated for the remaining concerns about infidelity and inaccuracy of his translation.[162] Félix Renouard de Sainte-Croix (1767–1840), who retranslated Staunton's *TTLL* into French in 1812, urged his readers to show the greatest faith in Staunton's commendable work.[163]

Essential to the authority of the English translator and translation was thus another kind of textual attitude, this time on the part of the Qing rulers in seeking to reduce myriad social and juridical complexities and variables into a highly selective body of legislation by codification. The textual attitude of both sides of the encounter created a kind of trans-textual interdependence and mutual subjectification: the Qing Code was often seen in the West as the Qing legal system or even Chinese legal tradition as a whole (despite all the changes and uncodified legal practices), and *TTLL* was then regarded as a faithful representation or substitution of that already textualized Chinese law. This kind of Chinese "self-essentialization" fed nicely into a similar tendency of Orientalism, indicating that the image of a "fixed and unchanging" body of Chinese law was "not just a Western fantasy" but a Chinese one as well.[164] I argue that it was through the operation of these double textual attitudes that Staunton's *TTLL* acquired its enormous influence. The following passage captures how all of this impacted readers of *TTLL*:

> It contains, as the title imports, the *authentic* text of the *whole* Penal Law of China; and, as their peculiar system of jurisprudence has attached a certain *public punishment* to the violation or neglect of almost every civil obligation, their Penal Law comprises an incidental view of *their whole system of legislation*. Now there is certainly no one document from which we may form a judgment of the character and condition of a nation with so much safety as from the body of their laws; and when these are presented to us, not in the partial abstracts of their admirers or detractors, *but in the original fullness and nakedness of their authentic statutes*, the information which they afford may be fairly considered as paramount to all that may be derived from other sources. The representations of travellers [even with unimpeachable fidelity] will almost always take a tinge from their own imagination or affections. . . . The laws of a people, however, are *actual specimens of their intellect and character*, and may lead the reflecting observer, to whom they are presented, *in any corner of the world*, to a variety of important conclusions that did not occur to the individual by whom they were collected. In such a work the legislator inevitably paints both himself and the people for whom he legislates; and, as nothing here depends upon the colouring of style or ornament, nothing short of intentional fabrication in the translator can prevent us from forming a correct notion of the original. In the case before us, however, we have not only every reason to believe that the translation is perfectly just and accurate, but think we can discover in the translator such candour and coolness of judgment as would entitle him to be trusted in a matter of far greater temptation.[165]

By such means, Western readers heartily echoed Staunton's assertion that *TTLL* would explain, more than all the volumes hitherto written in the West, the fundamental principles and operation of Chinese government, institutions, policies, national character, and society.[166] Along with its Indological counterparts, *TTLL* was considered a watershed in Western knowledge of the Orient. The British had no competitors in Indology since their colonization of India in the mid-eighteenth century, but they had yielded for centuries to their Continental European rivals in what came to be known as Sinology. Their national honor was now vindicated and the whole Western world, according to many British reviewers, was indebted to them for presumably gaining epistemic control over the largest empire and the most singular people on earth.[167] Even French, Spanish, and Italian reviewers thanked Staunton for making that impenetrable empire's peculiar laws and culture accessible.[168]

If the Macartney Embassy and the resulting China knowledge had enabled Britain "to recover a portion of the old [world]" by bringing that extraordinary empire under a new light, then Staunton was praised for venturing into "the dark and intricate windings of the oriental labyrinth" to produce *TTLL* as a fitting companion to Jones's *Institutes of Hindu Law*.[169] The epistemic terra incognita that was China, the last bulwark of the inscrutable Orient for curious Western intellectuals, was finally made known and explorable. The year after its publication, *TTLL* was already integrated into a comparative framework for the world's legal systems that compared Chinese, Indian, Roman, Muslim, and Jewish laws against the newly enacted, famous Code Napoléon. Featured in a number of influential intellectual journals and retranslated into other major European languages, *TTLL* was often cited in Euro-America as the authoritative text for comparing Chinese law and civilization well into the late twentieth century.[170]

CONCLUSION: *TTLL* IN A GLOBAL NETWORK OF KNOWLEDGE PRODUCTION

I would like to conclude this chapter by placing Staunton in the global context of imperial knowledge production. Staunton's translation of the Qing Code was partly inspired by contemporary Indological scholarship.

Before *TTLL*, Nathaniel Halhed published in English *A Code of Gentoo Laws* in 1776, based on a Persian compendium translated by a Bengali Muslim from a Sanskrit collection of Hindu law.[171] This circuitous process of retranslation did not inspire confidence. Upon becoming a judge of the Supreme Court of Calcutta in 1783, Sir William Jones planned for a full digest of Hindu and Muhammedan laws, modeled after Justinian's Pandects of the Roman Empire. From Sanskrit and Arabic texts, he published *Institutes of Hindu Law* (often known as *The Code or Ordinances of Menu*) in 1794, just months before his death. Four years later, Sir Henry Colebrooke completed Jones's plan to publish *A Digest of Hindu Law on Contracts and Successions*.[172] These works were "produced not simply in the context of colonial projects but as the culminations of what had been a long series of colonial projects."[173] Not only did Staunton cite Jones explicitly in *TTLL*, but he also cofounded the Royal Asiatic Society with Colebrooke in 1823, to which Staunton immediately donated 186 volumes of Chinese books, including multiple copies of the Qing Code and legal-case collections.

Another connection between *TTLL* and British India can be seen in Staunton's correspondence with Sir James Mackintosh (1765–1832). In the preface to *TTLL*, Staunton thanked two unidentified friends for encouraging his work. His unpublished letters show them to be James Mackintosh and John Barrow. Mackintosh, then recorder (i.e., chief judge) of Bombay (1804–1811) and later member of Parliament and leader of English legal reform in the 1820s to 1830s, wrote him on May 7, 1807, "My Dear Sir: . . . I particularly hope that we may see from you an abridgement of the system of law which you speak of [and] which will give us more insight into the state of China than all the volumes of the missionaries. Even a short abridgement will do instruction for our inspiration without costing you much labor."[174] Staunton was apparently convinced. In a letter to Barrow shortly thereafter, he explained that he had adopted a better plan to restart translating the Chinese laws. For a Chinese code of no fewer than 2,906 octavo pages, he believed that about ninety sheets of paper would suffice to show the essence of Chinese law and culture.[175] Mackintosh's interest thus played a role in Staunton's project, while the latter may have influenced subsequent British codification in India, as will be discussed.

In the decades following the publication of *TTLL*, Staunton continued to be an active member of the transnational networks comprising the founders of modern Orientalism. He and Robert Morrison were elected foreign members of the Société Asiatique in Paris, which was established partly through the exertions of Sinologists such as Jean-Pierre-Abel Rémusat (1788–1832, holder of the first European chair of Chinese literature and languages established at the Collège de France in 1814) and Julius Klaproth (1783–1835), who was originally from Germany. The latter two worked together in Paris in 1815–1832 and reviewed Staunton's *Ta Tsing Leu Lee*. In the 1820s, Klaproth sent Staunton his translation of Chinese texts as a supplement to the Chinese-Latin-French dictionary published by Joseph de Guignes (who "witnessed" the *Lady Hughes* case), while Staunton mailed his own work and Rémusat's *Chinese Grammar* to Morrison in Macao in 1822.[176] In contrast with its counterpart in Paris, the London Asiatic Society focused more on practical knowledge directly relevant to British interests in the East. This pragmatic orientation was also reflected in publications of contemporary missionaries or diplomats-turned-Sinologists, including John Davis, Thomas Meadows (1815–1868), Walter Medhurst (1796–1857), and Thomas Wade (1818–1895). Competing national or intellectual interests could and did cause bitter rivalry among these Sinologists, indicative of the lack of total uniformity in imperial or Oriental knowledge production.[177] Nonetheless, Staunton's *TTLL* and these transnational networks of knowledge production heralded modern Sinological Orientalism and transformed the modern image of China. I shall give just one example here. Together with tales of infanticide and foot binding as evidence of Chinese "barbarities," Italian translations of a British review of Staunton's *TTLL* and a French review of Rémusat's *Essai sur la language et la littérature chinoise* (1811) led the young, gifted Italian writer Giacomo Leopardi (1798–1837) to conclude in 1821 that the Chinese, possessing neither alphabet nor letters, did not have a "true civilization" in spite of their invention of "gunpowder, the compass, and even printing." For him, China's "strange immobility and *immutability*" were inevitable and the Chinese were "more marvellously stationary" than all other nations including India and Egypt.[178] Chinese law and language would remain two essential signifiers of China's irreducible barbarism and "otherness" in the modern world in the next 150 years.

In this chapter, we have seen that Staunton's translation of the Qing Code was embedded in Britain's imperial agenda and shaped by an imperative to mediate between different political and cultural traditions and practical interests rooted in tension-ridden Sino-British encounters. Although the Qing government still held on to its formal claim of sovereignty and administrative control over the Euro-Americans in China, the literal deterritorialization of the Qing Code from its homeland and its reterritorialization through the lens of Euro-American legal concepts, languages, and cultural assumptions were more than just an act of defiance of the Qing's authority. As British reviewers proudly proclaimed, it signified an epistemic conquest over the largest empire in the Orient. The benefits went beyond China itself, as Lord Macartney had predicted in 1794. Shortly after the First Opium War, Britain sent embassies to Japan, Vietnam, and Korea for similar commercial and political concessions, using *Chinese* as the language for the initial official communications.[179]

To be more specific, Staunton's translation was first and foremost motivated by the British desire to decipher the opaque operation of Chinese law and administration concerning foreigners in order to better secure their persons and trade. Accordingly, it resulted in a new body of Chinese legal knowledge that forced the Britons and others to search for a more sophisticated justification for extraterritoriality than a mere dismissal of Chinese law as arbitrary or barbaric, as noted near the end of chapter 1. Also as a result of the translation, Staunton invented a whole set of concepts, vocabulary, and categories in the West, defining the Qing Code *authoritatively* as a "penal code" for the first time. This characterization then led others, such as Sir Henry Maine and his Western and Chinese readers, to consider late imperial Chinese law as a signifier *and* a major cause of the "primitive" status of that society and civilization. As with India and the British colonies in Africa in the late nineteenth century, this conceptualization of "traditional" Oriental societies offered a culturalist justification for British "indirect rule" in lieu of the interventionist and costly policies of liberal imperialism.[180] For instance, in administering the "leased" territory of Weihaiwei in China's Shandong province from 1898 to 1930, the British authorities resorted to presumably indigenous practices such as village tribunals, summary justice, and collective responsibility in order to maintain law and order while refusing to grant Chinese prisoners access to the "benefits" of the touted English legal system.[181] Meanwhile, as will be discussed in the next chapter, *TTLL* became a crucial intervention in the European metropolitan debates over legal reform and modernity in the early nineteenth century.

3

CHINESE LAW IN THE FORMATION
OF EUROPEAN MODERNITY

Beginning in approximately the mid-eighteenth century, various European states started reforming their political and legal institutions as a result of a combination of sociocultural and political changes. Even absolutist rulers such as Frederick the Great of Prussia (r. 1740–1786) or Empress Catherine the Great of Russia (r. 1762–1796) came to be lauded as "enlightened despots" for promoting such reform programs. The actual results in terms of legislation and implementation were often limited and certainly uneven among European states over the next one and a half centuries.[1] Nevertheless, some of the disseminated ideas about the rule of law, justice, and penal practice later became key attributes defining a "modern" state and legal system. By the early twentieth century, the expansion of Western industrial powers such as Britain, France, Germany, and the United States had helped spread these ideas to India, Japan, China, and other parts of the world. In turn, legal modernity became one of the most powerful discourses used to legitimize Euro-American imperial domination as a new civilizing mission.[2] A most effective rhetorical strategy for many Chinese reformers in the early twentieth century was to claim that their proposed legal or social changes were necessary to make Chinese practices conform to the "universal" (*datong*) standards of Western modernity.[3]

Yet this grand narrative of global modernity eclipsed the multifaceted role of China and Chinese law in the formative stage of the conceptualization of the modern state and rule of law a century or so before Western institutions were reformed and then promoted as worldwide models of modernity. In this chapter, I first look at how Chinese law was differently read and invoked by Enlightenment writers and reformers around the mid-eighteenth century. Leading figures such as Baron de Montesquieu (1689–1755), Cesare Beccaria (1738–1794), Voltaire (1694–1778), Jeremy Bentham (1748–1832), and Sir William Blackstone (1723–1780) all directly or indirectly engaged with some of the core features of Chinese law, especially its rationality and proportionality, as they pondered whether and how to reform institutions in Europe. I then examine how Sir George Thomas Staunton's translation of the Qing Code generated another wave of enthusiasm about Chinese law and governance in the early nineteenth century. Such knowledge played a unique role in the heated debates in the British Parliament when reform and codification of English common law and criminal justice were proposed. Although codification was never completed in Britain *partly* because it was negatively identified with ancien-régime corruption, or Oriental despotism as signified by the Qing Code, at a crucial moment, such a negative association did not prevent British colonial administrators from drafting the famous Indian Penal Code in the 1830s as part of the attempt to introduce a modern legal system in India. I end with an account of how Max Weber (1864–1920) dealt with the conceptual tensions and Chinese law within his own classification of modern legal systems in the early twentieth century. My purpose is not to reclaim the direct, causal impact of Chinese law on some particular legal reforms or institutional changes in the West during the late eighteenth and nineteenth centuries. Rather, my argument is that Chinese law (as well as China) played a significant but rarely acknowledged role in shaping the Western discourse and imagination of modernity in different ways: it was frequently cited as a peculiar, paradigmatic, and at times indispensable example to establish the values and concepts that have since come to define modernity in the West and beyond. Used as either a negative or positive illustration, the peculiarity of Chinese law or culture thus performed an essential function in *legitimating* the universality of Western law or culture. This kind of legitimating or symbolic function of the Chinese example may be more worth investigating than instances of directly causing institutional changes. Critically reexamining the historical processes in which the seemingly anecdotal examples of China were repeatedly employed to instantiate the superiority or the necessity for change of Euro-American ideas and institutions, as Eric Hayot has argued in a similar context, helps us better understand how the Euro-Americentric narrative of globalization and modernity came into existence in the first place.[4] Many of the now taken-for-granted Western ideas of modern law and government would not have acquired their global credence or hegemony without manipulating such examples of Chinese or Oriental instantiation and particularity. The well-known fact that China was represented in an increasingly disparaging fashion after the mid-eighteenth century does not mean that China or Chinese law did not affect the Western conception of modernity.

Another goal of this chapter is to trace how information about Chinese law and society through Western missionaries, traders, diplomats, and Sinologists constituted an evolving "collective imperial knowledge" that conditioned the modern image of China. However, such knowledge did not coalesce into a coherent and united Western "language of domination" over China, even when it did traverse the "metropolitan politics and linguistic barriers" to spread in countries such as Spain, France, Italy, Britain, Russia, and Germany.[5] Sustained engagement with the unfamiliar ideas of Chinese law and society could have led a wide range of Western writers and readers to rethink the familiar ideas and institutions of their own societies. To be sure, the image of China in the West has been complex and multivalent and has changed considerably over time. Studying both the consistency and discrepancy in the pattern of interpreting China or Chinese law will tell us as much about Western commentators' imagination of that geographically remote country as about their evolving understanding of their own countries and traditions. By attending to these internal aporias and the *conflictual* processes of boundary making at the early stage of the dominant discourse of the modern state and rule of law, we can better appreciate the heterogeneous origins of global modernity and provincialize its ethnocentric narratives that have prevailed. This may help us turn the "discursive conditions of dominance into the grounds of intervention" in revisiting the history of the Sino-Western encounter.[6]

CONFLICTING VIEWS OF CHINESE LAW AND CULTURE IN ENLIGHTENMENT EUROPE

Montesquieu's Oriental Despotism and the Exception of Chinese Law

Whereas the "invented" European discourse of Confucianism had served as a medium for early Jesuit missionaries and their Sinophile readers like Leibniz to synthesize or accommodate Christian-Chinese differences before the mid-eighteenth century,[7] Oriental despotism became an influential analytical framework by which European commentators differentiated China as well as other Asian countries from their own by the end of the century.[8] In his 1748 work *The Spirit of the Laws*, Baron de Montesquieu, French jurist and leading philosopher of the Enlightenment, famously explicated many of the fundamental concepts of modern liberal governments, such as the separation of powers and rule of law. He classified the world's political regimes into republics, monarchies, and despotisms based on their animating spirit or principle of political virtue, honor, and fear, respectively. In contrast with the other two ideal types, a despotic government was ruled by a single person "according to his own will and caprice" without "established" or "fundamental laws."[9] Montesquieu's originality, as Brian Singer has explained, lies in "uncoupling of power from law" to define "power exclusively in terms of will and force"; perceived this way, despotism becomes totally unrestrained by law and driven only by power's "desire to free itself of all limits."[10] Montesquieu endowed "despotism" with a new significance and a very different meaning from its prior usages while making it almost "an inherently Oriental form of government" by attributing it to the particular climate and geography of Asia, Africa, and America.[11] In a despotic society, according to Montesquieu, people are political slaves without legal consciousness, civic virtue, honor, or security of private property. His reconceptualization of despotism "implied a theory of society and a rational analysis of the intellectual and moral capacity of Oriental" peoples as backward, servile, effeminate, and cowardly. As many scholars have shown, Asian countries including China, Japan, Turkey, and India were thereby redefined to mark the *outside* boundary of the rational, liberal, and law-based modern West.[12]

In calling China a despotism Montesquieu actually ran counter to the prevailing image of China in much of Europe. In the first half of the eighteenth century, historian Michael Adas has observed, "no culture or civilization has been as lavishly praised or as widely acclaimed as a model to be emulated as was Qing China." The influence of seventeenth-century chinoiserie, vividly reconstructed by Timothy Brook recently in *Vermeer's Hat*, extended into the next century through the imitated Chinese-style porcelain, gardens, paintings, wallpaper, and furniture on display in numerous wealthier European households.[13] From Matteo Ricci to later Jesuits, including Dominique Parrenin (1665–1741) (who served at the Kangxi emperor's court for four decades), most missionary publications, even when criticizing China's scientific stagnation and religions, extolled the achievements of Chinese civilization as a whole and praised its commerce, reason, and "superb law and administration" in particular.[14] For instance, the most comprehensive and authoritative source on China until well into the nineteenth century, *The General History of China*, first published in 1735 by the Jesuit historian Jean-Baptiste Du Halde (1674–1743), compared the Chinese judicial system favorably with its European counterparts, citing better prison conditions, more accessible courts, and mandatory reviews of serious criminal cases. In China, Du Halde wrote, "men may not be deprived of life and honour unjustly, yet criminals are severely punished in proportion to the enormity of their crimes," and no crimes would go unpunished.[15] Although Du Halde and earlier European writers often cringed at what they considered cruel forms of Chinese punishment, they never went so far as to suggest that China was a country devoid of established laws, honor, liberty, or reason. The Jesuit Louis Le Comte (1655–1728), who witnessed Chinese punishments and published probably the first description of *lingchi* (the severest form of punishment by slicing) in the West, described Chinese law in the 1690s as "wise, plain, and well understood, and exactly adequate to the particular genius and temper of that nation."[16] For these missionaries, as Montesquieu put it, the Chinese polity was "a proper mixture of fear, honor, and virtue."[17]

As noted in chapter 2, in order to maintain support for their controversial missions in China, these Jesuit authors tended to idealize or exaggerate the advantages of Chinese law and government, depicting Qing China as a different but civilized pagan society that was commensurable enough for Christian conversion. For secular Enlightenment intellectuals like Montesquieu, however, the examples of Chinese law and government were called upon to serve different purposes in their efforts to diagnose and remedy the problems in contemporary Western societies. To fit China as a despotism into his typology of governments, Montesquieu opted to cherry-pick the least flattering remarks from writings of European missionaries, diplomats, traders, or novelists (including Daniel Defoe). The recent Rites Controversy between the Qing government and the Vatican over the ultimate control over Chinese Christian converts also became a factor.[18] The resentment of his Chinese interlocutor, Huang Jialue (1679–1716), a native of Fujian and a Catholic convert then in Paris, about the Qing government's religious policies partly informed or reinforced his perception of China. Several conversations between them in late 1713 led Montesquieu to conclude that the Manchu conquerors ruled the Chinese with severe laws and "tyranny," wielding "completely unlimited" power in ecclesiastical and secular matters, and that the "goods and lives" of their subjects were always "exposed to all the caprices and untamed whim of a tyrant."[19] In *The Spirit of the Laws*, Montesquieu then took a conceptual leap from such scattered tales of the Manchu rulers' tyranny and cruelty to offering a world-famous, sweeping theory of *Chinese* or *Oriental* despotism.

Montesquieu's portrayal of China has been challenged by historians since the late twentieth century. Regarding the purported deficiency in private property and commerce in a "despotic" society, historians such as Bin Wong and Kenneth Pomeranz demonstrate the continued vitality and development of Qing China's economy and trade, in many ways comparable to their European counterparts well into the eighteenth century. Legal historians have shown the crucial importance of law to both rulers and ruled in late imperial China.[20] Because one of the key questions in this book revolves around representation of Chinese law against the backdrop of modern transformation of Western societies, I shall focus on the centrality of China to Montesquieu's conceptualization of despotism. My main claim here is that although Montesquieu cited China, especially its wide use of the threat of punishment, to illustrate features of despotism, he saw something in China's judicial system that complicated, if not subverted, his typology of governments. The malleability and unsettled nature of the trope of Chinese law, already evident in *The Spirit of the Laws*, was to shape the debates on modern legal reform in Britain and elsewhere in the next century.

China performed a unique function for Montesquieu in his dramatization of the nature and horror of despotic states in order to formulate his idea of modern liberal governments as the opposite. When asserting that the Chinese had no sense of honor, his most memorable statement actually appears in a footnote: "It is the cudgel that governs China." He attributed this quote to Du Halde's influential *General History of China*. Corporal punishments in late imperial China could be very harsh and were indeed imposed in a wide range of cases, as discussed in the next chapter, but this was a misquotation of a passing remark in Du Halde's ten-page discussion of China's legal system and proportionate justice.[21] Moreover, under imperial Chinese law, punishing certain minor or nonviolent offenses—including grand theft, which could subject the offenders to capital punishment under contemporary English law—by beating with the bamboo stick was designed to "shame" and admonish the offenders for self-reformation.[22] As some Western commentators also noticed, Montesquieu's interpretation of the prevalence of this penalty could thus be construed as evidence that contrary to Montesquieu's understanding, the value of honor and preventive justice was widely taken for granted in China. Voltaire wrote in the 1760s that "almost all Montesquieu's quotations are false" and that "the whole system" of *The Spirit of the Laws* was built upon a false "antithesis."[23] Nevertheless, this misquotation became a "decisive testimony on a fundamental constitutional and political issue" regarding China.[24] The cudgel or the bamboo, dramatized in Montesquieu's footnote, would remain an essentializing cultural symbol of China or Chinese despotism.

Still, classifying China as a despotism posed an analytical difficulty for Montesquieu. What mattered in a despotic country was the despotic will only, and yet China's government was characterized by a set of highly sophisticated laws. This contradiction was partially resolved by dismissing Chinese laws as futile attempts to restrain the unlimited power. Montesquieu put this memorably: "They wanted to make the laws reign in conjunction with despotic power; but whatever is joined to the latter loses all its force." It does not matter whether that power desired to be "fettered," because in that case "it armed itself with its chains, and is become still more terrible."[25] Even though Montesquieu did allow for the potential restraining influence of cultural tradition or customs on despotism, his radicalization of the nature of power and force in a despotic society effectively reduced law and other institutions to a spectral presence. His concepts and evidence were questioned by contemporaries such as François Quesnay (1694–1774), who considered China an enlightened "legal despotism" where even the emperor observed the irrevocable laws, but Montesquieu's framework would prevail in the next two centuries.[26] His influence on Hegel (1770–1831) was obvious in the latter's well-known *Philosophy of History*, which consigns non-Western countries like China and India to the outside of modern history for lacking the free spirit and capacity for historical progress as a result of their tyrannical laws and governments. Just as India now had Britain as its lord, Hegel predicted in the 1820s, so China should expect a similar future because it was these nations' "necessary fate" to submit to "Europeans of the modern world."[27] Hegel, whose work still exerts subtle influence on scholarship about Asia, as analyzed by Prasenjit Duara,[28] also implied here that by this point, "modernization" as a civilizing mission had firmly claimed its role as a powerful ideology of empire in conjunction with the discourses of free trade, law, and liberty.

The claim that law existed in China only as a specter of terror and oppression did not completely resolve the China paradox in Montesquieu's writings. Like his contemporaries, Montesquieu occasionally engaged with Chinese law as a source of critique of existing legal institutions in Europe. Importantly, some of the features of Chinese law were remarkably "modern." In a section of *The Spirit of the Laws* titled "Of the Just Proportion between Punishments and Crimes," he explicated what was to become a fundamental principle of modern law and justice: "It is an essential point that there should be a certain proportion in punishments" because a great crime, which is more harmful to society, should be prevented rather than a smaller one. He cited judicial practices in the Roman Empire, Britain, and Russia to illustrate the evils of indiscriminate punishment. Having elsewhere criticized the German states for that reason, he also lamented that it was a great abuse in France to mete out the same punishment to those who robbed on the highway and those who both robbed and murdered. In contrast, China was invoked to validate this point: "In China, those who add murder to robbery are cut in pieces, but not so the others; to this difference it is owing that though they rob in that country they never [add] murder." Although Chinese laws did stipulate different punishments for robbery with and without murder, the punishment for the latter was not as severe as slicing (*lingchi*). However, China was Montesquieu's only example of having written the principle of proportionality into the law.[29]

In illustrating a desirable legal system, Montesquieu also held that good legislators ought to be more interested in preventing crimes and inspiring good morals than in inflicting penalties on lawbreakers. For illustration, he again turned to China: "It is a constant remark of the Chinese authors, that the more the penal laws were increased in their empire, the nearer they drew towards a revolution. This is because punishments were augmented in proportion as the public morals were corrupted." He was proposing a theory of justice that punishments by design should be preventive or reformative, not simply retributive. After all, relying on severe punishments was more suitable for a despotic government due to its operative principle of terror. Realizing the self-contradiction in his depictions of China, he added a footnote: "I shall show hereafter that China is, in this respect, in the same case as a republic or a monarchy."[30] Buried in hundreds of pages, this note largely escaped the attention of his contemporaries and future generations of scholars; nevertheless, its implication for Montesquieu's overarching paradigm cannot be ignored. It revealed an important fissure in the paradigm's foundation that necessitated treating China simultaneously as a classic case of despotism representing a premodern stage of human society *and* as an exception to despotism so it could be appropriated to help reform European institutions. Through this strategy of bifurcation, China played a key, instructive role, as both a negative foil and a positive inspiration, in Montesquieu's articulation of modernity. The fact that the other footnote, about the cudgel as the ruler of China, soon became a catchphrase to characterize China also showed that a different interpretation of Chinese law and government could have been formed by this note about China as an exception to despotism. Ironically or not, we shall see more instances in which these possibilities of major significance were often assigned to the paratextual spaces of preface, appendix, or notes. A footnote may provide additional support for the argument of the main text, but it also "tends to heckle the main text, embarrassing and undermining its authority."[31] The completely different fates and roles of these two footnotes in shaping the subsequent Western image of China or Chinese law illustrate in a dramatic fashion how generalizations about a culture can sometimes depend on such anecdotal pieces of information.

At an anniversary meeting of the Royal Asiatic Society in London in May 1834, Sir Alexander Johnston (1775–1849), a former chief justice of Ceylon and founder and vice president of the society, told the Oriental specialists in attendance that according to Montesquieu's grandson, Charles-Louis de Montesquieu (1749–1824), "the only subject on which that distinguished writer felt at a loss, when preparing his admirable work [*The Spirit of the Laws*], was the system of Chinese jurisprudence."[32] As we parse the shifting roles that Chinese jurisprudence played in *The Spirit of the Laws*, this remark, anecdotal as it may sound, starts to make great sense. Montesquieu's typology of governments was premised on the creation of Oriental despotisms such as China, to which law was completely irrelevant except as a baton of the despotic will. In the meantime, principles of humane, rational, preventive, and proportionate law and justice, which Montesquieu illustrated by reference to Chinese jurisprudence, would later become some of the most essential criteria of modern legal systems in the West and beyond.

Such ambivalence, also evidenced in Sir George Thomas Staunton and many later writers, resulted in the mixed and sometimes phantomlike but persistent presence and effect of China in the formation of Western modernity. As we shall see, references to Chinese law and justice continued to appear in some of the key writings and debates leading up to, and in the midst of, the Euro-American legal reform. Many of these references were indirect or even marked by an effort to omit China totally, but the puzzle posed by this multivalent image of Chinese law is worth studying. It has been argued that Europe's "active engagement with the cipher of the foreign itself constitutes an act of cultural formation" and transformation. The examples that follow will help further illuminate the dynamics of the processes in which Europeans reacted to the unfamiliar Chinese law and culture or tried to *translate* them into familiar terms within the discourse of European modernity.[33]

Beccaria, Voltaire, Blackstone, and Catherine II on Modernity and Chinese Law

The decoupling of Chinese jurisprudence from discussions of legal rationality occurred in a highly influential work by Italian jurist Cesare Beccaria, *On Crimes and Punishments*. Along with *The Spirit of the Laws*, this treatise stimulated the transformation of Euro-American law and politics in the late eighteenth and nineteenth centuries. First published in 1764, it was translated into all the major languages and reprinted numerous times. A famous *Commentary* by Voltaire further helped make it a canonic text of modernity.[34] Drawing from contemporary theories of natural law, social contract, and utilitarianism (which privileges happiness over other values), Beccaria contended that the only justifiable purposes of punishment were to prevent offenders from repeating crimes and to deter potential offenders. The severity and method of punishment should be designed to have the most efficacious and lasting impression on spectators. For such purposes, punishment must be prompt, certain, preventive, and proportionate. It was the certainty rather than the severity of the punishment that created the most effective deterrence. Among other things, he strongly recommended that laws be codified in a clear and simple language and applied to the rulers and the ruled, and that criminal trials be conducted publicly according to rational rules of evidence instead of secret accusations or torture.[35]

Montesquieu's influence on Beccaria was evident. Beccaria acknowledged in the preface to *On Crimes and Punishments* that he was more inspired by that immortal thinker than anyone else, and he drew liberally upon the latter's ideas on natural law and rational justice. When criticizing undifferentiated capital punishment in Europe for robbers with and without violence, he asserted that the proposition that these two offenses were different in nature was "as certain in politics, as in mathematics." In the chapter "Of the Proportion between Crime and Punishment," he elaborated Montesquieu's ideas by arguing that just and effective punishment should be in proportion to the degree of harm that an unlawful act caused to the public good or happiness, and that there should be a corresponding scale of punishments between the highest and lowest degrees in seriousness of crime.[36] These ideas would help inspire British philosopher and jurist Jeremy Bentham to develop his legislative science and radical reform plans. However, whereas it had inspired Montesquieu's discussion of reformative and proportionate justice, Chinese law was erased by Beccaria when citing Montesquieu to promote the same ideas.

These widely read foundational texts of European modernity helped generate a discourse that would later privilege Europe as the origin and standard of modern civilization. When William Eden (1745–1814), later

Lord Auckland, published his acclaimed *Principles of Penal Law* in 1771, he cited the foregoing works by Montesquieu, Beccaria, and Voltaire to criticize English criminal justice and call for a more moderate and rational legal system. As in Beccaria's work, China now served only to illustrate what Montesquieu had warned Europe against: "The Japonese [*sic*] still submit to the daily discipline of the lash; and Japan continues the contempt of the world.—The cudgel (says du Halde) is the Governor of China; the Chinese (says the writer of Lord Anson's *Voyage*) are eminent for timidity, hypocrisy, and dishonesty."[37]

For many Enlightenment thinkers, however, European political and legal systems desperately needed reform to clean up all the confusion, arbitrariness, corruption, and above all cruelty that were said to characterize European law and criminal justice.[38] This recognition of the problems with their legal systems partially explains why the negation of China as an inspirational influence for legal reform was certainly not monolithic. In his famous *Commentary* on Beccaria's treatise, Voltaire referred to Chinese law as wise and humane, and one of the examples he cited was that multiple-level judicial reviews and imperial approval were required before capital offenders were executed. He remarked exasperatedly, "Must we go to the end of the world, must we have recourse to the laws of China, to learn how frugal we ought to be of human blood? It is now more than four thousand years that the tribunals of that empire have existed; and it is also more than four thousand years that the meanest subject, at the extremity of the empire, hath not been executed without first transmitting his case to the emperor, who causes it to be thrice examined by one of his tribunals; after which he signs the death warrant, alters the sentence, or entirely acquits."[39] As many intellectuals and legal reformers would read Beccaria's treatise in conjunction with, or through, Voltaire's famous commentary, such passages as these restored from Beccaria's omission the important, symbolic role of Chinese law in shaping the emergent discourse of modernity in Euro-America. The subsequent hegemony of this discourse and its representation of the West as the origin of global modernity can be more effectively challenged by reading these long-forgotten, counterhegemonic instances—in which the national or Occidental self was subject to severe criticism just as the Oriental Other had been—as symptoms of a more systematic tendency of dominant imperial powers to rewrite history and erase their messy past. In this sense, the Chinese example could have an epistemologically subversive effect even though it was often used to claim Western centrality or superiority.[40]

One may justifiably question the bias of Voltaire as a so-called Sinophile philosopher; however, it is crucial to note the context in which he uttered these praises of Chinese law. His inclination to see more of the positive aspects of Chinese law, government, and moral philosophy partly reflected his greater frustration with those aspects of contemporary France or Europe.[41] In this sense, Voltaire's rosier image of Chinese law is as valuable as Montesquieu's unflattering depiction of the Chinese government in indicating contemporary European sentiment toward Chinese *and* European institutions.

The trope of China resurfaced now and then, such as in the writing of Sir William Blackstone, the leading English jurist mentioned in chapter 1. Blackstone recommended the principle of proportionality in his monumental *Commentaries on the Laws of England* in 1765. After discussing Beccaria's "ingenious" proposal for a scale of crimes with a corresponding scale of punishments for every offense, he quoted Montesquieu directly in order to retain the sentence that praised English law:

> Thus in France the punishment of robbery, either with or without murder, is the same: hence it is, that though perhaps they are therefore subject to fewer robberies, yet they never rob but they also murder. In China, murderers are cut to pieces and robbers not: hence in that country they never murder on the highway, though they often rob. And in England, besides the additional terrors of a speedy execution, and a subsequent exposure or dissection, robbers have a hope of transportation, which seldom is extended to murderers. This has the same effect here as in China; in preventing frequent assassination and slaughter.

Omitting Montesquieu's admission of the lack of proportionality in English law in contrast with China, Blackstone equated England with China for possibly achieving the same result of deterrence *in practice*, suggesting that his compatriots should be proud of their own legal system as opposed to other Europeans. Ironically, England obtained that effect of deterrence only through a combination of the terror of a speedy execution and dissection of corpses with a hope of transportation.⁴² These English penal practices would soon be attacked as cruel and barbarous.

Blackstone was soon criticized by Bentham, in the words of modern jurist Richard Posner, as "a shameless apologist for the status quo, an enemy of all reform, a Pangloss blind to the shocking deficiencies of the English legal system."⁴³ But even Blackstone lamented that among those types of actions that people were daily liable to commit in England, no fewer than 160 were made felonies without benefit of clergy, and thus liable to death by parliamentary statutes. This dreadful list did not diminish but rather increased the number of offenders.⁴⁴ This explains why Chinese law, which certainly had its own share of serious problems, seemed to offer many Europeans an example of relative simplicity, certainty, moderation, and proportionality. Blackstone's passage quoted above has often been cited to credit him with being an advocate of "modernization," and by way of his writings, Chinese law remained relevant to the British debates on legal reform even before Staunton's *TTLL* was published.⁴⁵

Chinese law also figured in the "modernization" project of Catherine II. In 1767, she published the *Grand Instructions* as a blueprint for reform of the Russian legal system, and most of its 600 articles were taken verbatim from the works of Montesquieu and Beccaria discussed above. Despite its limited success in implementation, the *Instructions* earned her a reputation as an enlightened and humane monarch in Europe.⁴⁶ In the *Instructions*, Catherine declared it a general principle that some difference should be made in punishing robbery with or without murder, in the interest of general safety. Like Blackstone with regard to England, she did not mention Russia as Montesquieu's negative example for this principle, and she also omitted China as the positive illustration. Instead, she was led by Montesquieu to assert that customs rather than law were governing the Chinese, and that the law tyrannized the Japanese "with savage ferocity."⁴⁷

Nevertheless, influenced by *kitaishchina* (Russian equivalent of chinoiserie) and Voltaire (whom she admired and corresponded with), Catherine was also interested in the reportedly effective and enlightened government of Qing China and the Qianlong emperor. As she once stated, "To do nothing without principle or without reason, not to allow oneself to be led by prejudice, to respect religion, but not to give it any power in State matters, to banish everything that reeks of fanaticism and to draw the best of every situation for the public good, is the basis of the Chinese empire, the most durable of all those known on this earth."[48] She commissioned Aleksiei Leontiev (1716–1786) and other founders of modern Russian Sinology to translate the Qing Code (*Da Qing lüli*) and regulations (*Da Qing huidian*) of China. Their translation was published in 1778–1783, three decades before Staunton's English translation. Seldom noted by modern scholars, these Russian translation projects nevertheless testified to the widespread interest in Chinese law and institutions at the formative stage of Western modernity.[49]

Montesquieu and his theories on constitutionalism, separation of powers, and rational liberalism had an enormous influence on leaders of the American and French revolutions late in the eighteenth century. Likewise, Beccaria was often hailed as the founder of modern criminal justice and

КИТАЙСКОЕ

УЛОЖЕНІЕ,

Перевелъ сокращенно съ Манжурскаго
на Россійской языкъ коллегіи Ино-
странныхъ дѣлъ маіорскаго ранга

Секретарь Алексѣй Леонтіевъ.

ЧАСТЬ ПЕРВАЯ.

Цѣна 80 коп.

ВЪ САНКТПЕТЕРБУРГѢ
при Императорской Академіи Наукъ
1778 года.

FIGURE 3.1 Title page of the Russian abbreviated translation of the Qing Code (from Manchu), 1778–1779.

Courtesy of the University of London, School of Oriental and African Studies Library.

provided enduring inspiration for legal and political reformers, including drafters of the American Declaration of Independence (1776), Constitution, and Bill of Rights, such as Thomas Jefferson and John Adams.[50] The drafters of the French Code Pénal, promulgated by Napoléon in 1810 and lauded as the first *modern* code of criminal law, explicitly acknowledged their indebtedness to Montesquieu, Beccaria, Blackstone, and Bentham. This and other codes of the Napoleonic era became models for legal reformers, first in Euro-America and then in other countries, including Japan and China in the late nineteenth and early twentieth centuries.[51] All the contradictions examined thus far were often suppressed or forgotten amid the triumphant narrative of the spread of European law and culture as the origin of global modernity.

RECEPTION OF *TA TSING LEU LEE* IN EUROPE

Although imperial knowledge about presumably less civilized societies was frequently used to legitimize the rule and cultural superiority of the dominant empires, it also had the potential to destabilize the ideological foundation on which such cultural hierarchy hinged. Robert Travers, for example, has shown how British efforts to recover an ancient constitution from Indian culture to legitimize their rule turned up evidence that questioned the colonial stereotype of Oriental despotism.[52] Nicholas Dirks, Ann Stoler, James Hevia, and the earlier chapters of this book have all provided examples of how imperial archives could be read for traces of shame, rapacity, corruption, and incompetence of the colonizer and for the suppressed voices of the colonized.[53]

In a similar vein, the reception of Staunton's *TTLL* generated serious doubts and questions regarding conventional wisdom about Chinese law and government or about Sino-Western incommensurability. Even though the new knowledge was partially reincorporated into established categories, it also caused new tensions and was used by different voices in the British legal reform to advance contradictory arguments and agendas.

Staunton's translation was retranslated into Italian (1812), French (1812), and Spanish (1862, 1884) and was featured by a number of leading European intellectual journals, including the *Edinburgh Review*, *Quarterly Review*,

Monthly Review, British Critics, Eclectic Review, Critical Review, Literary Panorama, Selected Reviews (in the United States), *Journal général de la littérature de France,* and *Mercure de France,* and *Annali di scienze e lettere* (Italian).[54] Of these journals, the liberally oriented *Edinburgh Review* was one of the most prestigious intellectual venues in nineteenth-century Euro-America. Its subscribers grew from 750 to 9,000 within six years of its establishment in 1802, and to 12,000 by 1813; and its actual readership was significantly larger than its subscription number indicates since a copy of the magazine was typically read by more than one household at the time. In comparison, the London *Times* sold only 8,000 copies daily in 1816. An editor boasted in 1809 that each issue of the *Edinburgh Review* was read by 50,000 thinking people within a month after it was printed, and an author could become famous overnight by publishing in this journal.[55] The other major journals also had large readerships. In 1812, William Gilford (1756–1826), editor of the London-based *Quarterly Review,* which had been established by the Conservatives to oppose the reform agendas of the *Edinburgh Review,* made a similar claim about his journal's influence.[56] Like the *Times,* many of these leading newspapers and magazines were circulated widely through the network of empire, connecting metropoles such as London and Paris to imperial frontiers such as Calcutta, Singapore, and Guangzhou. The editor of the *Canton Gazette,* an English newspaper based in Guangzhou, noted in 1831 that the *Edinburgh Review* was widely quoted from China to America and that its assertions were generally assumed to be true simply because of its reputation.[57]

Publishing fairly long reviews of *TTLL,* these journals stimulated enormous interest in China's law and government in various Western countries. For instance, a famous review from the *Edinburgh Review* in 1810 was reprinted by an American periodical in the same year and was translated and published in an influential Italian journal in 1811.[58] Spread further by its Italian, French, and Spanish retranslations, *TTLL* or its variations became practically required reading for emerging modern Sinologists and many other authors, including jurists and philosophers, in order to compare and reclassify Chinese law and society.[59] An examination of *TTLL's* reception and assessment in these prominent periodicals sheds valuable light on how educated Westerners engaged with Chinese law and culture at a time when Western countries were seeking inspiration and paths to modernity. Since most of these commentaries have never been analyzed in prior studies, it may be worth discussing them at some length by sampling their views of Chinese law and society. It is worth emphasizing here that my discussion of some of the relatively "positive" Western views is not meant to valorize late imperial Chinese law or government, which had its own institutional disadvantages and defects. Rather, to highlight these views in the context of the increasingly "negative" portrayal of Chinese law and society is to draw attention to the serious contradictions and aporias in the dominant discourse of China in Euro-America.

In many ways, *TTLL* challenged reviewers to rethink the popular image of Chinese law or government as arbitrary and barbaric. In this text, reviewers saw evidence of highly developed codification and a spirit of rationality and liberality. That China had been using a uniform national law code since at least the sixth century was a great surprise to those who were familiar

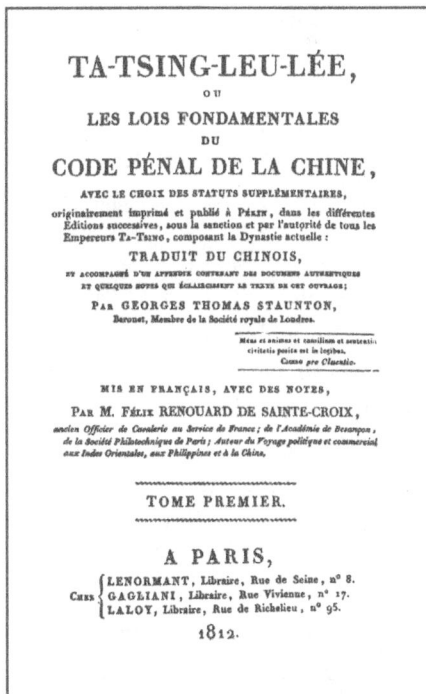

FIGURE 3.2 Title page of the French translation of Staunton's *Ta Tsing Leu Lee*, 1812.
Courtesy of Bayerische Staatsbibliothek digital (Bavarian State Library)/Google Books.

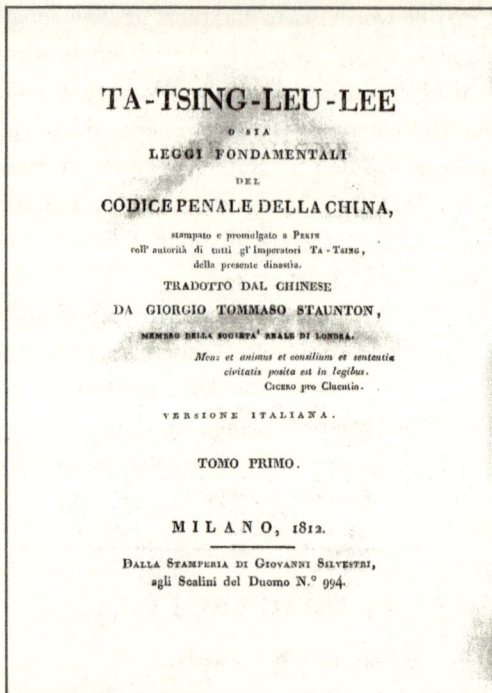

TA-TSING-LEU-LEE
O SIA
LEGGI FONDAMENTALI
DEL
CODICE PENALE DELLA CHINA,

stampato e promulgato a PEKIN
coll' autorità di tutti gl' Imperatori TA - TSING ,
della presente dinastia.

TRADOTTO DAL CHINESE

DA GIORGIO TOMMASO STAUNTON ,

MEMBRO DELLA SOCIETA' REALE DI LONDRA.

Mens et animus et consilium et sententia
civitatis posita est in legibus.
CICERO pro Cluentio.

VERSIONE ITALIANA.

TOMO PRIMO.

MILANO, 1812.

DALLA STAMPERIA DI GIOVANNI SILVESTRI,
agli Scalini del Duomo N.° 994.

FIGURE 3.3 Title page of the Italian translation of Staunton's *Ta Tsing Leu Lee*, 1812.
(Author's collection).

with the problems of the uncodified common law of Britain or the legal
confusion in Continental Europe. The *Eclectic Review* found it remarkable
that "the Chinese should have advanced so far beyond the most civilized
nations of the earth" in this respect. The French had had nothing like a code
of laws until very recently, and the national jurisprudence of England was
"anything but orderly and systematic." The commentator suggested that it
was important for both national honor and imperial interest to develop an
English code of law soon.[60]

Various specific statutes of the Qing Code were praised as relatively
more rational, advantageous, or lenient than their European counterparts,
including the strict requirements for bookkeeping and auditing of public
funds and those for preventing official embezzlement by punishing offenders in proportion to the assets embezzled.[61] The *Monthly Review* described

FIGURE 3.4 Title page of the Spanish translation of Staunton's *Ta Tsing Leu Lee*, 1862 (from the French translation).

Courtesy of the Biblioteca Virtual del Patrimonio Bibliográfico—España.

the Chinese rules of avoidance as sensible and likely to be effective in for-bidding officials to purchase land or marry within their own jurisdictions.[62] Despite their "vexatious minuteness," these laws seemed equitable and politic, from which even the "wiser and more liberal nations might derive advantage."[63] A Spanish commentator appreciatively highlighted the Chinese laws that mandated multiple judicial reviews in more serious cases, permitted litigants to appeal, and penalized officials for a wrongful judg-ment.[64] Another commentator found it noteworthy that women in China, despite their low social standing, enjoyed several legal indulgences, includ-ing redeeming themselves from banishment by a fine.[65] Publications such as the French *Journal général de la littérature*, the Spanish *Enciclopedia española de derecho y administración*, and even the overtly dismissive *Critical Review* mentioned these laws approvingly.[66] According to Bentham, it should be a key principle for modern legislation to consider the offender's age, sex, and social status in meting out punishments, so as to "conciliate the suffrages of public opinion."[67] Still, not all reviewers approved of such legislative leniency wholeheartedly. A British reviewer described such statutory leniency toward disabled or aged offenders in China as "merciful but somewhat fantastic,"[68] and a Russian author went so far as to consider it a great defect of Chinese law that a variety of corporal punishments were therefore commutable to monetary fines.[69]

Chinese legal principles were also cited to illuminate aspects of Western legal tradition. In Ming and Qing China, certain unintentional first-time offenders might be pardoned if they could demonstrate enough knowledge of the law.[70] The *British Critics* and the *Critical Review* found this statute useful for rethinking the English rule on the benefit of clergy, which had been criticized for encouraging illegality by reducing penalties for literate offenders. As the Chinese statute was designed to encourage the study of law among all classes of society, the *Critical Review* believed that a similar intention to promote literacy might be attributed to the benefit of clergy. Thus, what was being criticized as an ancient legal anomaly was rationalized as a worthy part of modern law through the invocation of Chinese law.[71] *TTLL* also brought some deficiencies in European legal systems into sharper focus. One reviewer wryly observed that the Chinese law on false accusation was what the "more civilized" states should have but still lacked. Under Chinese law, someone who caused another to die by false accusation would also suffer death. In contrast, that offense was treated as simple perjury in England and was punishable no more severely than the breach of an election oath. This was considered one of the greatest reproaches to every national code.[72] That *TTLL* made legal distinctions between principals and accessories in offenses and penalties was of great interest to some reviewers.[73] This was so because in English law, no distinction between principals and accessories was allowed in cases of high treason, manslaughter, and misdemeanor; in felony cases, the same punishment was stipulated for principals and accessories, and the distinction between principals and accessories before or after the fact mattered mostly to eligibility for the benefit of clergy *after* the sentencing.[74] In 1812, a French author found Chinese law unique in stipulating these distinctions, in contrast with French law on a very essential point.[75] Contrary to the dominant view, such examples led some reviewers to detect a "liberal" spirit in these parts of the Qing Code.[76]

Perhaps the most significant aspect of *TTLL* that caught the attention of Western readers was the meticulous attention to defining different shades of illegality in all foreseeable offenses and then matching them with graduated, proportionate penalties. We have seen above how this feature might have influenced Enlightenment thinkers in their advocacy of the principles of certainty and proportionality as key markers of modern law. The striking contrast with European law in this respect led even someone like John Barrow, who had written a most disparaging account of Chinese civilization in his *Travels in China* in 1804, to note that "the greatest care appears to have been taken in constructing this scale of crimes and punishments [in the Qing Code]; that they are very far from being sanguinary; and that if the practice was equal to the theory, few nations could boast of a more mild, and, at the same time, a more efficacious dispensation of justice of all the despotic governments existing, there is certainly none where the life of man is held so sacred as in the laws of China."[77] After reading Staunton's *TTLL* before it actually appeared in print to the public, Barrow noted in 1809 that China was perhaps the only country that had successfully adapted a scale of punishments to every species of crime, in a code that was written in such a concise and intelligible manner and was so widely distributed that no lawbreaker could plead ignorance of the law as an excuse.[78] It was no little surprise to Barrow and others that the Chinese, in a "despotic" state, had long attached so much importance to relying on *written and public laws* to regulate the conduct of the rulers and the ruled, more so than most of their European counterparts by then. Reviewing *TTLL* anonymously in the *Quarterly Review* in 1810, Barrow again praised this unique feature of the Chinese legal system.[79] Most British reviewers echoed his sentiment. For instance, the *British Critics* recognized the Chinese legislators' ingenuity in "the nice discrimination of the shades of difference in the degree of criminality," particularly in cases of life and death, including the six types of minutely distinguished homicides.[80] The reviewer found the Chinese emphasis on proportionality and certainty almost excessive, as the tearing away of a certain quantity of hair or the breaking of one, two, or more teeth, fingers, or bones of the body each had its proportional degree of punishment.[81] Many other British, French, and Spanish reviewers made similar observations.[82]

Most reviewers, however, remarked on what they saw as meritorious aspects of the Qing Code within a discursive environment that took for granted China's cultural inferiority or incommensurability. As a result, they often employed the strategy of bifurcation to create a series of dichotomies between the theory and the practice of Chinese law, between rationality and liberty in the same legal system, between European and Chinese laws, and between Chinese and other Asian laws. The first dichotomy minimized the subversive potential of acknowledging the *theoretical* merits of the Chinese legal system by pointing out how Chinese judicial practice differed from the codified law. The second helped maintain the Orientalist or ethnocentric conclusion regardless of whether the practice was consistent with the theory. The third allowed them to recognize some merits of the Chinese legal institution as distinct from the disavowed Oriental government or civilization to which that institution belonged. The fourth meant that such appreciative appraisals should be understood as relative only to other Oriental countries. However, these techniques of boundary drawing were not always successful, and the East-West cultural borders often proved difficult to maintain. The following famous passage from the *Edinburgh Review* in 1810 has frequently been quoted to suggest that Chinese law was highly regarded in Europe at the time.[83] However, a closer look at the entire review and the reviewer's overall assessment of China reveals a much more complex and ambiguous picture.

And here, we will confess, that by far the most remarkable thing in this code appeared to us to be its great reasonableness, clearness and consistency—the business-like brevity and directedness of the various provisions, and the plainness and moderation of the language in which they are expressed. There is nothing, here, of the monstrous *verbiage* of most other Asiatic productions—none of the superstitious deliration, the miserable incoherence, the tremendous *non sequiturs* and eternal repetitions of those oracular performances;—nothing even of the turgid adulation, the accumulated epithets, and fatiguing self-praise of other Eastern despotisms;—but a calm, concise, and distinct series of enactments, favouring throughout of practical judgment and European good sense, and, if not always conformable to our improved notions of expediency in this country, in general approaching to them more nearly than the codes of most other nations. When we pass, indeed, from the ravings of the [ancient Indian] Zendavesta, or the Puranas, to the tone of sense and of business of this Chinese collection, we seem to be passing from darkness to light,—from the drivellings of dotage to the exercises of an improved understanding: And, redundant and absurdly minute as these laws are, in many particulars, we scarcely knew any European code that is at once so copious and so consistent, or that is nearly so free from intricacy, bigotry and fiction. In everything relating to political freedom or individual independence, it is indeed woefully defective; but, for the repression of disorder, and the gentle coercion of a vast population, it appears to us to be, in general, equally mild and efficacious. The state of society for which it was formed, appears incidentally to be a low and a wretched state of society; but we do not know that wiser means could have been devised for maintaining it in peace and tranquility.[84]

This anonymous review was authored by Francis Jeffrey (1773–1850), a lawyer and renowned literary critic who would become lord advocate of Scotland, member of the British Parliament, and then lord justice of the Court of Session (i.e., the supreme civil court) of Scotland in the 1830s and 1840s. Having founded the *Edinburgh Review* in 1802, Jeffrey remained its editor and major contributor for twenty-six years.[85] He was a strong supporter of legal reform in the early nineteenth century, and in an earlier anonymous review of Barrow's *Travels in China*, he also expressed a strong disdain of the Chinese for their abject submission to a despotism upheld by "the sordid terrors of the lash," their incapacity and ignorance in modern sciences, and their defective language and national character.[86] Although his reformist inclination drew him close to the translated legal text for insights about law, his preconception of the Chinese as a whole rendered *TTLL* alien, a product "of a style of thinking and legislating the most remote from our own habits." Such ambivalence is brought to the fore in the foregoing passage. The passage began with an affirmative comment on *TTLL* for "its great reasonableness, clearness and consistency" and its "business-like brevity and directedness." According to the reviewer, the Qing Code embraced commendable "practical judgment and European good sense" better than not just other "Eastern despotisms" but also most European codes. Confirming the European standards of legal rationality resulted in making the Chinese law comparable or even superior in some respects to its European counterparts. At the same time, however, China remained firmly an Oriental society in "a low and wretched state" because of its lack of "political freedom or individual independence." If a sense of disjuncture arose from seeing China at once different and commensurable, it was ameliorated by interpreting the sophistication of the Chinese code as only necessary and suitable for maintaining a vast, benighted population in tranquility. To put it simply, a compelling argument was made that rational means served irrational or illiberal ends. Whether such rational means could and should be applied to the more "advanced" state of Western societies was to become a key point of debate during the British legal reforms, as we shall see.

Montesquieu's writings about China, Staunton's *TTLL*, and the many reviews of the translation and its retranslations could either corroborate or challenge one another. Staunton's translation of the Qing Code called into question Montesquieu's categorical claim that no established laws would exist or be respected in a despotic country. By bifurcating theory and practice and dichotomizing rationality and liberty, many British reviewers, including Barrow and Jeffrey, upheld that influential, Orientalist view in the end. While acknowledging some comparative merits or rationality of the Chinese code *in theory*, they often concluded that the Chinese legal system was doomed to fail *in practice* because despots eventually governed not by law but through their subjects' fear of corporal punishment. Typically, an essay in the *Eclectic Review* suggested that the Chinese, with no honor, conscience, or faith, would not hesitate to commit crimes whenever they felt safe from detection and the bamboo. As "cunning" was "the offspring of fear," China must necessarily be "a nation of cheats."[87] The theoretical assumption of the nature of despotism was accepted to preclude any need to suspend a general judgment either about the practical efficacy of *TTLL* compared with other legal systems or about Chinese civilization and national character. For these reviewers, *TTLL*, with its meticulous catalogue of corporal punishments, delineated a despotic society without honor or shame and filled with fear *through law*. Reiterating Montesquieu's famous footnote without even mentioning that author, Jeffrey stated that "[t]he bamboo is the great *panacea* of China."[88] Two French reviewers likewise wrote that subjecting officials to bamboo strokes for dereliction in their duties "particularly degraded the character of the [Chinese] nation."[89]

Such intercultural transactions in the metropole through the translated texts were still intimately connected with the transimperial encounter in southern China. As noted in chapter 2, Staunton appended a translated report of the 1807 *Neptune* case to *TTLL*. This paratext proved to be crucial in shaping the reception of the main text of the translation and the underlying Chinese legal system, just as Montesquieu's footnote had assumed such a disproportional significance in defining Chinese law and government in the West. For an ordinary Western reader, the original report would have been highly instructive in illustrating the typical judicial process in homicide cases involving European offenders. But Staunton's introductory comments placed it in a totally different light, telling the reader that the whole report was based on a fabricated story that turned the killing of a Chinese in a British riot into a pure accident. Like the *Lady Hughes* dispute, what this case illuminated was not so much the normal operation of the Chinese legal system as the erosion of the legal system by local Chinese officials and merchants and Westerners in a contact zone where imperial and local interests overrode legal concerns. Staunton stressed that the case should not be taken to reflect the general character of Chinese law. But his allusion to the Chinese judges' greed and corruption and his failure to mention any legal responsibility on the part of British agents (including himself) in circumventing the Chinese judicial investigation left his readers to read the report as indisputable proof of the prevalent corruption of the entire Chinese judicial system.[90]

For many reviewers, the *Neptune* report was one of the most "instructive documents" about the actual operation of the translated law code. Seen as a microcosm of Chinese legal practice, it was considered to reflect both the true state of Chinese society and the irrelevance of law despite a sophisticated legal code.[91] Although he repeatedly expressed appreciation of some aspects of the Qing Code, Barrow was led by Staunton's account of the *Neptune* case to conclude, "Certainly it is, that a more corrupt and profligate government than that of China does not exist in the universe; and that, however pure the source [i.e., the Qing Code], the streams become foul and muddy in proportion as they increase their distance from the fountain head."[92] Such corruption and injustice were said to be the fate of a nation without honor. Honor can be found in societies of almost all conditions and in every stage of progress, Jeffrey contended, but the Chinese were the only people completely destitute of it.[93] Regardless, even if the Qing Code might be followed in practice and be good enough for the Chinese, to impose it upon a presumably honorable and free people in Britain or the West would be to commit the cruelest atrocity.[94] Thus, from an otherwise diverse body of views about various aspects of Chinese law and society as a result of the publication of *TTLL*, many commentators reached a surprisingly unequivocal conclusion, often by following the logic of bifurcation, to maintain their preconceptions of cultural identity and superiority. Meanwhile, readers, including lawyers, politicians, and legislators, did get to learn a great deal about a very different but highly developed legal system, and gained new perspectives on their own cultural tradition and government at a time when major political and legal reforms were taking place in Euro-America.

About two decades later, Staunton himself offered specific examples to counter this kind of "broad assertion and vulgar prejudice" as an "inaccurate" description of both the theory and practice of the Chinese government. Direct contact had shown Staunton and other missionaries that the Chinese were not devoid of honor, honesty, virtue, or justice, despite all the known defects in their society. For him, to admit that practice differed greatly from theory in China, still based on limited information, was to admit only that their institutions were not immune in operation from the obstructions facing all human or even divine institutions anywhere due to "the ignorance and the evil passions of mankind." If all Christian nations "literally practiced what they professed," there would be no more war and civil strife. "The question therefore is only one of *degree*." Useful or just conclusions could not be drawn from even the best evidence of foreign immorality unless British observers compared that with the increasing "vices and crime" and delinquency in their own country. Staunton's sentiment here was still derived from his belief that the Chinese legal system was well suited to that people, but the same belief also led other British reviewers like Jeffrey to ultimately dismiss the legal system as a product of Oriental despotism not suited to Western nations.[95] Ten years after defending the British decision to wage the First Opium War in 1840, Staunton would reiterate his remarks while taking a further step to retract his earlier allusion, in 1810, to the corruption of the Chinese judges in the *Neptune* case.[96] Although these short notices, published privately decades later, would do little to change the negative reception of *TTLL* or Chinese law among many Europeans, they illustrate how cultural boundaries could be differently drawn and redrawn, as Staunton implied, depending on the viewers' agenda or degree of self-reflection.

THE INFLUENCE OF CHINESE LAW ON BRITISH LEGAL REFORM, 1810 TO 1830S

Having surveyed the reception of *TTLL* in Europe, I focus now on the hitherto unexamined role of Chinese law and justice in the debates over the reform of criminal law and codification in Britain in the early decades of the nineteenth century. As scholars have pointed out, by 1810 the British (primarily English) criminal justice system had frequently come under severe criticism for its lack of uniform structure, consistency, predictability, and efficacy. Hundreds of capital statutes, often of antiquated origin and based on ad hoc parliamentary acts, punished with death a variety of crimes ranging from murder to theft. In response to the socioeconomic and political transformation stimulated by the Industrial Revolution and the changing attitudes toward harsh punishments, which I discuss in chapter 4, British jurors and judges became less willing to enforce the law by convicting or sentencing petty property offenders to the "hanging tree," and cases of perjury and arbitrary judicial discretion became even more common than before. To many, the whole system had become quite arbitrary, as the same offender might face a totally different fate depending on when, where, and by whom he or she was prosecuted, tried, or sentenced. Contemporaries attributed many of the problems to the uncodified nature of British criminal law (which relied upon parliamentary statutes and common-law cases) and the virtually unregulated discretion of judges. Although there had been scattered suggestions for codification of the criminal justice system, the generation of Eden, Blackstone, and Bentham in the late eighteenth century was the first to generate enough intellectual and political support for substantial changes in the next century.[97] Their writings and those of Voltaire, Montesquieu, and Beccaria were avidly read in Euro-America and led many to call for legal and political reform. Among the leading legal reformers in Britain were Sir Samuel Romilly (1757–1818), Sir James Mackintosh (1765–1832), and Sir Henry Brougham (1778–1868), who were close friends and all reform-minded members of Parliament.[98] Beginning in February 1810, Romilly, a former judge of the Court of Chancery and former solicitor general, repeated his unsuccessful attempts of two years earlier to introduce bills to repeal capital statutes on stealing things worth five shillings in a shop or worth forty shillings in a dwelling house or on board a vessel in a navigable river.[99] These efforts and the debates they engendered are often considered as the start of the modern British legal reform. Substantial changes did not take place until the 1820s and 1830s, but even with these, the various law commissions appointed to codify the criminal law system have never accomplished that goal.[100] It is against this background that I trace the role of Chinese law throughout the process.

Before taking up the legal reform of the early nineteenth century, however, it may be helpful to get a sense of how some British jurists or writers felt about the state of their own legal system around the turn of the nineteenth century. In 1772, jurist Henry Dagge (1715–1784) lauded the jury system as the best means of protecting liberty and property, but wrote with a far more sober tone about other aspects of the legal system. To him, the criminal laws in Britain seemed designed more to terrorize slaves than to govern free people, despite the fact that liberty was supposed to be the foundation of the government. He held that those laws contradicted all notions of justice, confounded all distinctions of morality, and demonstrated the principles of despotism by making fear the incentive for obedience.[101] Blackstone made similar observations regarding the indiscriminate severity of punishments, rampant perjuries, and arbitrary judicial power in Britain. It would have been no little irony for Montesquieu (who favored Britain as an ideal of free governments) and Francis Jeffrey to see British law and government reduced to corrupt despotism. Dagge actually lamented that even despotism might lead to milder institutions than the British ones.[102] The comments of Blackstone and Dagge were included in the widely distributed pamphlets by advocates of legal reform in the early nineteenth century.

In 1810, Romilly introduced his legal reform bills with a memorable statement: "There is probably no other country in the world in which so many and so great a variety of human actions are punishable with loss of life as in England. These sanguinary statutes, however, are not [always] carried into execution."[103] Citing statistics over the past few decades, he maintained that the statutes were ineffective because they discouraged victims (as prosecutors), witnesses, juries, and judges from prosecuting or punishing criminals strictly according to the rule of law. Thus, judges neglected their duties or adjudicated cases quite unpredictably, and witnesses and jurors violated their oaths to tell and find the truth. Romilly suggested that all these factors had reduced the system of criminal law to almost a lottery of justice.[104] Such documented arbitrariness and widespread perjury in criminal justice contradicted the frequent assertions of British legal or cultural superiority such as those made by colonial judge Sir James Mackintosh in India in 1805 or by the English editors of the Shanghai-based *North China Herald* in the 1870s.[105] Opponents of the reform bills adopted the argument by Dr. William Paley (1743–1805), an influential British philosopher and archdeacon, that British law had achieved wise and beneficial results by purposefully enacting statutes that would not be regularly enforced but stand as objects of terror in the statute book to be applied only occasionally at the judge's discretion. Romilly and other reformers refuted such claims of benevolent design or effect of the British capital statutes. The current system was not a product of legislative wisdom or rationality, they countered, but a by-product of unauthorized adaptation to the growing popular and judicial antipathy toward harsh punishments found in those anachronistic statutes.[106]

For the reformers, the root of the problem lay in the indiscriminate severity of punishments and the unregulated discretionary power of judges in sentencing. Quoting Beccaria, Romilly declared as a universal maxim that the certainty of punishment would be much more efficacious than the severity of punishment in preventing crimes. Thus, he believed it imperative to have a police force, rational rules of evidence, clear laws, and "punishment proportioned to the guilt of offenders, to approach as nearly to that certainty as human imperfection will admit."[107] Certainty, uniformity, and proportionality in law and penalty were the focal points for both sides of the parliamentary debates on the reform bills. These were also the distinguishing features attributed to Chinese law by Jesuit historians and later Western reviewers of *TTLL*. Although Romilly did not cite Chinese law directly, he referred to Blackstone's passage that in turn cited Beccaria and

Montesquieu, who made proportionality fundamental to modern justice by invoking Chinese precedents.[108]

It is now very difficult to assess exactly how much direct influence Chinese law had on the actual legislative proposals of British or other Western reform programs in the nineteenth century. Sir James Fitzjames Stephen (1829–1894), a famous British jurist, observed that Bentham's writings "had a degree of practical influence upon the legislation of his own and various other countries comparable only to those of Adam Smith and his successors upon commerce," but later scholars have found it hard to trace any legislative act directly to Bentham's works.[109] If Bentham's reputation as a radical reformer explained the paucity of explicit reference to him in Euro-American legislative proposals, the stigma of China's Oriental despotism, symbolized by "the graduated bamboo" or cudgel, would have posed a far greater risk to the success of any Western reform program that explicitly invoked Chinese law as its inspiration.[110] In this sense, the representational strategy adopted by Montesquieu in *only footnoting* his recognition of Chinese law as an exception to his overall categorization of China as a despotism had already anticipated how Chinese law would be treated on such occasions. His other footnote—"It is the cudgel that governs China"—had long become the metonymic catchphrase for Chinese law and government by this time.

However, the practical need for reforming metropolitan institutions could result in a less-dismissive attitude toward Chinese law and culture. Earlier in this chapter, I noted the direct or indirect references by Enlightenment thinkers and jurists to Chinese law in developing some of the cardinal principles that came to define modern law and justice by the mid-nineteenth century. These ideas were so popular that even the author of *The Punishments of China* (1801), George Mason, noted that the Qing Code was compiled in such a way as to "have a punishment appropriate for every crime," which his watercolor paintings were supposed to illustrate.[111] This sentiment was echoed in many of the European reviews of Staunton's translation. Like Beccaria, British reformers such as Romilly, Mackintosh, and Brougham were evasive about Chinese law in their reform bills, but Bentham did cite Chinese practices to illustrate his legislative principles. Mackintosh had certainly read Staunton's translation, since it was he who had urged Staunton to undertake the project. Romilly and Brougham must have at least come across some of the reviews of that translation and the merits of the Qing Code.[112] By 1812, it would have been difficult to find a serious British legal reformer still totally ignorant about Chinese law and *TTLL*.

We do have some evidence of explicit engagement with Chinese law or *TTLL* in the British debates over legal reform. In 1811, for instance, a former member of Parliament published a pamphlet, *Hints for a Reform in Criminal Law*, addressed to Romilly, offering advice on how to reform the British legal system. Echoing Romilly's speech in the House of Commons that had just been published, this pamphleteer criticized British law for its ineffective severity and lack of uniformity and consistency. He cited Blackstone in declaring that no distinction in the gradations of the penalty meant no distinction in the gradations of the guilt, and thus no sense of justice. He recommended the newly published *TTLL* to all who were interested in the criminal jurisprudence of Britain. The fact that no one but the emperor himself could alter the punishment of any capital offense in China illustrated the value of limiting the discretion of judges in Britain.[113]

Like other readers, the pamphleteer found the Chinese system of household registration to be an effective mechanism for crime prevention. A short abstract of the scale of crimes and punishments, similar to that shown in the Chinese law code, was also recommended by the pamphleteer to enable people to acquire a basic knowledge of the penal law in a short time. Seeing the prevalent spirit of proportionality in that code, this former parliamentarian recommended adopting something similar to the Chinese system of graduated punishments, ranging from confinement to perpetual servitude and to execution, in order to replace the many capital statutes in Britain. While lamenting that the Chinese punished high treason so severely as to make human nature shudder, or even allowed torture in certain cases, he nonetheless considered the Chinese legal system one of the more moderate ones and praised its relatively more merciful treatment of female offenders. He urged British legislators to reform the statute that authorized execution of convicts who fled from the penal colonies, citing the more lenient Chinese legislation for such an offense as an example.[114]

Cheaply printed and accessible pamphlets were then a major tool for shaping public opinion on such matters as legal and political reform. Romilly published his own speeches in the House of Commons as a pamphlet in

1810, and some of his opponents did likewise.[115] The aforementioned *Hints for a Reform in Criminal Law* was reviewed in the *Monthly Review* and the *Critical Review* in the same year. The former journal thought that it would be a proud epoch in British history to see the reform of its criminal law, which the latter reviewer called "a very objectionable part" of the British constitution. Both reviews were silent on the pamphlet's recommendation of Chinese laws, although that aspect appears to be the only thing novel about the pamphlet. The two journals' reluctance to acknowledge Chinese law is understandable given their recent criticism of Chinese civilization when reviewing *TTLL*.

From February through April 1811, Romilly again moved to abolish the aforementioned capital statutes and another one on stealing from bleaching grounds in Great Britain and Ireland. These bills had support but also faced strong resistance in both houses of Parliament. A most vocal opponent, Colonel William Frankland (1761–1816), expressed the opinions of many in his speech in the House of Commons on March 29, 1811. Besides opposing abolition of those specific statutes, he criticized the general legislative principle underlying Romilly's proposals. In his view, the admittedly desirable certainty of punishment was unattainable in free states and must be supplied by severity, which then made the judges' discretion in sentencing essential. The current mode of judicial administration seemed to him best suited to this happy and free nation. A system based on codified law with "more mild, more definite, more proportionate, more certain, and more speedy" punishments would ruin Britons' freedom, happiness, and virtue.[116] What Montesquieu, Beccaria, and Bentham had proposed as a modern legal system was thus divided into two sets of opposing values: freedom, happiness, and honor vis-à-vis certainty, humaneness, and proportionality.

For legislators like Frankland, other legal systems, however efficacious for crime prevention, were inconsistent with Britain's constitutional tradition and national character. This has proved to be the most popular line of reasoning against codification in Britain ever since. Importantly, Frankland developed his arguments by citing *TTLL* as a new source of valuable information for all Europeans. After praising the translator's contribution, he recommended to his peers in Parliament the "enlightened" comments (by Jeffrey) in the *Edinburgh Review* in 1810, asserting,

[T]he excessive and unprofitable accuracy and minuteness of the regulations of the [Chinese] code are very ably exposed, as well as the constant desire to regulate everything, to interfere in every action and to fix
immutably, before hand, the effect of every shade of distinction which a
case may receive from its circumstances. By this code, the whole actions
of a man's life are submitted to the control of government: the legislator,
seeming to forget the suffering and debasement that was to result from
the destruction of individual freedom and seeming only to think of permanent control and complete superintendence. The commentator most
successfully points out the absurdity of the minute and anxious attempts
at accuracy in distinguishing cases and proportionate punishments, and
observes, that these minute regulations have their origin in '*unenlightened
presumption*,' experience proving, that *the exact apportionment of punishment is unattainable, and not even worth attaining.* In almost all cases . . . of
variable delinquency, the law need only fix the maximum of punishment,
leaving it to the judge to give effect to such circumstances of mitigation
as may arise: all beyond this is "foppery and childishness."[117]

What seemed to emerge from this account was a Foucauldian state in
which all the actions of a human's life were under permanent and total control. Michel Foucault analyzed the patrimonial nature of the modern state
that governs its people in "a form of surveillance and control as attentive
as that of the head of a family over his household and goods."[118] But long
before this attack on the modern (Western) state for undermining people's
freedom and subjectivity, John Stuart Mill (1806–1873) and Max Weber had
warned against those possible deprivations in the modernizing West by citing contemporary China (a patrimonial bureaucratic empire to them) as the
worst-case scenario to avert.[119]

In the early nineteenth century, this cultural dichotomization turned
the British debates on whether to reform domestic legal institutions into
a choice between British liberty and civilization vis-à-vis Oriental tyranny
and barbarity. Frankland and others criticized the Chinese code's "minute
and anxious attempts at accuracy in distinguishing cases and proportionate
punishments" as informed by an unenlightened presumption. Frankland
pointed out that this exact adaptation of pains to offenses was also recommended by Bentham. He suggested that all who heard him should read

the *Edinburgh Review* on *TTLL* and on Bentham's *Principles of Legislation* in 1804. The latter review, he noted, ridiculed Bentham's idea of exactly apportioning punishment and found "our undistinguishing grossness better than such foolery."[120] Both anonymous reviews were penned by Francis Jeffrey. Robert Southey (1774–1843), a famed poet who joined the staff of the Tory-oriented *Quarterly Review* in 1809, considered Frankland's speech admirable and "a fine specimen of pure philosophy, united with practical knowledge."[121] But Jeffrey, who with Brougham and Sydney Smith (1771–1745) founded the *Edinburgh Review* in 1802 as the mouthpiece of the Whigs' reform agendas, would have hated to see his attacks on Chinese law being used by the conservative politicians and lawyers to frustrate the legal reform efforts.

Legal historians have pointed out that for many Anglo-American opponents of codification, the uncodified common law "defines itself in terms of a 'codiphobia,' a morbid fear of those continental or civilian systems that have been codified." They often characterized a written law code in such a narrow fashion that any codification would appear so fanatical as to be antithetical to the presumably adaptable common law. In contrast, they viewed common-law judges as oracles of law and bulwarks of rights and liberties against tyranny, while regarding codification as a legacy of despotism and a corrupt old world order, which sometimes referred to Continental European states as well as the Oriental ones. Highly skeptical of the predictability and substantial certainty of a law code, they dismissed other real concerns about arbitrary or inconsistent judicial decisions of the common-law system.[122] These opponents apparently ignored what Staunton mentioned in his preface to *TTLL*, namely, that the codified Chinese legal system did not preclude judicial discretion or legislative flexibility but was operated on the basis of "systematization and codification without loss of practical adaptability," a feature attributed by Max Weber exclusively to modern European legal systems.[123] Although some Qing jurists such as Xue Yunsheng (1820–1901) lamented the shortcomings of the Qing Code that should have long been remedied, the periodic revision of the substatutes (*li*) and the issuance of ministerial circulars (*tongxing*) or precedential leading cases (*cheng'an*) in Qing China made the judicial system reasonably responsive to various socioeconomic and cultural changes.[124]

Supporters of the reform bills declared that the different gradations of every offense should be defined as much as possible. It was true that precise definitions adaptable to every shade of guilt were impracticable because of the subtlety and variety of human actions and the limitation of words. But statutory definitions to a certain extent were attainable, according to Sir John Anstruther (1753–1811), former chief justice of Bengal (1797–1806) and longtime Scottish member of Parliament, and until it became unattainable, judges should not be entrusted with the power to decide on people's life and death.[125] A similar rationale had informed the codification and legislations in imperial China. Romilly's call for certainty and proportionality in contrast with severe and discretionary punishments was criticized as a radically wrong attempt at speculative, theoretical improvements in legislation. He denied any connection between his bills and Bentham's legislative philosophy but, interestingly, made no attempt to refute the connection drawn by his critics between the rationale of his proposals and the Chinese code.[126] His critics did not think that he could deny it. When the bills were passed by the House of Commons in April 1811 after lengthy debates and moved for second reading in the House of Lords the following month, Lord Chief Justice Ellenborough (1750–1818), who was Warren Hastings's counsel in his impeachment trial near the end of the eighteenth century, maintained that the whole debate on the reform proposal might be reduced to two alternatives: either "there must be high punishment for the aggravated commission of a general crime bearing the intermediate degrees between that and the lowest penalty, to be supplied by the discretion of the judge; or there must be a graduated scale of punishment, proportionate to all the shades and difference of crime." He reminded his colleagues that the second alternative was based on a theory borrowed from the Chinese code under which, according to a recent pamphlet, all kinds of crimes were differentiated and "the blows of the baton were not only numbered, but the size and thickness of the instrument ascertained."[127]

By explicitly linking the Chinese code with the reform bills and by making them appear irrationally mechanical, the opponents could win the support of many people unfavorably disposed toward China or tyrannical, corrupt power. The specter of Oriental despotism alarmed many Britons about the larger consequences to their cherished cultural values. Lord Ellenborough ridiculed that kind of legal system as absurd in theory and nugatory in

practice. A whole century had proved that the current laws were necessary and should not be overturned "by speculation and modern philosophy."
They had been sturdily enforced in general and thus effective in punishing
offenders. It was his conviction that as long as human nature remained what
it was, the fear of death would be the most effective deterrent against crime.
To prevent crime, he believed it unwise to abandon the salutary influence
of that terror. Such terror was precisely why Dagge had suggested that the
legal system made Britain almost a despotism under Montesquieu's theory.
Moreover, the strong resistance to the reform bills was less about the specific statutes at issue than about the bills' potential to totally change the
underlying philosophy of the whole criminal justice system. And the core
principles of proportionality and certainty of punishments in the proposed
criminal code were explicitly attributed to the Chinese code and considered
features of *modern* legislation. The bill to abolish the death penalty for theft
from bleaching grounds passed, but those to abolish it for stealing in private
houses, shops, or navigable waters were defeated, twenty-seven votes to ten,
in the House of Lords in 1811.[128]

During the next decade or so, the Chinese code continued to be a sine
qua non on many occasions during the debates on codification and criminal law reform in Britain. Both proponents and opponents were mind-
ful of the Chinese model or stigma and invoked it for different purposes.
For instance, in an anonymous article in the *Edinburgh Review* concerning
Romilly's pamphlet based on his reform bills, Brougham, who would later
succeed Mackintosh as leader of the legal reform, maintained that certainty
and applicability should be the defining characteristics of a modern system
of jurisprudence. To recognize that absolute perfection in codification was
unattainable "even in China" did not mean that one should valorize the
existing imperfection of British law.[129] At the same time, others derided the
proposed reform as modern philosophical speculations that were ingenious
in theory but impossible to implement and absurd like the lately discussed
system of the Chinese code.[130] When the debate on the reform was renewed
in Parliament in 1819, it was emphasized again that the homegrown law
of Britain had no need to imitate "the fanciful accuracy of Chinese legislation" to anticipate and penalize every possible shade of crime with "a
precise degree of infliction from a graduated bamboo." These reform efforts
were seen as a threat to Britain's social and cultural fabric developed over

centuries, and no other kind of legal system was deemed capable of providing equally adequate protection for British property, individual liberty, and public tranquility.[131] This line of criticism was so powerful that reformers like Mackintosh and Brougham were compelled to repeatedly deny any intention to introduce a new criminal code or a legislative philosophy that was "so graduated" as to remove the judges' discretion.[132]

The so-called codiphobia had prevailed among Anglo-American legal professionals by the end of the nineteenth century, but its rationale had assumed a definitive form in the early nineteenth century, when codification was debated with unprecedented intensity.[133] Historian Keith Smith has suggested that the years from 1808 to 1818 were by far the most contentious period of British legal reform, during which Romilly's largely fruitless criminal law bills were deliberated. It was in 1810–1811 that Romilly's proposals sparked fierce debates in Parliament in which the Chinese code was invoked. A pattern of claim and counterclaim by the two sides also took shape during this period and continued in the subsequent British (and American) debates on codification.[134]

Romilly was credited with starting the movement that would eventually help consolidate the unsystematic criminal laws and abolish some of the capital statutes later in the century. Most of his proposals faced strong opposition in his time, however, and the task of codifying the criminal law has never been completed. Upon Romilly's death in 1818, Mackintosh and later Brougham continued to campaign for legal reform in Parliament. Brougham, as lord chancellor in the Whig government, appointed a Royal Commission on the Criminal Law in 1833 to reform and codify criminal justice as a whole. From 1834 through 1845, a series of reports were submitted to Parliament for the purpose. However, the resulting digest of British criminal law, to say nothing of any criminal code, was not adopted. The several commissions formed for similar purposes in the next century and a half met with scarcely greater success. Scholars have even announced the death of the modern codification project in Britain, where a modern criminal code remains as elusive as it was in 1811.[135]

A variety of factors contributed to the strong resistance to the proposed codification or fundamental legal reforms in the early nineteenth century, including the influence of conservatism in Britain and among many legal professionals.[136] There is little doubt, however, that Chinese law and *TTLL* played a unique, symbolic role in the British debate on legal reform and modernity.[137] Identifying codification and proportionate justice with the Chinese code enabled opponents to invoke all the negative imagery of China to defend the status quo. In this sense, modern Anglo-American codiphobia was partly attributable to growing Sinophobia during this period. The threat posed by the arguably more rationalized Chinese law to the British claim to modernity and superiority was temporarily neutralized by radicalization of cultural difference. This had the effect of further Orientalizing the Chinese while reifying (i.e., Occidentalizing) the British identity as rigidly defined by the anachronistically uncodified common-law system. It is important to recall that it was not the legal reformers or modernizers but the conservatives who attacked Chinese law in Parliament in defense of Britain's so-called Bloody Code. Ironically, about a century later Chinese legal reformers would use British law as one of their models in modernizing their own legal system.

COLONIAL LABORATORIES OF MODERNITY AND WEBER'S PREDICAMENT WITH LEGAL CLASSIFICATION

Although codification was rejected in Britain as being suited only to despotism, it was promoted as a "civilizing" institution in India and other British colonies. It has been remarked that "defects in England's legal system motivated the codification of Indian law."[138] In 1833, a Legislative Council was established to make laws for India, and Thomas Babington Macaulay (1800–1859), a recent member of Parliament for Leeds, became the first law member and president of the Indian Law Commission (1834–1838) to lead the project. In the next few decades, several commissions managed to enact the Indian Penal Code (1860), the Code of Civil Procedure (1859), and the Code of Criminal Procedure (1861).[139] Drafted in 1837, the Indian Penal Code was the first and arguably most important of these codes, known for its comprehensiveness, compactness, and meticulous definition and certainty of crimes and punishments. Although Macaulay consulted the French Code Pénal when drafting the Indian Penal Code, he claimed that the latter represented a truly scientific project that was not modeled on any existing system.[140] The chief colonial legislators such as Macaulay, Sir Henry Maine, and Sir James Fitzjames Stephen represented the new law codes as essential for progress and justice in India and necessary to bring law and order to the "subcontinental chaos by replacing the arbitrary and personal will of the Oriental despot with the rational and reliable objectivity of a universal law."[141] Elsewhere, thanks to European expansion, the French codes enacted during the period from 1804 to 1810 and the subsequent German codes and the Indian codes became the models for reformers all over the world by the early twentieth century. There emerged an influential narrative of modern law that defined codification as a major engine and marker of progress, modernity, and the rule of law. The essential components of the narrative about the origin and spread of legal modernity included the invented tradition of the Franco-Anglo-Germanic codes, the Enlightenment thinkers, and the Western legal tradition centered on Christian culture and Roman jurisprudence.

How were the contradictory views on codification in the British Isles and in British India reconciled? What turned a supposedly despotic institution in the metropole into an ideal of liberalism in the colony? The obvious contradiction was partly alleviated by invoking the line of culturalist and historicist arguments, developed by Sir William Jones in 1794 and later by James Mill in *History of India* (1818), that colonial law and administration would not be effective in achieving their goals unless they reflected the cultural prejudices of the people to be regulated thereby.[142] However, the recent British debates on Chinese law and despotism might also have played an instrumental role in convincing British legislators, intellectuals, and colonial administrators of different ideological persuasions that a codified Oriental legal system, though incompatible with the British tradition of liberty and honor, might be most suitable to the needs of British India. In this sense, the repertoire of Orientalism could provide very creative ideas for developing what Partha Chatterjee has called different "techniques of power" in the "actual practice" of empire.[143]

As noted earlier, pre-1840 China and colonial India obviously had different political relationships with Britain and other Western powers. This affected how the two countries' sociocultural institutions were interpreted in the West, but their geographical proximity and different historical developments also frequently brought them together for comparison within the same discourse of Orientalism in the eighteenth and nineteenth centuries. I mentioned in chapter 2 the close ties among the founding Indologists and Sinologists. Many British intellectuals in this period viewed both China and India as Oriental despotisms, but for different reasons. China was believed to possess too much legality without liberty, or too much equality and uniformity without differentiated individuality and freedom. In comparison, India was viewed as a despotic land with excessive religiosity and caste-based hierarchy instead of law, order, and equality.[144] When presenting the draft Indian Penal Code to Parliament in 1837, Macaulay maintained that no other country had so much need for law as India did.[145] In contrast with the popular image of a feeble and chaotic Mogul empire in India, European missionaries and commentators had long been impressed by the value of Chinese political and legal institutions in keeping that large pagan empire stable, unified, and independent of Western political penetration for centuries.[146] Recall that Francis Jeffrey and many other reviewers of *TTLL* considered the Qing Code more sophisticated and efficacious than other Asian legal systems, especially in the "repression of disorder and the gentle coercion of a vast population."[147]

Colonial administrators in India had been searching for such a model to keep that large country in tranquility and peace. Among others, Sir James Mackintosh, then chief judge of Bombay, recognized the value of studying the codified Chinese legal system when he urged Staunton to translate the Qing Code. Macaulay actually described the British colonial government as an "enlightened and paternal despotism" and told the House of Commons that codification might be the only thing that absolute governments could do better than popular governments.[148] India was not suited to having a free government, but it could have "the next best thing—a firm and impartial despotism."[149] Some of the key features of the colonial law codes resembled what British reviewers had attributed to the Qing Code. For instance, Sir James Stephen praised the Indian Penal Code for giving the plainest instructions to a small number of British administrators and for being so compact and small that the Indians knew its pocket editions better than the Scottish knew their Bibles. This colonial legal system was attended with evils, but Stephen thought it absolutely necessary in order to enable a few hundred civilians to rule a populous continent like India.[150] Despite the strong attack on the proposed codification of the common law at the home of empire, the affinity between India and China in the Orientalist discourse now justified the adoption of a Chinese or Benthamite type of codified legal order in the East Indies. While Bentham's legislative models were criticized as speculative, Staunton and others found the Qing Code instructive because it had been empirically tested as the foundation for governing a large empire, and was not just a product of the "untried theory of a legislator" or philosopher.[151]

The colonial law codes were promulgated speedily after the Great Rebellion of 1857, which had intensified the feelings of paranoia and besiegement among the vastly outnumbered colonial settlers in India. For leading intellectuals like Hegel and Maine, while excesses in both law and equality in China meant absence of the spirit of historical progress and sovereign subjectivity in the modern world, deficiency in both law and equality in India also justified denying its sovereignty, as India was formally colonized in 1858 and saw Queen Victoria becoming Empress of India two decades later. The new legal system, which purported to achieve universal justice and legal equality, actually helped perpetuate colonial rule and privileges.[152]

As a systematic national code came to characterize modern legal systems, for many the "partial and incomplete modernization" of the legal institutions in Britain and, to a lesser extent, in other Commonwealth countries and the United States appeared to have formed a counterpoint to this narrative of modernity.[153] However, Max Weber, one of the founding theorists of modernity, recalibrated his theory to include the Anglo-American legal systems as part of that modern family of law. In principle, Weber held that legal systems evolved from an earlier irrational state through increasingly sophisticated juridical and logical rationality and systematization to finally rational-formalistic jurisprudence. More problematic to him than the many antiformalist tendencies of modern legal developments in Continental Europe were the various nonformal or nonrational aspects of the Anglo-American systems: the continuing primacy of precedents (*stare decisis*) in the common-law regime manifested a charismatic kind of law finding; the British justices of the peace were "quite patriarchal, summary and highly irrational"; and the modern jury trial was often "kadi justice" in practice that was based on the jurors' personal sentiments rather than written law. He found no real legal science in England until very recently, and considered English legal thought essentially an empirical art rather than jurisprudence. Unlike critics of codification, he praised the French Civil Code as the first purely rational law based on Bentham's ideals. He concluded at one point, "All in all, the Common Law thus presents a picture of an administration of justice which, in the most fundamental formal features of both substantive law and procedure, differs from the structure of Continental law as much as is possible within a secular system of justice." Nonetheless, such huge differences ultimately became negligible for him since modern Western societies allegedly share a unique type of rationalized legal order. The world's great legal systems were thus composed of the French and German law codes (based on rational legislation), the Anglo-Saxon law (based on "juristic practice"), and the Roman common law (based on "theoretical-literary-juristic doctrine").[154] He apparently read the early twentieth-century geopolitical reality of European domination (and the resulting spread of their legal institutions) back into history as tautological proof of cultural or racial superiority, as he also did in using Protestant ethics to explain the success of Euro-American capitalism.

As for the Chinese code, Weber held that it appeared like a code only externally. Despite some elements of systematic classification, Chinese law was only a product of mechanical arrangements and had little to do with real codification.[155] In denying Chinese or other law as a legitimate alternative or counterpart to Western law, Weber reserved formal rationality and modernity for the latter by claiming its exclusive heritage from the Roman law codes of the sixth century. While rational-formalistic justice largely prevailed in "the modern Western world," Weber asserted, the Chinese legal system, like that of India and other Oriental countries, remained irrational "kadi justice," which was then cited as a major reason for China's lack of capitalist development and modernity. As he saw it, the Chinese emperor and his official-judges decided cases based on their free discretion and personal views on expedience or equity, without reference to any formally binding rules.[156] Besides challenging Weber's idealization of pre-1900 European states as liberal-rational in contrast with other contemporary countries, recent scholarship has refuted most of his arguments about late imperial Chinese law.[157]

In contrast with Weber's characterization of Chinese justice as being too irrational and subjective, influential jurists or philosophers such as Montesquieu, Hegel, and John Stuart Mill had criticized Chinese law precisely for being too rationalized and despotically meticulous in regulating everything (including the judges' discretion) to permit any development of individual liberty or moral conscience in China. For more than a century, both these diametrically opposed interpretations of the same legal or political system were prevalent in modern Western scholarship on China. We must analyze these hidden tensions and aporias in the Western discourse of China or Chinese law in order to better appreciate the history of the Sino-Western encounter and modernity. This chapter has shown that a critical study of their intersecting genealogies helps recover the multiple and shifting roles of China and Chinese law in shaping the entangled history of modern transformation of China and Euro-American countries over the past two centuries. Its analysis of the various instances of the constitutive or symbolic influence of Chinese law and institutions on the Western debates on legal and political reform illustrates what might have been suppressed by the Euro-Americentric historiography of global modernity that has since prevailed and persisted in reinforcing the discourse of racial or cultural boundaries and hierarchy.

4

SENTIMENTAL IMPERIALISM
AND THE GLOBAL SPECTACLE
OF CHINESE PUNISHMENTS

In 1876, an editorial in the Shanghai-based *North China Herald*, the leading English newspaper covering China, observed that the heathen Chinese were as peculiar in dying as in living because they preferred strangulation to decapitation in legal punishments. Whereas hanging in the West was carried out speedily, strangulation prolonged the Chinese prisoner's suffering. A recent Chinese execution was recounted in horrifying detail to show that China was still "guilty of such acts of barbarism" when other states were already making laws to protect even dogs and cats from wanton cruelty. The editorial lamented that the Chinese, despite their pretensions to civilization and recent efforts to import Western armaments, had learned none of the Western spirit of humanity.[1] It echoed a proposal made by the same paper two decades earlier: "Let European nations compel these real barbarians to fulfill their treaties and another order of things must gradually ensue."[2]

It was a huge leap from a description of technical differences in the methods of capital punishment between China and Western countries to an assessment of fundamental difference in the legal and political subjectivity of the nations. What made this leap possible was a sentimental discourse that endowed the technical differences in penal practice with profound implications for the status and rights of a sovereign state in international politics. In chapter 3, I discussed the Europeans' debates over Chinese law in relation to their political and legal reforms from the perspective of *rational liberalism* as theorized by philosophers such as Montesquieu and Bentham.

This chapter extends that discussion by showing how *sentimental liberalism* informed Euro-American representations of Chinese law and punishment and how it evolved into an imperial ideology, which I call *sentimental imperialism*, that shaped Sino-Western relations and policy making. I argue that the sentimental discourse served not only to create a speaking and feeling subject of modern humanity and civilization but also to define the sovereign subject of modern international law and politics. In this chapter, I explore how invocation of humanitarian sentiment was translated into moral and legal authority and cultural hierarchy, a practice still common among many neoconservative politicians and less-reflective advocates of "human-rights diplomacy" over the past century. But it is worth stressing that the sentimental discourse under discussion here cannot be reduced to only an instrument of nineteenth-century imperialism given that a great diversity of participants and agendas might be involved in its production and operation. What this chapter focuses on, instead, is what I believe to be a historically crucial but underexamined facet, function, and legacy of this discourse, and the analysis that follows should thus be understood without dismissing the internal fissures and other historical roles and legacies of this discourse. My goal is not so much to criticize the modern discourse of sympathy and humanity for being complicit with imperialism as to understand the mechanisms that produced or naturalized that discourse's underlying normative assumptions. These assumptions have since prevailed over the past two centuries regarding the epistemological relationship between (imagined) pain, sympathy, cultural, or social difference and national identity and international hierarchy

SYMPATHY, THE MODERN SUBJECT, AND PENAL REFORM

Over the past few decades, a number of historians have joined cultural critics and anthropologists in fruitful study of the role of emotions, affect, or sentiment in the historical, cultural, and political processes of identity and subject formation of both individuals and groups along social, racial, gender, and class lines.[3] This rapidly growing cross-disciplinary scholarly interest has been described as the "affective turn" and the emergence of "a new epistemology."[4] Although there is no denying the "biological substratum of emotions" in the body and the brain, emotions, just like the human body, are shaped by cultural and social contexts and transformations. According to American historian Barbara Rosenwein, "emotions are above all instruments of sociability" because they are "not only socially constructed and 'sustain and endorse cultural systems,' but they also inform human relations at all levels," including international relations.[5] In other words, emotions are not "pre-social, pre-ideological and pre-discursive psychological and individual states, but are social and cultural practices." This understanding permits historical inquiry into the dynamic relationship between power, emotions, subjectivity, and sentimentalism.[6]

Several historians and literary scholars have recently demonstrated the value of attending to the history of emotions and sentiment in Chinese studies. For instance, David Der-wei Wang has traced an influential literature of crime and punishment and of "the wounded and insulted" in twentieth-century China while Michael Berry and Eric Hayot have analyzed how the visualization of pain and Chinese judicial violence profoundly affected the modern subjectivity of both Chinese and their Western "spectators."[7] Likewise, Eugenia Lean's microhistory of the trial of a female assassin in the 1930s has shown the importance of passions in configuring modern Chinese politics and civil society.[8] Drawing upon these works in different fields, this chapter studies the sentimental dimension of the normative power of imperial culture and politics, and the normative implications of sentimentalism for empire in the Sino-Western encounter. It does so by investigating the relationship between the voluminous documented expressions of emotions and sentiment regarding Chinese law and society and the evolving imperial ideology and practice in the late eighteenth and nineteenth centuries.

At the center of sentimental liberalism was sympathy. Together with other leading intellectuals such as William Wollaston (1659–1724) and Francis Hutcheson (1694–1746), David Hume (1711–1776) and Adam Smith (1723–1790) maintained that the capacity and propensity for fellow feeling or sympathy with others in distress is inherent in human nature and is an essential index of universal humanity.[9] According to Smith, the source of our sympathy is imagination: we conceive and feel the emotions of another person by imaginarily placing ourselves in the latter's situation and adopting his or her pains or sensations as our own.[10] This natural capacity to see and imagine others' sufferings was dulled by custom and habit in premodern societies but can be regained through reason and education. The ability to sympathize "from the position of a generalized and necessarily disembodied observer" marked the birth of the modern subject and self.[11] Hume's and Smith's ideas of sympathy not only exemplified the rise of a new bourgeois sensibility and identity in European metropoles but also operated as an "epistemology and psychology," as Uday Mehta has noted, for "understanding experience and power, especially in the unfamiliar context of the empire."[12] This interlocking relationship between sentimentalism and liberalism—with the latter's conceptions of human dignity, liberty, and progress—came to produce a kind of sentimental liberalism that would profoundly shape the policy and practice of Euro-American empires both at home and abroad in the late eighteenth and the nineteenth centuries. It is crucial to recognize these cultural and ideological developments when studying the Sino-Western encounter during this period. As we shall see, China had a key role to play in the formation of this sentimental liberalism, and in many ways the discourse of Chinese law and society became almost an indispensable site where sentimental liberalism evolved into sentimental imperialism.

The juridical and political implications of the above-quoted editorials from the *North China Herald* or many similar accounts of Chinese punishments in the nineteenth century can thus be understood in the context of the sentimental culture (often known as the culture of sensibility) derived from the eighteenth-century Enlightenment discourses of moral sentiment and human nature. I use "sentimental culture" or "sentimental discourse" in this book to refer to the articulation of emotions and sentiment such as sympathy, pain, disgust, cruelty, or indignation in the representation of law and society, as well as to the associated aesthetic, moral, and cultural assumptions.[13]

With its broadening purchase among the polite classes and then other segments of the population by the late eighteenth century, this sentimental culture generated "a new set of attitudes and emotional conventions at the heart of which was a sympathetic concern for the pain and sufferings of sentient beings."[14] This led to strong criticism of the ancien régime systems of penal practices and judicial administration in Euro-America. Until then, the largest and most sensational gatherings in Western metropolises such as London, Paris, or New York were often occasioned by horrific public executions—by hanging, quartering, burning at the stake, or breaking on the wheel—with as many as tens of thousands of spectators.[15] These scenes of state-sanctioned violence had long served important functions by educating people on law and order, entertaining them as public carnivals, or bringing them closer to God as they witnessed the prisoners' dying confessions or relived Jesus Christ's pain on the Cross for their salvation.[16] As the sentimental culture developed, it was recognized that an ethical and civilized individual or community should sympathize with those suffering physical or mental distress, including previously despised types of people such as slaves or criminals, as well as animals. Deliberate infliction or display of pain was deemed both inhumane for the sufferers and brutalizing for the inflictors and spectators.[17] Even pragmatically oriented reformers wanted to abolish or at least privatize many types of punishments because public torments had lost their edifying effects: "civilized" people would no longer watch them while those who did would only be more brutalized by the spectacles.[18]

Although this sentimental culture has long been credited with mobilizing public support for reform of Euro-American criminal justice in the nineteenth century by propagating the panopticon prison system and moderating corporal punishments,[19] revisionist scholars have highlighted the gap between such humanitarian sentiment and the actual time and effects of the institutional changes. For British legal historian Vic Gatrell, humanitarianism or the so-called bourgeois civilizing process was not really the major cause of British penal reforms in the early nineteenth century. Michel Foucault and others have also contended that modern penal institutions often led to a "carceral society," with more intrusive disciplinary mechanisms than their predecessors. But even Foucault and Gatrell both noticed the influence of the sentimental culture in the late eighteenth and the nineteenth centuries.[20] As John Stuart Mill (1806–1873) observed in 1836, the regime of public opinion became averse to indecorous social activities such as public executions, resulting in improved decencies of life and progress of civilization.[21] Here, Mill drew attention to the social and cultural effects of emergent sentimental liberalism. Until very recently, scholars of China have paid little attention to how this new sensibility or its resulting imperial ideology came to shape the modern image of Chinese law and society.[22]

It is important to review the intellectual and political genealogy and transformation of this sentimental discourse. It was intertwined with modern world politics by helping redefine the legal and political status of a people in international relations; it influenced how the people's subjectivity was constituted. As Dipesh Chakrabarty has put it, "the person who is not an immediate sufferer but who has the capacity to become a secondary sufferer through sympathy [by imagination] for a generalized picture of suffering, and who documents this suffering in the interests of eventual social intervention—such a person occupies the position of the *modern subject*."[23] In imagining or lamenting another's pain, this subject of feeling assumes the moral or even legal authority to intervene on the primary sufferer's behalf. Founders of the law of nations such as Francisco de Vitoria and Hugo Grotius in the sixteenth and seventeenth centuries had sown the seeds of the modern-day doctrine of humanitarian intervention or human-rights diplomacy. Vitoria argued in the 1530s that the Amerindian governments' tyrannical or cruel treatment of their subjects (such as their reported cannibalism) constituted a cause of just war waged by a benevolent Christian state like Spain against the former on behalf of the native victims, regardless of whether the natives desired such intervention. The natives' will was disregarded because they had no such "legal independence [i.e., subjectivity] as to be able to consign themselves or their children to death."[24] The native governments' domestic cruelty was treated *implicitly* as an injury to both humanity in general and the presumably sympathetic foreign spectators in particular. In this sense, sentimental liberalism in the eighteenth and nineteenth centuries helped revive the earlier doctrine of humanitarian intervention to circumvent the formal recognition of the territorial sovereignty of independent states under the post-1648 Westphalian system of international relations.[25] How did this doctrine of injury and humanitarian intervention become relevant to China? In the rest of the chapter, I show that the spread of sentimentalism in representing Chinese law and society in this period made that possible. While genuine sympathy might erode national, social, or cultural boundaries, the enunciation of sentimental feelings could also further consolidate them. Lynn Festa has demonstrated an important function of eighteenth-century British and

French sentimental literature in accommodating imperial projects: "the sentimental becomes the privileged mode for discussing colonial activities because it allows for the provisional acknowledgement of the humanity of others while upholding differences between communities."[26]

EMOTIONAL COMMUNITIES AND POLITICS OF REPRESENTING CHINESE LAW AND SOCIETY

By the mid-nineteenth century, visual representation of Chinese society and judicial practice had become a popular source of ethnographical knowledge about China. Alongside the official archives and intellectual discourses, these visual materials worked in tandem with the printed media, travel accounts, and scholarly books to create an enduring picture of Chinese people and culture. Such visual and textual documentation shows that the epistemological, moral, and aesthetic frameworks underlying the sentimental culture were intertwined with how Chinese judicial violence was perceived, felt, imagined, and interpreted. The actual impact on individual readers was sometimes difficult to ascertain, but, as British historian Randall McGowen has argued, this new sensibility could and did often become beliefs for many people that conditioned their perceptions and emotions even though they might act upon them only partially or rarely.[27] To conceptualize how representations of Chinese judicial violence affected Western minds, I use the notion of "emotional community" and examine the *representational and emotional practices* of foreign communities that arose through the witnessing of Chinese legal and social practices. These emotional communities, as Rosenwein has explained, had their "system of feeling: what these communities (and the individuals within them) define and assess as valuable or harmful to them; the evaluations they make about others' emotions; the nature of the affective bonds between people that they recognize; and the modes of emotional expression that they expect, encourage, tolerate, and deplore." Emotional communities varied in size, ranging from a small number of individuals to national or international communities.[28]

The concept of emotional communities may shed new light on some important aspects of the historical representation of Chinese law and justice in the West that have otherwise escaped our attention. Following the stories of Portuguese captives in China from the 1530s, frightening accounts of Chinese prisons or punishments by missionary authors such as Juan González de Mendoza (1545–1618), Álvaro Semedo (ca.1585–1658), and Domingo Navarrete (ca.1610–1689) were circulated in the next two centuries. Given that many equally harsh forms of judicial torment were still widely practiced in Europe—recall the horrifying scene of the regicide François Damiens's quartering by horses in 1757 that opens Foucault's *Discipline and Punish*—mixed views of Chinese law and punishments existed well into the eighteenth century.[29] In their excellent survey of Western representations of Chinese punishments, Timothy Brook, Jérôme Bourgon, and Gregory Blue describe the general attitudinal change as follows: "During the seventeenth century, it became conventional to identify the bastinado and the cangue as characteristic Chinese punishments by which officials enforced order on behalf of the state." Such judicial practices were "transformed into a defining mark of despotic government" a century later, when Chinese penal practices began to be regarded as a product of Oriental despotism and evidence of a cruel and barbarous society.[30]

By 1800, therefore, a system of feeling, to use Rosenwein's term, seemed to have taken shape in much of this diverse body of Western literature on Chinese punishments to form an imperial or Orientalist emotional community (which was divisible into many smaller emotional communities). In such a community, the representation of and emotional expressions regarding Chinese judicial practice often came in the language of the Enlightenment theory of humanity and sentiments *and* the language of Oriental despotism and barbarity. The religious, cultural, or ethnic affinities produced, relatively speaking, affective bonds and shared emotional norms between the representers (reporters, artists and photographers, narrators, or commentators) and their audiences (viewers, listeners, or readers) vis-à-vis the Chinese. The dominant Orientalist discourse became a guiding (though not totalizing) influence or lens through which feelings about Chinese law and society were filtered, even though the actual representational and emotional practices, such as expressions of disgust, sympathy, or fascination, of particular individuals on a specific occasion might vary.

By claiming the sensibility and authority to exhibit and interpret the cruelty or pain of others, members of the emotional community recognized themselves as subjects of the "moral, civilized" human sociality or community while simultaneously being subjected to the "ideological regulation and subjugation" of the emotional conventions.[31] This is what Foucault has described as the duality of subjectivity, which entails that modern "man appears in his ambiguous position as an object of knowledge and as a subject that knows."[32] Building on earlier discussion of the archival, linguistic, and intellectual dimensions of the Western construction of Chinese law, the rest of this chapter focuses on the sentimental and discursive politics that characterized the transnational representation of Chinese punishments and national character. Through a series of case studies of these visual and textual documentations of Chinese judicial violence, I hope to investigate the ways in which emotions and sentiment were disciplined, standardized, and mobilized to serve particular cultural and political agendas.

The Punishments of China: *A Case Study of Visualizing the Pain of Others*

Sold in various studios and shops on Old China Street near the foreign factories just outside the city wall of Guangzhou, watercolor paintings on pith or rice paper were very popular among early nineteenth-century Euro-American visitors to China for their brilliant colors and exotic motifs, including grisly scenes of Chinese punishments. These paintings were so widely circulated that they have exerted an enduring impact on the Western image of China since the early nineteenth century.[33] In the same period, as historians of the British and other European empires have shown, arts, literature, and visual culture revolving around Oriental themes or societies played an important role in the construction of bourgeois subjectivity as well as gender, class, and racial identities, in both colony and metropole.[34] If it is true that such "art always encodes values and ideology," as Janet Wolff has suggested, then *The Punishments of China* illustrated how "[i]mperial power was asserted, redeployed, and negotiated in what seem to be relatively benign, even mundane paintings."[35]

First published in London in 1801, *The Punishments of China* consists of twenty-two engravings based on Chinese watercolor paintings, each accompanied by French and English textual explanations. The impact of this work on the popular imagination of Chinese law and society can be only partially extrapolated from its global circulation. It was reprinted at least in 1804, 1808, 1822, and 1830, and copies of its different editions are still available in numerous libraries, art museums, auction markets, and private collections all over the world.[36] It was already available to American readers in late 1801. A specific instance may indicate how such publications about China might intersect with the intellectual discourses discussed earlier. In October 1801, a bookstore in Philadelphia received from London and Dublin copies of this work together with *The Costume of China*, Montesquieu's *The Spirit of the Laws*, and Adam Smith's *The Wealth of Nations*. The Chinese watercolors were likely to make Montesquieu's passages about Oriental despotism more memorable to a curious reader than Smith's theory of free markets or division of labor.[37] That this collection of watercolor paintings was deemed worth importing—apparently on the basis of its title and the terse information in the publisher's advertisement—alongside these Enlightenment classics also testified to the extent of interest in such topics about China across the Atlantic. Although some readers raised questions about its veracity, *The Punishments of China* was virtually the only source on Chinese law for a four-volume comparative legal study by a British lawyer in 1810. In 1804, it was translated into German and reprinted a few times. In 1825, over half of its illustrations were included in a French book, whose editor inserted additional speculations regarding Chinese penal practices and culture.[38] Countless similar watercolors continued to be circulated, and many of them, dating from the 1820s through the early 1900s, are still available in private collections and public libraries.[39]

Flipping through this elegantly bound volume, a reader sees Chinese judicial procedures and penalties ranging from "A Culprit before the Magistrate" (plate I in figure 4.1), to "Punishment of the Wooden Collar" (plate XIII), and finally to "The Manner of Beheading" (plate XXII). On the surface, *The Punishments of China* did not seem very different from contemporary publications produced by European explorers. Its editor, Major George Henry Mason, a former British military officer in India, gathered the original watercolors during a short visit to Guangzhou for some fresh air to regain his health in 1789–1790, three years before the Macartney

FIGURE 4.1 *A Culprit before a Magistrate*, plate I of *The Punishments of China* (1801, reprint 1808).

Courtesy of the Thomas Fisher Rare Book Library, University of Toronto.

FIGURE 4.2 *Torturing the Fingers*, plate X of *The Punishments of China* (1801, reprint 1808).

Courtesy of the Thomas Fisher Rare Book Library, University of Toronto.

Embassy reached China. He also published *The Costume of China*, in 1800, which included sixty engravings based on the watercolor paintings he had acquired, featuring different kinds of Chinese occupations and social customs. He presented these collections as accurate representations of the Chinese to remedy the superficial European acquaintance with the religion, laws, manners, and arts of this people. These colorful images and his carefully prepared French and English notes were intended to update earlier accounts by travelers ranging from Marco Polo to George Leonard Staunton.[40]

Unlike many European travelogues and reports, however, Mason's publications relied upon watercolor paintings produced and sold by Chinese artisans. According to Samuel Williams, 2,000 to 3,000 people in Guangzhou were employed in this trade in 1848.[41] This fact was even captured by export watercolor paintings showing foreign buyers at the local Chinese studios.[42] Art historian Craig Clunas has suggested that local Chinese artists and artisans modified aspects of their own culture to cater to the Westerners' aesthetic sensibilities and preconceptions about China. Occupying "a space which is neither wholly Chinese nor wholly European," these visuals thus tell us less about China than about how it was imagined by the Europeans, or what Chinese artisans thought European clients would like to see of China.[43] In this middle ground in the contact zone of empire, "a set of aesthetic demands communicated through traders and marketing agents on both sides emerged through Chinese aesthetic and commercial practice for sale and exchange in Europe."[44]

As plates IX and XI show (see figures 4.3 and 4.4), human figures wearing exotic clothing are featured in brilliant colors against an empty backdrop. The empty space in which the twenty-two punishments are portrayed mark a major difference between these paintings and Western paintings of public executions as well as later photography of Chinese punishments. Without any trace of physical environment or social space, the paintings are radically decontextualized, showing nothing but Chinese torturers and the tortured. In two of the paintings, the unfortunate recipients of punishment are named, but the names in Chinese characters do more to exoticize the images than to inform. The spare layout of the images in the book is not unique to *The Punishments of China* but is a generic feature of contemporary export-oriented watercolor paintings.

It reflected the Chinese artists' efforts to meet a popular Western desire in the eighteenth and nineteenth centuries to simplify, decipher, and categorize the unfamiliar "Oriental" cultures and complex societies encountered. When viewed through the Euro-American interpretative frameworks, however, these images do not appear to depict just a particular historical event but rather serve to illustrate the general practice of Chinese law and culture.

Nevertheless, since the Chinese artists apparently intended these watercolors to simply satisfy the Euro-Americans' curiosity about Chinese law and punishment rather than support the latter's claim of civilizational or racial superiority over the Chinese, these export paintings often proved inadequate for the purposes of the foreign commentators or publishers. To be sure, the torturer is clearly shown in action, exercising brutal power over the passive tortured body; there are also indications that the tortured might be scared or in pain, including the teardrops on the woman's face in figure 4.2. Yet the tortured in these paintings are cleanly clad and look as well fed and healthy as the torturers. It is hard to tell from their facial expressions whether they are actually experiencing as much agony as the editor's textual notes lead us to expect. In contrast with later paintings and photographs dealing with the same motif, the visual images in this collection show no blood, severed limbs, or other concrete evidence of excruciating pain and terror. This impression would significantly reduce the ability of the images to evoke horror or cultural shock. If these Chinese export paintings do not fully convey the desired horror, the editor's textual notes that accompany them do.

Each painting in *The Punishments of China* has a lengthy bilingual caption that sometimes runs to 400 words, vividly describing how the punishments are executed, what they do to the body, and what they tell us about the peculiar Chinese culture or people. Plate IX in figure 4.3, for example, depicts a frozen moment in administration of the ankle squeezer (*jiagun*). In reality, subject to specific statutory limitations, this instrument was used as a technique of judicial interrogation, rather than a form of punishment, to obtain confessions in serious criminal cases such as murder and treason in late imperial China. After describing the dimensions of the instrument, Mason's note about plate IX compels the reader to relive the horrifying proceedings in slow motion:

The ankles of the culprit [are] held fast by two men. The chief tormentor then gradually introduces a wedge into the intervals, alternately changing sides. This method of forcing an expansion at the upper part causes the lower ends to draw towards the central upright, which is fixed into the plank, and thereby compresses the ankles of the wretched sufferer; who, provided he be fortified by innocence, or by resolution, endures the advances of the wedge, until his bones are completely reduced to a jelly.

This brief passage shows that Mason's captions function at different levels. It is first of all informative, explaining in great detail how the ankle squeezer actually deforms the ankle by compression; it triggers the reader's imagination by comparing the crushed anklebones to "a jelly"; it conveys sympathy with words such as "the wretched sufferer"; and finally, by referring to the ankle squeezer as the rack and a "horrible engine of barbarity and error," the caption serves as a powerful commentary, associating with this Chinese instrument the infamy and horror of the Inquisition in medieval Europe.

One may argue that the very selection of the topic of punishment reveals an Orientalist mind-set that saw China as a despotic state where individual liberty did not exist. A close reading of *The Punishments of China* further reveals the mechanism that turned an account of reportedly objective knowledge into an instructional manual of cultural difference and hierarchy. With information supplemented, and, more important, framed, by the editor's imagination, sympathy, and cultural assumptions, the collection exemplifies how sentiment played a key role in transforming a discussion of technical methods of punishment into one of cultural or racial difference. The imagination and sympathy of readers were called upon to recognize and indeed feel the pain inflicted by the torturers upon the body. Feeling the pain allowed the readers, according to Enlightenment thinking, to identify with the victim and to revolt against the institution that made such suffering possible. To the extent that the depicted tortures belonged to the Chinese, these paintings supposedly spoke volumes about Chinese culture in general. Indeed, Mason intended this collection not just to inform and amuse but also to "instruct" readers on the vast difference between Chinese law and culture and their own.[45] It was his hope, expressed in his preface, that the book would reinforce among British readers a "sensation of security" arising from the assurance that they were protected from prolonged agony or demonic cruelty resulting from "tyranny, fanaticism, or anarchy." In the aforementioned example of ankle squeezing, by invoking the specter of the European Inquisition, Mason transported Chinese jurisprudence back in time to the Middle Ages. Whereas in their criticism of judicial torture in Continental Europe, eighteenth- and early nineteenth-century British writers often differentiated their country from the former by pointing to their own jury trial and presumed absence of judicial torture.[46] But in the present instance, both the intra-European difference and the temporal difference between the Middle Ages and the present were discursively displaced by spatial and cultural differences between China and the West.[47] Commenting on two illustrations of capital punishment, the editor provided long expositions on Chinese philosophy regarding life and death. Hanging in Europe was considered a harsher penalty than the quicker execution by decapitation, but the Chinese deemed the latter the more disgraceful kind of death because of their belief that a Chinese man, presumably influenced by Confucian filial piety, was obliged to consign his body to the grave "as entire as he received it from his parents" (plates XXI and XXII). By emphasizing that hanging made death slower and more excruciating than decapitation, such commentary implied how peculiar and irrational the Chinese beliefs and judicial system were.

At the same time, Mason's information and commentary were often misleading or erroneous. Illegal or imaginary forms of torture were treated as if they were legal or typically practiced features of Chinese law and justice, such as in "Burning a Man's Eyes with Lime" in plate IX (figure 4.4) and "Hamstringing a Malefactor" in plate XVII. In another example in figure 4.2, plate X describes a woman subjected to the finger squeezer (*zanzhi*), which, like the ankle squeezer, was used as a method of judicial interrogation for women accused of serious crimes. But Mason depicts it as a punishment for women guilty of disorderly conduct such as wearing jewelry inappropriate for their social status, adding that there are "no people existing who pay so sacred an attention to the laws of [behavioral] decency as the Chinese."[48]

Informed by earlier and contemporary Western thinking and sentiment about China, the interpretative framework of *The Punishments of China* would influence subsequent Western reception of Staunton's translation of the Qing Code, as discussed earlier in this book. The emphasis on the Chinese peculiarity in such pictorial images had the effect of making judicial

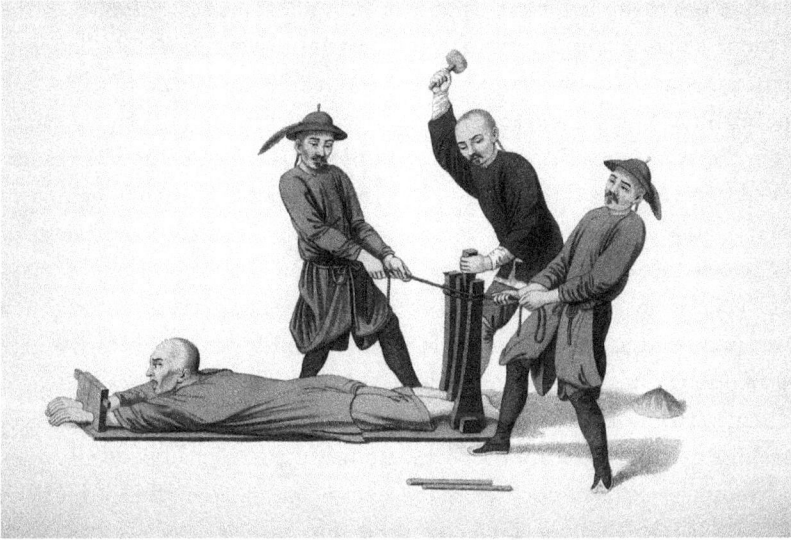

FIGURE 4.3 *The Rack*, plate IX of *The Punishments of China* (1801, reprint 1808).

Courtesy of the Thomas Fisher Rare Book Library, University of Toronto.

FIGURE 4.4 *Burning a Man's Eyes with Lime*, plate XI of *The Punishments of China* (1801, reprint 1808).

Courtesy of the Thomas Fisher Rare Book Library, University of Toronto.

torture or cruelty in general appear to be a phenomenon of China or the Orient alone. Emerging from these colorful visualizations of "Chinese" punishments was a modern subject presumably sympathetic to other suffering human beings and an imperial subject celebrating British or Western superiority. Whereas it was taken for granted that the editor and his readers would agonize over "the pangs of suffering humanity," the Chinese were said to have determined innocence by "the mental and corporeal power of enduring pain" through torture, exercised tyrannical control over society, and condoned the unrepresentable kinds of cruel punishments.[49] Sympathy was presumed as a universal capacity of humanity, but its invocation here served to exclude certain people from "modern" humanity. If in Sir George Thomas Staunton's translation of *Ta Tsing Leu Lee* we see a knowing subject seeking epistemic control over Chinese law, publications like *The Punishments of China* constitute readers as a sentimental subject while turning the Chinese into objects of foreign emotion and gaze, over whom the moral superiority of the gazing community is asserted.

To further contextualize how sympathy ended up creating or reinforcing the sense of alienation or hierarchy, we need to take a step back and reexamine sympathy in the Enlightenment context. The Enlightenment conception of the modern subject of sympathy developed from particular social and historical experiences in Europe around the time of Adam Smith, David Hume, and others, but this conception was later accepted often as a transhistorical, universal principle for humanity.[50] Smith himself recognized the particularity inherent in that universalizing theory: how and what we feel for another person depends on what *we* imagine to be the sentiment of the sufferer, even though the latter may not actually feel it that way; how much our feelings resemble those of the sufferer will be proportionate to "the vivacity or dullness" of the imagination.[51] *The Punishments of China* demonstrates that this need for imaginary identification posed a serious challenge when the representer and the audience presumed vast sociocultural or ethnic distance or difference.

Intriguingly, in the second edition of *The Theory of Moral Sentiments* (1761), Smith added a hypothetical scenario involving China: how might an ordinary European man react upon hearing that all people of the large Chinese empire had been "swallowed up" by a terrible earthquake? He might express sorrow for those unfortunate people, reflect upon "the precariousness of human life," and, if he was a man of speculation, ponder the potential implications for European commerce or even world trade. And then he would pursue his business or pleasure as usual and would "snore with the most profound security over the ruin of a hundred millions of his brethren" that night, even though a prospect of a "paltry misfortune" like losing his little finger might cause him more agonies. If all this made perfect sense to the reader, Smith tried to offer a more challenging moral experiment: "To prevent, therefore, this paltry misfortune to himself would a man of humanity be willing to sacrifice the lives of a hundred millions of his brethren, provided he had never seen them?" Smith answered in the negative because "reason, principle, and conscience," through education, will wake up the man's natural capacity for sympathy no matter how selfish he might be.[52]

It is no coincidence that Smith chose China to epitomize the greatest cultural distance or difference that was imaginable to contemporary Europeans. For him, China's presence in the hypothetical disaster might be most likely to dramatize the limitations of uneducated natural sentiment and the enlightening power of reason. Smith clearly recognized the enormous impact that physical *and* cultural distance had on the emotional reactions of even an "impartial spectator" toward a calamity in the Orient. Edmund Burke would later call the selective application of legal or ethical standards a practice of "geographical morality," but we also witness a practice of *geographical sympathy*, which withdraws sympathy from those removed *by spatial and cultural distance* from European metropoles.[53] Since our rational judgment cannot be totally insulated from our sociocultural milieus and personal interests, Smith's idealized *impartial* spectator often became an *imperial* spectator in transimperial contexts. In other words, despite the Enlightenment claim of its universal nature, sympathy is almost always differentially distributed along perceived national, social, or cultural boundaries.

Another way of understanding the impact of constructed distance on spectators of pain is to bear in mind the distinction between compassion and pity. In her study of the French and American revolutions in the heyday of sentimental culture, Hannah Arendt describes compassion as being "stricken with the suffering of someone else as though it were contagious," and pity as feeling "sorry without being touched in the flesh." Compassion is local, individual, and directed to the suffering person and cannot be triggered by the suffering of an entire class of people, let alone humanity as a whole. Unlike compassion, pity generalizes in order to overcome distance and becomes eloquent in expressing itself in emotion. Compassion is quiet, whereas pity is garrulous. As pity presupposes a net distance between the sufferer and the spectator, it focuses on *the spectacle of suffering* rather than the ethical reaction of the spectator, who does not experience the pain or distress directly with the sufferer.[54] If sentimental discourse enabled Westerners to ever recognize the pain of Chinese victims of judicial violence in *The Punishments of China* and similar representations, the sentiment that they experienced was more like pity than compassion. This explains why, as we shall see shortly in the study of Western reports of Chinese executions, the reports tended to emphasize the Western audiences' own emotions (such as repulsion or pain) and cultural superiority while treating the actual victims as unfeeling and speechless, and native spectators as cruel or indifferent. In this discourse, the actual sentiments of the Chinese often became unintelligible and irrelevant.

Chinese Executions and the Performative Role of Emotions in Shaping Identity

With technological developments in photography and telegraphy as well as the rapid expansion of the international news-gathering capacities of Western industrial nations, reports and images about China circulated globally at an increasing rate. Editorials, illustrated reports, or book excerpts on Chinese punishments or cruelty appeared frequently in many English-language newspapers based in China, Singapore, India, and Euro-America.[55] Depictions of Chinese cruelty from around 1800 continued to be recycled after the two Opium Wars. Fresh accounts of Chinese executions were churned out on a regular basis, first told by Western witnesses in Guangzhou or Shanghai and soon picked up in London, Boston, or Paris. To take just one example, in July 1877, the *Chicago Daily Tribune* reprinted a *New York World* article called "Sickening Scenes at a Chinese Court of Justice and Place of Execution," which was an expanded version of a report from the *Hong Kong Daily Press*. A letter from a French or Belgian gentleman in Guangzhou to a friend was added to give American readers an eyewitness account of Chinese executions.[56] Similar reports or commentaries, often headlined "Chinese Cruelty" or "Chinese Barbarity," were constantly distributed in numerous Western periodicals and newspapers.[57] Related images or tales then entered popular novels, movies, cartoons, and so on, and *Chinese cruelty* or *supplice chinois* had become a standard idiomatic phrase in the West by the early 1900s.[58] The constant flow of information helped create an *imagined emotional community* in which readers and spectators all over the world could fantasize about Chinese cruelty and articulate their sentiment. Just like the modern nation, this emotional community was also "solidified, imaged and imagined through the normativity of emotional bonds" and "acquired its performative force to reconfigure identities" for members of the community as citizens of a civilized nation or a larger Christian commonwealth.[59] This global spectacle of Chinese cruelty both contributed to and was produced by the transition of sentimental liberalism into sentimental imperialism, which negated the sovereignty and modern subjectivity of Chinese people and law in the process.

Execution represented a much-abhorred aspect of Chinese justice. Western reports of execution in nineteenth-century China almost invariably emphasized the absence of sympathy on the part of the Chinese. They portrayed the Chinese as unfeeling because of frequent exposure to such brutality. Even the victims did not seem to care about their own pain or horrible ending. Of an execution at Guangzhou in 1850, the *Chinese Repository* reported that no word, sign, or groan of pain came from any of the prisoners during the decapitation. The presiding local officials, executioners, and native spectators were portrayed as shockingly indifferent, if not amused.[60] Reports like this led the *Chicago Tribune* to conclude that human lives were treated like weeds in China, where callousness to human suffering was notorious and embodied in every section of the Chinese "Criminal Law Code."[61] In contrast with the natives, most foreign writers claimed that they put themselves through unusual pains to witness, report, or read about Chinese penal practices. Besides the emotional stress he endured, John Henry Gray (1823–1890), the archdeacon of Hong Kong, simply took it for granted that his description of Chinese criminal justice in 1878 would have filled the (Western) readers with "pain and indignation."[62] A number of missionaries, diplomats, and Sinologists who wrote about China during the nineteenth century, such as Robert Morrison, John Davis, Évariste Huc (1813–1860), and John Nevius, all expressed similar sentiments.[63]

Even more strikingly, according to these reports, Chinese executions were devoid of any effects of spiritual cleansing, for they supposedly did not have the moral, religious, or aesthetic elements that made similar occasions in the West ritualized religious events or public carnivals. The Chinese proceedings lacked the vociferous crowd of spectators flanking the streets from the prison to the execution ground, the elevated spectacle of the gallows in Paris or the hanging tree in London, the priest and the dying speeches of the prisoners, and the bloodied bodies in pain symbolizing the crucified Christ. This iconography of judicial violence and suffering had a long history in the West with widely understood religious symbolism and visual references, and shaped how Western viewers interpreted images of mutilated or tormented human bodies.[64] The absence of the expected religious signifiers led many foreigners in the nineteenth century to assume that Chinese judicial penalties served no rational or spiritual purposes but only reflected native cruelty and pagan depravity.[65]

One example was a widely circulated piece called "Executions of Criminals in China" in the first issue, in May 1817, of the Malacca-based *Indo-Chinese Gleaner*, the first English periodical focusing on China, established by Robert Morrison and William Milne of the London Missionary Society. Morrison, the anonymous author, reported the execution of forty offenders on two occasions outside the southern gate of the city of Guangzhou two months earlier, not far from the foreign factories there. He criticized the ostensible indifference of the local Chinese, as the executions excited little public attention and the Chinese official gazette only "coldly" mentioned that the offenders were beheaded. He was irritated by the peculiarity of the Chinese executions and what were missing from them: "There are no confessions, no dying spectacles, no account of the behavior of the unhappy victims of the offended laws, at the last awful scene; no minister of religion attends to urge them to repentance, in the hope of divine mercy, though human laws cannot forgive. The posture of execution is singular," with the prisoners kneeling in the direction of the Imperial Palace in submission and thanksgiving before their beheading. After this passage, Milne, editor of the *Gleaner*, added that such an awful spectacle would excite very different feelings in China than in any free and Christian country because even the most refined paganism was by nature unable to "cherish the nobler feelings of the human heart."[66] In 1832, the *Chinese Repository*, echoing Montesquieu, Adam Smith, and contemporary Euro-American legal reformers, cited a recent decapitation in Guangzhou to note that such frequent displays of cruelty would harden human hearts and make the cruel even more ferocious in a country where there was little moral feeling and no fear of God or of future retribution.[67]

It should be stressed that the Western emotional community that was brought into being by images and narratives of Chinese judicial barbarity was not monolithic. Different subject positions of the (real or imagined) spectators could affect the specific narratives or images, moral lessons, or coherence of the emotional practices or representational conventions. For instance, missionaries like Morrison, Milne, and Gray would insist that only Christians could genuinely and consistently show sympathy toward the condemned offenders in a foreign land, and that the Western nations should be grateful for living under a just and humane legal system imbued with the spirit of the Gospel.[68] Foreign free traders and diplomats with less evangelical enthusiasm tended to focus more on the mundane implications of the Chinese punishments, insisting on foreign extraterritoriality to protect them from the Chinese judicial system. Others might simply find them to be the most convincing evidence for the Western civilizing mission by all means, whether evangelical, economic, political, cultural, or scientific. National prejudices among the foreign community could also result in differing narratives. For instance, American readers might also draw on *The Punishments of China* or similar sources to make sweeping generalizations about China, but, unlike their British counterparts, they often contrasted Chinese cruelty and tyranny with the *American* legal and political systems as the best institutions of modern liberty and law.[69] The rise of social Darwinism and scientific racism in the late nineteenth century added another layer of interpretation. George Ernest Morrison (1862–1920), an Australian journalist who became the China correspondent of the London *Times* in 1897–1912 and then adviser to President Yuan Shikai of the Republic of China in 1912–1916, observed that the Chinese were genetically different from other peoples in that they were stoic in enduring the "physical pain" in surgical operation without anesthesia, undisturbed by the "foul and penetrating smells" and by all kinds of "noise." He stated in 1895, "No people were more cruel in their punishments than the Chinese," "obviously" because "the sensory nervous system of a Chinaman is either blunted or of arrested development."[70] So the spectacle of Chinese punishments was important for defining Chinese civilization and national character, no longer just because of the brutalizing effects on the Chinese but because it confirmed a larger pattern of Chinese backwardness or even genetic defect.

Whether through comments on watercolor paintings of punishments or press coverage of executions, a distinct Chinese cultural identity was constructed and cemented based on emotional representations of Chinese law and punishment. The emotional practices did not reflect the clash of some a priori cultural differences and boundaries. Instead, they were constitutive in that they helped establish or validate a *new* cultural or national identity. They were also performative in the sense that they sought to reenact similar scenes of Chinese cruelty to stimulate desired emotions or reactions.[71] It was *through the performance of this sentimental discourse* of humanitarianism and civilization that viewers and readers in the West were interpellated as a modern subject and the Chinese as the nonsubject Other who at the same time helped constitute the former by defining its outside limits. Having chosen to visit Chinese prisons and execution grounds in Guangdong in 1878, Mrs. Julia Gray, wife of Archdeacon John Henry Gray, declared, "These poor wretches [i.e., prisoners] *awoke my sympathy*, from the cruelties which had been used towards *them*, and my blood ran cold as I thought of the fate awaiting them. The jailors behaved with wanton cruelty towards them."[72] The sentimental subject "I" was formed through self-imposed encounters with the suffering natives and the cruel Oriental authorities. By evoking the normative markers of the emotional community such as sympathy and cruelty in describing these encounters, she became part of the prevailing sentimental discourse and, in the very process, claimed herself as the speaking and feeling subject "I" in contrast with the silent and presumably unfeeling Chinese (prisoners and jailers) as "them." This "performativity" of the nineteenth-century sentimental discourse on Chinese punishments, to quote Judith Butler in a different context, "must be understood not as a singular or deliberate 'act,'" but rather "as the reiterative and citational practice by which discourse produces the effects that it names." In this case, it means that scenes of Chinese punishments and cruelty had to be repeatedly reenacted in a familiar sentimental and Orientalist language to maintain the Western community's self-image as the modern and civilized.[73] The ceaseless efforts to depict and reconstruct similar spectacles of Chinese judicial violence thus performed the important function of simultaneously reinforcing the sense of superiority and generating new evidence of Chinese difference or barbarism.

In an influential essay of 1836 called "Civilization" that in a way signaled the transitioning of sentimental liberalism into sentimental imperialism through civilizational language, John Stuart Mill held that one thing that distinguished modern Western civilization from its premodern stage was that the spectacle and the very idea of pain were kept away from the more civilized people. For Mill and his contemporaries, civilization, an admittedly elusive term, simply meant what was not barbarism or savagery.[74] Thus, the savage or barbarous Other is necessary to signify the boundary and existential value of the civilized self-subject. As China or the Orient became the target of colonial expansion, the need to establish a modern identity by claiming a *temporal boundary* from one's own barbarous past came to be gradually replaced by a hardened *spatial boundary* from the contemporary Oriental Other. However, barbarity was such a recent part of judicial systems in Europe that cultural hierarchy premised on the presence or absence of judicial barbarity or savageness seems rather flimsy. For instance, suspected spy Francis Henry De la Motte was found guilty of high treason in London in 1781 and was sentenced to be drawn upon a hurdle to the execution ground, where he would first be hanged by the neck. He was then to be cut down alive and his bowels removed and burned before his face; finally his head would be severed and his body quartered. In 1814, this form of punishment was changed into hanging until dead before mutilation of the body, but gibbeting was not abolished in England until 1843, while drawing and quartering remained in the statute books until 1870.[75] A Chinese sailor, sentenced to hanging and dissection by the London-based Central Criminal Court in 1806 for stabbing another Chinese on an EIC ship in the Indies, apparently considered the British penalties more cruel than the Chinese punishment of decapitation or strangulation.[76] Britain was one of the Western countries least willing to abolish public executions; in fact, criminal law reforms in the 1820s left most of the "hanging statutes" intact. Public executions were not moved behind prison walls in Britain until 1868, in the German states until the 1850s, the United States until the 1830s, and France until 1939.[77] In light of these, the condemnation of Chinese executions, at least before the 1830s, cannot be fully explained by what some scholars have recently called the "trick of timing."[78] In this context, Western narratives about Chinese executions served a pedagogical-cum-ritual purpose, defining what would be a proper response to barbarity and how to perform such a response in order to become part of the civilized community vis-à-vis the Chinese. Such a disciplinary role for the narratives was especially crucial in light of the continued great fascination of Westerners with Chinese executions, which had long been condemned as being brutalizing to the spectators.

The Pedagogical Function of the Emotional Communities

Earlier in the chapter, I discussed the pedagogical effects of *The Punishments of China*. Many subsequent publications by diplomats, missionaries, and Sinologists in the next century had a similar effect of turning the emotional community into something like William Reddy's "emotional regime," in which the emotional norms and practices are subjected to systematic discipline or even "official rituals, practices, and emotives that express and inculcate them."[79] Many of the influential nineteenth-century Euro-American writers of China had official or semiofficial affiliation, and their depictions of Chinese law and society were often brought into direct alignment with the political agendas of their governments. For instance, Robert Morrison was Chinese interpreter for the British representatives in China from 1809 until his death in 1834, and Charles Gutzlaff played a similar role for the British expedition during the First Opium War. Thomas Meadows, Walter Medhurst, and Harry Parkes (1828–1885), all Chinese interpreters and then British consuls in China after the First Opium War, also published vivid accounts about Chinese punishments. For them, the Chinese punishments had a "barbarizing and decivilizing" impact on the Chinese, making them ready to commit "the most fiendish and atrocious acts" upon trivial provocation unless they were brought under the humanizing influence of Western civilization.[80] Their writings thus promoted a three-step ritualized emotional practice that moved logically from a portrayal of bloody Chinese penal practices to a reconfirmation of China's barbaric national character or culture, and then to the foreign powers' civilizing mission. As we shall see below, Parkes's claim that the Chinese officials in Guangzhou had insulted him and the British flag flying on the smuggling lorcha *Arrow* became the casus belli of the Second Opium War, and the sensational accounts of Chinese mistreatment of Parkes and other British and French captives later in the war became the grounds for the British destruction of the Old Summer Palace (Yuanmingyuan) in Beijing in 1860.

In the 1850s, Thomas Meadows articulated the political meaning of such sentimental narratives in the context of Sino-British relations. In a widely distributed account of the "horrible operation"—the execution of thirty-four Taiping rebels at Guangzhou—that he witnessed in July 1851, he explained that he attended this execution largely "as a matter of duty," because he was "desirous to inure [himself] to these sights (which [he] may be called upon to witness officially) as well as to watch closely the ordinary legal mode of procedure." As discussed below, he had indeed been ordered by Sir John Davis, then British plenipotentiary in China, to officially witness the execution, imposed by Davis, of four Chinese villagers for killing British subjects in Guangzhou in 1847.[81] It had by now become a "painful" duty of the more responsible members of this emotional community to bring to light the darkest but supposedly truest aspect of the Chinese national character and society. Henry Norman, author of the fairly popular *People and Politics of the Far East* (1895), insisted that only those who had witnessed Chinese public executions could tell the true character of that people to determine their status among the nations of the world. In his words, "I have looked upon men being cruelly tortured; I have stood in the shambles where human beings are slaughtered like pigs; my boots have dripped with the blood of my fellow-creatures;—repulsive as all this is, it is one of the most significant and instructive aspects of the real China, as opposed to the China of native professions and foreign imagination, and therefore it must be frankly described."This was followed by an account of the *lingchi* (or slicing) punishment he witnessed, accompanied by probably the first photograph ever taken of it, to authenticate that example of Chinese cruelty.[82] Despite the horrifying scenes, a few sets of such photographs from late 1904 were reprinted in various French, German, and English publications and became part of "the gruesome folklore" of Chinese cruelty in the West.[83]

By the mid-nineteenth century, numerous foreign visitors had found it difficult to resist the allure of Chinese execution grounds. In 1867, a popular travel guide by two British consular officers even included trips to such locales as recommended places of interest for visitors. After a description of the execution ground in Beijing, the omission of the sickening details of that "diabolic punishment" of *lingchi* might simply have enticed more readers into seeking that unique experience of repulsion and excitement at the pain of others.[84] According to a British doctor in 1849, foreigners actually risked physical danger from the local rabble in order to witness Chinese executions, and their Chinese servants or tour guides often refused to escort them to such events. He managed to find an execution ground and later published detailed observations.[85] Benjamin Ball, an American visitor, recounted three trips to the Guangzhou execution ground in his diary, family letters, and book. Two diary entries in February 1850 indicate that such visits had become a typical form of leisure or even a prebreakfast routine. "[After a tiresome trip elsewhere], I took a walk to the execution ground . . . and saw five bodies and five heads lying near each other." Two days later: "I passed through the execution ground as I went to breakfast this morning,

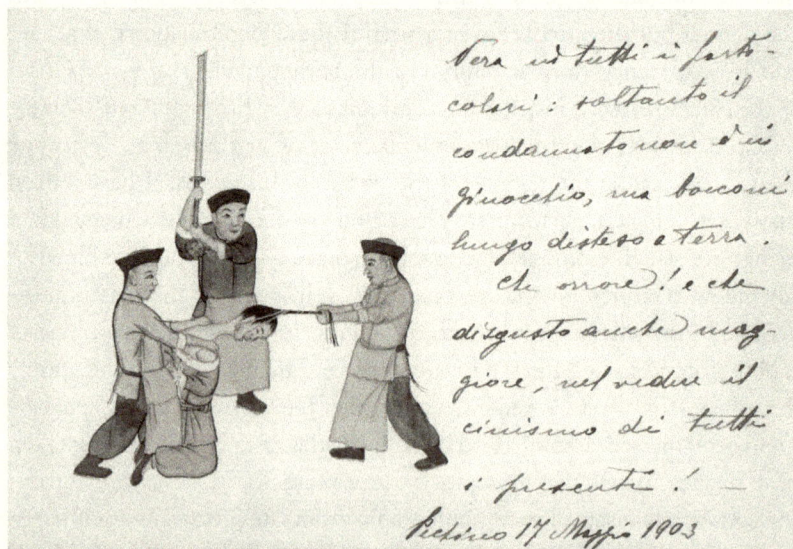

FIGURE 4.5 A postcard from an Italian soldier, Domenico Crespi, in the China expedition to comfort a young sister (then sick) at home, 1903.

Courtesy of Dr. Jérôme Bourgon.

to see if the bodies executed yesterday still remained there, and found them being tumbled into coffins of rough boards. The heads were thrown into the heap of forty or fifty heads in the little pen."[86]

Indeed, witnessing the horrifying spectacles appeared to have become both a ritual and cathartic obsession for many visitors to China in the nineteenth century. In 1877, an American visitor admitted having been so "haunted" by all the horrible tales of Chinese torture and execution that he had to visit the court, prison, and execution ground of Guangzhou to "relieve the impression of so much horror."[87] Men were not the only ones with hearts stout enough to bear frequent visits to the field of blood and horror. In 1873, Miss L. M. Fay, a missionary from the Episcopal Church, contributed to the Shanghai-based *China Review* a three-page account of Chinese *lingchi* and execution ceremonies. In 1877, Mrs. Julia Gray recounted for her mother in the United States the punishment of *lingchi* and other forms of cruelty that she witnessed at a Chinese prison and execution ground.[88] Even children were not spared this kind of indoctrination, or the flip side of what James Hevia has dubbed "imperial pedagogy." For instance, Elijah Bridgman mailed accounts of Chinese punishments in 1831 to the Sabbath School in Middleton, Massachusetts, to improve the students' Oriental knowledge.[89]

Despite the new photographic technology, watercolors had not lost their pedagogical value of vividly representing Chinese law and society. Among his collection of Chinese watercolors, Emil Vasilyevich Bretschneider (1833–1901), a physician of the Russian Legation in Beijing from 1866 to 1884, had a series of paintings of punishments. Clearly intending to use them for educational purposes, he translated the Chinese characters in the paintings into Russian and added textual notes in German. Indeed, the editors who published these paintings in 1995 found them to have "not only an aesthetic value, but to a much greater extent, ethnographic and historical importance." In spite of the ghastly human figures and bloody scenes, the editors believed them to be "authentic" reflections of the Chinese legal proceedings.[90] Two centuries after the publication of *The Punishments of China*, this genre of visualizing cruelty still enjoys artistic and scientific appeal.

The resulting surfeit of torment and pain "was not merely a seamy sideline to humanitarian reform literature but rather an integral aspect of the humanitarian sensibility."[91] If this sentimental culture indeed defined the

FIGURE 4.6 A stamped postcard featuring a photograph of Chinese decapitation around 1900.

Courtesy of Dr. Jérôme Bourgon.

modern human subject in an essential way, this modern subjectivity was constituted partly by simultaneously denying the Chinese (and most Oriental peoples) this capacity. By the mid-nineteenth century, China had been turned into a theater of cruelty and "a valley of death, a putrefaction of living death," in the words of Bridgman in 1847, where neither painting nor imagination could fully reveal for the Christian world that nation's horrible sins and abominations.[92] By the early 1900s, with pictures of Chinese capital punishment circulating worldwide as book covers, souvenirs, and postcards with homely messages through the official postal systems (see figures 4.5 and 4.6), many Western residents in China had agreed that an animal indifference to the suffering of others was a Chinese characteristic. Even sympathetic foreigners could compare the Chinese only to the ancient Greeks or Romans, who were polished but callous or hard-hearted, pushing China back by millennia in the evolutionary schema of civilization and race.[93] This was also the period of the Western scramble for China and Africa, and exhibiting Oriental barbarism would at least partly justify imperial rule as a civilizing mission. "Given this political context, these images have to be seen as documents of colonialism as well as evidence of Chinese [or Oriental] penal practice," Brook and his coauthors concluded succinctly. "They do show penal practice, to be sure, but they show it within a rhetorical frame that, by foregrounding the violence of the colonized, obscures the violence of colonialism. They also willfully neglect the history of earlier penal violence in Europe."[94]

Recently, Susan Sontag and Judith Butler both lamented the diminishing capacity, over the past few decades, of images of atrocity to shock modern viewers into ethical responsiveness to violence and suffering of others far away. If there is any other lesson to be learned from the past, however, it is that we should also guard against using moral indignation or humanitarian sentiment as a license to advance otherwise questionable political agendas. Sontag is fully aware of this pitfall and reminds us that sentimentality is fully compatible with brutality or even worse. The false sense of proximity between the privileged viewers and the faraway sufferers on the TV screen or the Internet is another "mystification of our real relations to power," because we might feel innocent of what has caused the suffering as long as we feel or express pity or sympathy.[95] These cautions are worth as much attention today as they were in the nineteenth century.

CULTURAL TRAUMAS AND SPECTACLES OF EXECUTION ON WESTERNERS' DOORSTEP

Sentiments regarding Chinese law and punishment were often at the center of international conflicts in the contact zone of southern China, especially in the years leading up to the First Opium War, when Western resentment of China's policies became increasingly intense and volatile. Not only did executions of Chinese opium traders directly implicate their Western partners, but Guangdong officials also brought these executions to the Westerners' doorstep. If the spectacles of Chinese punishment were intended by the Qing government to strike fear in the hearts of Western traders, they became the focus of vitriolic attack by the Western community, and indeed one of the factors that triggered the First Opium War. To understand the intensity of Western feelings over Chinese executions involving Western offenders, it is necessary to review several high-profile homicide cases that resulted in such executions.

The doctrine of secondary suffering, or what Adam Smith described as "adopted" suffering, is the flip side of the claim of *direct injury* to foreigners' feelings, rights, and property as a just cause for political or military intervention. The sense of direct injury can be traced back to the Sino-Western disputes analyzed in the earlier chapters of this book. From the Sino-Portuguese dispute in the Chen Huiqian case of 1743 to the Sino-American *Emily* case of 1821, executions of Euro-American offenders for killing Chinese persons were considered as both insult and injury to the Western community and triggered angry protests. The stakes were especially high for the British by the late eighteenth century, since the China trade had become enormously important to British India and the British empire, and they had a few thousand merchants and hard-to-control seamen in China every year. The fact that by the early 1800s the Portuguese, British, and Americans were increasingly relying upon importation of contraband opium into China to balance their trade deficits made the foreigners even more reluctant to submit themselves to Chinese jurisdiction and punishment.[96] Regarded as a serious threat not only to their economic interests and personal safety but also to their national honor, Chinese execution of Westerners constituted a "cultural trauma," a term used here to refer to "an invasive and overwhelming event that is believed to undermine . . . one or several essential ingredients of a culture or the culture as a whole."[97] It is traumatic because people believe, or are made to believe, that it is a threat to their collective or personal identity. A cultural trauma affects not just those individuals who witness the original incident in real time; it can become part of the collective memory and consciousness of a national or even international community through "affect-laden cultural representation" and other processes of public mobilization and education. A cultural trauma in this sense is a sociocultural construct in specific historical contexts.[98] In our case, Euro-American missionaries, travelers, merchants, diplomats, and Sinologists, as the "cultural carriers" who had the information, opportunities, and incentives, became the major players in establishing some of these events as cultural traumas in the contact zone.

The *Lady Hughes* case was one such event with traumatic effects on many contemporary observers. A Briton in China wrote to the Calcutta-based

India Gazette in December 1784, "Nature shudders at the recollection: The poor innocent Gunner, who, perhaps, did not fire the gun and certainly was a stranger to the man killed, was delivered up to the mercy of the Chinese. When I saw him led by an insulting rabble, the innocent victim of [British] pusillanimity, I absolutely blushed at the idea of being an Englishman." The writer felt that this incident proved once again that the British had sacrificed too much of their "national honor" for the sake of their commercial interests.[99] His sympathy and identification with the unknown "innocent" British offender was evident, and his sentiments of humiliation, injury, and injustice would be shared by many Britons in the next few decades.

Such a cultural trauma could also become a catalyst of transnational solidarity among Euro-Americans despite their conflicting interests or even internecine wars. In chapter 1, I mentioned the support of other Western nations for the British in the *Lady Hughes* case. Major Samuel Shaw, who had just arrived in China from the fledgling United States, stood by the British until the end of the dispute, purportedly for the sake of "humanity." Shaw's report to the U.S. government in 1785 of the unusually stringent Chinese control over foreigners and the harsh Chinese punishment for homicides regardless of circumstances constituted the first American official account of Chinese law and government.[100]

Shaw's invocation of humanity also reflected a popular tendency among the foreign community to treat Chinese judicial administration and assertion of sovereignty in such cases as "unjust and barbarous" and "contrary to all rules both of justice and humanity," as one Briton commented after the execution of a British pilot for killing his Chinese servant in Macao in late 1772.[101] French sojourners in China had their own traumatic experiences and expressed similar views about Chinese justice. Charles de Constant, a French veteran trader and consular officer in China until 1794, maintained that the *Lady Hughes*'s gunner was delivered to Chinese "barbarism" and that the Chinese had committed the "most atrocious of all barbaric acts" in executing the French sailor in the *Success* case of 1780, mentioned in chapter 1. His anger and disgust, even years later, were in large part attributable to his imagination of a scene where the local people were busy caning and stoning the corpse of the strangled Frenchman on a side street in Guangzhou before being reportedly dispersed by the English sailors who were "outraged by this spectacle."[102] It is this kind of spectacle—where a Westerner was a victim of not just merciless Chinese law but also "cruel" Chinese spectators—that seemed to traumatize the Western community most. These emotions were not simply spontaneous expressions but were generally mediated by the discourse of cultural incommensurability. European writers often prefaced their criticism of Chinese law and justice by challenging earlier missionary accounts and stressing that China was a "despotic state" where "tyranny and oppression" prevailed and the people were immoral and strangers to liberty and progress.[103] In this way, those earlier executions became almost indelible negative memories for the foreign community in the nineteenth century. As cultural traumas, they were recycled, remembered, and reimagined to define or revise the collective identity.[104] Besides hardening the assumed cultural difference, experiencing these traumas by imagination helped generate public support for extraterritoriality in China. Portraying criminal offenders as victims of a barbaric Chinese government, the cultural traumas lent moral legitimacy to demands for extraterritoriality that would make China an exception to the presumably universal principle of territorial jurisdiction.

One of the effects of such constructed cultural traumas was to stigmatize anyone who would allow their repetition. The Americans unfortunately became the target of public scorn in the *Emily* case of 1821. Francis Terranova, an Italian sailor on that American opium ship, killed a Chinese woman vendor during a quarrel by dropping or throwing a jar at her forehead and knocking her overboard. After a long delay (following the British precedents), the American merchants and captains finally gave him up to the Chinese officials. He was later convicted and strangled.[105] That the Americans submitted to Chinese jurisdiction four decades after the *Lady Hughes* case made them a laughingstock. Testifying in the House of Commons in 1830, Sir Charles Marjoribanks (1794–1833), president of the EIC Select Committee in China, stated that the Americans gave up an entirely innocent sailor to a sham trial and summary execution to save their trade.[106] Sir John Davis, who succeeded Marjoribanks in 1832, contrasted this with the *Topaz* case of the same year, in which the British managed to protect all their suspects from Chinese investigation for killing two villagers in an affray. For him, Terranova had been abandoned by those who should have protected him against Chinese barbarous conduct. This was a disgraceful American counterpart to the British humiliation in the *Lady Hughes* case.[107]

The Americans found British ridicule offensive and unwarranted. Refuting the assertion that Terranova was innocent and citing as a defense the cliché that Chinese law demanded life for life in all homicide cases, the *North American Review* noted that under the law of nations, a foreigner voluntarily entering a country was subject to that country's laws. The journal further reasoned,

> [I]f a Chinese sailor, from on board a Chinese vessel in the Thames, (supposing it possible a Chinese vessel should get there), had gone on shore at night, and stolen a sheep [as the Britons did in the *Topaz* case], he would, unless the law has been lately changed, in Great Britain, have been arrested the next day, for a capital offence. Had his voluntary delivery been withheld, he would have been taken by force. Had that force been resisted by the Chinese captain and his crew, they would have been deemed partakers of the crime, and treated accordingly. . . . If the [Chinese] sovereign . . . had thought of remonstrating against this usage of his wandering subject, the remonstrance would have been considered a proof, that his majesty was . . . no better than a barbarian.[108]

Even though the Americans and the British alike had resisted Chinese jurisdiction by portraying Chinese judicial administration as arbitrary and cruel, the British were reminded here that their treatment of foreigners in similar cases might well be worse in reality, and that China's efforts to enforce its law did not justify denying its sovereignty and jurisdiction under international law. Interestingly, this case itself would become a cultural trauma for many Americans as it seriously damaged their national honor and reputation. The fact that they had surrendered one of their sailors (albeit an Italian national) to suffer the ignominious Chinese strangulation scandalized them. Probably in retaliation, John Quincy Adams, who as secretary of state (1817–1825) had read the report on the *Emily* case from the American consul in Guangzhou, defended the British in 1841 as fully justified in waging the First Opium War to end China's injurious and "anti-social" policies against the Western nations. Despite Americans' refutation of the British allegations regarding Terranova's death, the United States became one of the first nations to demand extraterritoriality in China as a result of the British victory, ironically by citing the *Emily* case.[109]

On the eve of the First Opium War, spectacles of execution increasingly involved the Western community. On April 7, 1838, Guo Yaping, an opium shop owner and broker in Guangzhou, was executed by strangulation near the gate to the walled Portuguese settlement in Macao. His immediate execution without the Autumn Assizes was one degree more severe than the punishment stipulated in the Qing Code for colluding with foreigners at the coastal frontier—an unmistakable warning to the foreigners. The strangulation was witnessed by a large crowd, including many Euro-Americans, and was widely reported in Guangzhou and elsewhere through foreign newspapers and diplomats. Although the prisoner showed no sign of pain during the quick execution, several foreign commentators manifested unusual sympathy with the opium offender in describing him as someone with an excellent character and a victim of Chinese judicial corruption. The editor of the *Canton Press* was disgusted by Portuguese apathy in allowing the execution at Macao.[110]

The threat of the death penalty did not send an effective warning to opium traders. On December 12 that same year, Guangdong officials

FIGURE 4.7 View of the Hongs at Canton, 1825–1835, ca. 1835. Oil paint, canvas; frame 22½ × 32 × 2 in. (57.15 × 81.28 × 5.08 cm), Lamqua (ca. 1825–1860).

Museum purchase, 1931. Courtesy of Peabody Essex Museum, M3793.

planned to execute another offender, He Laojin, to pressure the foreigners into quitting the contraband opium trade. This time, they intended to
bring that notorious spectacle of Chinese justice to the square in front of
the foreign factories at Guangzhou. As local officials attempted to set up a
tent and other implements for strangling the prisoner near the American
flagpole (see figure 4.7), about seventy foreign residents rushed out to stop
them. William Hunter (1812–1891), a partner in the American opium firm
Russell & Company, declared that the square was leased to the foreigners,
who would not permit its "desecration by a public execution!" A group of
British seamen tore down the tent and implements and attacked the officials, putting them to flight. The foreign mob went on to beat the spectators
with sticks to clear the square; the Chinese crowd, now numbering almost
10,000, fought back with bricks and stones. A violent riot ensued, resulting
in a few broken heads and a siege of the foreign factories for a few hours
before Chinese soldiers arrived to restore order. He Laojin was strangled
elsewhere later that day.[111]

The American consul struck the flag in anger. In an official protest to
Governor-General Deng Tingzhen (1776–1846), the foreign Chamber of
Commerce called the attempted execution a violation of the foreigners'
contractual and customary property rights. The foreign residents would
have opened fire in self-defense, Deng was warned, if the Chinese soldiers
had arrived a bit later. The Chamber of Commerce attributed the violence
to "the novel spectacle" of a public execution in the square that had hitherto
been reserved for the foreigners' use, while ignoring the cause of the riot.
Deng replied that He's death resulted from the pernicious introduction of
opium by depraved foreigners, and that the execution was meant to make
them think hard and warn one another to respect Chinese law. He dismissed
any implicit challenge to China's sovereignty and jurisdiction: the ground,
whether before or behind the foreign factories, "is all the territory of the
empire, and is merely granted by the emperor, from motives of extraordinary
grace and clemency, as a temporary resting place for all the foreigners." He
found no grounds for foreigners to question whether or not a local convict
should be executed there. Instead, the petitioners should dissuade their fellows from selling the drug for selfish gain at the expense of numerous lives;
they would be expelled if they were so presumptuous as to come forward
to hinder future executions there.[112] On February 26, 1839, Deng executed

another opium offender near the foreign factories but not exactly opposite them, with a large number of troops present to maintain order. Two days earlier, an order to arrest the leading foreign opium merchants had reached Guangzhou from Lin Zexu, the newly appointed imperial commissioner, to suppress opium smuggling. War would soon break out.[113]

For the foreign community, the imposed spectacle of execution was the latest instance of Chinese outrage and injury, designed to intimidate and degrade them in the eyes of the local people.[114] In his official protests to Governor-General Deng, Charles Elliot conceded China's right to execute native criminals anywhere in the empire, but argued that because of the foreigners' different genius, nothing could be more offensive to them than the execution of a criminal before their doors. His government would view that unprecedented action as "an outrage upon the feelings and dignity of all the Western governments" concerned.[115] These emotionally charged correspondence and reports were forwarded to the British Foreign Office, Parliament, and newspapers, and later shaped the debate over the First Opium War.[116]

How do we make sense of the Westerners' outrage over the strangulation of opium offenders at their doorstep? Protestations on the grounds of national honor aside, one interpretation that can be easily overlooked concerns the unavoidable implication of the West in the creation of spectacles of cruelty. When executions did not involve Westerners, the latter were able to maintain a distance that sustained their sense of security and cultural superiority. However, when executions took place at their doorstep, foreigners themselves became part of the spectacle. They could no longer watch in safety and contemplate the pain and death of the native Other and then excuse themselves for such voyeurism by condemning the native authorities or spectators. After all, most members of the Western community were involved in the opium trade that led to the executions. Indeed, they could almost see themselves in the human figures of the condemned. The effect of seeing one of their local business partners strangled near their residences was both terrifying and traumatizing. If Lin and Deng continued to enforce the law, foreign opium traders might take center stage in that spectacle, with the despised natives becoming the "fresh gazers."[117] Their strong emotional reactions to these Chinese strangulations agitated the whole Western community, leading them to take an uncompromising approach to the Chinese anti-opium campaign and contributing to the outbreak of the First Opium War soon after.

THE IMPOSED SPECTACLE OF *NATIVE* CRUELTY
AS PART OF IMPERIAL PEDAGOGY

While vilifying the Chinese for using the spectacle of pain and the resulting emotional responses to enforce law and order, the foreign powers did not shy away from adopting a similar approach to assert political supremacy after the First Opium War. This was found necessary when the relatively small number of foreigners felt besieged by a hostile native population that had not yet been reduced to total submission by the war. The Huangzhuqi incident was a telling example.

On December 5, 1847, six Britons on a bird-hunting trip were killed at Huangzhuqi village, several miles north of the city of Guangzhou, after they got into a fight with the local people, who had been disturbed by their intrusion, killing one villager (Chen Yazhen) and shooting another (Li Yajian) through the chest. British officials and interpreter Thomas Meadows initially recorded the six deaths as resulting from "an affray" but later changed the narrative to call it a case of cold-blooded "murder."[118] Warning that an imminent war would cost thousands of lives, Sir John Davis, British plenipotentiary and governor of Hong Kong, demanded that Imperial Commissioner Qiying (1787–1858) execute all the principal suspects in the presence of British officers and demolish Huangzhuqi and two neighboring villages to punish their "extreme wickedness."[119] According to the Chinese judicial investigation, the local villagers killed the Britons probably in self-defense or upon being provoked by the latter's intrusion and gunshots; the case was an affray (*hu'ou*) with casualties on both sides, rather than premeditated murder; the principal offenders were unidentifiable since hundreds of people had gathered at Huangzhuqi as a marketplace that day; and six of the fifteen jailed villagers confessed to participating in the affray but denied, even under torture, striking the fatal blows that would make them the principal offenders. Davis rejected the findings and refused to extend the deadline for carrying out his threat. To avoid another war and the destruction of the three villages, Qiying and Governor-General Xu Guangjin (1797–1869) decided to execute four of the prisoners without going through the normal judicial reviews, and to sentence the other eleven to more serious penalties than they deserved under Chinese law. All the arbitrariness and injustice that the foreign community had complained of were now considered necessary to teach the Chinese a lesson. Such harsh punishments did not fully satisfy the British representatives. Davis, however, agreed to the Chinese proposal with the proviso that the four villagers be executed at Huangzhuqi as the crime scene, because, he argued, the only object of punishment was to set an example for the future.[120] Except revenge and colonial deterrence, there was no mention of due process of law, justice, or humanitarian sympathy.

On December 21, 1848, three senior British officials, Mr. Alexander Johnston (Davis's secretary), Vice-Consul Adam Elmslie, and Thomas Meadows, together with three dozen British officers and soldiers with drawn cutlasses, witnessed the four decapitations before the ancestral hall of Huangzhuqi village. Among the various eyewitness reports in official dispatches and newspapers in China, Britain, Canada, and the United States, the London *Times* described one of the four decapitations this way:

> This criminal [was] a stout-bodied man. The policemen were obliged to force his body into the coffin by stamping it in with their feet, which, from the cool way in which they did it, was to me the most disgusting sight I witnessed during the morning. . . . The head when suspended by the tail in the air had, from its ghastly paleness and the dropping of the under jaw, a peculiar lengthy horrible appearance, which, when once seen, will, I think, be long remembered.[121]

The Chinese officials and executioners were blamed for the disgusting spectacle, whereas the British officials who had compelled it were lauded for obtaining such swift retribution and for their leniency in not demanding more lives.[122]

It was made clear that this imposed spectacle of Chinese cruelty was to simultaneously interpellate the foreigners as the subjects of imperial domination and the Chinese (including the officials) as the subjugated and uncivilized subjects. Davis informed Foreign Secretary Lord Palmerston that executing the suspects at the offending village was "one of the greatest pollutions of the locality according to Chinese ideas."[123] The *Chinese Repository* further explained, "Having quietly suffered a disgraceful execution to take place before their ancestral temple, at the instance and in the presence of the hated English, it may be doubted whether they are beyond the control of their own authorities [and, indirectly, of the foreign powers]."The imposed executions were supposed to humiliate and intimidate the Chinese into submission. The entire execution process was carried out in silence and no Chinese villagers were allowed near the scene.[124] Except the Chinese on official duty, the spectators with a clear view were all foreigners. In other words, the foreigners created this spectacle of Oriental barbarism for their own consumption. In instances like this, however, humanitarian sentiments were overshadowed by political interests. The London *Times* observed that even the life for life demanded by Davis had failed to achieve the desired effects because the Chinese cared little about life, and that more vigorous policies must be adopted to make "these willful barbarians pay the costs of their own chastisement."[125] All the one hundred or so British residents in China also urged their government to use this "sad" event to prevent imminent danger to their lives and properties. A "salutary lesson" to the Chinese would turn their hostility or passive toleration into submission and eventual goodwill. The petitioners averred that their dignified existence in China depended on "a moral as well as physical ascendancy."[126]

By the 1840s, therefore, the now racialized discourse of sentimental liberalism regarding China or Chinese law had assumed the mantle of sentimental imperialism on occasions such as the Huangzhuqi incident. Its role in the debate over the First Opium War is analyzed in the next chapter, but it may be useful to briefly mention how this sentimental discourse of Chinese cruelty also shaped post-1842 Sino-Western relations and conflicts, including the Second Opium War. Although historian John Wong argues that the economics of empire played the "pivotal" role in shaping the British government's decision to wage this war, he also highlights the important role played by "the public passion of imperial Britain" in shaping public opinion and parliamentary debates over the war.[127] Directly triggered by the *Arrow* incident engineered by Acting Consul Harry Parkes and British plenipotentiary John Bowring (1792–1872), the Second Opium War was justified as a war to vindicate "every sort of insult, outrage, and atrocity" that the British had suffered in China. After the Whig government of Lord Palmerston was defeated in Parliament on a motion over the China war, a general election became necessary in 1857. Palmerston reduced the election to a vote of support for either the opposition, which would let Britain abjectly submit to the "barbarians" who had murdered and mistreated respectable

British citizens, or those who would avenge the atrocities suffered by their compatriots.[128] Major English newspapers also cited century-old stories about Chinese uncleanness, sensuality, avarice, prejudice against women, and despotism to confirm that China should not be treated as "a civilized state."[129] Besides their injuries to the British, the "cold-blooded, machine-like" Chinese should also be punished for their offense to humanity. Both Parkes and Bowring contributed to that growing body of literature on Chinese punishment.[130] It was contended that the Chinese were "outside the pale of all laws" and should be dealt with "as wild beasts in human shape." It was useless to talk to them of international law, and only "a law of severe, summary, and inexorable justice" was applicable.[131]

This discourse helped generate enough public sympathy and support for a war whose legality was questioned by no less than the attorney general of Britain. The fact that Palmerston's party won a landslide victory against the pacifists and other critics of the war policy further validated the notion of Chinese barbarity as a dominant frame of representation.[132] The same sentimental discourse later also served to justify the Anglo-French forces' looting and destruction of Chinese civilians and of the Old Summer Palace. The French plenipotentiary, Baron Gros, denied any plundering in the technical sense because the allies took over the Old Summer Place in time of war and shared the booty as victors according to the laws of war (*droits de la guerre*).[133] The British officers avoided the plundering issue and maintained that the destruction, though a serious blow to the stubborn Qing rulers themselves, was still a punishment moderate enough to be consistent with the spirit of "humanity."[134] According to James Bruce (1811–1863), eighth earl of Elgin, who led the China expedition in 1857–1860 as British plenipotentiary, this was the only effective means of avenging the Chinese mistreatment of English and French prisoners (including Parkes) during the war because it would be futile to demand punishment of the responsible officials in China, where innocent persons would be substituted for execution under its cruel and corrupt judicial system.[135] Sinologists such as Robert Douglas, keeper of Oriental books at the British Museum and professor of Chinese at King's College, would incorporate this kind of official narrative into scholarly history three decades later.[136]

China was defeated by the Anglo-French forces and signed the Treaty of Tianjin in June 1858 and then the Convention of Beijing in late

October 1860 with Britain, France, Russia, and the United States. China had to pay millions of dollars in indemnity, about a dozen more ports and the interior were also opened up, and the opium trade was finally legalized.[137] The treaties and concessions further undermined China's sovereignty.

CONCLUSION

To sum up, this chapter has shown that the sentimental discourse, structured by the core concepts of *primary injury* and *secondary injury*, was essential to the reclassification of Chinese law and sovereign status in relation to Western powers in the eighteenth and nineteenth centuries. Even after China had been reduced to a "semicolonial" country as a result of the two Opium Wars, the Western empires rarely based their China policies on their military or political domination. Instead, those policies were most effectively represented as necessary for redressing or preventing *injury* to life, property, treaty rights, or national feeling. This narrative of native injury to the dominant power was by no means confined to the Sino-Western relationship. Its popularity and efficacy in modern politics lies precisely in its *liminal* position—just like sentiment itself—which enables it to appeal to affect and emotions without being fully bound by formal legal or moral norms, and to claim legal and moral authority without losing its emotional power.

By such means, sentimental liberalism joined rational liberalism to become a powerful ideology of nineteenth- and twentieth-century imperialism. This can be seen in John Stuart Mill's efforts to integrate these two discourses in developing new legitimating doctrines for Euro-American domination in the late nineteenth century. In his celebrated essay *On Liberty* (1859), Mill singled out China as *the* negative foil for his conceptualization of modern subjectivity and liberty, warning that Europe, despite its noble antecedents and Christianity, might well become another China, lacking in any individuality. The Chinese once excelled in discovering the secret of human progress, but they had become stationary and remained so for thousands of years. Mill held that if the Chinese were "ever to be farther improved, it must be by foreigners."[138] At the end of the Second Opium War, Mill was even more convinced that it was in the interest of an Oriental people to submit to a more civilized foreign country in order to remedy their defective national character and sensibility to attain rapid progress.[139]

The discourse of Chinese or Oriental cruelty and apathy helped naturalize the earlier bifurcation, advocated by Euro-American international lawyers, of the world into a community of "civilized" states that were full sovereign subjects of international law and another group of states, including China, whose legal subjectivity was only recognized for the purpose of fulfilling their obligations under unequal treaties with the former states. The ideas of universal liberty, humanity, and sympathy thus generated the moral authority and theoretical framework for creating an international pecking order that assigned different degrees of sovereignty and humanity among different nations or communities.[140]

Studying the post-9/11 visual frames of the U.S.-led wars on terror, Judith Butler postulates that the "differential distribution of grievability across populations has implications for why and when we feel politically consequential affective dispositions such as horror, guilt, righteous sadism, loss, and indifference" toward human degradation or destruction.[141] In the context of this book, this discourse of humanity and sympathy helped construct racial and cultural hierarchy, which then informed the representational frames about whose death or pain was more worth grieving or revenging. In 1900 and 1901, for instance, the ceaseless reports of China's barbarity and injury toward its own people and to foreigners during the Boxer Rebellion served to dehumanize the Chinese, often leading to pillaging and the lynching of civilians by the foreign armies as well as forced summary execution of senior Qing officials supposedly sympathetic to the Boxers.[142]

Nevertheless, when the foreign authorities and soldiers became the de facto instigators or supervisors of the otherwise condemned forms of local execution of Chinese officials around 1900, or when foreign officers became part of the same spectacle of cruelty by leisurely taking photographs of dismembered native bodies while exposing themselves to other photographers or viewers, as seen in figure 4.8, many foreign commentators began to worry about the decivilizing impact of imperial war and the civilizing mission itself, as noted earlier. If civilization, as John Stuart Mill observed in 1836, exists only by distancing itself from the spectacle of pain and brutality, would the widespread practice of colonial violence and oppression since the

FIGURE 4.8 Europeans photographing a beheaded Chinese boxer, Beijing. From Giuseppe Messeroti Benvenuti, "Un italiano nella Cina dei Boxer—Lettere e fotografie (1900–1901)," May 1901.

Courtesy of Dr. Jérôme Bourgon.

fifteenth century have also barbarized builders of the colonial empires? In a chapter on civilization inspired by Mill's essay, Thomas Meadows indeed admitted that the Anglo-Saxons, French, and Chinese were all "still in the bonds of those truly barbarous and barbarizing or discivilizing habits."[143] Such tensions within sentimental liberalism never seem to be fully resolved in the practice of empire. In 1891, the *New York Times* ran an editorial titled "Enlightened Barbarism." Sensational reports of injuries suffered by a few foreigners in Tianjin at the hands of the provincial peasantry had led leaders of public opinion in Euro-America to threaten various military actions that could kill hundreds of thousands of Chinese, actions that even "savages" would shrink from. The editorial asked whether or not the Chinese people and government were also entitled to any consideration of honesty, humanity, and justice by what was conventionally called the civilized world.[144] Ann Stoler has described this kind of refusal to care about or recognize the pain of others as a "negative space" of imperial disposition, or an act of "imperial disregard."[145] When emotions and imagination have been so mobilized as to harden the cultural, racial, or social boundaries and *frame* other people as both a serious threat and a despicable kind—whether labeled barbarians, infidels, class enemies, or terrorists—that are not worthy of full recognition under our legal and ethical principles, it then becomes much easier to condone or support otherwise unacceptable treatment of the latter, often in the name of humanity, liberty, international law, or civilization.

5

LAW AND EMPIRE IN THE MAKING
OF THE FIRST OPIUM WAR

I n May 1840, an article in the *Eclectic Review*, an influential British journal, urged its readers to publicly protest "the *Opium* War, as an outrage on justice, on public principle, and on the independent rights of nations." The recent British parliamentary debate had traced the primary cause of the war to the opium traffic, which was found to be "immoral" for destroying human lives, "criminal" in its unlawful means, and "injurious" to Britain's national interests and reputation.[1] At the same time, many other people in the British press and government maintained that the purpose of the military expedition was *only* to obtain redress under international law for the "insults and injuries" inflicted on British subjects in the past and to secure their lives and property in the future.[2] What factors enabled a morally and legally questionable war over the contraband drug to become a "just war" waged not only to redress recent injuries and insults but also to redefine the Sino-Western relationship? I argue that the prevailing discourse of Chinese law and society was indispensable for this re-presentation of the nature and origins of the first Anglo-Chinese war in 1839–1842, better known as the First Opium War, and that the discourse also influenced the decision of the British government to flout the increasingly stringent Chinese anti-opium laws and campaigns, contributing to the eventual showdown and military conflict in 1839.

In what is still considered the standard reference on this event, Hsin-pao Chang characterized this war as resulting from an "inevitable" "clash between two cultures": an "agricultural, Confucian, stagnant" Qing China versus an "industrial, capitalistic, progressive, and restless" Britain.[3] Despite the fact that he was influenced by this now seriously challenged overarching framework, Chang did point out that "the Opium War could only have been avoided by the legalization of the opium trade and by China's relinquishment of her legal jurisdiction over foreigners." He concluded that "the direct origins" of this conflict were the contraband drug and Britain's quest for extraterritoriality in China.[4] Law was central to both issues. If we no longer see this Sino-British war as an inevitable clash between two essentialized cultural traditions, it becomes imperative for us then to reexamine how competition and negotiation over law and imperial sovereignty and interests contributed to the First Opium War and the subsequent institutional rearrangement of Sino-Western relations.

Many scholars have written about this landmark event, but few have extensively analyzed the *legal* origins, dimensions, and implications of the war.[5] Drawing upon my earlier discussions, this chapter analyzes these legal issues as key sites and moments in which the constructed ideas of Chinese and Western laws, cultures, and identities were invoked, contested, and reconfigured. In fact, these sites provide us with a valuable window through which to explore the nature and complexities of the tensions of empire in practice and ideology. Among other things, what emerges from the analysis is not a *monolithic* picture of a Western empire determined to invade China with no regard for international law or morality, as nationalist historiography of China has tended to suggest. As we shall see, both legal and moral considerations were crucial for the British debate and policy-making process, and many British commentators and politicians expressed serious reservations about or scathing criticism of the war with China. This analysis will also show that the conventional portrayal of this war as an inevitable conflict that was primarily about diplomatic equality, free trade, or national honor has been misinformed by uncritical use of historical sources, conflation of ideology and practice of empire, or a partial picture of the First Opium War that barely extends beyond the one or two decades preceding the war.[6]

QING EFFORTS TO ENFORCE THE ANTI-OPIUM LAWS

It is certainly true that economic and political interests were of crucial importance to this conflict, but in many ways the First Opium War was also a war over law, imperial sovereignty, and cultural boundaries. On the one hand, the national crisis in China caused by the opium trade not only seriously damaged the finances of the Qing empire and the physical condition of its military and civilian populations but also threatened to ruin the reputation of its law and government as the basis of the Qing ruling house's legitimacy and sovereignty. On the other hand, the growing danger and moral stigma associated with the opium trade, heightened by the Qing campaigns to crack down on the drug in the late 1830s, led foreign merchants and officials to feel that the time had come to fundamentally shake up the current structure of the Sino-Western relationship. The enormous economic interests at stake, which had served as a restraining force over the more aggressive members of the foreign community in the past, now enabled the opium merchants, free traders, and British diplomats and politicians to gather enough support for changing the status quo of the China trade.

Despite their grievance over the restrictive Canton System, many Euro-Americans enjoyed a flourishing trade with China in the late eighteenth and early nineteenth centuries. To maximize their profits and offset their trade deficits, the foreign merchants resorted to the opium trade, which had ballooned to a gigantic scale by 1830. The British remained predominant among Western nations in China's maritime trade, and the British EIC had controlled and encouraged opium production in India as a government monopoly since 1773.[7] The Qing government had banned the nonmedicinal sale of opium in 1729, criminalized opium cultivation, consumption, and distribution in 1796, and further increased the penalties for offenders in 1813.[8] However, a combination of rampant corruption and negligence on the part of local Qing officials and the violent resistance of Chinese and foreign opium dealers equipped with faster boats and more powerful weapons made it almost impossible for the government to enforce the anti-opium laws by ordinary means. The Qing authorities' well-known reluctance to cause violent confrontation with the foreigners further diminished the deterrent effect of these laws and anti-opium campaigns.[9]

The rapid spread of the addictive drug had led to a national crisis for the Qing government by the early 1830s, including a serious fiscal problem due to the outflow of millions of taels of Chinese silver every year.[10] In 1836, there was a well-reported debate on whether to legalize opium, based on a proposal by an official named Xu Naiji (1777–1839) and backed by the provincial officials of Guangdong.[11] However, other officials, such as Vice-Minister of War Zhu Zun (1791–1862), strongly objected to the proposal for both moral and practical reasons. Zhu also warned the emperor about the long-term danger to the empire, suspecting that the British were using the drug to enfeeble China just as the Europeans had done with Southeast Asian natives before colonizing them.[12] In 1838, Censor Huang Juezi (1793–1853) proposed that a new law be promulgated to punish Chinese opium smokers with capital punishment if they refused to quit the drug after the one-year grace period. Senior officials submitted more than two dozen written responses; all agreed on the urgency of the opium crisis but most found Huang's proposed death penalty for smokers too harsh and there was no consensus as to the best solution. Lin Zexu (1785–1850), governor-general of Hunan and Hubei, was one of the most enthusiastic advocates of taking extraordinary means to deal with the extraordinary situation. For him, the threat of death for unrepentant offenders would actually save the vast majority in the same way that "a raging fire" tended to scare people away.[13] On October 28, 1838, the Daoguang emperor (r. 1820–1850) finally pronounced the legalization proposal "unsuited to the character of the polity" (*bude zhengti*) of the empire and declared his abhorrence of the spread of opium as a "flowing poison" that must be fully eradicated to prevent any further harm. On the last day of the year, Lin Zexu was appointed imperial commissioner (*qinchai*) to lead the campaign against opium in southern China.[14] However, what the Daoguang emperor and Commissioner Lin apparently failed to acknowledge or realize was that decades of ineffective law enforcement by Qing officials and the enormous amount of vested interest on the part of the foreigners had made the opium problem too deeply entrenched to resolve peacefully.

In *The Inner Opium War*, James Polachek has argued that it was the Qing government, not the British, that "took the really active role in forcing a diplomatic and military showdown over the drug question in 1840 . . . under the influence primarily of *internal* political pressures [from literati officials of the Spring Purification party engaged in a power struggle], and not foreign economic or military threat."[15] His nuanced analysis of factional politics among Qing bureaucrats provides a useful alternative perspective on what might have transpired in the Qing decision-making process on the eve of the First Opium War. Nevertheless, his effort to trace the outbreak of the war to a domestic power struggle appears to be at the expense of due consideration of other domestic factors and *external* pressures. Among other things, the Qing authorities would probably not have toughened their stance on opium if foreign and Chinese opium dealers had been less daring in challenging Chinese laws and regulations in the 1830s or if the British government had been more willing to control its own subjects or India opium production.[16] As discussed in chapter 4, Governor-General Deng Tingzhen, who had supported legalization of opium in 1836, staged a few executions of Chinese opium offenders in late 1837 and 1838 near the residences of the foreign traders in order to compel them to quit the opium trade, but the lure of profit and anticipation of support from their governments emboldened most foreign traders. The expected risks even encouraged some foreigners, such as James Matheson (1796–1878), a senior partner in the leading opium syndicate, Jardine Matheson & Co., and a future member of Parliament (1843–1868), to take advantage of the opportunity in the belief that the best time for speculation was when other competitors had become disheartened and given it up.[17] In the meantime, the Chinese crackdown on opium had already pushed tensions in the Western community to a high level, months before Xu Naiji's legalization proposal was vetoed or Commissioner Lin was appointed.[18] These tensions spilled over into Lin's tenure. On March 22, 1839, British superintendent of trade Charles Elliot wrote Deng that he was seriously disturbed by the Chinese executions and the more recent assembly of troops near the foreign factories, and demanded to know whether the Chinese wanted to make war with his nation.[19] These incidents and widely shared sentiments are important for understanding both why Lin and his colleagues felt it necessary to take more drastic steps and why Elliot and other foreigners responded as adamantly as they did in 1839.[20] This is discussed in greater detail below.

A summary of what happened afterward is in order here. After the foreign traders refused to surrender their opium as required on March 18, 1839, Lin imposed an embargo on the trade and, after March 24, forbade the foreigners to leave their factories in Guangzhou before compliance. Charles Elliot came up from Macao to intervene, and later, in the name of his government, ordered the surrender of just over 20,000 chests of opium, which were then destroyed by Lin. All the foreigners were eventually allowed to leave. Following Elliot's refusal to allow British traders to sign a pledge to quit opium smuggling or otherwise submit to Chinese punishment in the future, and the dispute over the killing of Lin Weixi at a village near Macao in July 1839, tensions escalated into a military skirmish, and the first shot of the First Opium War was fired in September 1839.[21] The Whig ministry in Britain decided to send a military expedition to China in October. In early April 1840, the Tories, through Sir James Graham (1792–1861), introduced a motion in Parliament to censure the Whig government for causing the rupture because it had failed to give enough power and guidance to the superintendents of trade in China. An intense debate ensued in the British Parliament and press over the economic, political, legal, and moral implications of the conflict. The Whigs survived the motion.[22] The war with China continued until August 1842, when the Treaty of Nanjing was signed.

TENSIONS BETWEEN INTERNATIONAL LAW AND RESISTANCE TO CHINESE JURISDICTION

It is well known that the First Opium War, through its resultant treaties, led to Qing official recognition of foreign consular jurisdiction and extraterritoriality in China after 1843. There has been much less discussion, however, about how this war led to the reconceptualization of Chinese law and sovereign status and in turn contributed to the transformation of modern international law. The pre-1830 Sino-Western legal disputes studied in earlier chapters had involved a strong desire on the part of Western traders and diplomats for exemption from Chinese law and jurisdiction. However, they had never *formally* denied that China was a sovereign country. It was the First Opium War that validated and codified, by force and treaty, the idea that China was *an exception* to the general principle of territorial sovereignty because its law and government were barbaric or despotic or, regardless, incommensurable with Western notions of justice and diplomacy. The earlier representation of Chinese law and punishment played an indispensable role in helping rationalize the British decision to wage the war and legitimate the British, French, and American demand for treaty-based extraterritoriality after the war.

A naturalist conception of the law of nations, informed by universalist understandings of human reason and natural justice, had prevailed among European countries from the sixteenth through the eighteenth centuries. Thanks to the influence of jurists such as Jeremy Bentham (1748–1832), who coined the term "international law" in the 1780s, John Austin (1790–1859), and their disciples, legal positivism, which regarded the consent of sovereign states as the only legitimate source of international public law, had become the dominant framework for international relations by the mid-nineteenth century.[23] Under both the naturalist and positivist theories, Qing China, as a fully independent country with sophisticated political and legal institutions, would be considered a sovereign state and one of the subjects of international law.[24] On the eve of the First Opium War, even the most aggressive politicians, free traders, and opium merchants repeatedly acknowledged China's unquestionable right to manage its foreign trade according to its own law and interest.[25] This was also the official stance of the British authorities. According to the British Crown's law officers in 1839, China's sovereign rights could not be interfered with except by a treaty or permitted usage.[26] In the parliamentary debate in April 1840, for instance, Sir Thomas Macaulay, the newly appointed secretary at war (1839–1841) and a Whig member of Parliament for Edinburgh (1838–1847), enthusiastically supported the war with China but still acknowledged that the Chinese government was entitled to prohibit opium importation and silver exportation by all means consistent with the principles of public morality and of international law.[27] Without resorting to force, diplomacy and bilateral treaties remained the only means of getting China to concede its territorial sovereignty. However, all earlier attempts had failed to obtain such treaties or concessions.

For those eager to change the nature of the Sino-Western relationship, it became necessary to reconsider whether and when international law should apply to China. In an 1836 pamphlet, James Matheson made such an attempt. In response to China's recent efforts to regulate foreigners by threatening to stop trade, Matheson cited passages from *The Law of Nations*, by the eighteenth-century Swiss jurist Emer de Vattel (1714–1767), to argue that China had no right under international law to terminate the foreign trade. In this famous treatise, Vattel maintained that nations as well as individuals were "obliged to trade together for the common benefit of the human race, because mankind stands in need of each other's assistance." At the same time, he also held that because our duty to ourselves should override our duty to others, a state that found foreign commerce dangerous to its national interest could discontinue and prohibit it. To exemplify this important principle, he specifically mentioned that the Chinese had done this for a long time. No country had any right to sell things to another against the latter's will.[28] In 1609, long before Vattel, Hugo Grotius had stated that the rights to self-defense and self-preservation were the most fundamental ones in the immutable or primary law of nature and nations. Privileges based on other international customs or positive law—let alone English municipal law—were the secondary law of nations and inapplicable when in conflict with the primary law.[29] Matheson echoed Vattel in suggesting that international commerce was agreeable to human nature and thus constituted a general obligation of all nations, including China. He disregarded, however, what Vattel considered an even higher principle—namely, that an independent state had an inalienable natural right to prohibit foreign trade for self-preservation. Citing English legal customs as his authority of international law, he contended that China had long surrendered such sovereign rights vis-à-vis Britain. In his view, China's long benefit from foreign trade constituted adequate consideration under English contract law that obligated China to continue the trade. Implicitly referring to the English legal doctrine of *easement* or *adverse possession*, which created a legal title to another's land after nonpermissive use for a certain period of time, Matheson added that China, in allowing foreign trade for two centuries, had imposed upon itself certain "liabilities" from which justice and the law of nations forbade it to retreat. He concluded that the municipal law gave Britain "perfect rights" to compel China to fulfill its obligations.[30] The doctrine of easement or adverse possession of private property was analogous to the legal doctrine of *prescription* invoked by earlier Europeans to claim sovereignty over the land of Amerindians based on a prolonged period of usage without protest from the original owners. Nevertheless, contemporary international lawyers found Matheson's arguments problematic because the Qing government had never relinquished jurisdiction over the foreigners or their residences in China, as seen in Governor-General Deng Tingzhen's rejection of the foreigners' protests over executions near the foreign factories.

Probably aware of the flaws of Matheson's reasoning, other writers tried to exclude China completely from the benefits of international law. This was essentially the advice of Hugh Lindsay (1802–1881) to Lord Palmerston on China policies found in a letter to the latter in 1836. Lindsay, a former EIC supercargo and future British member of Parliament (1841–1847) who had led the controversial voyage aboard the *Lord Amherst* in 1832 in an illegal attempt to open trade in other Chinese ports north of Guangzhou, suggested that the best policy, without making "humiliating concessions of national inferiority," would be to send a military force to demand redress for past injuries and security for the future. He denied any intention to dispute the general principle of international law that foreigners in another country must obey that country's laws and regulations. But that principle, he asserted, always presupposed the other country to be a "civilized" nation. China did not qualify as such because of its barbarous homicide laws and its other forms of unjust and oppressive treatment of foreigners, including the use of the Chinese term *yi* (which he adamantly insisted on translating as "barbarian") to refer to them insultingly, as Lindsay had protested in 1832. Influenced by Thomas Staunton, Robert Morrison, and John Davis, who had called for extraterritoriality on similar grounds, Lindsay added that Chinese judicial administration was inconsistent with humanity, reason, and Chinese law itself. Published later that year, this letter also advised Palmerston on how to prepare for a military expedition. As explained below, Lindsay's advice played a key role in Palmerston's deliberation over the First Opium War.[31]

Given China's size and geopolitical influence over other Asian countries, such as Japan, Korea, and Vietnam, the construct of a *China exception* was crucial for legitimating Western international law and imperialism worldwide. In a leading treatise also published in 1836, Henry Wheaton (1785–1848), a prominent American diplomat and jurist, was one of the first to fully elaborate "a constitutive theory of recognition," a doctrine that limited international law only to those *recognized* as civilized sovereign states.[32] Wheaton defined jus gentium as a particular law that was applicable only to a distinct set or family of nations. Although he quoted

Vattel and Grotius extensively, he departed from their naturalist conception of international law to make it a culturally or racially defined system. In his words, "the international law of the civilized, Christian nations of Europe and America is one thing; and that which governs the intercourse of the Mohammedan nations of the East with each other, and with Christian, is another and a very different thing."[33] European extraterritoriality in Turkey and the Barbary States as well as other Asian countries, as Martti Koskenniemi has pointed out, then became just a natural conclusion of this ethnocentric reading of international law and national sovereignty.[34] However, the presumed universality of European international law and diplomatic norms was not accepted by the Qing authorities until long after the First Opium War. As Wheaton himself recognized in 1836, Qing China had not even recognized the "national character" of Westerners in southern China, treating them only as employees of foreign trading companies rather than subjects or representatives of foreign states with equal sovereignty.[35] The occurrences discussed in the preceding section that directly led to the First Opium War both dramatized the perils of the status quo for the foreign community and made them feel it imperative to fundamentally change it.

Although Wheaton and others tried to racialize international law and ethics, Commissioner Lin and his colleagues assumed certain principles of justice, morality, and humanity to be universal, even though their notions of universality might be influenced by Sinocentrism as much as their Western counterparts were by Euro-Americentrism. In spite of all their differences, therefore, there existed substantial basis for comparing their decision-making processes rather than simply dismissing the Chinese thinking as irrational. They invoked those principles to urge Queen Victoria, in an imperially sanctioned letter (or proclamation, *xi*) drafted in July–August 1839, to enjoin British subjects from sending opium to China. Despite enormous profits from the China trade for two centuries, they informed the Queen, some greedy British traders had brought the contraband drug to poison numerous innocent Chinese. That was unconscionable and repugnant to heavenly principles and human reason (*renqing*). They asked rhetorically, "Let us suppose that foreigners came from another country, brought opium into England, and seduced the people of your country to smoke it, would not you, the sovereign of the said country, look upon such a procedure with anger, and in your just indignation endeavor to get rid of it?" As a humane monarch, the Queen should put an end to this evil, especially given that the smugglers were now subject to the death penalty. They reminded the Queen of China's sovereign right: if a foreigner who came to England to trade must comply with English laws, why would the case be different in China?[36]

However Sinocentric such official edicts might sound to the foreign community, these Qing officials actually used Vattel's *Law of Nations* to support their arguments. In July 1839, Lin had his English interpreter, Yuan Dehui, and an American doctor, Peter Parker (1804–1888), translate several passages from Vattel's treatise. The translated passages showed that foreigners in China should be subject to Chinese law and jurisdiction, and that China was justified in confiscating contraband goods, imposing embargoes, or even waging war against the foreign smugglers when its national interest was in danger.[37] Whereas Wheaton tried to deny China rights under international law, Lin wanted to use international law to serve Chinese interests. Hoping to balance coercion and persuasion in order to avoid military conflict, he attempted to obtain foreign cooperation and written consent to submit to Chinese penalties if the foreigners brought opium into China after the grace period. By translating foreign newspapers and books, Lin and his colleagues in Guangdong were better informed than their predecessors about the Westerners in China.[38] An unofficial English translation of Lin's letter was circulated in English newspapers as early as January 1840, and it was reprinted by the *Canton Press* and the *Chinese Repository* in February and in the *Times* on June 10, five days before the British Foreign Office rejected Lin's official letter, which was delivered by a British merchant on Lin's behalf.[39] The contents of the letter would be a public embarrassment to the British government. A London newspaper found it "impossible for any right feeling mind" to read the letter "without admiring the noble sentiments which they contain, and blushing for the character which the villainous [had] entailed upon this Christian land."[40] Although they might often be interpreted differently for competing political interests, certain notions of legality, justice, and morality seemed to strike a common chord among people on both sides of the constructed cultural or racial boundaries. But such sentiments alone could not prevent the upcoming war.

REDEFINING THE LEGAL NATURE
OF THE FIRST OPIUM WAR

The Moral Challenge Posed by the Illegal Opium Trade

To a great extent, the issue of law was important to the debate over the First Opium War because many Britons considered it unjustifiable to wage a war for compensation for seized contraband opium; the cause of the war would thus have to be construed differently under British or international law. Just as the Qing authorities felt it necessary to resort to the extraordinary means they employed in 1839 to deal with the opium crisis, the British representatives and home government found themselves struggling for extraordinary means to redefine the legal nature of the opium trade and Chinese seizure of the drug. In other words, it was the legal discourse that helped displace the moral questions regarding the opium trade and the war over it. It is true that for their own political purposes, both the British and Chinese governments have since manipulated the narrative of the First Opium War, either forgetting it or commemorating it in a nationalistic fashion.[41] However, our postmodern sensibility should not lead us to dismiss the value of reexamining how this event was actually understood or rationalized by its participants and contemporary witnesses in the nineteenth century.[42]

In the *Cambridge History of China*, John King Fairbank called the opium trade "the most long-continued and systematic international crime of modern times" that provided "the life-blood of the early British invasion of China."[43] Such a view expressed in the late twentieth century might sound too harsh and unwarranted to many nineteenth-century British observers, but Fairbank's characterization of the opium trade was not very different from that of a number of British critics at the time of the First Opium War. As indicated by the *Eclectic Review* article quoted at the beginning of this chapter, this conflict was already called "the Opium War" almost twenty years before Karl Marx famously used that term in his scathingly critical reports of the two Opium Wars in the *New York Daily Tribune*.[44] Many Britons were scandalized by the opium trade and their government's complicity in it. In a widely read book published in early 1839, the Reverend Algernon Thelwall provided numerous testimonials, facts, and Chinese official documents from the *Chinese Repository* concerning the physical and social harm resulting from the contraband opium trade. He warned readers of the enormous damage caused by the opium trade to British national honor and welfare and to the "interest of religion and humanity."[45] Featured in the London *Times* as early as May 1839 and in other newspapers, publications like this influenced the subsequent public and parliamentary debates.[46] As word of the rupture and a possible war with China spread rapidly throughout the British Empire, Christian philanthropists, Chartist activists, pacifists, and many other Britons joined in the criticism of the opium trade and war. Public meetings were held in cities such as London and Leeds in 1840 to condemn the immorality of the opium trade and petition Parliament to avoid hostilities with China.[47] Equally harsh commentaries appeared in leading newspapers in London, Liverpool, Manchester, Bombay, Guangzhou, and Singapore during this period, even though it might have been expected that these commercial or manufacturing centers would enthusiastically welcome the forcible opening of China to foreign trade.[48] For instance, an article in the *Liverpool Mercury* expressed outrage that the opium traders got Britain into a war that was owing "clearly and indubitably to the traffic in a deadly drug, carried on in shameless and daring violation of the express laws of the country." An editorial in the London *Times* even compared the opium trade to the slave trade, against which "a high-toned outcry" was expected to rise up among all British political parties and Christian denominations until its abolition.[49] As Sir George Thomas Staunton (1781–1859) lamented in the House of Commons on April 7, 1840, contemporary newspapers condemned the war with China as "the most atrociously unjust and dishonourable" war.[50]

The British government and parliamentarians generally recognized that Britain did not have a legal or moral right to prevent China from carrying out its anti-opium campaign. Only a small number of them, such as Henry Ward (1797–1860), a leading Radical member of Parliament for Sheffield (1837–1849), who was interested in free trade and opening up China to manufactures from his constituency, would cite the testimonies of opium traders to note in passing that the evils of the opium trade were much exaggerated because the drug, *when used in moderation*, was not so injurious to health or morals.[51] Even those who supported the war stated that it was inconsistent with the "most sacred obligations" between nations and between humans for the British to profit financially by fostering trade in something that caused the destruction of hundreds of thousands of people.[52] Thomas Macaulay, one of the staunchest advocates of the military operation, noted that he had the highest respect for those who supported the Tories' motion of disapproval of the opium trade, which he regretted as much as they did. He considered it ridiculous even to imagine, as the British press did, that the government would attempt to "force an opium war" on the public.[53] Foreign Secretary Palmerston likewise claimed that he had always tried his utmost to discountenance the traffic.[54] Critics of the government cited evidence regarding the harmful effects of opium on both Indians and Chinese, while others castigated the war in very strong terms.[55] The imminent war was considered unjustifiable, as one British parliamentarian put it, because the Chinese had done nothing more than they had to, unless they were willing to let opium smugglers carry the drug up to the very doors of Guangzhou.[56] For Sir Sydney Herbert (1810–1861), Tory member of Parliament for Wiltshire, anyone unprejudiced by party feelings or faked sympathy for the opium smugglers would conclude that Britain "started a war without just cause" and that the British had proved themselves to be "the less civilized nation of the two" in its relationship with China.[57]

If there was consensus that China had the legal and moral right to enforce its laws against opium trafficking, then what turned such law enforcement into a "crime against Britain" and gave Britain the cause of just war against China? The most popular line of reasoning was that China was "guilty" and punishable under international law not because of its prohibition of opium or punishment of smugglers but because of its insult and injustice to the "innocent" British representatives and merchants and its unjustified destruction of British "property."[58] It was through this juridical discourse of Chinese injury to British persons, property, and national honor that the moral dilemma regarding the opium trade was transformed into a primarily legal issue of just war under international law.

Transforming Contraband Opium Into Legal Property

Let us first examine why and how contraband opium was transformed into property. The word "property" was frequently used in British diplomatic correspondence and in parliamentary and public debates after the Chinese seizure of opium in 1839. This term had important legal, economic, and moral implications. In fact, according to the orthodox theories of the law of nations since the seventeenth century, the two most fundamental causes of just war under the law of nations were defense of one's life and property against injuries (or threatened injuries) and revenge for such injuries or wrongdoings.[59] This natural right to defend property entitled one "not only to offer resistance but also to dispossess others." It is worth noting that, as Grotius explained in the early 1600s, property should be understood not just in a material sense but also as referring to "every right, including that right to a good name which is justly the possession of virtuous persons and of which they ought by no means to be deprived."[60] Therefore, insult to national reputation or honor could be construed as injury to property rights and thus a just cause of war as well. I have insufficient space to survey the large body of literature on the intellectual genealogy of the modern concept of property. Suffice it to say that through the influential theorization of John Locke and others, property acquired such moral, legal, and political-economic significance that it played an indispensable role in the expansion of European territories and capital from the seventeenth century onward. Among other things, it generated a new economic and ethical justification for colonial acquisition and appropriation of other peoples' labor, land, and resources even where such actions might be otherwise inconsistent with the law of nations or other applicable laws.[61] The influence of the Lockean ideas about the natural rights to life, liberty, and property was illustrated by their codification, with only a minor alteration, as the inalienable rights to life, liberty, and happiness in the United States Declaration of Independence and Constitution. It is in this sense that we should understand the carefully chosen terms "injury," "property," "national honor," and "just war" in the British debate on the First Opium War.[62]

Given that opium had long been outlawed in China, what did it take to establish it as legal property? In a dispatch to Palmerston on April 13, 1839, Elliot reasoned that the legalization proposed by Xu Naiji, the Qing court's prior laxness in law enforcement, and the local officials' connivance should have given this "property," on every ground of justice and policy, a totally different treatment from that given by Commissioner Lin.[63] This argument was refuted by contemporary British commentators since an analogous situation of continued rampant smuggling on the British coast would neither acquit the foreign smugglers nor invalidate the relevant British laws.

It turned out that what eventually obliged the British government to treat the contraband drug as property was Elliot's intervention at the most critical moment of Lin's efforts to compel the foreigners to turn in their opium.

We need to review some of the key details related to the surrender of foreign opium from March to May 1839. According to witnesses, the foreign merchants refused to turn over the contraband drug, which they often claimed was the property of Indian owners. Except for the American Russell & Co., which suspended its opium operation temporarily, Euro-Americans decided to brave the storm, using the time-honored tactics of denial, procrastination, and evasion. The foreign Chamber of Commerce made only a token surrender of 1,036 chests of opium before the March 21 deadline. Like James Matheson, Lancelot Dent, a founding partner of the second-largest British opium firm, Dent & Co., objected vehemently to compliance while dissuading others from promising to quit the drug trade. The commissioner demanded to see Dent within the city of Guangzhou. Fearing his detention and citing Chinese treachery in early legal cases, the foreign representatives refused to let Commissioner Lin take Dent from the foreign factories without force or without Lin's written guarantee of Dent's safe return. William Wetmore, an American trader and chairman of the General Chamber of Commerce, advised the foreigners not to testify against any other foreigner for smuggling the drug. As in earlier disputes, the Chinese use of persuasion rather than force carried little weight. Finding his ultimatum snubbed, Lin pressed for compliance by blocking trade and communications on the Pearl River between Guangzhou and Huangpu, the anchorage of the foreign ships.[64]

Elliot had actually anticipated this showdown. In January 1839, he once again warned Lord Palmerston that Britain would be driven by necessity into "urgent, expensive, and hazardous measures upon the most painful grounds" in consequence of the reckless opium smuggling lately. He wanted the British traders to stop bringing the drug within the heavily guarded Pearl River or, dangerously, to the foreign factories of Guangzhou. Neither the British opium traders nor his superiors in London heeded his concerns and he lacked effective means or power to control the traders; nevertheless, he felt that he had to protect the traders from the wrath of Chinese law. In the same letter to Palmerston, Elliot pledged that, even if the traders were wild enough to forcibly oppose the Chinese authorities, he considered it his obligation to prevent British subjects, regardless of their crime, from falling into Chinese hands. For him, it was a well-established "general principle" that any such Chinese action that affected British subjects required the consent of British officers.[65]

On March 22, upon hearing of Lin's blockade of the Pearl River, Elliot wrote Palmerston that he would go to the Humen entrance of the Pearl River and demand to know whether the Chinese wanted to have a war with Britain. He was sure that a firm tone would make the provincial authorities relent.[66] Later that evening, after having sent his two children back to England, he sent a secret note, asking Captain Blake of the HMS *Larne*, stationed near Lingding, to rescue him and other Britons if Blake heard nothing about their safety in six days. He left Macao on March 23 and went further than he had promised, landing at the foreign factories near the city wall of Guangzhou the next evening after forcing his way through the many Chinese junks that blocked the Pearl River.[67] After hoisting the British flag, Elliot immediately took Dent under his protection within the British Superintendent's Hall, declaring that Dent was one of the most respectable foreign gentlemen. Suspecting that Elliot was trying to sneak Dent out, Lin withdrew all Chinese servants from the factories and stationed troops around them. Thus began what Elliot and others called their "imprisonment."[68] Before heading for Guangzhou, Elliot had asked the thirty or so British private opium ships to come to anchor near the British naval warship the *Larne* at Macao for their protection.[69] Elliot and the foreign community thus never allowed Lin to distinguish the guilty from the few innocent foreigners, but this would later become a key justification for the war, as discussed in the following.

Like Qing officials in earlier Sino-Western legal disputes, Commissioner Lin refrained from forcing his way into the foreign factories or ships to seize the foreign smugglers or their accomplices. He chose to pressure them into compliance by surrounding the foreign factories with soldiers and confining the 350 or so foreigners to an area of about 80,000 square yards for the next six weeks. Services and provisions by local Chinese were partially resumed after Elliot promised on March 27 to deliver about 20,000 chests of British-owned opium. In a public notice of March 27, Elliot demanded that all the British traders deliver their opium to him, guaranteeing that the surrendered opium would be paid for. Most foreigners were allowed to leave on May 2, whereas sixteen leading opium dealers stayed until May 21, when the pledged amount of opium was fully delivered.[70]

Several important questions need be addressed: Why would Elliot force his way from Macao to Guangzhou, reportedly at the risk of his life, when Lin had already blockaded the Pearl River after the foreign traders at Guangzhou refused to surrender either opium or Dent? Why did he later think it advisable to surrender all the British opium even though he saw no real danger to the lives of those detained in the foreign factories? And why did he insist that all the opium be delivered *through him* to the Chinese government?

Historian Robert Blake has suggested that Elliot put his head in a trap when he arrived at Guangzhou on March 24, and that he later surrendered the opium abjectly.[71] This seems to be a serious underestimation of Charles Elliot, who, as a British diplomat from a powerful aristocratic family, made a tough, risky, and calculated decision under unusual circumstances with little guidance from London except some earlier instructions and a general pattern of Britain's China policies. Elliot explained to Palmerston that he considered it his duty to let Commissioner Lin deal with him rather than with Her Majesty's subjects because the "forced and separate surrender of all this immensely valuable property by individual merchants, without security or indemnity and protection, must have led to some desperate commercial convulsion in India and England, which might have embarrassed the Queen's Government in an incalculable degree."[72] This was partly why he went to Guangzhou, prevented Lin from taking Dent, and offered to surrender the opium in the name of his government instead of allowing Lin to confiscate it from individual traders. Besides these immediate financial and economic concerns, the current situation and the pattern of the Chinese government's recent actions toward the Western nations had also convinced Elliot that some fundamental changes to the Sino-Western relationship were due. These were apparently what Elliot meant by "other very weighty causes" besides the alleged concern for the lives and liberty of all the foreigners at Guangzhou when he explained in his public notice of March 27 why all British-owned opium should be surrendered through him to the Chinese.[73] Although they had rarely listened to Elliot's instructions when it was against their interests, the British traders this time agreed to deliver their opium stored not only within the

Pearl River but also in their ships securely moored at Lingding, outside the Pearl River.[74]

Elliot was not just making up retrospective excuses for his unauthorized guarantee of payment for the delivered opium. In a letter to his wife on April 4, he reiterated that Lin obviously intended to "bully the merchants into forced and separate surrenders of their property," which would have produced terrible shock in the Pacific and in India. He "burst in upon" Commissioner Lin so that the latter's actions against the opium traders would now come up against the British Crown's officer, with all the diplomatic and political consequences. Elliot expected the Chinese to pay for everything he surrendered. He was not too worried about losing the trade at Guangzhou since he believed that London would easily find another Chinese port. He might have "bowed" to Lin for now, but he assured his wife that the British government would vindicate him soon. It is worth noting that in this private letter, the term "opium," which he used to refer to the contraband drug before its delivery to the Chinese, became "property" when he was talking about Chinese indemnity.[75]

What exactly did Elliot mean by the incalculable embarrassment or consequences that he had to avoid by all means? In a lengthy dispatch to Lord Palmerston on February 2, 1837, Elliot explained about the economic interest at stake as a result of the recent Chinese crackdown on the drug: the British imports of opium to China in 1836 had amounted to almost eighteen million dollars, nearly a million dollars more than the whole value of teas and silk exported on British accounts during the same period. The stake had become much higher by mid-1839. Interruption of the opium trade and its related cash flow jeopardized the whole British trade with China and India. As Elliot told his cousin, Lord Auckland, then general-governor of India, in another letter he wrote the same day, "The interception of the opium traffic must have the effect not merely of temporarily crippling our means of purchasing in this market at all; but undoubtedly of placing us in respect to the prices of the export staples completely in the power of . . . native dealers. The failure of the opium deliveries is attended with an almost entire cessation of money transactions in Canton and in the glutted condition of this, your Lordship will judge how peculiarly mischievous the present stagnation must operate on the whole British Commerce with the Empire." For these reasons, he obtained authorization from Lords

Palmerston and Auckland to order British warships to frequent the China coast for purposes of making the Chinese authorities relent in the anti-opium campaigns.[76]

From private conversations, James Matheson believed that Elliot originally wanted to gather all the foreign opium to protect rather than surrender it, expecting that the Chinese would be taken aback by the huge quantity of the drug. Elliot and the opium traders later decided to deliver all their opium (more than they had to) on the assumption that the Chinese would be compelled to compensate them. It was a necessary and calculated gamble. Matheson was actually worried that the Chinese officials might reject the offer. There had been no market at all for the rapidly growing stock of unsold drug over the past few months. Matheson praised Elliot's opium surrender as "a large and statesmanlike measure, more especially as the Chinese [had] fallen into the snare of rendering themselves directly liable to the British Crown." Had they declined to receive it, he believed, the result would have been far less favorable, or even "disastrous," to the traders, who would then have been burdened with a huge stock under a new law that threatened capital punishment for drug dealers. Indeed, the longer the foreigners were held in confinement, the better the situation would be as it would add to the grievances for which the British could claim redress. Instead of worrying about his safety or liberty, Elliot, still in confinement, started to compile meticulous documentation about the quantity and rates of the confiscated opium for future indemnity. He was clearly anticipating a war in which Britain would be victorious and then be in a position to determine the compensation scheme. He discussed with Matheson whether to colonize a place like Zhoushan or Formosa (Taiwan) (the latter of which Matheson recommended but Elliot found too expensive to maintain). He even drafted a future public proclamation that threatened to impose trade stoppage unless the Chinese promised to avoid similar hostile measures and to give the British extraterritorial privilege in China.[77] As a witness put it, the British government was now bound to compensate its subjects for the opium surrendered by Elliot, and the only option, Elliot suggested, was to let China pay.[78]

The problem is that neither Elliot nor Palmerston had the power to commit the British government to an obligation of two to three million pounds sterling (which would require the approval of Parliament), let alone indemnify opium *smugglers*. Thus, Elliot's guarantee placed the government in a very difficult position. When he signed the certificates guaranteeing payment for the surrendered opium, Elliot took it for granted that his government would *eventually* force China to foot the bill. His certificates expressly stated that he would "hold Her Majesty's Government responsible for the value" of the opium. It was not the Chinese seizure but this guarantee that provided the legal basis for the British merchants to demand indemnity from the *British* government. These claimants, often through law firms in London, almost invariably argued that their "property" was surrendered not to the Chinese but to Elliot himself, "for the service of Her Majesty's Government."[79] The government could choose to force China to pay, or pay the huge sum out of the British Treasury, or do nothing and face a political backlash from numerous constituencies. Since the government had no fund for such indemnities and refused to even submit a budgetary request to a Parliament that was unlikely to approve of it, the British ministers naturally preferred the first option, especially since Elliot's intervention had created a plausible justification for the China expedition.[80] Although Elliot's unauthorized actions could result in a political disaster for Palmerston and the Whig government, it could also provide an unprecedented opportunity for the more ambitious political or commercial adventurers, of whom Elliot himself was not necessarily the most aggressive one.

In early April 1839, speaking as a witness and victim to his government, Elliot decried the forcible detention of foreigners and their threatened deprivation of fresh water and food. The Chinese opium suppression campaign was described as "unprovoked" and constituting "aggressive measures against British life, liberty, and property, and against the dignity of the British Crown."[81] The popular discourse of Chinese despotism, corruption, cruelty, and injustice made it much easier to establish a strong case against China. Even though several members of Parliament noted that Elliot had placed himself under restraint by going to Guangzhou,[82] his intervention led Macaulay and others to declare it the British government's *obligation* to avenge the confinement of their "innocent countrymen" and the insult to "the Sovereign in the person of her representative."[83] Such sentimental representation of injury and insult helped transform the seized contraband opium into legitimate property. In a series of dispatches to Lord Palmerston in late March and April, Elliot took pains to defend his decision to implicate his government in the conflict by stressing Chinese injustice and the long-term benefits for Britain. He condemned Lin's measures as unexpected and thus unjustifiable, and as an act of "public robbery" and "wanton violence" on the Queen's officers and subjects and the entire foreign community in China. This gave Britain "the right of full indemnity and future security."[84] This line of reasoning would become the linchpin of government and popular defense of the war with China.

Economic and Political Implications of the Opium Crisis

Represented this way, the opium crisis made it possible for opium merchants, free traders, and the British government and parliamentarians to work out a compromise that suited their own interests. British commentators and politicians generally agreed on the crucial importance of retaining the China trade. Besides the now almost universal consumption of Chinese tea in British households, nearly £6 million, or one-tenth of the combined annual revenue of Britain and British India, was derived from exporting opium to China (worth £2 million for India) and from importing Chinese goods such as tea and silk. In addition, China had become a market for British products worth £1.5 million annually, while the China trade created employment for thousands of British seamen as well as numerous British and Indian merchants, workers, and farmers concerned with the trade.[85] According to one estimate, from 1795 to 1830, British India alone sold more than 162,000 chests of opium to China, worth about 200 million Spanish dollars, or £48.3 million.[86] This enormous revenue from opium was crucial for balancing Britain's global trade, fueling its Industrial Revolution, and funding its "imperial expansion and maintenance in India" and elsewhere in the nineteenth century.[87] The vital importance of the China trade caused many Britons to worry about the consequences of losing it in the event of a military confrontation, but it also led opium merchants and free traders to welcome the opportunity to put the commercial relationship on a more secure and favorable foundation.[88]

Along with many other interest groups, James Matheson in China and William Jardine in London, through their allies or business partners such as John Abel Smith (1802–1871), member of Parliament for Chichester and a personal friend of Lord Palmerston's, and the East India and China

Association of London, lobbied the government tirelessly. From August 7, 1839, to February 1840, at least seven private interviews were arranged with Palmerston, mostly through Smith, to discuss how to deal with the rupture with China. Although Palmerston never explicitly disclosed his plan for the military expedition at those meetings, Smith and his allies became increasingly convinced that the government would compel China to pay for their losses.[89] At the same time, numerous other mercantile communities in India, China, and Britain also attempted to influence the British government and public by adopting the arguments of Elliot and the opium merchants. For a few months starting in August 1839, hundreds of firms interested in the China trade or Chinese markets sent signed petitions and memorials to the Foreign Office and Parliament from commercial or manufacturing centers such as London, Liverpool, Glasgow, Manchester, Lancaster, Newcastle, Blackburn, and Leeds. For instance, thirty-four firms from Blackburn and Lancaster protested the unwarranted imprisonment of Her Majesty's subjects, the wanton seizure of British property, and the complete suppression of the valuable China trade. They urged immediate and vigorous actions to secure "redress for the dishonor done to the British name, and compensation for the loss sustained by British interests in consequence of the arbitrary and iniquitous proceedings."[90]

Framing the crisis as an issue of national interest and of international law served to ennoble the opium trade and the war and in turn reduced partisan dissonance and secured empire-wide political support for the war. Although opposition members of Parliament had tried to take advantage of this crisis to oust the Whigs from power, they were themselves considered partially responsible for the current crisis. Both opium merchants and critics of the opium trade pointed out that the contraband drug traffic, if a crime at all, was a "national crime," committed by the governments of India and Britain with the explicit approval of the bipartisan legislature in London.[91] In a memorial to Palmerston, the East India and China Association of London wrote,

When we find the growth of opium within the territories of the East India Company is a strict monopoly, yielding a large revenue; that the drug is sold by the Government of India in public sales [destined for China]. When we observe that Committees of the House of Lords and

Commons have inquired minutely into the subject . . . [and arrived] at
the conclusion "that it did not appear advisable to abandon so important a source of revenue." When we look at the persons composing
these Committees, and those examined before them, consisting of
Ministers, Directors of the East India Company, former Governors
of India, etc., men of all parties of the highest moral character; when
we know [that the British government] might prevent what it did not
approve—we must confess that it does seem most unjust to throw any
blame or odium attaching to the opium trade upon the merchants,
who engaged in a business thus directly or indirectly sanctioned by the
highest authorities.[92]

Many British merchants in India heartily echoed these sentiments and
thus felt fully justified in demanding that the British government compensate them for the seized opium or else compel China to do so.[93] It was
pointed out in the parliamentary debates in April 1840 that the Tory parliamentarians had had the opportunity in 1810 and 1832 to abolish India's
opium trade but twice refused to do so because of the "desirable" financial benefits to the Indian government.[94] This was why, according to Sir
John Hobhouse (1786–1869), president of the Board of Control in charge
of Indian affairs, and other supporters of the Whig government, Sir James
Graham's motion to censure the government for mishandling China matters was completely silent on the opium question and the war with China.
After all, Graham and other former Tory ministers had also been responsible for encouraging the infamous opium trade.[95] Indeed, at closed-door
meetings in March 1840, the Tory leaders carefully worded the motion to
be "vague, amounting to little more than a general censure and avoiding
the expression of an opinion on the Opium Trade, and on the nature of the
quarrel with the Chinese."[96] As the *Eclectic Review* observed, evasion of
those central issues of the opium trade and war with China rendered the
parliamentary debate a "jejune and unsatisfactory performance," just as if a
performance of *Hamlet* had left out the part of Hamlet. According to this
journal, the reason for the politicians' reticence on these issues was evident:
both parties in Parliament were "equally guilty of the Chinese war" and
responsible for the "blunders and crimes which [had] brought this country
into its present disgraceful position."[97]

As the opium crisis came to be recognized as affecting the national interest and reputation, political support for the war coalesced across party lines.
Even opponents of the Whig government, including the Duke of Wellington (Arthur Wellesley, 1769–1852), who was prime minister in 1828–1830
and foreign secretary in 1834–1835, raised no objection to the war, believing
that Britain's footing in China could not be reestablished without military
force.[98] In his closing speech against the Whigs in the House of Commons
on April 9, 1840, Sir Robert Peel (1788–1850), Tory leader and former and
future prime minister (1834–1835, 1841–1846), also noted that the military
expedition, "however culpably" it originated, had become unhappily necessary to reclaim the China trade.[99]

Nevertheless, the opium trade and the anticipated war were so controversial that there was a general feeling, according to William Jardine, that the
Whig government would have to resign. Palmerston confidentially admitted to John Smith the Whigs' fears of being defeated on Graham's motion
unless they could keep all their friends and supporters with them. Smith
and his allies agreed to help out if, among other things, the government
would arrange to pay half of Elliot's guaranteed opium indemnities as a loan
to the claimants before China was compelled to pay the full amount. The
proposal was eagerly accepted by Palmerston and Lord John Russell on the
evening of March 30, 1840, and even the prime minister, Lord Melbourne,
was willing to entertain it. On April 4, Smith agreed to vote with the Whig
government on the motion.[100] On April 9, the government narrowly escaped
defeat in the Commons by nine votes (271 to 262). Hobhouse observed that
the Whigs were fortunate in being able to keep the party together on this
occasion.[101] Even after the Tories replaced the Whigs in government in 1841,
the war with China continued unabated. The fact that it was understood as
being waged to avenge the injury and injustice sustained by British officers
and subjects in China afforded British decision makers much-needed solace
in the face of the harsh criticism they received from those with a liberal
conscience, Christian philanthropy, or humanitarian sensibility.

International Law Versus Imperial Common Sense

Earlier in this chapter, we looked at various attempts to establish that
international law regarding territorial sovereignty did not apply equally to

China. If China were beyond the pale of international law, however, could a foreign government claim that Commissioner Lin's treatment of its persons and property constituted a violation of international law? This section shows how the First Opium War enabled promoters and theorists of empire to develop a workable resolution of this dilemma through a two-pronged argument: (1) the Chinese anti-opium law or its administration was illegitimate according to universal or Western notions of reason, justice, and humanity, and (2) such unacceptable law or enforcement violated China's obligations under international law even though China might be ineligible for rights under such law. The representations of Chinese law and society examined in this book again proved indispensable to this effort.

In 1836, Staunton still felt uneasy about Lindsay's blunt call for military invasion to obtain Chinese concessions. He thought Lindsay's arguments "wholly inconsistent with any interpretation" of the law of nations that he knew of. Unlike Lindsay, however, he saw no reason to shrink from the opportunity to take possession of Chinese islands as colonial depots if such hostilities indeed arose.[102] Four years later, his speeches in the House of Commons endorsed not only Lindsay's militant approach but also Matheson's invented legal doctrines for Sino-British relations discussed earlier. In defense of Palmerston's China policy, Staunton told the House of Commons on April 7, 1840, that during his tenure as an EIC official in China, he had always adhered to the principle that foreigners had no right to interfere with Chinese laws, but he considered the present case to be totally different: the dispute over the opium trade was no longer a question of morality or policy but of a breach of international rights or international law.[103] He made two major arguments typical of supporters of the China expedition. Relying on the stories of Elliot, Lindsay, and the opium merchants, he contended first of all that since the Chinese governors-general had allowed their own vessels to be used to transport the opium, foreigners were not bound to strictly obey Chinese laws.[104] In addition, he protested Commissioner Lin's enforcement of the "new" law against foreigners who had come under the old law as an act of "the most atrocious injustice" that alone fully justified the expedition to exact reparation.[105] For his audiences, Staunton's speech boiled down to the simple idea that Lin had resorted to "violent measures, never sanctioned by law & usages of China."[106] Speaking as the leading authority on Chinese government and national character, Staunton suggested that the British demand for reparations must be accompanied by a competent force.[107] Hobhouse observed that Staunton "spoke very feebly but his Chinese education gave him weight."[108] Both he and Macaulay echoed the view that Lin's measures were unjust and "unlawful" and called for a British response to Lin's "atrocities."[109]

Contemporary media and commentators refuted both lines of justification. The *Singapore Free Press* found it astounding for anyone to assert "a prescriptive right to smuggle . . . founded upon the forbearance or connivance" of the Qing customs officers, an assertion that would be similar to a London thief's claim of legal immunity because "the Bow Street [Police] Officers either were or chose to be blind to pilfering."[110] As for the second argument, the *Eclectic Review* cited Charles King, an American trader in China and "an unimpeachable eye-witness," to show that the Guangdong officials spared no means to get the foreign merchants to voluntarily leave China with their opium before resorting to the seizure. None of the Chinese "warnings, threats, entreaties, and the public execution of native accomplices" could "convince the smugglers of the reality of the danger."[111] Tory members of Parliament echoed these arguments in challenging Staunton. They pointed out that Lin had reiterated on various occasions that his government had shown foreigners extraordinary favor in confiscating only the contraband drug actually on board their store ships in Chinese waters while forgiving their prior misconduct. The foreigners could continue legitimate trade if they signed a pledge not to return with opium. The new law prescribing capital punishment for foreign opium smugglers would not take effect until after an eighteen-month grace period.[112] It was observed in the House of Commons that the Chinese authorities had exhibited extraordinary patience and had adopted other measures in March 1839 only after Elliot had disclaimed authority to secure British subjects' compliance and even denied that his government had any knowledge of the opium trade in China.[113] Frederick Thesiger (1794–1878), a British jurist and newly elected Tory member of Parliament for Woodstock, agreed that Staunton had misinterpreted Chinese forbearance as sanctioning the opium trade and then had accused the Chinese of cruelty in enforcing the law. The Chinese might have committed acts of cruelty toward their own people caught in the illicit traffic, but Thesiger found no evidence of cruelty to the British.[114]

One popular claim by supporters of the Whig government was that the Chinese violated international law in punishing or even threatening with death by starvation the innocent along with the guilty. A number of newspapers and pamphlets tried to reinforce this by evoking the popular image of Chinese despotism and cruelty.[115] William Gladstone (1809–1898), a pious Christian and the young Tory member of Parliament for Newark who would later become Liberal leader and four-time prime minister, observed in Parliament that when he first heard of the opium confiscation, he also thought that the Chinese had committed a cruel and monstrous act. Upon further inquiry, however, he learned that almost the entire British community had been engaged in the opium trade. Regarding the complaint that not all the detained Britons had been *proven* guilty of opium smuggling, Gladstone believed that Commissioner Lin had been justified in acting against the entire community, especially when it was impossible to fix guilt upon individuals because of Elliot's refusal to let the Chinese try any British subject.[116] As Peel also pointed out, Elliot himself had told Palmerston in January 1839, "Whilst such a [drug] traffic existed, indeed, in the heart of the regular [lawful] commerce, I had all along felt that the Chinese Government had a just ground for harsh measures towards the lawful trade, upon the plea, that there was no distinction between the right and the wrong."[117] Nevertheless, when the Chinese actually began enforcing their laws against the opium traders, Elliot vowed to protect British persons and property by all means.[118] Even a British journal that advocated a more aggressive policy toward China declared that Elliot's conduct in this rupture showed him to be an "overseer and director of an illegal traffic" or an "abettor and defender" of those who carried it out, including "his friend Dent, the chief smuggler."[119]

Although Elliot may have acted in this case far beyond his official capacity as superintendent of the British trade, his intervention did have the expected effect of redefining this dispute for many contemporary Britons. For instance, on October 21, 1839, Captain John Campbell, a British veteran in the China trade, wrote Palmerston that Britain had a cause of just war because Commissioner Lin did not obtain British "property" by a legal seizure (as they were militarily too weak to do so) but extorted it as a ransom from Elliot for the lives of foreigners unjustly imprisoned. Campbell argued that Elliot had ordered the delivery of British opium because he considered it the only means of rescuing him and others from death by starvation.[120] This narrative turned Elliot, as the British Crown's representative, into the *primary* subject and victim of Chinese injustice, while the original targets of Chinese law enforcement, the opium smugglers, now became secondary. This was precisely how Palmerston, in his official instructions to the British plenipotentiary in May 1841, and how the Treaty of Nanjing in 1842, justified the demand of full compensation (totaling eighteen million dollars) for the opium "extorted" as a "ransom for the superintendent and for the British subjects imprisoned *in company with* him" and for the British expenses for the war itself.[121] The fact that Lin did not use force to seize the opium or the smugglers thus became the legal grounds for retaliation and demand for compensation. Samuel Williams, one of the Americans at Guangzhou during the incident, wrote nine years later, "Might makes right, or at least enforces it, and if the Chinese had had the power to destroy every ship found violating their laws, although the loss of life would have been dreadful, no voice would have been raised against the proceeding."[122]

Contemporary witnesses and modern historians have suggested that people confined to the thirteen foreign factories during the blockade might have suffered humiliation, anxiety, boredom, or "obesity" from too little exercise but were not exposed to other serious physical harm or real danger to their lives. Save for mental distress and losing some domestic comforts and the liberty to leave Guangzhou, their condition was materially different from "imprisonment."[123] In various letters that were sneaked out, Elliot confirmed that there was no need to worry about the safety of the foreigners; he even had the mood to write to John Backhouse, undersecretary of the Foreign Office in London, explaining why one of his earlier dispatches should be numbered fourteen instead of thirteen.[124] By the end of 1839, this so-called siege and imprisonment had been magnified by the propaganda machine of the opium merchants and free traders into an equivalent of the Black Hole of Calcutta, which had played a major role in legitimating British colonization of India after the 1750s.[125]

In a subsequently published "corrected" or revised version of his parliamentary speech, Staunton redefined international law and ethics to suit the needs of the peculiar situation with China: "Though the Chinese are no parties to the specific usages of international law amongst European nations, they cannot but be bound by that law of nations, which is founded on the law of nature and of common-sense."[126] Sir Stephen Lushington (1782–1873), a lawyer and Whig member of Parliament, further suggested on April 9, 1840, that the law of nations could not be directly applied to a half-civilized, half-barbarous country like China. Instead, he proposed that Sino-Western relations should be governed by the principle of "ordinary sense."[127] This imperial common sense, informed by the dispatches or testimonies of people such as Elliot, Lindsay, and Matheson, convinced these British politicians that China had breached international law and justified the upcoming war. It also made moot the issue of the admittedly detestable traffic of opium.[128]

Years before this debate, as noted earlier in the book, the Britons in China, including Sir Charles Marjoribanks (1794–1833), former president of the EIC Select Committee in China, had called for British extraterritoriality and refusal to apply the general principles of international relations to China on the grounds that China stood alone among the nations and was in many ways diametrically opposed to civilized nations in its laws, customs, and institutions.[129] This notion of incommensurability helped redefine the legal universalism of the modern empire through insistence that China, though not qualified as a civilized nation insofar as rights under international law were concerned, was bound by its obligations toward the Christian nations under that same law. Instead of law or ethics, imperial common sense and sensibility became a convenient means for some (though not all) empire builders to legitimate imperial policies and practices when a vastly different and supposedly inferior people were concerned. What has characterized empire over the past two centuries, according to Partha Chatterjee, is the fact that "the imperial prerogative . . . lies in the claim to declare the colonial exception."[130] In the present case, declaring China as an exception to international law and justice carved out the necessary theoretical space for restructuring the preexisting Sino-Western relationship. Until then, the Westerners felt oppressed and insulted and their legal and political subjectivity were unrecognized by the Chinese authorities. The First Opium War now made it possible to actually enforce this imperial prerogative through a treaty-based system of international relations.

International Treaty as the New Legal Order for Sino-Western Relations

As explained in chapter 1, attempts to obtain extraterritoriality in China through bilateral treaties dated from at least the 1720s for the British (or the

1520s for the Portuguese). For different reasons, the Cathcart, Macartney, and Amherst embassies had all failed to achieve the goal of placing the Sino-British relationship on a new footing based on an international treaty, but this goal remained a top priority for many Britons interested in the China trade.[131] How and when that would actually take place was anyone's guess. Lord Macartney noted in early 1794 that it was practically impolitic and morally unjust to use force to change the status quo unless some future contingencies made such forbearance unbearable.[132] For many Britons, the opium crisis in 1839 was such a juncture, at which a revamping of the relationship with China became inevitable and critical. As British political commentators observed in 1840, a combination of the issues of (perceived) past injuries, trampled national honor, and current and future economic and political interests were all "now finally at stake," making it imperative to combine the "ancient and lasting purposes of security with the accidental purposes of the moment" to obtain a permanent guarantee against future injuries to British character and property.[133] Although John Barrow in 1834 had also strongly objected to the proposals of Lindsay and Marjoribanks to forcibly open China to British trade and opium, he wrote anonymously in the *Quarterly Review* in March 1840, "The time has come when China can no longer be allowed, from whatever jealousy or haughtiness, to refuse to bind herself to something like the diplomatic *jus gentium*" as defined by "a solemn treaty."[134]

For that reason, leading opium traders hoped that Charles Elliot would refuse to accept payment from the Chinese Hong merchants for the destroyed opium. Otherwise, the British government would take no notice of the British subjects' "insult" and leave them to carry on the business as well as they could, while the Chinese officials would become even more arrogant and tyrannical than before. William Jardine reminded people of the horror of the *Lady Hughes* case: "Should an accident (or death) occur and the Englishman connected with it make his escape, Elliot would in all probability be (seized) upon and told unless you give up the murderer in ten days or three days, we shall strangle you." He invited his Western fellows to just imagine what would happen if future governors-general were as determined and despotic as Lin Zexu was.[135] Likewise, in a letter forwarded to the Foreign Office and to Parliament, Captain Andrew Henderson (1800–1868), a Liverpool merchant who had been in the China trade for over two decades, considered the current rupture actually "fortunate for British interests" because the Chinese action had given Britain "just cause for war," enabling it to gain a position to "dictate" the terms of its relationship with China. If the recent outrages were left unaddressed, Henderson wrote, British life and property would be as precarious in China as it had been in Algiers, and Britain would be held in contempt among both the Chinese and other Asian nations, over whom the Chinese had a lot of influence.[136] In other words, besides obtaining compensation for opium and prying China open, the war was also to restructure the Sino-British relationship in the long run and facilitate British expansion in Asia and the Pacific. This was why Elliot also believed that changing China's foreign policy would help lift other East and Southeast Asian states' restrictions on Westerners.[137]

In a dispatch dated April 3, 1839, Elliot wrote Palmerston that no effort of the British government could restore the past confidence or security for foreign trade to be carried on at Guangzhou. The recent Chinese measures had demonstrated the unlimited danger of placing "the lives, liberty, and property of the foreign community in China, with all the vast interests, commercial and financial," at the mercy of this government.[138] This dispatch was enclosed in the first package of Elliot's confidential reports about the rupture, which reached the Foreign Office in London on August 29, 1839. However, in the collection of such *Chinese Correspondence* about the rupture (often known as the Blue Book) that was printed for Parliament's information in March 1840, only the above-quoted passage was included, while the most important contents of this "secret" dispatch were deliberately left out. Although one of the most significant documents shaping the British government's decision on the First Opium War, this dispatch has rarely been noted in modern scholarship. What Parliament and the public did not see were Elliot's detailed explanations of the justification, necessity, and strategic goals of a war with China. Elliot suggested to Palmerston that a military expedition was fully justified by the Chinese provocation, would be best suited for prompt redress of all the injustices suffered by the British, and would be the most likely to put future relations with China on "a sure and extending basis." Britain's response must be a swift and heavy blow, unprefaced by any written communication to the Chinese government. The expeditionary forces would achieve the fastest relief by occupying the Zhoushan

Islands and blockading the ports of Guangzhou and Ningbo and the Yang-tze River up to its juncture with the Grand Canal. The British government should also send an "ultimatum" to Beijing, demanding punishment of Commissioner Lin Zexu and Governor-General Deng Tingzhen, ample apology for insulting the Queen, payment for British losses, formal cession of the Zhoushan (Tchusan) Islands, and permission for local people to trade with the British at those islands and all Chinese seaports. The blockade would not end until all the demands had been met. Elliot suggested an indemnity of no less than five million pounds sterling, part of which could be forgiven if British goods were given ten years of free access to the ports of Guangzhou, Ningbo, Xiamen (Amoy), and Nanjing. He warned that the British military forces must be sufficient to proceed vigorously in this first attack of its kind ever made upon China "by the nations of the Western world." In a postscript also omitted from the printed *China Correspondence*, Elliot asked His Lordship to excuse his bad handwriting since he did not want to divulge the contents of the dispatch by asking anyone else to copy it. Indeed, while keeping it top secret, Palmerston and the Foreign Office carefully studied the dispatch and highlighted the key passage about the indemnity and the desirable treaty ports in the original copy.[139] Elliot's proposal made it clear that what he and many others had in mind was not merely compensation for the destroyed opium but also a complete rearrangement of the Sino-British or even Sino-Western relationship on a system of international treaties. Although it was considered "a high duty to the cause of civilization" to force China to pay for all the losses suffered by the British, Elliot reminded Lord Palmerston that "the time has arrived when this [Chinese] government must be made to understand its obligations to the rest of the world."[140]

Earlier scholars such as Hsin-pao Chang and Peter Fay have suggested that Palmerston was primarily influenced by William Jardine, who had an interview with him on September 27, 1839.[141] Jardine certainly provided useful information for Palmerston's preparation for the China expedition, by bringing maps and charts of China to the interview and then sending two memoranda four weeks later regarding the naval and military forces necessary for the expedition.[142] In late 1842, Palmerston indeed thanked John Abel Smith, Jardine, and their friends for their valuable "assistance and information," which enabled the government to prepare detailed instructions for British officers in China during the First Opium War. But Palmerston also mentioned the contribution of "the various other persons" he and the government consulted in the autumn of 1839.[143] As explained earlier, Elliot's dispatches had already given Palmerston detailed advice on the China expedition four weeks before Jardine first met with Palmerston. On September 20, Palmerston sent a copy of Elliot's secret dispatch of April 3 to Sir John Hobhouse in a "secret" packet.[144] Three days later, he sent Prime Minister Lord Melbourne a list of six practical questions about the opium crisis. Besides discussing whether and how the British government should assume legal responsibility for Elliot's undertaking to obtain compensation for the opium merchants, Palmerston indicated that a treaty should be demanded to place the intercourse with China "on a footing of security for the future," and an "apology for reparation of some kind for the gross indignity" suffered by Superintendent Elliot.[145] Palmerston's *concrete* plan for the military operation and strategies of the First Opium War was significantly influenced by Hugh Lindsay's letter of March 1836 and Elliot's secret dispatch,[146] but it is important to note that Palmerston himself also saw the current rupture as a rare, if a bit risky, opportunity to settle the "China question" that had troubled him for years. He refused to tell John Abel Smith and his allies whether the government would send a military expedition, partly because of the scandalous issue of opium; however, the questions he asked at their first meeting, on August 7, 1839, indicate that he was already inclined to compel China to pay for the surrendered opium and presumably to sign a treaty also.[147]

The decisive cabinet meeting on October 1, 1839, illustrates how a legal technicality, as a result of Elliot's intervention, could displace the moral issue in the most crucial moment of the British government's decision-making process regarding the First Opium War. During this closed-door meeting of the Whig ministers at Windsor Castle, Palmerston began by reading portions of Elliot's dispatches and then reiterated his plan for the China expedition, as noted earlier. Despite concerns about the lack of enough military forces from India, Sir Thomas Macaulay was "exceedingly eloquent against the Chinese" and eagerly supported hostile measures. There was an implicit consensus at the meeting that the opium had been surrendered to "save the lives of Elliot and the other English." Lord Melbourne made it clear that the British government should not pay for the seized opium, especially since Parliament would not agree. Francis Baring (1796–1866), chancellor of the exchequer, suggested that the Indian government should pay, but both Macaulay and Palmerston recommended seizing Chinese property for the opium indemnity, and their view eventually prevailed. During the discussion, the issue of the opium trade was overshadowed by the "main" issue of obtaining redress for the outrage suffered by Elliot, which all the cabinet members deemed "undisputable for the national honour and character."[148]

On October 18, Palmerston notified Elliot that a military expedition would reach China the following March, blockade the China coast, and seize some islands or ports to protect British commerce and interests. Even in this "secret" internal dispatch, the foreign secretary avoided including opium among the causes of the war: "Her Majesty's Government feel that it is impossible for Great Britain not to resent the outrages which have been committed by the Chinese upon British subjects, and upon the Queen's officer; and they are of opinion that it is absolutely necessary that the future of Great Britain with China should be placed upon a definite and secure footing" through an international treaty.[149] As confirmed by the Whig government's cabinet meeting and Palmerston's famous letter to the minister of the emperor of China in February 1840, the military conflict with China would thus be officially classified as a just war under international law, to defend and recover British property and redress all the insults, injustices, and insecurity endured by British officers and subjects. Hostilities would not end until a treaty was signed on terms entirely satisfactory to Britain.[150] All these deliberations of the Whig government were kept secret. News about preparations for the China expedition was finally brought to the attention of Parliament in March 1840, and Sir James Graham soon gave notice of his motion against the government on the rupture with China, leading to the parliamentary debate in April 1840 discussed earlier.[151]

During this debate, those who supported the military expedition often invoked the archival, intellectual, and popular discourses about Chinese law, government, and national character examined earlier in this book. A litany of earlier disputes with China, beginning with the unsuccessful first British attempt to establish direct trade with China in 1637, through the various legal cases and the British embassies and first superintendents of trade, to the current rupture, was cited to show that the long, humiliating history of British "slavish submission" to Chinese aggression had to be reversed. The cumulative lesson was that only a display of formidable power could make sense to an Oriental people like the Chinese, who were "incapable of true civilization" and "incurably savage" in the moral sense.[152] Through the lens of the sentimental discourse of sympathy, cruelty, and injury, the cultural traumas of earlier cases such as the *Lady Hughes* became a rallying cry for British patriots to defend and recover their national dignity. It was a belated opportunity to resolve their long-standing "moral guilt" and vindicate their "humiliation and national crime" of having contributed to the "atrocity of the poor old gunner voluntarily given up by his own countrymen."[153] These narratives added emotional power and legal cogency to the arguments of Elliot, Jardine, Palmerston, and others about the origins and meaning of this war. Macaulay's speech in the House of Commons captured this very well:

> The Imperial Commissioner began by confiscating property; his next demand was for innocent blood. A Chinese was slain [in the Lin Weixi case].... Great Britain [refused to] be party to so barbarous a proceeding [of turning over a British national for punishment]. The people at Canton were seized; they were driven from Macao, suspected or not. Women with child, children at the breast, were treated with equal severity..., an English gentleman was barbarously mutilated, and England found itself at once assailed with a fury unknown to civilized countries.... Conscious of her power, England could bear that her Sovereign could be called a barbarian, and her people described as savages, destitute of every useful art. When our Ambassadors were obliged to undergo a degrading prostration [in the kowtow ritual], in compliance with their regulations, conscious of our strength, we were more amused than irritated. But there was a limit to that forbearance. It would not have been worthy of us to take arms upon a small provocation, referring to rites and ceremonies merely; but everyone in the scale of civilized nations should know that Englishmen were ever living under the protecting eye of their own country.[154]

He reminded his compatriots that Britain was the country that had humbled the bey of Algiers for its insulted consul, had avenged the horrors of the Black Hole of Calcutta on the battlefields of Plassey, and had not regressed since its great protector vowed to make the name of an English person as respected as the name of a Roman citizen had ever been.[155] Hobhouse thought that Macaulay answered Graham in "a very eloquent and argumentative harangue," and Lord John Russell told the Queen that Macaulay spoke in a most satisfactory way to his audience.[156] The allusion to the Black Hole of Calcutta, the most famous tale of Oriental brutality in the British imperial chronicle, served as an effective *alibi of empire* by casting the current war as one fought in the interests of humanity, civilization, and imperial honor.[157]

Staunton maintained that given the character of the Chinese, no one could doubt the necessity of accompanying a treaty proposal with a competent physical force. The expedition would lead to a national treaty between the two countries and to the end of the detestable opium traffic. Reminding others that British honor and interests were at stake, he warned, "Let it finally be recollected that our high position throughout the whole eastern world is mainly founded on the moral force of public opinion." If such outrage and commercial degradation in China were not vindicated, the day would not be far off when Britain's political ascendancy in India would also be fatally undermined.[158] Indeed, a large portion of the expeditionary troops and logistical support came from British India during this war, and the governor-general of India had general superintendence over the military operations and treaty negotiations in China.[159] Resolution of the China question was considered essential to securing the British Empire itself.

In his concluding speech on April 9, 1840, Lord Palmerston quoted British and American opium traders to make an equally effective and emotionally charged argument. He ended it by saying that a mere demonstration of the British forces would bring the Chinese emperor to a sense of reason and justice. The noble lord sat down amid loud and protracted cheering.[160] After seventeen and a half hours of debate in the House of Commons, extending from April 7 to 9, Graham's motion to censure the government was defeated.[161] Macaulay and Hobhouse were correct in predicting that the Tories would not abandon the war. After replacing the Whigs in August 1841, Sir Robert Peel's Tory government continued the war until China signed the Treaty of Nanjing and its supplementary agreements in 1842–1843. China was to pay twenty-one million taels of silver in indemnity; open the five ports of Guangzhou, Xiamen, Fuzhou, Ningbo, and Shanghai to foreign trade with low tariffs; cede Hong Kong; and give Britain most-favored-nation status and extraterritoriality. The United States and France secured similar privileges through treaties in 1844.[162] Thus a new international order commenced.

Although the First Opium War had its *direct* origins in disputes over opium and jurisdiction, the prevailing discourse of Chinese and international law transformed a scandal of empire into an enabling discourse that legitimated and created new opportunities for the imperial project. As the British government had already made up its mind about the war before the parliamentary debate in April 1840, much of the debate, to quote Nicholas Dirks in a different but analytically related context, "ironically made empire seem a natural extension of British sovereign and commercial rights and interests."[163] Moreover, the war and the treaty-port system were believed to be beneficial not just to the British but also to the Chinese and humanity in general.[164] Elliot was quick to make this argument. Prompt and powerful British interference to avenge all past wrongs would be the only means of saving the Chinese empire from the desperate smugglers and other crimes as well as a devastating war with foreign powers. The expedition was therefore the British government's "high obligation" toward the Chinese as well as the public interest and national character of Britain. There would be no safety or honor for either government until Her Majesty's flag was flying over the China coast from a secure position.[165] Other memorialists to Palmerston and Parliament echoed these sentiments, stressing that it was in the interest of justice, global commerce, and British merchants and reputation to "chastise" China and teach its rulers how to observe the "reciprocal duties" as observed by civilized nations.[166] Even Elliot's critics tended to think that the grandest revolutions in an unchanging China might be accomplished by the meanest means, and that Elliot's questionable decisions had stirred "a smuggling quarrel into a national war, which [is] destined to confer the light of freedom, civilization, and religion, on three hundred millions of our race."[167] But what really excited these British empire builders was the prospect that was explained by Palmerston to Smith privately in late 1842: "There can be no doubt that this Event, which will form an Epoch in the Progress of the Civilization of the Human Race, must be attended with most Important advantages to the Commercial Interests of England; and these advantages will not be temporary and transient, but permanent and continually increasing."[168]

CONCLUSION AND SUMMARY
OF POSTWAR DEVELOPMENTS

In this chapter, at the risk of some repetition, I have tried to demonstrate in detail the different ways in which a set of core arguments, imageries, and rhetorical strategies regarding China and Sino-British or Sino-Western relations were developed, widely distributed, and recycled by a large number of British traders, politicians, and commentators for various purposes. I have focused on the underanalyzed legal issues and implications of the First Opium War to illustrate how the discourse of law or Chinese law, as examined in earlier chapters, came to influence the direct causes, decision-making process, and long-term results of this landmark event. The popular perception of Chinese judicial administration as despotic and barbaric not only encouraged defiance of Chinese anti-opium laws and campaigns but also led to a rethinking of China's sovereign status under international law. Elliot's intervention helped convert Commissioner Lin's confiscation of contraband opium into an unjust aggression against British lives, liberty, property, and national dignity. The contingencies of the opium crisis, influenced by economic interests, party politics, and representation of past injuries and national honor, provided an opportunity for key British actors in this event—such as Elliot, Matheson, Jardine, Palmerston, and Macaulay—to push for a military solution to the China question. The kinds of major factors that contributed to the British decision to wage this war were similar to those that historian John Wong has discussed for the Second Opium War in 1856–1860.[169] Among other things, the debate over and results of the First Opium War fundamentally changed the legal infrastructure of the Sino-Western encounter, replacing the Canton System, which was in principle defined by Chinese law and sovereign power, with the treaty-port system, based on international treaties whose terms were largely dictated by the dominant foreign powers. A positivist international legal and political order was thus established on the basis of agreements between Sino-Western "sovereign" countries even as China was relegated to a status of exception to the "universal" principle of equal, territorial sovereignty and treated as a subject of modern international law and relations only in a crippled sense. The constructed images of Chinese law and justice were codified in this process. The post-1842 development of the treaty ports, extraterritorial courts, and gunboat diplomacy helped establish the domination of the foreign empires in China over the next century. However, some of the legal and moral issues debated in 1840 were never fully resolved then or in the subsequent debates over the Second Opium War. To help situate this chapter within the larger context of this book in relation to earlier discussions, I highlight some of those issues here.

Even when advising Palmerston on the war with China, Staunton admitted that he had a strong feeling against opium and would support a motion condemning the existing Indian production of the drug for Chinese markets.[170] Three years after his defense of the war in April 1840, Staunton stated in the House of Commons that he "never denied the fact that if there had been no opium smuggling, there would have been no war." Without the British government's support, which quadrupled opium production in India, he noted, it would never have excited such an unusual alarm in the Chinese authorities as to cause them to adopt the controversial measures to suppress it in 1839.[171] The fact that the British government was eager to have China legalize the opium trade but chose not to make it a precondition of the Treaty of Nanjing also reflected an awareness of this tension between imperial interest and liberal conscience or ideology. In 1842, foreign secretary Lord Aberdeen asked the British representatives in China to detach British diplomats from all connection with this "discreditable" traffic.[172] When the commanders of the China expedition were later unanimously honored by Parliament for their gallantry in the military campaigns in China, no parliamentarians or cabinet ministers would touch upon the origin of that "sad war." To defend the First Opium War, Palmerston had to cite stories of Chinese shock at the British troops' alleged benevolence and forbearance during the war; and for such moral examples and the introduction of Christianity, other politicians claimed that the results of the war would ultimately be more beneficial to the Chinese (despite their temporary sufferings) than to the British.[173]

For many, the efforts of foreign missionaries to suppress opium in China later in the century served to justify empire as a civilizing mission, just as the British antislavery movement, according to former U.S. president John Quincy Adams (1767–1848), better qualified Britain to bring China to Western terms of international relations. Adams held in 1841 that the British had a righteous cause in its war with China to ensure that future commerce would be conducted upon terms of equality and reciprocity, so that each side would retain the right (ironically) to interdict articles or trading activities injurious to itself, such as opium.[174] By the same token, Henry Wheaton revised his treatise on international law to suggest that the contact between Christian nations in Euro-America and Muslim and pagan nations in Asia and Africa had led the latter to renounce their peculiar international usages and adopt those of Christian states. China, he added, had recently been compelled to "abandon its inveterate anti-commercial and anti-social principles, and to acknowledge the independence and equality of other nations in the mutual intercourse of war and peace." A Chinese translation of Wheaton's treatise by an American missionary in 1864 became a textbook for the Chinese (and other East Asians) on modern diplomacy and was cited as "the most remarkable proof of the advance of Western civilization in the East."[175]

Claiming native benefit or invoking a religious or secular civilizing mission sounded ironic to contemporary observers such as philanthropic Christian Reverend Algernon Thelwall, American merchant Charles King, and British statesman William Gladstone.[176] After being pressured by Tory leaders to withdraw his objection to the British demand for Chinese compensation for the confiscated opium, Gladstone lamented in his diary in May 1840, "I am in dread of the judgments of God upon England for our national iniquity towards China. It has been to me a matter of most painful & anxious consideration." Prime Minister Peel dismissed the opium question in 1843 as just a minor subject compared with other imperial interests constantly considered by the government that Gladstone would join as a cabinet member,[177] but that minor subject haunted those concerned about the empire's legitimacy. Elliot and other supporters of the war had admitted that the drug was injurious to the British character and reputation. The Baptist Missionary Society of England even had to transfer 5,000 pounds of its funds to the presumably less-stigmatized American missionaries for purposes of preaching the Gospel in China.[178]

After the First Opium War, Lord Aberdeen was advised that every means should be adopted to win Chinese confidence and, if possible, to compensate for all the evils inflicted by British opium and guns.[179] It was imperative for Britain to suppress the contraband trade to secure a friendly relationship with China on an honorable basis. Peel and others sided with the opium merchants, however, and rejected the motion to suppress the drug, claiming that the best solution was to have China legalize it.[180] As long as the British Empire was financially dependent on opium, its growing stigma made its legalization more urgent. Lord Elgin told American plenipotentiary William Reed in September 1858 that the opium trade had such a corrupting influence on the producer, importer, and official, whether foreign or Chinese, that it should be legalized rather than banned under the ineffective Chinese laws or Sino-American treaties. Besides protecting the huge Anglo-American interest in opium, Chinese legalization would resolve the pernicious difficulty with this "anomalous opprobrium."[181] As noted in chapter 4, the widespread reports of Western violence and pillaging in the two Opium Wars and then in the suppression of the Boxer Rebellion around 1900 reminded people of the inherent contradictions between the professed Western values of the rule of law, humanitarianism, and civilization and the actual practices of the dominant empires. Along with opium addiction among the Chinese, perceived racial or cultural differences led to exclusionary laws targeting Chinese immigrants in the United States, Canada, Britain, and other Western countries in the late nineteenth and early twentieth centuries.[182] A similar "state of apprehension" about the "Yellow Peril," as James Hevia has argued, informed the popular literary trope of Dr. Fu-Manchu as a diabolic symbol of the crafty, unruly, and dangerous Chinese or "Red China" in Euro-America from World War I through the Cold War period.[183] It is tempting and convenient to attribute such racialized anxieties or fears to the clash of civilizations, as Samuel Huntington and many others have done.[184] However, recent scholarship has shown that this kind of constructed "otherness" is "neither inherent nor stable" and has to be politically "defined and maintained" through the operation of essentialism and exclusionary logic.[185] This book's analysis of the formation and transformation of Western knowledge of Chinese law and society in the contact zones has illustrated some of the historical possibilities and experiences that were erased or forgotten by the once-dominant historiography.

CONCLUSION

Variations of the image of China as a quintessential Oriental despotism without law, honor, and liberty or democracy have remained influential (though less so in the past three decades than before) among commentators and scholars of China since Montesquieu popularized this idea in *The Spirit of the Laws* in 1748. The underlying discourse and assumptions about Chinese law and society have also profoundly impacted the Sino-Western relationship over the past few centuries. However, the historical genealogy of this powerful discourse had received little critical attention until recently. Through a combination of case studies and broader analyses, this book has offered an empirically grounded history of how Chinese legal tradition and modernity came to be represented, imagined, and interpreted, often very differently by Euro-Americans even of the same period or country. It has shown how the discourse of Chinese law and society significantly shaped the ideological formation and policy making of the British Empire and some other Western powers in relation to China during the eighteenth and nineteenth centuries. In the process, its analysis calls for reexamination of the received wisdom about various Sino-Western legal and political disputes that contributed to the outbreak of the Opium Wars and the subsequent treaty-port system and (semi)colonialism. This book does not provide a comprehensive coverage of the history of Sino-Western, or even Sino-British, cultural or political relations during the period under study. It is also very different from a typical historical study of international relations or comparative law.

Nonetheless, I hope that its analysis has demonstrated that studying the unfolding processes and power politics of boundary making in the multidimensional contact zones of empire may help broaden our understanding of the history of not just Sino-Western relations but also other transcultural or transimperial encounters.

Using a wide array of sources, this study has been organized around the different but related aspects of the production, distribution, and institutionalization of the discourse of Chinese law and society in the eighteenth and nineteenth centuries. It began by examining the imperial archives of Sino-Western legal disputes to reinterpret the historiography of extraterritoriality in chapter 1 before moving on to explore how such disputes led to the production of Western knowledge of Chinese law and society in the next chapter. Chapter 3 then analyzed the reception and multifaceted influence of such knowledge on Euro-American debates about the ideals of modern law and government in the eighteenth and early nineteenth centuries. Related to such archival and intellectual discourses was the rise of popular and sentimental representations of Chinese judicial punishments that came to redefine Chinese and Western law and subjectivity in the nineteenth century, which was the subject of chapter 4. Chapter 5 illustrated the influence of these archival, intellectual, and popular discourses on the decision making of British diplomats, traders, and politicians in waging the First Opium War and developing the subsequent China policies. Now let me take this opportunity to highlight some of the analytical issues and historiographical debates that this book has tried to investigate or flesh out.

The fact that China was repeatedly defeated by Western powers after 1840 and reduced to a semicolony later in the century has led many modern students of history to assume that the story of early modern Sino-Western encounters is primarily one of the clash of civilizations or one of Western domination. While joining the recent revisionist scholarship in refuting the clash-of-civilizations thesis, this book has argued that the history of Sino-Western relations cannot be reduced to just intractable conflicts or the *clash of empires*. Constant negotiation and mutual accommodation were also an important part of the story. Without glossing over the oppressive nature of colonial rule or imperialism, I have also cautioned against the tendency in earlier postcolonial scholarship to overemphasize the internal coherence and totalizing hegemony of colonial power and discourse. This book illuminates the various ways in which certain constructs of China as the inferior or incommensurable Other of the modern West acquired epistemological authority both in spite of and because of their inherent contradictions. It calls for more attention to the practice of self-Occidentalization by Euro-Americans who sought to maintain their cultural identity by essentializing and dehistoricizing their cultural tradition in contradistinction to Chinese law or culture.

Moreover, many of the still influential Western ideas of China or Chinese law did not acquire the normative power that they have had until well after the First Opium War. In the century prior to 1840, Western ideas about China and Sino-Western boundaries were far more ambivalent, contested, and incoherent. In fact, the increasingly negative portrayal of China and Chinese law before 1840 arose more directly from the embarrassing and precarious status of Western explorers and interests in China than from Western political or military domination. China's tight control over the Sino-foreign trade and relationship from the 1520s through the 1830s had made Euro-Americans in China and their supporters at home frequently feel insecure and insulted, leading to outcries against Chinese law and government. In other words, the processes of Sino-Western knowledge production and boundary making were neither monolithic nor unilaterally dominated by the Western empires. What this book set out to do was to recover and analyze such instances of contestation, anxieties, and internal contradiction at the formative stage of such universalizing discourses as liberalism, humanitarianism, international law, free trade, and modern civilization.

This study has helped restore the centrality of law in the history of modern Sino-Western relations by showing that law was not only pivotal in many major conflicts, including the two Opium Wars, but also a key site where imperial sovereignty, cultural boundaries, and international order were asserted, negotiated, and reconfigured during this formative period. Its findings have revealed that one of the often neglected but most enduring consequences of the First Opium War is that it served to forcibly perpetuate the prewar narratives about Sino-Western incommensurability. This and subsequent wars and gunboat diplomacy helped transform the Sino-Western relationship from one governed by Chinese law to one controlled primarily by Western law and interpretation of treaty rights in the language of international law and modern diplomacy.

In this book, we saw how the humanitarian sentiment or visualization of the pain of others came to become a crucial part of the liberal ideology of modern empires. The worldwide circulation of visual and textual depictions of Chinese judicial torture and punishments, interpreted through the Enlightenment concepts of sympathy and universal humanity, turned Chinese law and people into a global spectacle of barbarism and cruelty. A transnational "emotional community" emerged to provide the rhetorical and emotional conventions for the Western viewers and readers to claim their modern subjectivity while excluding the Chinese as well as other "natives" from the privileged space of modern civilization and international law.

Reexamination of the representation of the pre-1840 Sino-Western legal disputes in the imperial archives, dominant narratives, and modern historiography challenged the received wisdom on the origins of foreign extraterritoriality in post-1843 China, popularly attributed to the incommensurability between Chinese and Western law and civilizations. Careful study of the "primary" sources of these disputes against the backdrop of a longer history of European colonial expansion has demonstrated that Western resistance to Chinese jurisdiction had little to do with the actual differences between Chinese and Western laws and procedures. Revisiting these cases also highlighted the fact that much of the modern historiography about these early Sino-Western conflicts or disputes adopted the dominant popular narratives that were contradicted by even the official archives, which were in turn influenced by the self-serving agendas of imperial agents on the ground. It is worth noting that the jurisdictional politics in the contact zone of southern China created a kind of legal limbo in which the complicity of foreign and local Chinese merchants and officials caused gradual erosion of Qing law and sovereignty despite efforts of the Qing emperors to enforce Qing laws and jurisdiction in some cases.

This book has provided the most extensive study of the production, reception, and legacy of Sir George Thomas Staunton's underanalyzed but enormously influential translation of the Qing Code to trace the historical emergence of modern comparative study of Chinese law. This canonical text of modern Sinology resulted from a complicated process of cultural translation and translingual practice. The unquestionably authoritative status of the

Qing Code, viewed as the "fundamental law" that supposedly captured the unchanging essence of Chinese civilization and national character, allowed Staunton and other writers to believe that they had finally reduced the inscrutable China into a docile Western text. This marked a major epistemological milestone in Western knowledge of China, by domesticating and reclassifying Chinese law through Western languages, categories, and sensibilities. Staunton's English translation and its retranslations were widely cited in Euro-America in the next two centuries, allowing Hegel, Maine, Max Weber, and other philosophers, jurists, anthropologists, sociologists, and linguists to fit China into their various comparative frameworks.

Nonetheless, cultural appropriation or transculturation in the Sino-Western contact zones has been a two-way process. Contrary to the once-dominant theory of "Western impact and Chinese response" used to explain the post-1840 Chinese transformation, this book has shown that knowledge of Chinese law and government played a important and potentially transformative role in Euro-American imaginations of modernity before Chinese reformers drew inspiration from the West in the twentieth century. Enlightenment leaders such as Montesquieu, Voltaire, Beccaria, and Blackstone in the late eighteenth century and European intellectuals and jurists in the nineteenth century wrestled with and often appropriated ideas of Chinese law and society when developing their visions of modern legal and political institutions. It is also worth reiterating that China, viewed as an archetypal state of Oriental despotism, likewise exerted a profound influence upon Western modernity, by negatively defining what was not a modern civilization or a modern political or legal system. To put it rather simplistically, both such "positive" and "negative" Chinese impact should be taken into account when discussing Sino-Western encounters and cultural exchanges. What further complicated the situation is the fact that many Chinese later utilized various Orientalist representations of Chinese law or civilization to push for "modernization" of China, ironically, in order to end foreign domination.

To conclude, I would like to briefly mention how the Western perceptions of Chinese law, with all their internal fissures and contradictions, came to affect the Chinese experience with modernity. Chapter 2 mentioned that the representation of the Qing Code or the entire Chinese legal system as exclusively penal led influential intellectuals like Sir Henry Maine to consider China stationary and primitive in contrast with

Western countries. In 1904, Liang Qichao (1873–1929), a famous late Qing reformist scholar, cited Maine to suggest that late imperial Chinese law was too backward to survive the competition of modern civilizations because of its excessive attention to criminal punishments rather than civil laws and rights.[1] During the late Qing reform in 1902–1911, the legal system was restructured along the Western categories of civil law, civil procedural law, criminal law, criminal procedural law, constitutional law, commercial law, and so on.[2] Contemporary Britons proudly proclaimed that "English schooling and an English legal training have been in a measure at the bottom of Chinese legal reform." Wu Tingfang (1842–1922), appointed in 1905 to lead the reform with Minister of Justice Shen Jiaben (1840–1912), turned out to be an English barrister who had studied law at Lincoln's Inn thirty years earlier and once sat at the feet of Sir James Stephen for lectures on criminal law.[3]

Nevertheless, the Euro-Americentric discourses could also be used by dominated people for different purposes. Yan Fu (1854–1921), an influential intellectual during the early twentieth century, translated the works of Montesquieu, Adam Smith, John Stuart Mill, Thomas Huxley (1825–1895) and Herbert Spencer (1820–1903) and helped popularize their ideas of liberty, democracy, or progress as the universal criteria for Chinese modernity. When translating Montesquieu's *The Spirit of the Laws*, however, Yan Fu highlighted the complexities of Chinese history in rejecting Montesquieu's "classification of China as the prototype of despotism." The evolutionist ideas of social Darwinism that Yan Fu also introduced helped legitimate Western domination but could also inspire the dominated to seek wealth and power in order to make their nation the fittest to survive.[4] Likewise, apparently invoking the sentimental discourse of Chinese cruelty, discussed in chapter 4, Lu Xun (alias Zhou Shuren, 1881–1936), a founder of modern Chinese literature, dramatized the now clichéd spectacle of Chinese indifference and barbarity around scenes of execution to attack China's "cannibalistic" tradition on the one hand and to urge the nation to wake up and arm itself against domestic and foreign oppression on the other. Literary scholars have extensively analyzed the political cogency as well as the embedded ambivalence of Lu Xun's writings in this regard. However, what has been less often noticed was the century-long genealogy of the transnational discourse of modern (Western) sympathy and humanity versus Chinese (legal) cruelty and barbarity. Lu Xun and other Chinese reformers in the twentieth century tried to cultivate a new national subjectivity by appealing to this dominant discourse of modern civilization, but their frustration with and ambivalence toward both the discourse and their own people and civilization appear almost inevitable since the former had generally posited the Chinese as culturally and racially incommensurable with the modern values it promoted.[5]

When attempting to appropriate Western concepts or institutions, Chinese intellectuals and reformers in the late nineteenth and early twentieth centuries often adopted the strategy of bifurcation—splitting the idea of the West into a "metropolitan West (Western cultures in the West) and the colonial West (the cultures of Western colonizers in China)." As Shu-mei Shih and other scholars have shown in relation to Chinese modernity, this strategy enabled Chinese intellectual or social elites to represent the metropolitan West "as an object of emulation, which often resulted in diminishing the [colonial West] as an object of critique." Thus, Chinese intellectuals could promote Westernization without being seen as "collaborationists."[6] However, they did become cultural brokers or mediators in the contact zones of a new era. It is worth recalling that many European intellectuals in the eighteenth and early nineteenth centuries— such as Montesquieu, Staunton, John Barrow, and Francis Jeffrey—had also utilized a similar bifurcation strategy, recommending some Chinese laws or legal principles as worthy of being borrowed by European countries even while dismissing the legal system as suitable only for Oriental despotism. Interestingly, both the bifurcation of China or Chinese law by European intellectuals and the later bifurcation of the West by Chinese intellectuals were considered problematic by a small number of Euro-Americans and Chinese who had substantive knowledge of both Chinese and Western legal systems.[7]

Meanwhile, many Chinese critics of Westernization also ended up adopting various Orientalist characterizations of Chinese law and society. In the early twentieth century, it was popular to argue that China was a country ruled by Confucian morals and ritual or propriety (*li*) and was not suited to the Western-influenced legal system. In the second half of the twentieth century, an effective objection to political liberalization and the rule of law was often made in the language of nationalism and the peculiarity of a modern Chinese state and society founded on a Communist revolution against Western imperialism.[8] Such self-essentialization might ostensibly help resist foreign domination, but, as Arif Dirlik has observed, "in the very process it also consolidates 'Western' ideological hegemony by internalizing the historical assumptions of Orientalism."[9] What has been erased or overlooked by the Eurocentric, Orientalist, or Chinese cultural-ist or nationalist narratives of modernity and Sino-Western contact is, in the words of Dipesh Chakrabarty, the more complex history of the "con-tradictory, plural, and heterogeneous struggles whose outcomes are never predictable, even retrospectively, in accordance with schemas that seek to naturalize and domesticate this heterogeneity," which also characterized other transcultural or transimperial encounters.[10] It is this kind of history of Sino-Western encounters that this book has sought to analyze.

As China is regaining its status as a major world power thanks to decades of rapid economic development since the late 1970s, the prospect of China's rise to global domination or use of force to challenge the status quo of the world order has generated widespread anxieties and fears around the globe, particularly in the previously dominant industrialized countries such as Britain and the United States. This sense of anxiety and precariousness has resulted from, and further contributed to, the continued tendency to reduce the Sino-Western historical relationship to one of fundamental incom-mensurability and inevitable clash. The growing interdependence of China and Western countries in a globalized world has significantly changed the power dynamics underlying Sino-Western relations. But for many observ-ers, China's law and government appear almost as totalitarian and objec-tionable as they did one or two centuries ago. If anything, this book has shown how this impulse to essentialize and politicize racial, cultural, or national difference could hold the Sino-Western relationship hostage and eventually lead to catastrophic conflicts. We need to rethink rather than reify the historical constructions of boundary and hierarchy in international relations to prevent the concerns about the clash of civilizations or empires from becoming self-fulfilling prophesies again.

Abbreviations

AMJLJZ: Yin Guangren and Zhang Rulin, eds. *Ao'men jilue jiaozhu* (*Annotated Edition of the Brief Records of Macao*). 1751. Annotated by Zhao Chunchen. Macao: Aomen wenhuasi shu, 1992.

CBEIC: Hosea Ballou Morse, ed. *The Chronicles of the British East India Company Trading to China, 1635–1834*. 5 vols. Oxford: Clarendon Press, 1926–1929.

COT: Jin Guoping and Wu Zhiliang, eds. *Correspondência oficial trocada entre as autoridades de Cantão e os procuradores do Senado: Fundo das chapas sínicas em português (1749–1847) (Yue'ao gongdu lucun)*. 8 vols. Macao: Fundação Macau, 2000.

CRTC: "Correspondence Relating to China [01/1834–09/1839]." In *Parliamentary Papers*. London: House of Commons, 1840.

DFUSCC: Despatches from United States Consuls in Canton, 1790–1906. Vol. 1790–1834. National Archives, College Park, Maryland.

FO: Foreign Office Records. National Archives, Kew, London.

GEDF: "Ta-tsing-leu-lee, o sia Leggi fondamentali del Còdice penale della China." *Giornale enciclopedico di Firenze* 4 (1812): 23–24.

HCT: Edward Hertslet and Godfrey E. P. Hertslet, eds. *Hertslet's China Treaties: Treaties, &c., between Great Britain and China; and between China and Foreign Powers; and Orders in Council, Rules, Regulations, Acts of Parliament, Decrees, &c., Affecting British Interests in China, in Force on the 1st January, 1908*. 3rd ed. 2 vols. London: His Majesty's Stationery Office, 1908.

IOR: India Office Records. British Library, London.

JJCLFZZ: Junjichu Lufu Zouzhe (Grand Council Copies of Memorials). First National Historical Archives, Beijing.

JMC: *China Trade and Empire: Jardine, Matheson & Co. and the Origins of British Rule in Hong Kong, 1827–1843*. Edited by Alain Le Pichon. Oxford: Oxford University Press, 2006.

MQHQH: *Ming Qing huanggong Huangpu midang tujian* (*Illustrated Secret Archives on Huangpu in the Ming and Qing Imperial Palaces*). Compiled by Zhongguo Diyi Lishi Dang'anguan and Guangzhou Huangpuqu Renmin Zhengfu. Guangzhou: Jinan daxue chubanshe, 2006.

MQSQA: *Ming Qing shiqi Aomen wenti dang'an wenxian huibian* (*Archival Material on Macao in the Ming-Qing Period*). Compiled by Zhongguo Diyi Lishi Dang'anguan et al. 6 vols. Beijing: Renmin chubanshe, 1999.

PRUSC: *Political Relations Between the United States and China*. U.S. Department of State, no. 71. Submitted to the 26th Cong., 2nd sess., January 25, 1841. Washington, D.C.: GPO, 1841. Printed edition of DFUSCC, 1790–1834.

PTYDP: Liu Fang and Zhang Wenqin, eds. *Putaoya dongpota dang'anguan chang Qingdai Aomen zhongwen dang'an huibian* (*Collections of Chinese Documents on Qing-Dynasty Macao at the National Archives of Portugal*). Macao: Aomen jijinhui, 1999.

QGJJD: Qingdai Gongzhongdang Ji Junjichu Dangzhejian (Qing Palace Memorials and Archives of the Grand Council). Palace Museum, Taipei.

QGYGA: *Qinggong Yue Gang Ao shangmao dang'an quanji* (*Complete Records from the Qing Imperial Archives on the Foreign Trade at Canton, Hong Kong, and Macao*). Compiled by Zhongguo Diyi Lishi Dang'anguan. Beijing: Zhongguo shudian, 2002.

QLCSYD: *Qianlongchao shangyudang* (*Imperial Edicts of the Qianlong Emperor*). Compiled by Zhongguo Diyi Lishi Dang'anguan. 18 vols. Beijing: Dang'an chubanshe, 1991.

SP: Sir George Leonard and George Thomas Staunton Papers [diaries, letters, etc.], 1743–1885. William R. Perkins Library, Duke University, Durham, N.C.

TTLL: George Thomas Staunton, trans. and ed. *Ta Tsing Leu Lee*. London: Cadell & Davies, 1810.

WWC: "War with China." In *Hansard's Parliamentary Debates*, 3rd ser., vol. 53, 3rd sess., 13th Parliament, March–May 1840. London: Thomas Curson Hansard, 1840.

XFAMS: Jin Guoping, ed. *Xifang Aomen shiliao xuancui (15–16 shiji)* (*Selected Western Historical Sources on Macao, 15th and 16th- Centuries*). Guangzhou: Guangdong renmin chubanshe, 2005.

YPZZD: *Yapian zhanzheng dang'an shiliao* (*Archival Sources of the Opium War*). Compiled by Zhongguo Diyi Lishi Dang'anguan. Tianjin: Tianjin guji chubanshe, 1992.

NOTES

INTRODUCTION

1. Thousands of people from various countries posted comments on the execution within hours to the BBC bulletin board. For the quotations and other details about this case, see Chris Hogg, "British Anger at China Execution," *BBC News*, December 29, 2009, http://news.bbc.co.uk/2/hi/uk/8433704.stm (accessed December 30, 2009); "Akmal Shaikh: China Refers to Controversial Opium Wars with Britain," *Telegraph*, December 29, 2009 (the Chinese ambassador attributing China's drug policy to "the bitter memory of history"); "Britain, the Drug Pusher," *Daily Mail*, January 4, 2010; Isaac S. Fish, "All Politics Is Local," *Newsweek*, January 4, 2010. Shaikh's supporters claimed, based on his e-mails and ex-wife's statements, that he might be a patient of bipolar disorder. For the medical definition, see David J. Miklowitz, *Bipolar Disorder: A Family-Oriented Treatment Approach* (New York: Guilford Press, 2008), 23–24.

2. Before this, Antonio Riva, an Italian citizen, was the last European executed by China, with a Japanese named Ruichi Yamaguchi, in 1951 for allegedly plotting to assassinate Mao Zedong and other Chinese leaders. See Chris Hogg, "China Executions Shrouded in Secrecy," *BBC News*, December 29, 2009, http://news .bbc.co.uk/2/hi/asia-pacific/8432514.stm (accessed December 30, 2009); Frank Dikötter, *The Tragedy of Liberation: A History of the Chinese Revolution, 1945–57* (London: Bloomsbury, 2013), 103–4.

3. For such recent studies, see, e.g., Teemu Ruskola, *Legal Orientalism: China, the United States, and Modern Law* (Cambridge, Mass.: Harvard University Press, 2013); Pär Cassel, *Grounds of Judgment: Extraterritoriality and Imperial Power in Nineteenth-Century China and Japan* (Oxford: Oxford University Press, 2012); Eric Hayot, *The Hypothetical Mandarin: Sympathy, Modernity, and Chinese Pain* (New York: Oxford University Press, 2009); Timothy Brook, Jérôme Bourgon,

and Gregory Blue, *Death by a Thousand Cuts* (Cambridge, Mass.: Harvard University Press, 2008); Lydia H. Liu, *The Clash of Empires: The Invention of China in Modern World Making* (Cambridge, Mass.: Harvard University Press, 2004); James L. Hevia, *English Lessons: The Pedagogy of Imperialism in Nineteenth-Century China* (Durham: Duke University Press, 2003); John Y. Wong, *Deadly Dreams: Opium, Imperialism, and the Arrow War (1856–1860) in China* (Cambridge: Cambridge University Press, 1998).

4. Except publications on the Macartney Embassy in 1793, few works have extensively analyzed the pre-1840 century since Earl Pritchard did so in 1936.

5. See the discussions about Montesquieu, Hegel, Henry Maine, Max Weber, and so on in chapters 2 to 4.

6. For such revisionist scholarship, see the works cited in chapters 2 and 3 and in Li Chen and Madeleine Zelin, eds., *Chinese Law: Knowledge, Practice, and Transformation, 1530s–1950s* (Leiden: Brill, 2015), esp. 2–3.

7. See chapters 2 and 3. Also see Jérôme Bourgon, "Uncivil Dialogue: Law and Custom Did Not Merge into Civil Law under the Qing," *Late Imperial China* 23, no. 1 (2002): 50–90; Jianpeng Deng, "Classification of Litigation and Implications for Qing Judicial Practice," in Chen and Zelin, *Chinese Law*, 17–46.

8. See Ruskola, *Legal Orientalism*, 35; Arif Dirlik, *Culture and History in Postrevolutionary China: The Perspective of Global Modernity* (Hong Kong: Chinese University Press, 2011); Ruth Rogaski, *Hygienic Modernity: Meanings of Health and Disease in Treaty-Port China* (Berkeley: University of California Press, 2004); Shu-mei Shih, *The Lure of the Modern: Writing Modernism in Semicolonial China, 1917–1937* (Berkeley: University of California Press, 2001).

9. William P. Alford, "Law, Law, What Law? Why Western Scholars of Chinese History and Society Have Not Had More to Say about Its Law," *Modern China* 23, no. 4 (1997): 398–419; Ruskola, *Legal Orientalism*.

10. Hosea B. Morse, *The International Relations of the Chinese Empire*, 3 vols. (New York: Longmans, 1910), 1:41–255. For similar views in later works, see George W. Keeton, *The Development of Extraterritoriality in China*, 2 vols. (London: Longmans, 1928); Earl H. Pritchard, *The Crucial Years of Early Anglo-Chinese Relations, 1750–1800* (1936), reprinted in *Britain and the China Trade, 1635–1842*, ed. Patrick Tuck (New York: Routledge, 2000); John K. Fairbank, *Trade and Diplomacy on the China Coast: The Opening of the Treaty Ports, 1842–1854* (Cambridge, Mass.: Harvard University Press, 1964); Hsin-pao Chang, *Commissioner Lin and the Opium War* (Cambridge, Mass.: Harvard University Press, 1964); Alain Peyrefitte, *The Collision of Two Civilisations: The British Expedition to China in 1792–4*, trans. Jon Rothschild (London: Harvill, 1993); Harry G. Gelber, *The Dragon and the Foreign Devils: China and the World, 1100 B.C. to the Present* (London: Bloomsbury, 2007).

11. Fairbank, *Trade and Diplomacy*, 4–23; John K. Fairbank and Ssu-yu Teng, "On the Ch'ing Tributary System," *Harvard Journal of Asiatic Studies* 6, no. 2 (June 1941):

135–246; John K. Fairbank and Edwin O. Reischauer, *China: Tradition and Transformation* (Boston: Houghton Mifflin, 1989), 277. For critiques of these American Sinologists in the Cold War era, see Tani Barlow, "Colonialism's Career in China Studies," in *Formations of Colonial Modernity in East Asia*, ed. Tani Barlow, 373–412 (Durham: Duke University Press, 1997); James L. Hevia, *Cherishing Men from Afar: Qing Guest Ritual and the Macartney Embassy of 1793* (Durham: Duke University Press, 1995), xi–25; Hevia, *English Lessons*, 9–11.

12. See Paul A. Cohen, *Discovering History in China: American Historical Writings on the Recent Chinese Past* (New York: Columbia University Press, 1986); Joseph W. Esherick, *The Origins of the Boxer Uprising* (Berkeley: University of California Press, 1988); William T. Rowe, *Hankow: Commerce and Society in a Chinese City, 1796–1889* (Stanford: Stanford University Press, 1984); Arif Dirlik, "Chinese History and the Question of Orientalism," *History and Theory* 35, no. 4 (1996): 102 (seeing this as an anti-Eurocentric potential of "Orientalism"). Cf. Hevia, *English Lessons*, 9–11 (noting that the China-centered approach could cause neglect of the Sino-Western contact and reify the West as a given).

13. Hevia, *Cherishing Men*, 25, 28 (challenging "the view that constructs culture as a realm primarily of beliefs and ideas").

14. Wong, *Deadly Dreams*, esp. 32–34, 476, 484–85; see 457–85 for his critique of earlier literature.

15. Liu, *Clash of Empires*, 2; see also 31–106.

16. E.g., Lie Dao, ed., *Yapian zhanzheng shi lunwen zhuanji* (*Essays on the History of the Opium War*) (Beijing: Sanlian shudian, 1958); Xia Li, *Di erci yapian zhanzheng shi* (*History of the Second Opium War*) (Shanghai: Shanghai shudian chubanshe, 2007).

17. Xia, *Di erci yapian zhanzheng shi*, 61–71; He Wenxian, *Wenming de chongtu yu zhenghe—Tongzhi zhongxing shiqi zhongwai guanxi chongjian* (*Clash and Reintegration of Civilizations: Reconstructing Sino-Foreign Relations during the Tongzhi Restoration*) (Xiamen: Xiamen daxue chubanshe, 2006), esp. 316, 325; also see chapters by Zhang Shunhong and Wang Tseng-tsai in Robert A. Bickers, ed., *Ritual and Diplomacy: The Macartney Mission to China, 1792–1794* (London: Wellsweep Press, 1993).

18. Li Wenhai, *Cong minzu chenlun dao minzu zhenxing* (*From the National Decline to the National Revival*) (Beijing: Renmin daxue chubanshe, 2012). For more recent works still so influenced, see, e.g., Mao Haijian, *Tianchao de bengkui: Yapian zhanzheng zai yanjiu* (*Collapse of the Heavenly Dynasty: Reexamining the Opium War*), 2nd ed. (Beijing: Sanlian shudian, 2005), esp. 5–26. For a survey, see Huaiyin Li, *Reinventing Modern China: Imagination and Authenticity in Chinese Historical Writing* (Honolulu: University of Hawai`i Press, 2012).

19. For critiques of nationalist historiography, see Prasenjit Duara, *Rescuing History from the Nation* (Chicago: University of Chicago Press, 1995); John Fitzgerald,

Awakening China: Politics, Culture, and Class in the Nationalist Revolution (Stanford: Stanford University Press, 1996); Hevia, *Cherishing Men*, 239–48; Hevia, *English Lessons*, 332–45 (on "national humiliation" or "anti-imperialism"); Wong, *Deadly Dreams*, 38, 481.

20. This is very different from what Fairbank meant by "synarchy" in post-1842 China.

21. Mary Louise Pratt, *Imperial Eyes: Travel Writing and Transculturation* (New York: Routledge, 1992), 4, 6.

22. Ibid., 38.

23. Natalie E. Rothman, *Brokering Empire: Transimperial Subjects between Venice and Istanbul* (Ithaca: Cornell University Press, 2012), 4; see also 3–84.

24. See, e.g., David Porter, *Ideographia: The Chinese Cipher in Early Modern Europe* (Stanford: Stanford University Press, 2001).

25. Edward Said, *Orientalism* (New York: Random House, 1994), 3, 5 (focusing on "the internal consistency of Orientalism and its ideas about the Orient"), 116–20 (uniting latent Orientalism with manifest Orientalism under a uniform intentionality for colonial hegemony). For critiques, see Robert Young, *White Mythologies: Writing History and the West* (New York: Routledge, 2001), 120–26; Homi Bhabha, *The Location of Culture* (New York: Routledge, 2006), 101–20; Patrick Williams, ed., *Edward Said*, 4 vols. (London: Sage, 2001).

26. Edward Said, *Culture and Imperialism* (New York: Knopf, 1993), 10, 16. For a similar critique, see Catherine Hall, "Introduction: Thinking the Postcolonial, Thinking the Empire," in *Cultures of Empire: Colonizers in Britain and the Empire in the Nineteenth and Twentieth Centuries*, ed. Catherine Hall (Manchester: Manchester University Press, 2000), 15.

27. Said, *Culture and Imperialism*, 77; Said, *Orientalism*, 3–5, 12.

28. Ann Laura Stoler and Frederick Cooper, "Between Metropole and Colony: Rethinking a Research Agenda," in *Tensions of Empire: Colonial Cultures in a Bourgeois World*, ed. Frederick Cooper and Ann Laura Stoler (Berkeley: University of California Press, 1997), 33.

29. Dirlik, "Chinese History," 99–101, 112–17; Dirlik, *Culture and History*, 154–55. See Xiaomei Chen, *Occidentalism: Theory of Counter-Discourse in Post-Mao China* (New York: New York University Press, 1994), 3–26.

30. See Dirlik, *Culture and History*, 160–61.

31. Stuart Hall, "Who Needs 'Identity'?" in *Identity: A Reader*, ed. Paul du Gay, Jessica Evans, and Peter Redman (London: Sage, 2000), 19.

32. See, e.g., Gayatri Chakravorty Spivak, "Can the Subaltern Speak?" in *Marxism and the Interpretation of Culture*, ed. Cary Nelson and Lawrence Grossberg (Urbana: University of Illinois Press, 1988), 202, 278; Dipesh Chakrabarty, *Provincializing Europe: Postcolonial Thought and Historical Difference* (Princeton: Princeton University Press, 2000), 3–46.

33. Michel Foucault, "What Is an Author," in *The Foucault Reader*, ed. Paul Rabinow (New York: Pantheon, 1984), 118.

34. Ruskola, *Legal Orientalism*, 35–36.

35. For recent debates on sovereignty, see, e.g., Hent Kalmo and Quentin Skinner, eds., *Sovereignty in Fragments: The Past, Present and Future of a Contested Concept* (Cambridge: Cambridge University Press, 2010). For a comparative study including chapters on China, see Stefanos Geroulanos, Zvi Ben-Dor Benite, and Nichole Jerr eds., *The Scaffold of Sovereignty: A Global Interdisciplinary Approach* (New York: Columbia University Press, forthcoming).

36. See Pamela Crossley, *A Translucent Mirror: History and Identity in Qing Imperial Ideology* (Berkeley: University of California Press, 2002). About the Qing as a "colonial empire," see Laura Hostetler, *Qing Colonial Enterprise: Ethnography and Cartography in Early Modern China* (Chicago: University of Chicago Press, 2005).

37. Hevia, *Cherishing Men*, 116–33; Cassel, *Grounds of Judgment*, 9–12, 15–84.

38. For a new, illuminating study of the evolution of Qing frontier policy into Qing foreign policy by the end of the period under study, see Matthew W. Mosca, *From Frontier Policy to Foreign Policy: The Question of India and the Transformation of Geopolitics in Qing China* (Stanford: Stanford University Press, 2013).

39. Martin Chanock, *Law, Custom, and Social Order: The Colonial Experience in Malawi and Zambia* (Portsmouth, N.H.: Heinemann, 1998), 4. See John Comaroff, "Colonialism, Culture, and the Law: A Foreword," *Law & Social Inquiry* 26, no. 2 (2001): 305–14.

40. See, e.g., Andrew Fitzmaurice, *Humanism and America: An Intellectual History of English Colonization, 1500–1625* (Cambridge: Cambridge University Press, 2003), 102–94.

41. By the first century c.e., the Roman Empire had been identified with the world, its people with the human race, its law with universal law for mankind. Those outside the *civitas* were considered barbarian and less than human. Later Christian European powers and medieval theologians adopted these discourses. See Anthony Pagden, *Lords of All the World: Ideologies of Empire in Spain, Britain and France, c. 1500–c. 1800* (New Haven: Yale University Press, 1995), 8–31; James Muldoon, *Empire and Order: The Concept of Empire, 800–1800* (New York: Palgrave MacMillan, 1999), 87; Robert A. Williams, *The American Indian in Western Legal Thought: The Discourses of Conquest* (Oxford: Oxford University Press, 1992), 15–34.

42. Reprinted in Frances G. Davenport, ed., *European Treaties Bearing on the History of the United States and Its Dependencies to 1648* (Washington, D.C.: Carnegie Institution of Washington, 1917), 12 and 23; see also 9, 22–24, and 34 for references to "the Indies."

43. See the Treaty of Tordesillas of 1494 and the bull *Inter caetera* (II) of May 4, 1493, from Pope Alexander VI (r. 1492–1503), in Davenport, *European Treaties*, 9, 27–100.

44. Pagden, *Lords*, 64, 33–35 (French colonialism), 8–9; David Armitage, *The Ideological Origins of the British Empire* (New York: Columbia University Press, 2000), 8; Fitzmaurice, *Humanism and America*, 58–101, 138–66; Brian C. Lockey, *Law and Empire in English Renaissance Literature* (Cambridge: Cambridge University Press, 2009), 80–218.

45. Henry P. Biggar, ed., *The Precursors of Jacques Cartier, 1497–1534: A Collection of Documents Relating to the Early History of the Dominion of Canada* (Ottawa: Government Printing Bureau, 1911), 8–10; Francesco Tarducci, *John and Sebastian Cabot*, trans. Henry F. Brownson (Whitefish, Mont.: Kessinger, 2007), 65–66, 320–22. Identical language was used in the letter patent of Queen Elizabeth I (r. 1558–1603) for Sir Walter Raleigh's expedition to North America in 1583.

46. *A Brief Account of the Privileges and Immunities Granted by the French King to the East-India Company, &c. of France* (London: Ambrose Isted, 1671), 4; Glenn J. Ames, *The Globe Encompassed: The Age of European Discovery, 1500–1700* (Upper Saddle River, N.J.: Pearson Prentice Hall, 2008), 102–3 (for the Dutch East India Company charter); John Shaw, *Charters Relating to the East India Company from 1600 to 1761* (Madras: R. Hill, 1887), 7–15 (for the 1600 English East India Company charter); Charles H. Alexandrowicz, *An Introduction to the History of the Law of Nations in the East Indies (16th, 17th and 18th Centuries)* (Oxford: Clarendon Press, 1967), 27, 36–37.

47. Pagden, *Lords*, 24; Armitage, *Ideological Origins*, 66–76; Fitzmaurice, *Humanism and America*, 139–46. Theologian Juan Ginés de Sepúlveda (1489–1573) defended Spanish colonialism by claiming the Amerindians as barbarians and natural slaves as defined by Aristotle in Book I of *Politics* (Williams, *American Indian*, 82–93).

48. Franciscus de Victoria (Vitoria), *De Indis et de ivre Belli Relectiones, Being Parts of Relectiones Theologicae XII*, trans. John Pawley Bate (Washington, D.C.: Carnegie Institution of Washington, 1917), 156–62; see also 15–55 and 187 ("natural society and fellowship"), 79–100 (preaching); cf. 120–39 (refuting universal papal jurisdiction). This influential treatise, published in 1557, was based on his lectures in 1532 and remains a canonic text. Also see Williams, *American Indian*, 82–93, 41–52.

49. Hugo Grotius, *The Free Sea; or, A Disputation Concerning the Right Which the Hollanders Ought to Have to the Indian Merchandise for Trading* (1609), ed. David Armitage (Indianapolis: Liberty Fund, 2004), 10–39, 43, 51–60. See Hugo Grotius, *Commentary on the Law of Prize and Booty* (ca. 1604), trans. Gwladys Williams, ed. Martine Julia van Ittersum (Indianapolis: Liberty Fund, 2005), 89–189 (on just war), 426–28 (on injuries), 27 (on limits of such freedoms); Hugo Grotius, *The Rights of War and Peace* (1625), ed. Richard Tuck (Indianapolis: Liberty Fund, 2005). The manuscript of *Commentary*, showing Grotius as author of *The Free Sea*, was found in 1864 and published in 1868.

50. Richard Tuck, *The Rights of War and Peace: Political Thought and the International Order from Grotius to Kant* (Oxford: Oxford University Press, 1999), 103, also 78–108.

51. Armitage, *Ideological Origins*, 91–124; Williams, *American Indian*, 13–192, 218–21; Pagden, *Lords*, 29–103.

52. Pagden, *Lords*, 2, 10. See Stoler and Cooper, *Tensions of Empire*.

53. Pagden, *Lords*, 156–77; Fitzmaurice, *Humanism and America*, 136; Kathleen Wilson, *The Island Race: Englishness, Empire, and Gender in the Eighteenth Century* (London: Routledge, 2002), 49–53. The term "international law" was reportedly coined by Jeremy Bentham in the 1780s, but the term "the law of nations" remained in use well into the nineteenth century.

54. For the shifting theories of law and empire, see Antony Anghie, *Imperialism, Sovereignty, and the Making of International Law* (Cambridge: Cambridge University Press, 2004), 13–31 (on the sixteenth century), 34–114 (on the nineteenth century); Fitzmaurice, *Humanism and America*, 137–66. For sovereignty doctrines, see Ken MacMillan, *Sovereignty and Possession in the English New World: The Legal Foundations of Empire, 1576–1640* (Cambridge: Cambridge University Press, 2009).

55. Armitage, *Ideological Origins*, 125 (quotations), 8–9, 143–47. For the growing intellectual support of empire by the 1830s, see Jennifer A. Pitts, *A Turn to Empire: The Rise of Imperial Liberalism in Britain and France* (Princeton: Princeton University Press, 2005).

56. James Epstein, *Scandal of Colonial Rule: Power and Subversion in the British Atlantic during the Age of Revolution* (New York: Cambridge University Press, 2012) (about the Trinidad scandal); Rande W. Kostal, *A Jurisprudence of Power: Victorian Empire and the Rule of Law* (Oxford: Oxford University Press, 2008), 460–88 (about the trial concerning colonial brutalities in Jamaica).

57. Williams, *American Indian*, 218–21.

58. Stoler and Cooper, "Between Metropole and Colony," 2–3; Wilson, *Island Race*, 29–48.

59. Kathleen Wilson, "Introduction," in *A New Imperial History: Culture, Identity and Modernity in Britain and the Empire, 1660–1840*, ed. Kathleen Wilson (Cambridge: Cambridge University Press, 2004), 2.

60. See, e.g., Stoler and Cooper, "Between Metropole and Colony," 3–4, 7.

61. Donald Ferguson, *Letters from Portuguese Captives in Canton, Written in 1534 and 1536* (Bombay: Education Society, 1902), 1–2. Marco Polo's *Travels* was published in Portuguese in 1502. See Charles R. Boxer, *The Christian Century in Japan: 1549–1650* (Berkeley: University of California Press, 1951), 4–5.

62. *Archivio storico italiano: Appendice* (Florence: G.P. Vieusseux, 1846), 3:85–87 (account by Giovanni de Empoli in 1515); Ferguson, *Letters*, 2, 5, 7. On Chinese whiteness, see Tomé Pires, *The Suma Oriental of Tomé Pires: An Account of the*

East, from the Red Sea to Japan . . . in 1512–1515 (1944), ed. Armando Cortesão, 2 vols. (Burlington, Vt.: Ashgate, 2010), 1:116–17.

63. For the Iberian proposals to invade China from the 1520s to the 1580s, see, e.g., Ferguson, *Letters*, 115–66; Jin Guoping, ed., *Xifang Aomen shiliao xuancui* (*Selected Western Historical Sources on Macao*) (Guangzhou: Guangdong renmin chubanshe, 2005) (*XFAMS*), 93–120, 258–70 (1569–1587); "Copia de carta del P. Martín de Rada al Virrey de México, dándole importantes noticias sobre Filipinas," Cebú, July 8, 1569, Archivo General de Indias (Seville) (AGI), Audiencia de Filipinas, 79, 2 folios; "Declaración de Urdaneta de 1566," AGI, Patronato, 49, R.12; Francisco Cabral to Philip II, June 25, 1584, AGI, Patronato, 25/21, Doc. 11 (*XFAMS*, 259–63); Alonso Sánchez, "De la entrada de la China en particular," AGI, Patronato, 24/66. For more about the last proposal and about the British attempts in 1802 and 1808, see chapter 2.

64. *XFAMS*, 234, 239–41, 255–57; George B. Souza, *The Survival of Empire: Portuguese Trade and Society in China and the South China Sea, 1630–1754* (Cambridge: Cambridge University Press, 2004), 16–17. See T'ien-tse Chang, *Sino-Portuguese Trade from 1514–1644* (1934; repr., New York: AMS Press, 1973), 97 (on the population); Andrew Ljungstedt, *An Historical Sketch of the Portuguese Settlements in China* (London: Munroe, 1836), 78–79.

65. *XFAMS*, 254. On Chinese exercises of sovereignty, see *MQSQA*, 1:217 (1746), 3:1–562; *AMJLJZ*, 68–95; *PTYDP*, 637–770. See Jin Guoping, *Zhongpu guanxi shidi kaozheng* (*An Evidentiary Study of the Historical Geography in Sino-Portuguese Relations*) (Macao: Aomen jijinhui, 2000), 100–15 (refuting Portuguese claims of legal title based on conquest or a Ming "gift"). The Spanish knew that Macao was "lent" to the Portuguese (see Emma H. Blair and James A. Robertson, eds., *The Philippine Islands, 1493–1898*, 55 vols. [Cleveland: Arthur H. Clark Co., 1903–1909], 6:303 [Santiago de Vera to Philip II in 1586]).

66. See "Historical Landmarks of Macao," *Chinese Recorder and Missionary Journal* 18, no. 7 (1887): 264–70; John E. Wills Jr., "Maritime Europe and the Ming," in *China and Maritime Europe, 1500–1800: Trade, Settlement, Diplomacy, and Missions*, ed. John E. Wills Jr. (Cambridge: Cambridge University Press, 2011), 67–75.

67. See the memorials by Censor Pang Shangpeng in 1564, Governor-General Wu Guifang in 1572, and Governor-General Zhang Minggang in 1614, in *MQSQA*, 1:7; see also 5:77–78, 41–45 (1629–1632).

68. *MQSQA*, 5:92–93 (1569), 72–73, 8–9, 1:12–14; *MQHQH*, 1:5, 10. About *huairou*, see Zhu Kejing, comp. *Rouyuan xinshu* (*A New Book on Cherishing Men from Afar*), 4 *juan* (Changsha, 1881), 1:1–11. For Ming and Qing invocations of this doctrine, see *MQSQA*, 5:46 (1632), 26–30 (1653), 1:171. For a recent study, see Hevia, *Cherishing Men*, 7–28.

69. For the regulations, see Antonio Bocarro, ed., *Decada 13 da historia da India*, 2 vols. (Lisbon: Academia das Ciências de Lisboa, 1876), 2:728–37; Jin, *Zhongpu*

guanxi, 71–81 (1613); *AMJLJZ*, 22; Dai Yixuan, *Mingshi Folangji zhuan jianzheng* (*Corrections for the Section on Portugal in the Ming History*) (Beijing: Shehui kexueyuan chubanshe, 1984), 156. For later Ming regulations, see *MQSQA*, 1:11–13, 16–20 (1634), 5:77–78.

70. Four stations were set up, in Guangdong, Fujian, Zhejiang, and Jiangsu, to regulate the maritime trade. See *Qinggong Guangzhou shisanhang dang'an jingxuan* (*Selected Imperial Records of the Thirteen Hongs of Guangzhou*), comp. Zhongguo Diyi Lishi Dang'anguan (Guangzhou: Guangdong jingji chubanshe, 2002), 36–40; *MQSQA*, 6:684. For Tong Yangjia's 1647 proposal to allow the Portuguese to trade again, see *MQSQA*, 1:22–24, 119.

71. Quoted in 1806 by Yu Zhengxie, in *AMJLJZ*, 250. See *MQSQA*, 6:688–92.

72. *MQSQA*, 6:117, 105, 1:144–46; *MQHQH*, 1:44–45, 81 (1736), 168; *Qinggong Guangzhou shisanhang*, 83–84.

73. John L. Cranmer-Byng and John E. Wills Jr., "Trade and Diplomacy with Maritime Europe, 1644–c. 1800," in Wills, *China and Maritime Europe*, 199, 228, 252; see also 184–222 (on early Qing trade).

74. *MQSQA*, 1:295–340 (1749, 1755–1758); *MQHQH*, 1:101–9, 1:10 (mapping out the tollhouses and forts).

75. For all such discussion, see chapters 1, 2, and 5.

76. See, e.g., *PTYDP*, esp. 320–62.

77. See Peter J. Marshall, "Introduction," in *The Oxford History of the British Empire: The Eighteenth Century* (Oxford: Oxford University Press, 2009), 2:25.

78. "Free Trade with China," *Chinese Repository* 2, no. 8 (1833): 362; George Thomas Staunton, *Miscellaneous Notices Relating to China, and Our Commercial Intercourse with That Country* [Part 2] (London, 1828), 171 (for "extremely precarious") (testifying in the House of Lords in 1813); *Corrected Report of the Speeches of Sir George Staunton on the China Trade, in the House of Commons, June 4, and June 13, 1833; with an Appendix by George Thomas Staunton* (London: Edmund Lloyd, 1833), 6, 23 ("precarious"), 48 (also quoting a 1831 petition from forty one Britons in China).

79. Palmerston to Rear Admiral George Elliot and Captain Charles Elliot, February 3, 1841, IOR/L/PS/9:47, 69.

80. Samuel P. Huntington, *The Clash of Civilizations and the Remaking of World Order* (New York: Simon & Schuster, 1997).

1. IMPERIAL ARCHIVES AND HISTORIOGRAPHY OF WESTERN EXTRATERRITORIALITY IN CHINA

1. For European ships there in 1783–1787, see Robert B. Forbes, *Remarks on China and the China Trade* (Boston: S.N. Dickinson, 1844), 18–19; IOR/G/12/79:116. For Chinese exports, see "China Goods," *India Gazette*, January 17, 1785;

IOR/G/12/27 (1728). On the importance of the China trade, see Anthony Wild, *The East India Company: Trade and Conquest from 1600* (London: HarperCollins, 2000), 11.

2. See Samuel Shaw's "Letter to John Jay," May 19, 1785, in John Jay, *The Correspondence and Public Papers of John Jay, 1782–1793*, ed. Henry P. Johnston (New York: G. P. Putnam's Sons, 1891), 3:147.

3. In the *Neptune* case of 1807, the British did not turn the suspects over to the Chinese. See discussions below. For the skirmish during the first British expedition to China led by Captain John Weddell in 1637, see Sir Richard Carnac Temple, ed., *The Travels of Peter Mundy in Europe and Asia, 1608–1667*, vol. 3, part 2 (London: Hakluyt Society, 1919).

4. E.g., Earl H. Pritchard, "The Origin of Extraterritoriality in China," *Northwest Science* 4, no. 4 (1930): 108–14; also see the last section of this chapter.

5. Jonathan D. Spence, *The Search for Modern China*, 2nd ed. (New York: Norton, 1999), 126–27 (noting the *Emily* case as the American counterpart event); R. Randle Edwards, "Ch'ing Legal Jurisdiction Over Foreigners," in *Essays on China's Legal Tradition*, ed. Jerome A. Cohen et al. (Princeton: Princeton University Press, 1980), 238.

6. Foreign extraterritoriality continued in China even after Turkey, Persia, Siam, and Egypt had abolished it. For this and the quotation, see Ching-Chun Wang, "China Still Waits the End of Extraterritoriality," *Foreign Affairs* 15, no. 4 (July 1937): 747; also see 745. For debates on extraterritoriality, see Shihshun Liu, *Extraterritoriality: Its Rise and Decline* (New York: Columbia University Press, 1925); Edmund S. K. Fung, "The Chinese Nationalists and the Unequal Treaties 1924–1931," *Modern Asian Studies* 21, no. 4 (1987): 793–819. For more recent studies about its post-1842 operation or later abolition, see Eileen P. Scully, *Bargaining with the State from Afar: American Citizenship in Treaty Port China, 1844–1942* (New York: Columbia University Press, 2001); Turan Kayaoğlu, *Legal Imperialism: Sovereignty and Extraterritoriality in Japan, the Ottoman Empire, and China* (Cambridge: Cambridge University Press, 2010), 149–90; Pär Cassel, *Grounds of Judgment: Extraterritoriality and Imperial Power in Nineteenth-Century China and Japan* (Oxford: Oxford University Press, 2012). On the British and American efforts to induce Chinese reforms in exchange for the abolition of extraterritoriality, see *HCT*, 1:171 (1902), 575 (1903).

7. See discussion below and in the last section of the chapter.

8. The EIC officials' *Narrative*, abbreviated in Hosea Ballou Morse, *The Chronicles of the East India Company Trading to China, 1635–1834*, 5 vols. (Oxford: Clarendon Press, 1926–1929) (hereafter cited as *CBEIC*), has been the main primary source for subsequent commentators and modern scholars including Randle Edwards. But Morse never went back to revise his earlier and influential books on Qing foreign relations. Many of my sources for the *Lady Hughes* case and

other Sino-Western disputes have seldom or never been used by prior scholars, including some Chinese, English, and French accounts.

9. For the quoted words, see Premesh Lalu, "The Grammar of Domination and the Subjection of Agency," *History and Theory* 39, no. 4 (2000): 48.

10. Ann Laura Stoler, *Along the Archival Grain: Epistemic Anxieties and Colonial Common Sense* (Princeton: Princeton University Press, 2009), 1–102 (for the method); Nickolas Dirks, *Castes of Mind: Colonialism and the Making of Modern India* (Princeton: Princeton University Press, 2001); Premesh Lalu, *The Deaths of Hintsa: Postapartheid South Africa and the Shape of Recurring Pasts* (Cape Town: HSRC Press, 2009).

11. IOR/G/12/79:118 (December 9, 1784). For another two identical copies, see IOR R/10/14:90–107, and "A Particular Account of the Unfortunate Accident Which Happened at Whampoa 24th Nov. 1784," in IOR/G/12/18:49–83 (ff. 25–42). The EIC managed its affairs in China by a council of twelve supercargoes after 1775 and by the Select Committee from 1786. See *CBEIC*, 1:viii.

12. The *Narrative* was entered in the record of December 9; IOR/G/12/79:102–3, 118; IOR/R/10/14:78.

13. IOR/G/12/79:119. This British proposal was re-presented as a Chinese demand for a substitute. See Philip C. F. Smith, *The Empress of China* (Philadelphia: Philadelphia Maritime Museum, 1984), 195. Morse's assertion that this was "quite customary" was supported only by hearsay (*CBEIC*, 2:10, 72, 1:270; cf. IOR/R/10/3:276–79).

14. Charles Macfarlane, *A History of British India from the Earliest English Intercourse to the Present Time* (London: Routledge, 1853), 7; Edward Balfour, *The Cyclopædia of India and of Eastern and Southern Asia*, 3 vols. (London: Bernard Quaritch, 1885), 1:1018–24.

15. IOR/G/12/79:118–19. On the EIC agents' "absolute and arbitrary" power over British traders in the East, see WWC, 678 (1840); John Francis Davis, *The Chinese: A General Description of the Empire of China and Its Inhabitants*, 2 vols. (London: Charles Knight & Co., 1836), 1:47–48; Peter Auber, *China: An Outline of Its Government, Laws, and Policy* (London: Parbury, 1834), 190; IOR/G/12/79:175. For a Chinese rebuttal, see FO233/189/f1 (October 2, 1781); *CBEIC*, 2:65 (1781).

16. The council members suspected that the Chinese might seize President Pigou to get the gunner if the seizure of Smith failed to achieve that purpose. There is no conclusive proof of such intention except for hearsay. IOR/G/12/79:120 (for the council's report), 136. Cf. *MQSQA*, 1:449 (December 1, 1784).

17. IOR/G/12/79:121–22; Josiah Quincy, *The Journals of Major Samuel Shaw* (Boston: Wm. Crosby and H. P. Nichols, 1847), 187. See Jay, *Correspondence*, 147. A native of Boston, Shaw had served as an aid-de-camp to Henry Knox in the American Revolution and left Guangzhou or Canton on December 27, 1784.

18. IOR/G/12/79/:122–23; "Riot at China," *Universal Register* (renamed the *Times* after 1788), July 8, 1785; Quincy, *Journals*, 187–88; Donald Campbell, *A Journey Overland to India* (London: Cullen and Co., 1795), 174.

19. IOR/G/12/79:124 (Sun's message dated QL49/10/15).

20. Ibid., 125; Quincy, *Journals*, 188.

21. IOR/G/12/79:126; "English Mistakes Respecting China," *Evangelical Magazine and Missionary Chronicle* 13 (1835): 202.

22. Quincy, *Journals*, 188–91; IOR/G/12/79:126–27; See Jay, *Correspondence*, 147–48.

23. Quincy, *Journals*, 188–92 (Shaw noted that the French bowed out first).

24. This was in addition to roughly one million dollars of proceeds from imports by British country traders in 1785. See *CBEIC*, 2:94–95 (1784), 110–11 (1785). The currency and weight conversions are based on the conventional rates listed in *CBEIC*. For the pressure, see IOR/G/12/79:126–32.

25. IOR/G/12/79:128–29, 133. *CBEIC*, 2:103.

26. IOR/G/12/79:129–31; Quincy, *Journals*, 191–92.

27. Hoping to use the rumor, Mackintosh judged it wise to "make the appearance of having searched," so he had sent a boat downriver to the Second Bar and was just about to return to Guangzhou when Williams delivered the gunner to him; IOR/G/12/79:129–34; Quincy, *Journals*, 192. Morse's *Chronicles* omitted Mackintosh's original plan (*CBEIC*, 2:103–4). The *Neckar* sailed without customs clearance and reached Calcutta on January 12, 1785 ("Calcutta [News from the *Neckar*]," *India Gazette*, January 17, 1785).

28. Quincy, *Journals*, 192. In comparison, the council's *Narrative* further asserted that the Chinese deputy promised that care be taken to represent this case most favorably and that he had no doubt that the man would be sent back in about sixty days; IOR/G/12/79:134–36.

29. Ibid., 136, 118.

30. Ibid., 153–56; Auber, *China*, 187.

31. IOR/G/12/79:169 (January 1785); *CBEIC*, 2:105, 1:102.

32. Sir William Blackstone, *Commentaries on the Laws of England*, 13th ed., 4 vols. (London: Cadell and Davies, 1800), 4:198; also see 26, 181–82, 200. See Frank J. McLynn, *Crime and Punishment in Eighteenth-Century England* (New York: Routledge, 1989), 38–39. Cf. William C. Jones, trans., *The Great Qing Code* (New York: Oxford University Press, 1994), 268–310; Tian Tao and Zheng Qin, eds., *Da Qing lüli* (*The Great Qing Code*) (1740) (Beijing: Falü chubanshe, 1998), 420–46.

33. See Tian and Zheng, *Da Qing lüli*, 433; Ernest Alabaster, "Illustrations of Chinese Criminal Practices," *China Review* 25, no. 2 (1900): 93; Jennifer M. Neighbors, "Criminal Intent and Homicide Law in Qing and Republican China" (Ph.D. diss., University of California, Los Angeles, 2004), 29–33. On judicial practices, see Zhu Qingqi et al., eds., *Xing'an huilan sanbian* (*Conspectus of Legal Cases in Three Installments*) (1886) (Beijing: Beijing guji chubanshe, 2003), 1144–50.

34. *QLCSYD*, 1:128 (1736); Davis, *The Chinese*, 1:45 (1670). British bribery undermined its enforcement. See *CBEIC*, 1:259–60 (1737), 14, 297 (1754); JJCLFZZ, 03-156-7613-54 (QL2/3/19).

35. IOR/G/12/79:102, 118, also 116; *CBEIC*, 2:94–97; Paul A. Van Dyke, *The Canton Trade: Life and Enterprise on the China Coast, 1700–1845* (Hong Kong: Hong Kong University Press, 2006), 14, 29–30.

36. See Leon Radzinowicz, *The Movement for Reform, 1750–1833* (London: Stevens & Sons, 1948), 631, 49–79; McLynn, *Crime and Punishment*, 38. On Qing law, see Tian and Zheng, *Da Qing lüli*, 437.

37. See *CBEIC*, 1:82 (1689), 168 (1721), 175 (1722), 231 (1735), 236 (1735), 253 (1736), 270 (1739), 5:14 (1754), 2:59 (1780), 72 (1784), 334 (1800), 3:40 (1807), 318 (1817), 4:18 (1821), 232 (1830); Edwards, "Ch'ing Legal Jurisdiction," 233–43. The British called most cases accidental and claimed self-defense in two cases (1780, 1807).

38. IOR/G/12/21:41–43 (1722). For the 1736 cases, see *CBEIC*, 1:253; cf. *MQHQH*, 60–61; *CBEIC*, 1:235–36. For the 1800 case, see IOR/G/12/128:30–240 and chapter 2.

39. IOR/R/10/3:223 (August 28, 1754).

40. These killers could be punished by exile to 3,000 Chinese miles away plus one hundred strokes with the heavy bamboo; see Zhu et al., *Xing'an huilan sanbian*, 1180–82; Tian and Zheng, *Da Qing lüli*, 437 and 433 (on the statutes).

41. In two other cases involving British casualties in affrays, the Chinese suspects were also accused of murder and executed by the Chinese officials under foreign pressure. See IOR/R/10/21:25 (July 28, 1785) (the Chinese was strangled six weeks later); *CBEIC*, 2:148 (1787), 289 (1796) (a local stall keeper executed after a trial attended by Europeans).

42. See, e.g., *PTYDP*, 331 (1790), 333 (1792), 339 (1805).

43. Jack P. Greene, "Empire and Identity from the Glorious Revolution to the American Revolution," in *The Oxford History of the British Empire: The Eighteenth Century*, ed. Peter J. Marshall (Oxford: Oxford University Press, 2009), 2:208–11, 216–17, 222–30.

44. CRTC, 318 (Palmerston to Elliot, March 23, 1839), 258, 325. Also see *CBEIC*, 3:40 (1806).

45. Donald Ferguson, *Letters from Portuguese Captives in Canton, Written in 1534 and 1536* (Bombay: Education Society, 1902), 138, 20, 53–55, 122–23; Tomé Pires, *The Suma Oriental of Tomé Pires: An Account of the East, from the Red Sea to Japan . . . in 1512–1515*, ed. Armando Cortesão, 2 vols. (Burlington, Vt.: Ashgate, 2010), 1:199–21. Cf. *XFAMS*, 42–44.

46. Besides refusing to restore the recently colonized Malacca, a tributary state of Ming China, the Portuguese had also forced their way to the city of Guangzhou, fired cannons (in salute), built a fort and executed someone on Chinese soil, kidnapped or smuggled out Chinese children, and refused to pay tariffs.

See Ferguson, *Letters*, 8–31, 104–18; *XFAMS*, 78–106, 144–56, 187–88; *MQSQA*, 5:99–101; T'ien-tse Chang, "Malacca and the Failure of the First Portuguese Embassy to Peking," *Journal of Southeast Asian History* 3, no. 2 (1962): 50–53. Also see Armando Cortesão, *Primeira embaixada europeia à China* (*Ouzhou diyige fuhua shijie*) (Macao: Instituto Cultural de Macau, 1990), 132–58.

47. Reprinted in Anthony Farrington, ed., *The English Factory in Japan, 1613–1623*, 2 vols. (London: British Library, 1991), 1:83–85; spelling modernized.

48. Elizabeth had tried to communicate with the Chinese court in 1596 and 1602. *CBEIC*, 1:194.

49. "Contract for Settling an English Factory at Taiwan (10 September 1670)," in Hsiu-jung Chang and Anthony Farrington, eds., *The English Factory in Taiwan, 1670–1685* (Taipei: National Taiwan University, 1995), 56–57. See Davis, *The Chinese*, 1:45.

50. IOR/G/12/28:9 (June 1729); Auber, *China*, 153–54; *CBEIC*, 1:60–84; Edwards, "Ch'ing Legal Jurisdiction," 235 (calling this alleged agreement on extraterritoriality "ineffective").

51. IOR/G/12/22:41 (1721), 43–44. The offender was David Griffiths. See Captain George Shelvocke, *Voyage Round the World by Way of the Great South Sea* [1719–1722] (London: J. Senex, 1726), 11:445–54 (calling this shooting an "accident," though it was likely a capital felony under English law); "Seamen in the Port of Canton," *Chinese Repository* 2, no. 9 (1834): 423. For English law on this kind of homicide as a murder, see Sir Matthew Hales, *Pleas of the Crown, in Two Parts* (London: Giles Jacob, 1716), 1:45–46.

52. IOR/G/12/72:20 (1780).

53. See *CBEIC*, 2:86 (1783).

54. For their shared sentiments in the 1754 Lord Anson case, see IOR/R/10/3:297–98, 272. Also see IOR/G/12/72:18–20 (1781); *PTYDP*, 410 (1792), 411 (1793); *CBEIC*, 2:60 (1780); *MQSQA*, 1:253–54 (1750), 369 (1763); Paul A. Van Dyke, trans., and Cynthia Vialle, rev., *The Canton-Macao Dagregisters, 1762* (Macao: Instituto Cultural do Governoro da R.A.E. de Macao, 2006), 75–84; *Gongzhongdang Qianlongchao zouzhe* (*Secret Palace Memorials of the Qianlong Period*), 75 vols. (Taipei: National Palace Museum Press, 1982–1988), 9:762–64 (1754).

55. IOR/R/10/3:297–98, 272.

56. IOR/G/12/72:17–21 (1781) (for the quotations). The London courts often disclaimed jurisdiction, and the only few recorded trials there involved Britons killed by Britons, or Chinese killed by Chinese on British ships.

57. Lauren Benton, "Colonial Law and Cultural Difference: Jurisdictional Politics and the Formation of the Colonial State," *Comparative Studies in Society and History* 41, no. 3 (2000): 563–88; Lauren Benton, *Law and Colonial Cultures: Legal Regimes in World History, 1400–1900* (Cambridge: Cambridge University Press, 2002).

58. See "First [Official] Edict Concerning the European Trade at Canton," issued in 1755 by the governor-general of Liangguang and the commissioner of foreign trade, in *CBEIC*, 5:37, 1:40, 29.

59. IOR/G/12/79:125; Quincy, *Journals*, 188.

60. "English Mistakes," 201.

61. Chrétien-Louis-Joseph de Guignes, "Détail d'une affaire survenue entre les Européens et les Chinois, en 1784, à l'occasion de deux hommes tués à Wampou par un coup de canon" (Details of a Case Arising between Europeans and Chinese, in 1784, on the Occasion of Two Men Killed at Huangpu by a Cannon), in *Voyages à Peking, Manille et l'île de France faits dans l'intervalle des années 1784 à 1801* (Paris: Imprimerie imperiale, 1808), 292–93. Concerning de Guignes, see Henri Cordier, "Le consulat de France à Canton au XVIII siècle," *T'oung Pao* 9, no. 1 (1908): 92–94.

62. For English law, see Hales, *Pleas*, 1:32; Blackstone, *Commentaries*, 4:199–201.

63. Robert B. Forbes, *Personal Reminiscences*, rev. ed. (Boston: Little, Brown, 1882), 375.

64. Davis, *The Chinese*, 1:66.

65. Blackstone, *Commentaries*, 4:28–30, 33–39. See *Regina v. Howe*, 1 A.C. 417 (1987), 417–59, http://www.bailii.org/uk/cases/UKHL/1986/4.html. Under Qing law, the officer (as the abettor, or *zaoyi*) would be the principal in a case of murder or intentional killing (both punishable by decapitation) but would be an accessory in a killing in an affray and thus punishable by exile to 3,000 *li* away. See Tian and Zheng, *Da Qing lüli*, 420, 430–31, 320.

66. "English Mistakes," 202; de Guignes, "Détail d'une affaire," 292. Cf. *QGYGA*, 2829 (recording the prisoner as thirty-five years old).

67. "Calcutta" (on the *Lady Hughes* case), *India Gazette*, February 7, 1785; "Extract of a Letter from China, Dec. 6," *India Gazette*, January 31, 1785.

68. Ann Laura Stoler, "'In Cold Blood': Hierarchies of Credibility and the Politics of Colonial Narratives," *Representations* 37 (1992): 154.

69. "English Mistakes," 248, 247 (on the execution). See reports about this case in the *India Gazette*, April 25, 1785, and January 3, 1785.

70. The three memorials were delivered together; JJCLFZZ, 03-7820-003 (Muteng'e's memorial, dated QL49/10/19) (reprinted in *MQSQA*, 1:447); 03-7820-002 (Sun's memorials, QL49/10/19). Also see *MQSQA*, 1:451–52 (Qianlong's reply, QL49/11/11, or December 22, 1784) (reprinted in *QLCSYD*, 12:361) (this published edict is Randle Edwards's only Chinese document directly related to this case in his 1980 essay). About Qianlong's activities that day, see *Qianlongchao junjichu suishou dengjidang (Register of the Grand Council in the Qianlong Reign)*, comp. Zhongguo Diyi Lishi Dang'anguan, 46 vols. (Guilin: Guangxi shifan daxue chubanshe, 2000), 36:748.

71. JJCLFZZ, 03-7820-002 (Sun's memorial, QL49/10/19, rescripted QL49/11/11). This document is still classified as concerning sensitive issues of foreign relations

and the archivists in Beijing made an exception in allowing me to take note of a temporary copy of the original in the summer of 2013. I am thankful for their help. Some of the resulting new details shall be taken here as an update of my earlier article about this case.

72. Muteng'e glossed over the local officials' negligence in enforcing the ban on foreign firearms at Huangpu when he noted that the foreign custom of saluting each other's arrival or departure had long been tolerated at Guangzhou; JJCLFZZ, 03-7820-003; *MQSQA*, 1:447.

73. *MQSQA*, 1:199, 461.

74. JJCLFZZ, 03-7820-002. See *MQSQA*, 1:451, 459–61; *QGYGA*, 2825–29. For Qianlong's recent pardon of a missionary, see *MQSQA*, 1:445–46 (December 1, 1784).

75. See QGJJD, 037721 (December 17, 1785) (Sun Shiyi's census); Ezra C. Seaman, *Essays on the Progress of Nations in Civilization, Productive Industry, Wealth and Population* (New York: Charles Scribner, 1868), 559–63 (British population). For challenges facing local officials, see Wang Zhi, *Chongyatang gao* (*Drafts from the Chongya Hall*), 8 vols. (1759), 4:32–40 (1734).

76. See, e.g., Peter J. Marshall, *The Making and Unmaking of Empires: Britain, India, and America, c. 1750–1783* (Oxford: Oxford University Press, 2005); Nicholas Dirks, *The Scandal of Empire: India and the Creation of Imperial Britain* (Cambridge, Mass.: Harvard University Press, 2008), 206, 215. For the empire's impact on ordinary Britons, see, e.g., Kathleen Wilson, *The Sense of the People: Politics, Culture, and Imperialism in England, 1715–1785* (Cambridge: Cambridge University Press, 1995).

77. See, e.g., JJCLFZZ, 03-7604-01 to 03-7604-27 (JQ13–14); *MQSQA*, 6:95–96; *CBEIC*, 2:370–72 (1802); FO233/189:93–98 (1802).

78. IOR/G/12/79:127, 136.

79. "Riot at China"; Jay, *Correspondence*, 147; Quincy, *Journals*, 186.

80. Liangguang governor-general Ruan Yuan had varying degrees of success in handling four legal cases in 1818–1821, including the *Emily* case. Also see Betty Peh-t'i Wei, *Ruan Yuan, 1764–1849: The Life and Work of a Major Scholar-Official* (Hong Kong: Hong Kong University Press, 2006), 149–61.

81. See, e.g., the *Providence* case in 1800 and the *Neptune* case in 1807, discussed in chapter 2.

82. For some of the legal disputes and the foreigners' tactics in resisting Chinese jurisdiction or punishments, see, e.g., FO233/189/ff. 114–33 (1810), 177–93 (1807–1808); *PTYDP*, 714–30; *COT*, 1:55–57 (1768), 73–77 (1773), 247–52 (1789), 492–506 (1793), 4:52, 69–77 (1807); Van Dyke and Vialle, *Canton-Macao Dagregisters, 1762*, 75–84.

83. For the secret memorial system, see Zhuang Jifa, *Qingdai zouzhe zhidu* (*The Qing Palace Memorial System*) (Taipei: Gugong bowuyuan, 1979); Silas H. L. Wu, *Communication and Imperial Control in China: Evolution of the Palace*

Memorial System, 1693–1735 (Cambridge, Mass.: Harvard University Press, 1970).

84. See, e.g., Peter C. Perdue, *China Marches West: The Qing Conquest of Central Eurasia* (Cambridge, Mass.: Harvard University Press, 2010); Mark C. Elliot, *The Manchu Way: The Eight Banners and Ethnic Identity in Late Imperial China* (Stanford: Stanford University Press, 2001).

85. Philip A. Kuhn, *Soulstealers: The Chinese Sorcery Scare of 1768* (Cambridge, Mass.: Harvard University Press, 1990), 187–222.

86. *MQSQA*, 1:198–99.

87. *AMJLJZ*, 89–91; *MQSQA*, 1:198–99. For later application, see *MQSQA*, 1:383 (1766), 390–93 (1768–1769), 400 (1773), 505–8 (1790–1792). For domestic cases of *xianxing zhengfa* (immediate execution), see *Gongzhongdang Qianlongchao zouzhe*, 57:767, 851 (1783), 60:60, 80 (1794).

88. *MQSQA*, 1:241 (November 23, 1748), 238–48. See QGJJD, 003341 (October 21, 1748), 004080 (March 20), 004073 (March 18), 002406 (June 13), 004772 (August 30, 1749), 005156 (January 26, 1750). Cf. Andrew Ljungstedt, *An Historical Sketch of the Portuguese Settlements in China* (London: J. Munroe, 1836), 105–7.

89. *Qing shilu: Gaozong shilu* (*Veritable Records of the Qing Dynasty: The Qianlong Period*), 60 vols. (Beijing: Zhonghua shuju, 1986), 13:620, 13:708–9; Lo-shu Fu, *A Documentary Chronicle of Sino-Western Relations (1644–1820)*, 2 vols. (Tucson: University of Arizona Press, 1966), 1:187 (translation modified). See Edwards, "Ch'ing Legal Jurisdiction," 255–59 (for punishment of Chinese offenders).

90. These regulations were engraved in Chinese and Portuguese on stone tablets in Macao; *AMJLJZ*, 92–94. Pär Cassel was probably misled by Fu's translation to read the 1744 substatute as suggesting that "the defendant be tried together by Qing and Portuguese officials and executed under 'joint supervision,' if found guilty" (Cassel, *Grounds of Judgment*, 41). The 1744 substatute itself did not give foreign officials a right to a joint trial, and it permitted the foreign representatives to witness or assist the execution.

91. Cassel seems to suggest that foreign extraterritoriality was an extension of Qing "legal pluralism," and that the Europeans had obtained de facto extraterritoriality in most legal matters except for homicide cases involving Chinese victims as early as the mid-eighteenth century, and that Qing officials generally did not object to foreign exercise of "personal jurisdiction." See, e.g., Cassel, *Grounds of Judgment*, 41–43, 161–62.

92. See the cases cited in note 82. In the Lin Weixi case of 1839, Lin Zexu repeatedly affirmed the principle that China had jurisdiction over foreigners within its territory. Even a Hong merchant made this argument explicitly to the British superintendent of trade: if Englishmen who went to France "were amenable

to the justice of that country," why should the case be "different when English-men came to China?" See Elliot to Palmerston, September 26, 1837 (received March 19, 1838), in CRTC, 231. For the Qing sense of territoriality and jurisdiction, see R. Randle Edwards, "Imperial China's Border Control Law," *Journal of Chinese Law* 1, no. 33 (1987): 33–62.

93. In this case, the Guangdong officials suggested that the French offender should be strangled for killing the English sailor according to the Qing Code. See *Gongzhongdang Qianlongchao zouzhe*, 762–64 (November 23, 1754); *Shiliao xunkan* (*Historical Documents Published Every Ten Days*), ed. Gugong Bowuyuan, 40 vols. (Taipei: Guofeng chubanshe, 1963), 12:425; *Qing shilu*, 14:1145. Cf. Fu, *Documentary Chronicle*, 1:193–94 (translation not completely accurate). See *MQSQA*, 1:198 (on the term *banli*). The Dutch proposed to send their offender back home for punishment in a homicide case of 1750 (*MQSQA*, 1:253–54).

94. Cassel, *Grounds of Judgment*, 42.

95. See, e.g., *PTYDP*, 258–778; IOR/G/12/73:94–96 (1781); *COT*, 1:73–77 (1773), 4:69–77 (1807).

96. IOR/G/12/72:18–19 (1780). See also *PTYDP*, 723–24 (1814); *COT*, 1:75–76 (1773).

97. See FO233/189:1–2 (1781); IOR/G/12/72:17–19; *PTYDP*, 726, 411, 321–62. Cf. Cassel, *Grounds of Judgment*, 40–49. At one point, Cassel did note that China "retained ultimate jurisdiction over both the territory and its inhabitants" of Macao (41).

98. See, e.g., the *Emily* case and the *Topaz* case in 1821 and the case of Lin Weixi in 1839, in chapters 4 and 5.

99. For Qing judicial leniency to foreigners, see FO233/189:1 (1781); Fu, *Documentary Chronicle*, 1:188 (1751), 196 (1755), 216–20 (1759), 275 (1775), 276–80 (1777), 279, 291 (1780), and 299 (1785).

100. *QLCSYD*, 12:254 (49/8/20), 260, 373–75, 394, 405, 415, 422; Edwards, "Ch'ing Legal Jurisdiction," 241; *MQSQA*, 1:445–46, 450–53.

101. Kuhn, *Soulstealers*, 220–22.

102. *MQSQA*, 1:452; *QLCSYD*, 12:361. On court letters reflecting the imperial mind, see Kuhn, *Soulstealers*, 124.

103. As the British often argued in cases in which local Chinese were killed by Europeans, the French officials also claimed that the accused (Frenchman) acted in self-defense or only accidentally killed the (British) victim in this case. See IOR/R/10/3:225–313, 263–65 (quotations). Cf. *Gongzhongdang Qianlongchao zouzhe*, 9:762–64 (November 23, 1754); *QGYGA*, 1265–73 (for a report with testimonies). When the Chinese made the same argument later to justify prosecuting Europeans, the British dismissed it as a false principle (IOR/G/12//72/1781:20, 18–19 [December 11, 1780]).

104. JJCLFZZ, 03-9259-054 (December 30, 1784); *MQSQA*, 1:452; *QLCSYD*, 12:361, 417, 385.

105. Kuhn, *Soulstealers*, 220–22.

106. Thomas M. Buoye, "Suddenly Murderous Intent Arose: Bureaucratization and Benevolence in Eighteenth-Century Qing Homicide Reports," *Late Imperial China* 16, no. 2 (1995): 70–75, 75.

107. *QLCSYD*, 12:361. For similar cases, see Zhu et al., *Xing'an huilan sanbian*, 3:1546–48, 1639–42; Li Zhiyun, *Cheng'an xubian erke* (*A Second Anthology of Leading Cases*) (1763).

108. JJCLFZZ, 03-7820-005 (QL49/12/18, or January 28, 1785); 03-7820-007 (for confession of the accused); *QGYGA*, 2825–29.

109. Kuhn, *Soulstealers*, 220. The earliest Sino-British legal disputes were dated in the 1680s in the EIC records.

110. IOR/R/10/14 (1784–1785):131–32.

111. Quoted in Davis, *The Chinese*, 1:62; George W. Keeton, *The Development of Extraterritoriality in China*, 2 vols. (London: Longmans, 1928), 1:39–40. See discussion below.

112. IOR/R/10/33, court letter, February 24, 1786, para. 8. See George Thomas Staunton, *Miscellaneous Notices Relating to China, and Our Commercial Intercourse with That Country* (London, 1828), 285–310 (1814).

113. Court letter, February 24, 1786, IOR/R/10/67:297. For another copy, see IOR/R/10/33, court letter, February 24, 1786, paras. 11–24.

114. IOR/R/10/67:298–300. See IOR/G/12/79:124–25 (for the original).

115. IOR/R/10/67:304–5.

116. IOR/R/10/14:121 (commenting on the consultation dated January 13, 1785).

117. IOR/R/10/67:302–6.

118. IOR/R/10/14:131 (on the consultation dated Jan 13, 1785). In case the council indeed had to turn in a murderer, the court claimed solace by citing the Bible that "Thou shalt do no murder." See IOR/R/10/67:306 (words penciled after the instructions of February 1786).

119. Sun Shiyi delivered a memorial at a rate of 400 *li* per day. See *QGYGA*, 2827. It took fifteen days to deliver at a daily traveling speed of 600 *li*. See *Gongzhongdang Qianlongchao zouzhe*, 60:718 (1786); *MQSQA*, 1:445–46. For the secret memorial system, see works cited in note 83.

120. See chapters 4 and 5 on these wars.

121. On the prohibition, see IOR/R/10/33, court letter, January 27, 1786, para. 12; de Guignes, "Détail d'une affaire," 297. On the confirmation of power, see 26 Geo. III, c. 57, sect. 35 (passed in 1787), in Auber, *China*, 190–91; Keeton, *Development of Extraterritoriality*, 1:44. Cf. IOR/G/12/79:175 (1785).

122. IOR/R/10/33, court letter, January 27, 1785, paras. 10, 11.

123. Jay, *Correspondence*, 147–49, 147 (quotation).

124. "Riot at China"; see *The New Annual Register for the Year 1785* (London, 1786), 40, 47–48.

125. See IOR/G/12/90 (1787–1789); *CBEIC*, 2:154–60; Earl H. Pritchard, *The Crucial Years of Early Anglo-Chinese Relations, 1750–1800* (New York: Routledge, 2000), 236.

126. *Three Reports of the Select Committee* [of the EIC] (London: J.S. Jordan, 1793), 94–95.

127. See, e.g., IOR/G/12/91:121–26, 233–48 (Qianlong's letter to George, October 3, 1793), 271–98 (Qianlong's answer to British requests); see also IOR/G/12/92:233–58, 271–98. For the Chinese versions, see *Yingshi Majia'erni fanghua dang'an shiliao huibian* (*Archival Records about the Macartney Embassy to China*), comp. Zhongguo Diyi Lishi Dang'an guan (Beijing: Guoji wenhua chuban gongsi, 1996), 173–73, 55–60; *MQSQA*, 1:540–42, 553–56. For more about the Macartney Embassy, see also IOR/G/12/91– IOR/G/12/93 (for the archival records); James L. Hevia, *Cherishing Men from Afar: Qing Guest Ritual and the Macartney Embassy of 1793* (Durham: Duke University Press, 1995), 184–91, 116–33 (for importance of the guest ritual); Li Chen, "Universalism and Equal Sovereignty as Contested Myths of International Law in the Sino-Western Encounter," *Journal of the History of International Law* 13, no. 1 (January 2011): 94–97.

128. *CBEIC*, 2:68 (1781), 156 (1787), 215 (1792). For the Qing court's concerns, see Liang Tingnan, *Yue haiguan zhi* (*Gazetteer of the Guangdong Customs Station*) (Taipei: Chengwen chubanshe, 1966), 571–72, 1667, 1688–89.

129. Pei-kai Cheng, Michael Lestz, and Jonathan Spence, *The Search for Modern China: A Documentary Collection* (New York: Norton, 1999), 108 (for the translation); *MQSQA*, 1:535–36 (1793) (for the Chinese original); Liang, *Yue haiguan zhi*, 1683, 1679–88. For more analysis, see Chen, "Universalism and Equal Sovereignty," 94–97.

130. Hosea B. Morse, *The International Relations of the Chinese Empire*, 3 vols. (New York: Longmans, 1910), 1:244. For later cases, see Edwards, "Ch'ing Legal Jurisdiction," 241–50.

131. Davis, *The Chinese*, 1:388, 392–94; see 1:66–68 (citing the *Lady Hughes* case).

132. [Robert Morrison], "The Law of Homicide in Operation," *Chinese Repository* 3, no. 1 (1834): 38–39 (also reprinted in Keeton, *Development of Extraterritoriality*, 2:252–53); Robert Morrison, "Thoughts on the Conduct of the Chinese Government Towards the Honourable Company's Servants at Canton" (1819), in *Memoirs of the Life and Labours of Robert Morrison*, ed. Eliza A. Morrison, 2 vols. (London: Longman, 1839), 2 (appendix): 7. On the authorship of publications in the *Chinese Repository*, see Samuel Wells Williams, *General Index of Subjects Contained in the Twenty Volumes of the Chinese Repository* (Tokyo: Maruzen Co., 1851).

133. See chapter 4 on the image of Chinese legal barbarity and chapters 2 and 3 on Staunton's translation.

134. Quoted in Davis, *The Chinese*, 1:395. See Morrison, "Thoughts," 2 (appendix): 8–9.

135. Davis, *The Chinese*, 1:388–89, 392–95 (including quotations from Robert Morrison). For anti-Chinese legislations, see, e.g., Martin B. Gold, *Forbidden Citizens: Chinese Exclusion and the U.S. Congress; A Legislative History* (Alexandria, Va.: TheCapitol.Net, 2012); also see relevant works cited in chapter 5.

136. Davis, *The Chinese*, 1:63, 390–95. See Morrison, "Thoughts," 2 (appendix): 9–10.

137. Davis, *The Chinese*, 1:392.

138. Charles H. Cameron, *An Address to Parliament on the Duties of Great Britain to India, in Respect of the Education of the Natives and Their Official Employment* (London: Longman, Brown, 1853), 4.

139. George Thomas Staunton, *Corrected Report of the Speeches of Sir George Staunton on the China Trade, in the House of Commons, June 4, and June 13, 1833; with an Appendix by George Thomas Staunton* (London: Edmund Lloyd, 1833), 25, 41–42. After his first attempt failed in June 1833, Staunton moved again in July, and his motion was passed in August 1838. His idea was then incorporated in article six of the Act of Parliament in August 1838 and the Order in Council. See FO17/4:66–75; FO17/5:52–53, and V. K. Wellington Koo, *The Status of Aliens in China* (New York: Columbia University Press, 1912), 234–39. Palmerston quoted Staunton again in 1838 in an attempt to expand this court's jurisdiction to civil matters. See *Papers Relative to the Establishment of a Court of Judicature in China, Presented to the House of Commons, 1838* (London: J. Harrison & Son, 1838); "China Courts Bill," *Canton Press*, December 15, 1838.

140. Samuel Wells Williams, *The Middle Kingdom: A Survey of the Chinese Empire and Its Inhabitants*, 2 vols. (New York: Wiley & Putnam, 1848), 2:454–59. It has gone through at least twenty-five reprints or new editions since.

141. Peter W. Fay, "The French Catholic Mission in China during the Opium War," *Modern Asian Studies* 4, no. 2 (1970): 116, 115 (on Morse's use of "culture").

142. Morse, *International Relations*, 1:117, 109–10. Morse did not use the EIC archives for his earlier works (see ibid., 101–3 [citing only Davis and Auber]). See Pritchard, *Crucial Years*, 220–30, and "Origin of Extraterritoriality," 109–13; Peter W. Fay, *The Opium War, 1840–1842* (Chapel Hill: University of North Carolina Press, 1975), 38–39. For Hsin-pao Chang, see chapter 5.

143. For the quotations, see John K. Fairbank, *China Watch* (Cambridge, Mass.: Harvard University Press, 1987), 1, 3. For critiques of the Fairbank school, see works by Paul Cohen, Barlow, Hevia, and others cited in the introduction.

144. Frederic E. Wakeman Jr., "The Canton Trade and the Opium War," in *The Cambridge History of China: Volume 10, Late Ch'ing 1800–1911, Part 1*, ed. John K. Fairbank (London: Cambridge University Press, 1992), 180, 189–90. See also Frederic E. Wakeman Jr., *Strangers at the Gate: Social Disorder in South China, 1839–1861* (Berkeley: University of California Press, 1997), 81.

145. IOR/G/12/79:118–37; Davis, *The Chinese*, 1:65. Cf. *CBEIC*, 2:99–107; Auber, *China*, 183–84 (Auber was then secretary to the Secret Committee of the Court

of Directors); Keeton, *Development of Extraterritoriality*, 1:404; Pritchard, *Crucial Years*, 226–27.

146. Derk Bodde and Clarence Morris, *Law in Imperial China* (Cambridge, Mass.: Harvard University Press, 1967), 43, 331. For likely sources of their assertion here, see M. H. van der Valk, *Interpretations of the Supreme Court at Peking, Years 1915 and 1916* (Batavia: Sinological Institute, University of Indonesia, 1949), 20–21; Sybille van der Sprenkel, *Legal Institutions of Manchu China* (London: Athlone Press, 1962), 127; Joseph Needham, *Science and Civilisation* (Cambridge: Cambridge University Press, 1965), 2:528.

147. For critiques of this traditional view, see Dao-lin Hsu, "Crime and Cosmic Order," *Harvard Journal of Asiatic Studies* 30 (1970): 111–25; Geoffrey MacCormack, "Issues of Causation in Homicide Decisions of the Qing Board of Punishments from the Eighteenth and Nineteenth Centuries," *Bulletin of the School of African and Oriental Studies* 73, no. 2 (2010): 285–310. About its continued influence, see, e.g., Spence, *Search for Modern China*, 126–27; Johanna Waley-Cohen, *The Sextants of Beijing: Global Currents in Chinese History* (New York: Norton, 1999), 101; Wei, *Ruan Yuan*, 148, 153–54. The 2013 edition of Spence's *Search for Modern China* has retained the old narrative about this case (124–25) after adding a citation to Cassel, *Grounds of Judgment*. Cassel called the case accidental homicide while citing my article (2009), which actually argues against that traditional characterization.

2. TRANSLATION OF THE QING CODE AND COLONIAL ORIGINS OF COMPARATIVE CHINESE LAW

1. Sir George Thomas Staunton, *Ta Tsing Leu Lee; Being the Fundamental Laws, and a Selection from the Supplementary Statute of the Penal Code of China* (London: Cadell and Davies, 1810) (*TTLL*).

2. John Francis Davis, *Chinese Miscellanies: A Collection of Essays and Notes* (London: John Murray, 1865), 51.

3. Norman J. Girardot, *The Victorian Translation of China: James Legge's Oriental Pilgrimage* (Berkeley: University of California Press, 2002), 15. On Davis's ambivalence, see Peter J. Kitson, *Forging Romantic China: Sino-British Cultural Exchange, 1760–1840* (Cambridge: Cambridge University Press, 2013), 106–24.

4. See Edward Said, *Culture and Imperialism* (New York: Knopf, 1993), 194–95.

5. See, e.g., Patrick Petitjean, Catherine Jami, and Anne Marie Moulin, eds., *Science and Empire: Historical Studies about Scientific Development and European Expansion* (Dordrecht: Kluwer Academic, 1992); Fa-ti Fan, *British Naturalists in Qing China: Science, Empire, and Cultural Encounter* (Cambridge, Mass.: Harvard University Press, 2004). About imperial archives, see Thomas Richards,

Imperial Archives: Knowledge and the Fantasy of Empire (New York: Verso, 1998); James L. Hevia, *The Imperial Security State: British Colonial Knowledge and Empire-Building in Asia* (Cambridge: Cambridge University Press, 2012).

6. Richard Drayton, "Knowledge and Empire," in *The Oxford History of the British Empire: The Eighteenth Century*, ed. Peter J. Marshall (Oxford: Oxford University Press, 2009), 2:234, 237–49; Richard Drayton, *Nature's Government: Science, Imperial Britain, and the "Improvement" of the World* (New Haven: Yale University Press, 2000), 237–44, 248–49; John Gascoigne, *Science in the Service of Empire: Joseph Banks, the British State and the Uses of Science in the Age of Revolution* (Cambridge: Cambridge University Press, 1998), 178–82 (on the earlier "informal structure of empire").

7. "Ta Tsing Leu Lee," *Literary Panorama* 10 (1811): 25.

8. John W. Witek, "Catholic Missions and the Expansion of Christianity, 1644–1800," in *China and Maritime Europe, 1500–1800*, ed. John E. Wills Jr. (Cambridge: Cambridge University Press, 2011), 140–62; Joanna Waley-Cohen, "China and Western Technology in the Late Eighteenth Century," *American Historical Review* 98, no. 5 (1993): 1525–44. For changes over time, see Benjamin A. Elman, *On Their Own Terms: Science in China 1550–1900* (Cambridge, Mass.: Harvard University Press, 2005).

9. Witek, "Catholic Missions," 148 (for the quotation), 155–77; David E. Mungello, ed., *The Chinese Rites Controversy* (Nettetal, Ger.: Steyler Verlag, 1994).

10. Roger Hart, *Imagined Civilizations: China, the West, and Their First Encounter* (Baltimore: Johns Hopkins University Press, 2013), 255–56, 51–75 (refuting assertions of Sino-Western incommensurability), 195–263; Witek, "Catholic Missions," 143, 155–58. For Ricci's manipulation of such ambiguities, see Willard J. Peterson, "Learning from Heaven: The Introduction of Christianity and Other Western Ideas into Late Ming China," in Wills, *China and Maritime Europe*, 91–102.

11. Peterson, "Learning from Heaven," 92.

12. John Barrow, *Travels in China* (London: Cadell and Davies, 1804), 27 (quoting Jones).

13. Tejaswini Niranjana, *Siting Translation: History, Post-Structuralism, and the Colonial Context* (Berkeley: University of California Press, 1992), 1–4; Natalie E. Rothman, *Brokering Empire: Transimperial Subjects between Venice and Istanbul* (Ithaca: Cornell University Press, 2012), 16.

14. Donald F. Lach, *Asia in the Making of Europe, Volume II: A Century of Wonder* (Chicago: University of Chicago Press, 1994), 490–543.

15. Thomas Macaulay, "Minute on Indian Education" (February 2, 1835), in Charles H. Cameron, *An Address to Parliament on the Duties of Great Britain to India, in Respect of the Education of the Natives and Their Official Employment* (London: Longman, Brown, 1853), 80, 78, 75.

16. Macaulay's speech on July 10, 1833, quoted in Eric Stokes, *The English Utilitarians and India* (New York: Oxford University Press, 1990), 45.

17. Alonso Sánchez, "De la entrada de la China en particular," in Archivo General de Indias (Seville), Patronato, 24/66; "The Proposed Entry into China, in Detail," in Emma H. Blair and James A. Robertson, eds., *The Philippine Islands, 1493–1898,* 55 vols. (Cleveland: Arthur H. Clark Co., 1903–1909), 6:197–233, esp. 218–28.

18. Manel Ollé, *La invención de China: Percepciones y estrategias Filipinas respecto a China durante el siglo xvi* (Wiesbaden: Harrassowitz, 2000), 136–59.

19. Armando Cortesão, *Primeira embaixada europeia à China (Ouzhou diyige fuhua shijie)* (Macao: Instituto Cultural de Macau, 1990), 149.

20. Jin Guoping, *Zhongpu guanxi shidi kaozheng (An Evidentiary Study of the Historical Geography in Sino-Portuguese Relations)* (Macao: Aomen jijinhui, 2000), 29–32. For early Jesuit study of Chinese, see M. Howard Rienstra, ed., *Jesuit Letters from China, 1583–84* (Minneapolis: University of Minnesota Press, 1986), 18, 22, 24; *MQSQA,* 1:88–89, 93 (1710).

21. Jin, *Zhongpu guanxi shidi kaozheng,* 184–85; John E. Wills Jr., *Embassies and Illusions: Dutch and Portuguese Envoys to K'ang-Hsi, 1666–1687* (Cambridge, Mass.: Harvard University Press, 1984), 118–22.

22. Mark C. Elliott, *The Manchu Way: The Eight Banners and Ethnic Identity in Late Imperial China* (Stanford: Stanford University Press, 2001), 290–304; Pamela Crossley and Evelyn S. Rawski, "A Profile of the Manchu Language in Ch'ing History," *Harvard Journal of Asiatic Studies* 53, no. 1 (1993): 63–102.

23. In practice, exceptions to these rules were sometimes made by individual officials. On these rules and legal obligations, see FO233/189:4–7 (1759–1761); *MQSQA,* 1:325–40; *PTYDP,* 411 (1792) (attributed the regulated steps of petition to 1744), 414 (1803/3/14) (noting that local officials would receive only the Chinese translation of foreign petitions), 724–25 (1814/12/18); FO1048/35/8 (1813–1814); FO1048/14/55 (1814). See also *CBEIC,* 1:40 and 297 (1755), 3:232 (1810) (language), 4:235 (1830). For the petitions, see *AMJLJZ,* 79; *CBEIC,* 5:77–78 (1759); Paul A. van Dyke, *The Canton Trade: Life and Enterprise on the China Coast, 1700–1845* (Hong Kong: Hong Kong University Press, 2006), 20–21; Crossley and Rawski, "A Profile of the Manchu Language," 87–90 (on missionaries' use of Manchu).

24. *PTYDP,* 724 (1814).

25. *MQSQA,* 1:337–40 (1759); *CBEIC,* 5:94–98. See FO233/189:5 (1760). About late imperial China's *huairou* policy, see Zhu Kejing, comp., *Rouyuan xinshu (A New Book on Cherishing Men from Afar),* 4 *juan* (Changsha, 1881).

26. *PTYDP,* 667, 680, also see 414 (1803), 410–13; *CBEIC,* 3:219 (1810). For an exception made by Guangdong officials in 1814 after Staunton and EIC officials bargained hard for it, see sources cited in note 57.

27. Lydia H. Liu, *The Clash of Empires: The Invention of China in Modern World Making* (Cambridge, Mass.: Harvard University Press, 2004). For the Macartney Embassy, see James L. Hevia, *Cherishing Men from Afar: Qing Guest Ritual and the Macartney Embassy of 1793* (Durham: Duke University Press, 1995). For the Amherst Embassy, see George Thomas Staunton, *Notes of Proceedings and Occurrences during the British Embassy to Pekin, in 1816* (London: Havant Press, 1824); Robert Morrison, *A Memoir of the Principle Occurrences during an Embassy from the British Government to the Court of China in the Year 1816* (London: Hatchard & Son., 1820).

28. See item 5 of the Sino-British agreement (*shanding shiyi*), August 15, 1842 (DG22/7/10), FO682/1975/65. For similar stipulations on the language policy in Sino-Western diplomatic correspondence, see also Article 11 of the Treaty of Nanjing and Article 50 of the Treaty of Tianjin, in *HCT*, 1:11, 33.

29. On Flint's training beginning in 1736 and subsequent services, see *CBEIC*, 1:276–305, 5:12, 49–80; Charles F. Noble, *A Voyage to the East Indies in 1747 and 1748* (London, 1765), 119–22, 262, 306.

30. JJCLFZZ, 04-01-12-0088-025 (QL22/12/26), 03-01-04-15128-07 (QL23/12/23), 03-1293-040 (QL24/8/19); FO233/189:6–7, 14–16; *MQSQA*, 1:337 (on prohibition), 319 (1759). The Qing court did punish the accused customs superintendent, Li Yongbiao.

31. Bevan arrived to study Chinese in 1753. See Susan Reed Stifler, "The Language Students of the East India Company's Canton Factory," *Journal of the North China Branch of the Royal Asiatic Society* 69 (1938): 48–51; *CBEIC*, 1:296.

32. Sir George Leonard Staunton, *An Authentic Account of an Embassy from the King of Great Britain to the Emperor of China*, 3 vols. (London: G. Nicol, 1797), 2:136–43, 1:38, 50; Barrow, *Travels*, 5–6 (quoting a French missionary's opinions); Stifler, "Language Students," 51–54; cf. *CBEIC*, 2:209. For the translation issue of the Macartney Embassy, see Wang Hongzhi, "Majia'erni shihua de fanyi wenti (The Problem of Translation of the Macartney Embassy to China)," *Zhongyang yanjiuyuan jindaishi yanjiusuo jikan* 63 (2009): 97–145. Johann Christian Hüttner (1766–1847) was attached to the embassy and served as Thomas Staunton's tutor.

33. Rienstra, *Jesuit Letters*, 20 (1580s); Van Dyke, *Canton Trade*, 77–93, 12–13 (licensing from 1731 on), 23–26. Also see R. E. Pritchard, *Peter Mundy: Merchant Adventurer* (Oxford: Bodleian Library, University of Oxford, 2011), 124 (on a Chinese interpreter named Nortetti in 1637); *CBEIC*, 1:82 (1689), 140–43. Three linguists were listed in 1760 (Lin Cheng, Lin Wang, and Cai Jing), and four were listed in 1800 (Xiao Ao, Lin Jie, Cai Quan, and Lin Guang) (see FO233/189:5, 39); FO1048/32/17 (mentioning three Chinese linguists in 1832).

34. Noble, *Voyage*, 261, 210, 224–56. The chronicle was compiled in 1745–1751. See *AMJLJZ*, 186, 79; see also 153, 187–200 (vocabulary).

35. *MQSQA*, 1:337.

36. *CBEIC*, 1:187 (1728), 179 (1724), 3:134 (1810).

37. A British veteran trader in Guangzhou used the term "terra incognita" ("Free Trade with China," *Chinese Repository* 2, no. 8 [1833]: 374). For earlier European efforts to master Asian languages, see Lach, *Asia*, 490–543.

38. Edward Said, *Orientalism* (New York: Random House, 1994), 122.

39. See Staunton, *Authentic Account*, 2:129–35; Barrow, *Travels*, 3–8; John L. Cranmer-Byng, *An Embassy to China: Lord Macartney's Journal, 1793–1794*, in *Britain and the China Trade, 1635–1842*, vol. 8, ed. Patrick Tuck (New York: Routledge, 2000), 220–78, 343–52, 42 (on Macartney's library, including works by George Anson and Voltaire); John Barrow, *Some Account of the Public Life, and a Selection from the Unpublished Writings, of the Earl of Macartney*, 2 vols. (London: Cadell and Davies, 1807), 2:530. For biographies of Staunton and Macartney, see Sydney Lee, ed., *Dictionary of National Biography* (London: Macmillan, 1898), 114–15.

40. Cranmer-Byng, *Embassy*, 208–13, 276–77.

41. [Francis Jeffrey], "John Barrow's Travels in China," *Edinburgh Review* 5, no. 10 (1805): 259–83, 283. See Barrow, *Travels*, 366–86 (on Chinese law), 366–70 (on the identity of the translator).

42. Cranmer-Byng, *Embassy*, 277; Staunton, *Authentic Account*, 2:235, 501. See Thomas Staunton's diaries, SP, September 14, 19, and November 12, 1793 (on copying Chinese letters).

43. Warren Hastings and John Davis both started as EIC writers.

44. George T. Staunton, *Memoirs of the Chief Incidents of the Public Life of Sir George Thomas Staunton* (London: L. Booth, 1856), 26, 17 (appointed a writer in April 1798 and leaving for China in June 1799), 22. See IOR/G/12/128:12 (1800); Thomas Staunton's letter, SP, January 20, 1800.

45. See, e.g., FO233/189:34–40, 38–39 (Chinese account); IOR/G/12/128:26–123, 82–87 (about the trial), 83, 116, and 119. Cf. *CBEIC*, 2:333–41, 428–29.

46. See IOR/G/12/128:85; *CBEIC*, 2:368, 339. See also IOR/G/12/128:120, 123; George T. Staunton, "Communications from China," *Monthly Visitor* 13 (1801): 153; see also 153–55; George W. Keeton, *The Development of Extraterritoriality in China*, 2 vols. (London: Longmans, 1928), 1:46.

47. *TTLL*, 328.

48. *CBEIC*, 2:342, 338 (on the "joint" trial); Keeton, *Development of Extraterritoriality*, 1:43–47; Earl H. Pritchard, "The Origin of Extraterritoriality in China," *Northwest Science* 4, no. 4 (1930): 112; see also 109–13.

49. Staunton, *Memoirs*, 27.

50. See IOR/G/12/128:47, 84–90, 118–35, 147, 207, 213, 220. Thomas Staunton's letters, SP, March 20, 27, and May 26, 1800. About the meetings, see IOR/G/12/128:211–14 (April 7 and 9).

51. Thomas Staunton's letters, SP, May 26, 1800. See, e.g., IOR/G/12/128:208–9 (April 3, 4), 220–21 (April 16).

52. James Flint still had to rely on a Chinese to write the complaint for him in 1759.
53. IOR/G/12/131:28. On Staunton's Chinese skill, see Thomas Staunton's letters, SP, May 26, 27, and 20, 1800; also see FO233/189:40 (no. 34) (March 3, 1800) (on his Chinese letter quoted there).
54. See IOR/G/12/128:136 (March 22, 1800), 211–13 (April 7, 9), 128 (for the committee's advice on Chinese legal procedure); Staunton, *Memoirs*, 28; *CBEIC*, 2:342–43.
55. FO233/189:23 (or f29) (Qianlong 60/3/26).
56. Thomas Staunton's letters, SP, March 27, 1800, January 20 and 25, 1800 (for Staunton's Chinese study). See IOR/G/12/128:211 (April 7, 1800).
57. For Staunton's role on a few important occasions besides the Amherst Embassy, see FO1048/11/18–26 (1811); FO1048/35/8 (1813–1814); *PTYDP*, 724–26 (1814); FO1048/14/73–105 (on the negotiation in 1814).
58. The others included Francis H. Toone, Thomas Manning, and Alexander Pearson, with James Bannerman behind at the factory; *CBEIC*, 3:259. See Stifler, "Language Students," 55–69.
59. IOR/G/12/132:10; Cranmer-Byng, "First English Sinologists," 255.
60. *TTLL*, 315.
61. See *Fajia jingtian lei* (Shulin xiyuan, 1800?), Special Collections, Chinese, R.A.S. 124; *Fajia toudan han* (by Buxiangzi, 1 vol.), R.A.S. 123; *Xinzeng fayu jinnang/zhu mingjia hexuan* (6 vols., similar in contents to *Fajia jingtian lei*), R.A.S. 122, now at the library of the University of Leeds. These three titles were listed in the Royal Asiatic Society's catalogue by 1838 (Samuel Kidd, *Catalogue of the Chinese Library of the Royal Asiatic Society* [London: John W. Parker, 1838], 36–39) and were most likely purchased in 1800–1801, when Staunton also got two copies of the Qing Code and other law books among the 1,000 volumes (Thomas Staunton's letter, SP, January 9, 1801).
62. Regarding such handbooks, see Melissa Macauley, *Social Power and Legal Culture: Litigation Masters in Late Imperial China* (Stanford: Stanford University Press, 1998), 18–46; Susumu Fuma, "Litigation Masters and the Litigation Systems of Ming and Qing China," *International Journal of Asian Studies* 27, no. 1 (2007): 79–111.
63. *TTLL*, 315–16, 563–65, and another case he translated in Barrow, *Travels*, 370.
64. For the relevant archives, see JJCLFZZ, 04-01-26-0020-024 (JQ12/10/16); IOR/G/12/152–63 and IOR/G/12/269; FO233/189:136–58; FO1048/7; IOR/R/10/39/no. 3 of 1808 (April 29, 1808); *CBEIC*, 3:40–53. George Thomas Staunton, *Miscellaneous Notices Relating to China, and Our Commercial Intercourses with That Country* (London: John Murray, 1822), 261–82. For English law on riots, see Sir William Blackstone, *Commentaries on the Laws of England*, 13th ed., 4 vols. (London: Cadell and Davies, 1800), 4:199. Regarding the nature of this incident as a riot, see John F. Davis, *The Chinese: A General Description of*

the Empire of China and Its Inhabitants, 2 vols. (London: Charles Knight & Co., 1836), 1:82.

65. *TTLL,* 521–24 (appendix).

66. Archibald Campbell, *A Voyage Round the World, from 1806 to 1812* (New York: Van Winkle, Wiley & Co., 1817), 200, 198–204 (quoting the *Morning Chronicle*). For the attacks on Macao, see *CBEIC,* 2:369–85.

67. Staunton, *Miscellaneous Notices* (1822), 268.

68. Ibid., 271–72.

69. Staunton, *Memoirs,* 34–35 (misdating the court's comments to February 1808). For the directors' letter, see IOR/R/10/39/no. 3 of 1808 (April 29, 1808), paras. 46–47.

70. Niranjana, *Siting Translation,* 2.

71. See Lydia H. Liu, *Translingual Practice: Literature, National Culture, and Translated Modernity—China, 1900–1937* (Stanford: Stanford University Press, 1995), 26–27; Liu, *Clash of Empires,* 31–139, 110 (for the quotations). See Gayatri Chakravorty Spivak, "The Politics of Translation," in *Outside in the Teaching Machine,* 179–200 (New York: Routledge, 1993).

72. William C. Jones, trans., *The Great Qing Code* (New York: Oxford University Press, 1994), v–vi. Reviewers of Jones's translation agreed with him on the problems with Staunton's translation; see reviews by Nancy Park, *American Journal of Legal History* 39, no. 4 (1995): 514–15, and Thomas M. Buoye, *Journal of Asian Studies* 54, no. 4 (1994): 1242–43.

73. See James St. André, "'But Do They Have a Notion of Justice?' Staunton's 1810 Translation of the Great Qing Code," *Translator* 10, no. 1 (2004): 23–24, 2–3, and 13–27; Timothy Brook, Jérôme Bourgon, and Gregory Blue, *Death by a Thousand Cuts* (Cambridge, Mass.: Harvard University Press, 2008), 174–77.

74. Gérard Genette, *Paratexts: Thresholds of Interpretation,* trans. Jane E. Lewin (Cambridge: Cambridge University Press, 1997), 2 and 1–16 (for distinctions between different types of paratexts).

75. For the popular accounts by Lord Anson in the 1740s and Daniel Defoe in the 1720s, see Jonathan D. Spence, *The Chan's Great Continent* (New York: Norton, 1998); George Anson, *A Voyage round the World, in the Years 1740–44,* ed. Richard Walter (London: John and Paul Knapton, 1748).

76. *TTLL,* xxx.

77. Ibid., lxiii–lxxvi. On such technical changes, see St. André, "'But Do They Have a Notion of Justice?'" 7–11.

78. See *TTLL,* lxxiii–lxxiv, 1–2, 383, and 449; lxxiv–lxxvi. Cf. Tian Tao and Zheng Qin, eds., *Da Qing lüli (The Great Qing Code)* (1740) (Beijing: Falü chubanshe, 1998), 42–74.

79. Cf. tables in *TTLL,* lxxv–lxxvi, 487–88; for the implications of Staunton's translation strategies, compare *TTLL,* 343–57 with Tian and Zheng, *Da Qing lüli,*

64–74. See also St. André, "'But Do They Have a Notion of Justice?'" 11. On implications of the mourning relations, see *TTLL*, 371–74; Jones, *Great Qing Code*, 322–24, 255–56, 349, 269–73.

80. *TTLL*, xiii–iv.

81. *North China Herald*, October 4, 1889, 405–6, quoted in David Wright, "The Translation of Modern Western Science in Nineteenth-Century China, 1840–1895," *Isis* 89, no. 4 (1998): 659. On the different attributes of classical Chinese, see Liu, *Clash of Empires*, 191–208, 183–86 (on the Western discourse on Chinese).

82. Lach, *Asia*, 518–30 (for the universal language). For such a view dating back to the 1700s, see Noble, *Voyage*, 136, 125, 262; Voltaire, *The Works of M. de Voltaire*, 35 vols. (London: J. Newbery, 1761–1765), 1:22; Barrow, *Travels*, 356 (quoting Sir Jones). Also see Liu, *Clash of Empires*, 186–87 (on similar views by Wilhelm von Humboldt [1767–1835], Friedrich von Schlegel [1772–1829], and William Whitney [1827–1894]).

83. *TTLL*, xiv.

84. Ibid., xxxii.

85. Ibid., xv.

86. Ibid., xxxii–xxxiii.

87. Cf. ibid., 313 (sect. ccxcii), with Jones, *Great Qing Code*, 278; Tian and Zheng, *Da Qing lüli*, 433.

88. *TTLL*, xxxi–xxxii.

89. Ibid., i.

90. Ibid., xxix, i.

91. Francis Jeffrey, "Ta Tsing Leu Lee," *Edinburgh Review* 16, no. 32 (1810): 476–99, 495. For authorship of this anonymous review, see Lord Henry Cockburn, *Life of Lord Jeffrey, with a Selection from His Correspondence*, 2nd ed., 2 vols. (Edinburgh: Adam and Charles Black, 1852), 1:420, 93; Walter E. Houghton, ed., *The Wellesley Index to Victorian Periodicals, 1824–1900* (Toronto: University of Toronto Press, 1966–1989), 1:436.

92. Teemu Ruskola, *Legal Orientalism: China, the United States, and Modern Law* (Cambridge, Mass.: Harvard University Press, 2013), 51–54.

93. *TTLL*, lxiii.

94. "Ta Tsing Leu Lee," *Monthly Review* 64 (1811): 114, 117.

95. For the relevant discussion of title and subtitle, see Genette, *Paratexts*, 90–94, 55–100.

96. Yang Yifan, *Hongwu falü dianji kaozheng (Evidentiary Study of the Law Books of the Hongwu Reign* [1368–1398]) (Beijing: Falü chubanshe, 1992), 55–56 (praising this structure as a Ming innovation); Su Yigong, *Ming Qing lüdian yu tiaoli (Laws and Regulations in the Ming and Qing Periods)* (Beijing: Zhongguo zhengfa daxue chubanshe, 1998), 93–109 (on the six-board structure), 108 (on its possibly Yuan-dynasty origin).

97. Philip C. C. Huang, *Civil Justice in China: Representation and Practice in the Qing* (Stanford: Stanford University Press, 1996), 220, 218–21. Cf. Jérôme Bourgon, "Uncivil Dialogue: Law and Custom Did Not Merge into Civil Law under the Qing," *Late Imperial China* 23, no. 1 (June 2002): 50–90. On Chinese "civil" justice, see, e.g., Linxia Liang, *Delivering Justice in Qing China: Civil Trials in the Magistrate's Court* (Oxford: Oxford University Press, 2008); Madeleine Zelin, Jonathan Ocko, and Robert Gardella, eds., *Contract and Property in Early Modern China* (Stanford: Stanford University Press, 2004).

98. "Ta Tsing Leu Lee," *Critical Review* 21, no. 4 (1810): 343–44.

99. Jones, *Great Qing Code*, 7–8.

100. See, e.g., Zhang Jinfan, *Zhongguo falü de chuantong yu jindai zhuanxing (Tradition and Modern Transformation of Chinese Law)*, 2nd ed. (Beijing: Falü chubanshe, 2005), 204–28, 209 (mentioning Maine specifically).

101. For earlier views, see William Winterbotham, *An Historical, Geographical, and Philosophical View of the Chinese Empire* (London: J. Ridgeway, 1795), 280–86 (on "civil laws"), 286–91 (on "criminal laws"); Staunton, *Authentic Account*, 2:490–96.

102. *TTLL*, 360.

103. Jennifer M. Neighbors, "Criminal Intent and Homicide Law in Qing and Republican China" (Ph.D. diss., University of California, Los Angeles, 2004), 10; Jones, *Great Qing Code*, 7–8.

104. William P. Alford, "Of Arsenic and Old Laws: Looking Anew at Criminal Justice in Late Imperial China," *California Law Review* 72 (1984): 1180–95, 1190 (quotation). See also William P. Alford, "The Inscrutable Occidental? Implications of Robert Unger's Uses and Abuses of the Chinese Past," *Texas Law Review* 64, no. 5 (1986): 915–72.

105. IOR/G/12/131:26–27 (May 26); also IOR/G/12/128:220 (April 16), 211–12. For the reissuance, see, e.g., "From the Indian Gazette," *Providence Gazette*, June 6, 1801; "From the Boston Centinel: Chinese Criminal Laws," *Genius of Liberty*, April 29, 1817; "China—Copy of a Translation," *New York Mirror* 3, no. 2 (1823): 11. For the watercolor paintings, see chapter 4.

106. FO233/189:40 (for the Chinese original). For the translation, see IOR/G/12/128:240–41 (May 4, 1800); *CBEIC*, 2:343. For the background, see IOR/G/12/128:211, 213.

107. IOR/G/12/128:211–13 (April 7–9), 240 (May 14, 1800); IOR/G/12/131:27 (in a report of May 26 to the directors); Staunton, "Communications," 155.

108. Barrow, *Travels*, 366.

109. Ibid.; Thomas Staunton's letters, SP, May 7, 1807 (from Mackintosh), August 25, 1807 (to Barrow),

110. "Literary Intelligence," *British Critic* 33 (1809): 96; [John Barrow], "[Review of] *Voyages à Peking, Manille, et l'Isle de France, faits dans l'intervalle des années 1784 à 1801. Par M. de Guignes* (Paris, 1808)," *Quarterly Review* 2, no. 4 (1809): 273. On

the reviewer's identity, see http://www.rc.umd.edu/reference/qr/index/04.html. Also see Jonathan Cutmore, *Contributors to the Quarterly Review: A History, 1809–1825* (London: Pickering & Chatto, 2008).

111. "Ta Tsing Leu Lee," *Monthly Review*, 117; "Ta Tsing Leu Lee," *Critical Review*, 3rd ser., 21, no. 4 (1810): 344, 346.

112. See the title pages of the retranslations in chapter 3; "Ta Tsing Leu Lee, ou les lois fondamentales de la Chine," *Journal général de la littérature de France* 14, no. 10 (1811): 336–41; ibid., 15, no. 1 (1812): 27–29, 29; "Ta-tsing-leu-lee, o sia Leggi fondamentali del Còdice penale della China," *Giornale enciclopedico di Firenze* 4 (1812): 23–24 (*GEDF*), 23; Saluges, "Ta-Tsing-Leu-Lee, ou les lois fondamentales du Code pénal de la Chine," *Mercure de France: Journal littéraire et politique* 50 (1812): 210–18, 217 (finding "little order" in the code).

113. Ernest Alabaster, *Notes and Commentaries on Chinese Criminal Law and Cognate Topics* (London: Luzac, 1899), viii–ix, 517–600 (on the "Law of Property"). On the etymology of Chinese terms such as *lü, xing,* and *fa,* see, e.g., Liang Qichao, *Liang Qichao faxue wenji* (*Liang Qichao's Essays on Jurisprudence*), ed. Fan Zhongxin (1904. repr., Beijing: Zhongguo zhengfa daxue chubanshe, 1997), 787–79; Li Li, *Chutu wenwu yu xianqin fazhi* (*Excavated Artifacts and the Legal System of the Qin Dynasty*) (Beijing: Daxiang chubanshe, 1997), 78–79.

114. Jones, *Great Qing Code*, 7–8; Neighbors, "Criminal Intent and Homicide Law," 10.

115. Sir Henry Sumner Maine, *Ancient Law: Its Connection with the Early History of Society, and Its Relation to Modern Ideas*, 2nd ed. (New York: Charles Scribner, 1864), 328–31, 355–57, 22–23. On Maine, see Karuna Mantena, *Alibis of Empire: Henry Maine and the Ends of Liberal Imperialism* (Princeton: Princeton University Press, 2010).

116. Hugh T. Scogin Jr., "Civil 'Law' in Traditional China: History and Theory," in *Civil Law in Qing and Republican China*, ed. Kathryn Bernhardt et al. (Stanford: Stanford University Press, 1994), 26.

117. E. Adamson Hoebel, *The Law of Primitive Man* (Cambridge, Mass.: Harvard University Press, 1954), 28.

118. Sally F. Moore, *Law as Process: An Anthropological Approach* (London: Routledge, 1977), 56–58, 74.

119. Valerie Hansen, *Negotiating Daily Life in Traditional China: How Ordinary People Used Contracts 600–1400* (New Haven: Yale University Press, 1995), 3, 7–8.

120. *TTLL*, vi–x.

121. Sir William Jones, "The Second Anniversary Discourse, Delivered 24 February, 1785, by the President, at the Asiatick Society of Bengal," in *The Works of Sir William Jones*, ed. John Shore (London: John Stockdale and John Walker, 1807), 13; see also 11–23; Sir William Jones, "The Third Anniversary Discourse, Delivered 2 February 1786 by the President," ibid., 24. For Macartney, see Cranmer-Byng, *Embassy*, 44.

122. Nathaniel Brassey Halhed, *A Code of Gentoo Laws, or, Ordinations of the Pundits* (London, 1776), xii, xxii–xxxi (languages), xxviii–xxxii (poetry), xliv–xlix (religion), xlii–xlix (antiquity), lxiv (punishments); xiii and lxiv (excusing native practices); Sir William Jones, *Institutes of Hindu Law: Or, the Ordinances of Menu* (London: J. Sewell, Cornhill, 1796), iv–xi.

123. Spence, *Chan's Great Continent*, 52–80; Lydia H. Liu, "Robinson Crusoe's Earthenware Pot," *Critical Inquiry* 25, no. 4 (1999): 728–57. See Barrow, *Travels*, 161–83; Jeffrey, "John Barrow's Travels in China," 262–82.

124. *TTLL*, x; George Thomas Staunton, *Miscellaneous Notices Relating to China, and Our Commercial Intercourse with That Country* [Part 2] (London, 1828), 261–67.

125. *TTLL*, xxvi–xxvii, 269, 92, 186, 315.

126. Ibid., x–xi, 347.

127. Staunton, *Miscellaneous Notices* (1828), 271–76 (1828), 294 (1814).

128. Although he did vote for some moderate reform bills later in his Parliamentary career, he disliked radical, unnecessary changes to the status quo. For his defenses of the EIC's monopoly over the China trade, see Staunton, *Miscellaneous Notices* (1828), 167–262 (1813 and 1821).

129. Cranmer-Byng, *Embassy*, 208–13, and 276–77.

130. On the Amherst Embassy, see IOR/G/12/196–98; letters to Amherst, British Library, MSS Eur F140/38–39; Staunton, *Notes of Proceedings*; Gongzhongdang Quanzong, First National Historical Museum (Beijing), 05-0585-042 to 05-0585-075 (JQ21/6/1-7/3).

131. See, e.g., Thomas Staunton's letters, SP, August 18 and November 8, 1800; November 5, 1805; June 8, 1807; Staunton, *Memoirs*, 16–17. Also see WWC, 675, 682–83.

132. Kitson, *Forging Romantic China*, 95–97.

133. *TTLL*, x.

134. Ibid., xii. On Davis, see Kitson, *Forging Romantic China*, 105–24.

135. *TTLL*, xxv–xxvi. Cf. St. André, "'But Do They Have a Notion of Justice?'" 5, 23.

136. Said has treated such sympathetic identification as "latent Orientalism" united with "manifest Orientalism" by a will to power and domination (Said, *Orientalism*, 116–20, using Jones's *Institutes of Hindu Laws* as an example). Staunton's case complicates the picture.

137. *TTLL*, xii, xix

138. Ibid., xxvii.

139. Frederick E. Pargiter, ed., *Centennial Volume of the Royal Asiatic Society of Great Britain and Ireland, 1823–1923* (London: Royal Asiatic Society, 1923), viii. Jones, "Second Anniversary Discourse," 13–14.

140. Penderel Moon, *Warren Hastings and British India* (New York: Macmillan, 1949), 352.

141. *TTLL*, xi, xv, xvii–xx, xxiv.

142. See chapter 3.

143. Bernard S. Cohn, *Colonialism and Its Forms of Knowledge: The British in India* (Princeton: Princeton University Press, 1996), 62–66. See Halhed's elaboration on this, in Halhed, *Code of Gentoo Laws*, ix, xi. This was echoed by contemporary Britons ("Review of *A Code of Gentoo Laws*," *Annual Register* [1778], 246).

144. Halhed, *Code of Gentoo Laws*, xi.

145. Ta-Van Tai, "Vietnam's Code of the Lê Dynasty (1428–1788)," *American Journal of Comparative Law* 30, no. 3 (1982): 525; P. L. F. Philastre, *Le code annamite, nouvelle traduction complète* (Taipei: Ch'eng-wen Pub. Co., 1967).

146. Staunton, *Miscellaneous Notices* (1828), 162 (considering use of force impossible).

147. Thomas Staunton's letter, SP, March 27, 1800. On cooperation of Indian elites, see Moon, *Warren Hastings*, 103; Garland Cannon, "Sir William Jones's Indian Studies," *Journal of the American Oriental Society* 91, no. 3 (1971): 418–25, esp. 419. Cf. Barrow, "[Review of] *Voyages à Peking*," 274–75.

148. In fact, about 30 or 40 percent of the statutes in the Qing Code of 1740 could be traced back to the Tang Code of 653, but as Bodde and Morris noted in 1967, the other 60 or 70 per cent did change over time. See Derk Bodde and Clarence Morris, *Law in Imperial China* (Cambridge, Mass.: Harvard University Press, 1967), 63.

149. *TTLL*, xxx, xxiii, xxxv.

150. David Porter, *Ideographia: The Chinese Cipher in Early Modern Europe* (Stanford: Stanford University Press, 2001), 6, 8.

151. The substatutes totaled 1,456 in 1761 and 1,603 in 1801. See Tao Jun and Tao Nianlin, *Da Qing lüli zengxiu tongzuan jicheng* (*Comprehensive Edition of the Revised Qing Code*), vol. 22 (Shanghai: Wenyuan shanfang, 1900); Bodde and Morris, *Law in Late Imperial China*, 67, 32.

152. Edward H. Parker, *China: Past and Present* (London: Chapman & Hall, 1903), 383–88; Alabaster, *Notes and Commentaries*, v. Only those who studied Chinese law in depth recognized this; see, e.g., Parker, *China*, 314–43, but cf. 311–12 (influence of the penal-civil dichotomy); Elijah C. Bridgman, "Penal Laws of China," *Chinese Repository* 2, no. 1 (1833): 1–19, 10, and "Penal Laws of China," *Chinese Repository* 2, no. 3 (1833): 97–100.

153. See, e.g., Barrow, *Travels*, 27–30.

154. Cranmer-Byng, *Embassy*, 226.

155. Michael Adas, *Machines as the Measure of Men* (Ithaca: Cornell University Press, 1989), 107, also 103–8. On anachronistic space, see Anne McClintock, *Imperial Leather: Race, Gender and Sexuality in the Colonial Contest* (New York: Routledge, 1995), 30, 40.

156. Jeffrey, "Ta Tsing Leu Lee," 480–81; "Ta Tsing Leu Lee," *Critical Review*, 339.

157. Adas, *Machines*, 71–74. Echoing Jones's words about India, Staunton also noted that China did not have Newton, Locke, or Bacon, or tolerable proficiency in the sciences (*TTLL*, x).

158. Halhed, *Code of Gentoo Laws*, lxxiii–lxxiv. For more about Indology and colonial study of Indian law, see Cohn, *Colonialism*, 66–75; Ludo Rocher and Rosane Rocher, *The Making of Western Indology: Henry Thomas Colebrooke and the East India Company* (London: Routledge, 2008); Rosane Rocher, *Orientalism, Poetry, and the Millennium: The Checkered Life of Nathaniel Brassey Halhed, 1751–1830* (Delhi: Varanasi, 1983). About Jones, see Cannon, "Sir William Jones's Indian Studies," 423.

159. Said, *Orientalism*, 92–96, 19.

160. Fan, *British Naturalists*, 103–6; Fa-ti Fan, "Hybrid Discourse and Textual Practice: Sinology and Natural History in the Nineteenth Century," *History of Science* 38, no. 1 (2000): 25–56.

161. *TTLL*, xv (quotation). See Edward Gibbon, *The Decline and Fall of the Roman Empire*, 6 vols. (London: Strahan and Cadell, 1781–1788), esp. vol. 4. Gibbon was often credited as the first modern historian.

162. Lorenzo Arrazola, "Codigo: China," in *Enciclopedia española de derecho y administración* (*Spanish Encyclopedia of Law and Administration*), ed. Lorenzo Arrazola, 367–69 (Madrid: Imprenta de la Revista de Legislacion y Jurisprudencia, á Cargo de J. Morales, 1856), 367; *TTLL*, i.

163. See the French translator's preface in George Thomas Staunton, *Ta-Tsing-Leu-Lée, ou les lois fondamentales du Code pénal de la Chine*, trans. Félix Renouard de Sainte-Croix, 2 vols. (Paris: Lenormant, 1812).

164. Ruskola, *Legal Orientalism*, 51.

165. Jeffrey, "Ta Tsing Leu Lee," 478, 495 (emphasis added). Also see "Ta Tsing Leu Lee," *British Critics* 36 (1810): 224; "Ta Tsing Leu Lee," *Critical Review*, 340.

166. *TTLL*, i; Barrow, *Travels*, 366; Jeffrey, "Ta Tsing Leu Lee," 283; Barrow, "Ta Tsing Leu Lee," 273–74.

167. See "Ta Tsing Leu Lee," *British Critics*, 209–11; "Ta Tsing Leu Lee," *Critical Review*, 337–42; Jeffrey, "Ta Tsing Leu Lee," 476–77; "Ta Tsing Leu Lee," *Monthly Review*, 113–14.

168. See Arrazola, "Codigo: China," 367 (quotation); Saluges, "Ta-Tsing-Leu-Lee," 210–12, 218; *GEDF*, 23.

169. *TTLL*, viii (for the first quotation); Barrow, "Ta Tsing Leu Lee," 273–74 (for the second quotation). On Jones's ambition, see Garland Cannon, ed., *The Letters of Sir William Jones* (Oxford: Clarendon Press, 1970), 2:751 (1787).

170. See the translator's long "Introductory Discourse" in *The Code Napoléon*, trans. Bryant Barrett, 2 vols. (London: W. Reed, 1811). For *TTLL*'s reception, see chapter 3, and John M'Arthur, *Principles and Practice of Naval and Military Courts Martial*, 4th ed., 2 vols. (London: J. Butterworth, 1813), 210–11, 325;

Theodric R. Beck, *Elements of Medical Jurisprudence*, 2 vols. (Albany: Webster and Skinner, 1823), 1:93, 281; Francis Lieber, *Manual of Political Ethics: Designed Chiefly for the Use of Colleges and Students at Law*, 2 vols. (Boston: Charles C. Little and James Brown, 1838–1839), 1:154; Adolphe Chauveau and Faustin Hélie, *Théorie du Code pénal*, 4th ed. (Paris: Imprimerie et librairie générale de jurisprudence, 1861), 1:196, 201, 458; George Ives, *A History of Penal Methods: Criminals, Witches, Lunatics* (London: S. Paul, 1914).

171. Halhed, *Code of Gentoo Laws*; see also Said, *Orientalism*, 116–18. Halhed studied Arabic at Oxford, where he met Jones, and was one of the first to study Sanskrit's affinities with other languages; Cohn, *Colonialism*, 66.

172. About this plan, see William Jones's last anniversary discourse as president of the Asiatic Society of Bengal, quoted in *A Digest of Hindu Law, on Contracts and Successions*, by H. T. Colebrooke, 3rd ed., 2 vols. (Madras: J. Higginbotham, 1864), 1:vii–xi. For more on Jones's efforts, see Cohn, *Colonialism*, 69–74; Nandini Bhattacharyya-Panda, *Appropriation and Invention of Tradition: The East India Company and Hindu Law in Early Colonial Bengal* (Oxford: Oxford University Press, 2008), 89–242.

173. Nickolas Dirks, *Castes of Mind: Colonialism and the Making of Modern India* (Princeton: Princeton University Press, 2001), 191.

174. Thomas Staunton's letter, SP, May 7, 1807; see June 30 and August 15, 1805 for earlier correspondence. See also *TTLL*, xxxiv; Staunton, *Memoirs*, 40 (about Mackintosh).

175. Thomas Staunton's letter, SP, August 25, 1807; *TTLL*, xxix, xxxiii.

176. For the exchanges, see Eliza A. Morrison, *Memoirs of the Life and Labours of Robert Morrison*, 2 vols. (London: Longman, 1839), 2:95, 171–73, 231. Also see Hartmut Walravens, *Zur Geschichte der Ostasienwissenschaften in Europa: Abel Rémusat (1788–1832) und das Umfeld Julius Klaproths (1783–1835)* (Wiesbaden: Harrassowitz, 1999).

177. For their rivalry or disputes, see Morrison, *Memoirs*, 2:252–57; Barrow, "[Review of] *Voyages à Peking*," 264–66.

178. Giacomo Leopardi, *Zibaldone*, ed. Michael Caesar and Franco D'Intino (New York: Farrar, Straus and Giroux, 2013), 1091, 444–46 (quoting Staunton on Chinese "natural incapacity and indisposition" to undertake "ambitious projects and foreign conquests"), 665 (on foot binding). About the Italian reviews of Staunton's *TTLL*, see notes 57 and 58 in chapter 3.

179. E.g., FO1080/54 and 56 (on the mission to Annam and treaty in Chinese in the 1850s); FO1080/58 (on the correspondence in Chinese with Japan in 1858); FO1080/60 (November 17, 1858); FO1080/67/2 (letter to Japan).

180. Partha Chatterjee, *The Black Hole of Empire: History of a Global Practice of Power* (Princeton: Princeton University Press, 2012), 212–15. For Maine's influence on indirect rule, see Mantena, *Alibis*.

181. Carol G. S. Tan, *British Rule in China: Law and Justice in Weihaiwei, 1898–1930* (London: Wildy, Simmonds & Hill, 2008). See my review of the book in *Law and History Review* 28, no.2 (2010): 573–75.

3. CHINESE LAW IN THE FORMATION
OF EUROPEAN MODERNITY

1. See Günter Birtsch, "Reform Absolutism and the Codification of Law: The Genesis and Nature of the Prussian General Code (1794)," in *Rethinking Leviathan: The Eighteenth-Century State*, ed. John Brewer and Eckhart Hellmuth (Oxford: Oxford University Press, 1999), 343–58.

2. See, e.g., Daniel V. Botsman, *Punishment and Power in the Making of Modern Japan* (Princeton: Princeton University Press, 2005).

3. But Chinese reformers were not passive victims of foreign impact. As noted earlier, the other major argument was to abolish foreign extraterritoriality through reform. See memorials of ministers of justice Shen Jiaben and Wu Tingfang for reforming the Qing Code and certain punishments in JJCLFZZ, 539-7225-57 (GX29/12/7), 539-7228-5 (GX32/4/2). For general discussion of the late Qing reform, see Xiaoqun Xu, *Trial of Modernity: Judicial Reform in Early Twentieth-Century China, 1901–1937* (Stanford: Stanford University Press, 2008), 25–53.

4. Eric Hayot, *The Hypothetical Mandarin: Sympathy, Modernity, and Chinese Pain* (New York: Oxford University Press, 2009), 27–29, 11–12.

5. Ann Laura Stoler and Frederick Cooper, "Between Metropole and Colony: Rethinking a Research Agenda," in *Tensions of Empire: Colonial Cultures in a Bourgeois World*, ed. Frederick Cooper and Ann Laura Stoler (Berkeley: University of California Press, 1997), 13.

6. Homi Bhabha, *The Location of Culture* (New York: Routledge, 2006), 154.

7. David E. Mungello, *Curious Land: Jesuit Accommodation and the Origins of Sinology* (Honolulu: University of Hawai`i Press, 1989), 16–17. See John W. Witek, "Catholic Missions and the Expansion of Christianity, 1644–1800," in *China and Maritime Europe, 1500–1800: Trade, Settlement, Diplomacy, and Missions*, ed. John E. Wills Jr. (Cambridge: Cambridge University Press, 2011), 172–82. On the invention of Confucianism, see Lione M. Jensen, *Manufacturing Confucianism: Chinese Traditions and Universal Civilization* (Durham: Duke University Press, 1997).

8. Jürgen Osterhammel, *Die Entzauberung Asiens: Europa und die asiatischen Reiche im 18. Jahrhundert* (Munich: C.H. Beck, 1998), 297.

9. M. de Secondat, Baron de Montesquieu, *The Spirit of the Laws*, trans. Thomas Nugent, 4th ed., 4 vols. (London: J. Nourse and P. Vallant, 1766), 1:10–47; 2:177–81.

The original title of this 1766 translation is *The Spirit of Laws*, but I have adopted the current title, which is more common in later translations.

10. Brian Singer, *Montesquieu and the Discovery of the Social* (London: Palgrave MacMillan, 2013), 45–46.

11. Montesquieu, *Spirit of the Laws* (1766), 1:390–99 (on climate); Aslı Çırakman, "From Tyranny to Despotism: The Enlightenment's Unenlightened Image of the Turks," *International Journal of Middle East Studies* 33 (2001): 49–68, 56 (quotations). For earlier meanings of "despot" and "despotism," the latter of which appeared in French only in the late seventeenth century, see Franco Venturi, "Oriental Despotism," *Journal of the History of Ideas* 24, no. 1 (1963): 133–35. For more about Montesquieu, see Teemu Ruskola, *Legal Orientalism: China, the United States, and Modern Law* (Cambridge, Mass.: Harvard University Press, 2013), 16; Timothy Brook, Jérôme Bourgon, and Gregory Blue, *Death by a Thousand Cuts* (Cambridge, Mass.: Harvard University Press, 2008), 163.

12. Çırakman, "From Tyranny to Despotism," 56.

13. Timothy Brook, *Vermeer's Hat: The Seventeenth Century and the Dawn of the Global World* (London: Profile Books, 2009); Michael Adas, *Machines as the Measure of Men* (Ithaca: Cornell University Press, 1989), 79.

14. Adas, *Machines*, 85 and 83; see also 79–85. Parrenin made maps and served as interpreter for international negotiation with Russia for Kangxi and founded the first Latin school for Kangxi.

15. Jean Baptiste Du Halde, *The General History of China: Containing a Geographical, Historical, Chronological, Political and Physical Description of the Empire of China*, trans. Richard Brookes, 4 vols. (London: J. Watts, 1736), 2:223–34. The work's other notable readers included, among others, Nicolas-Gabriel Clerc (1726–1798), Oliver Goldsmith, the Encyclopedists, and Rousselot de Surgy. See Hyobom Pak, *China and the West: Myths and Realities in History* (Leiden: Brill, 1974), 56.

16. Louis Le Comte, *Memoirs and Remarks . . . Made in above Ten Years Travels through the Empire of China* (1696) (London: Olive Payne, 1737), 270 and 249 (quotations), 271–314. For earlier European accounts of China, see Jonathan D. Spence, *The Chan's Great Continent* (New York: Norton, 1998), 21–27; Brook et al., *Death*, 155–63.

17. Montesquieu, *Spirit of the Laws* (1766), 1:181.

18. He followed the controversy closely and questioned Du Halde's work in his reading notes around 1739. See Xu Minglong, "Mengdesijiu dui liyi zhizheng de jiedu (Montesquieu's Understanding of the Rites Controversy)," *Shijie lishi* 4 (2011): 29–38. He might also have been influenced by a meeting with Father Jean-Francois Foucquet in 1729. See John W. Witek, *Controversial Ideas in China and in Europe: A Biography of Jean-François Foucquet, S.J., 1665–1741* (Rome: Institutum Historicum S.I., 1982), 312–13.

19. Huang Jialue, alias Arcade Hoangh or Arcadius Hoange, journeyed with a French missionary to Rome in the early 1700s. Once a Chinese interpreter to King Louis XIV in Paris, he then worked with two French Sinologists on a Chinese dictionary; Xu Minglong, *Huang Jialue yu zhaoqi faguo hanxue* (*Huang Jialue and Early French Sinology*) (Beijing: Zhonghua shuju, 2004); Spence, *Chan's Great Continent*, 88–91 (quoting "Geographica," in Montesquieu, *Oeuvres complètes*, ed. André Masson [Paris, 1955], 2:927–41), 90 (for the English quotations).

20. R. Bin Wong, *China Transformed: Historical Change and the Limits of European Experience* (Ithaca: Cornell University Press, 1997); Kenneth Pomeranz, *The Great Divergence: China, Europe, and the Making of the Modern World Economy* (Princeton: Princeton University Press, 2001).

21. Montesquieu, *Spirit of the Laws* (1766), 1:184, 181, 120. Du Halde wrote, "It is the common custom of the Chinese justices not to inflict any punishment . . . , which is not preceded or succeeded by the bastinado, insomuch that it may be said that the Chinese government subsists by the exercise of the battoon" (Du Halde, *General History*, 2:229). He saw it mostly as a measure of proportionality (226–28). See Le Comte, *Memoirs*, 292–94; Alvaro Semedo, *The History of That Great and Renowned Monarchy of China* (London: John Crook, 1655), 141–42, 148–50; Brook et al., *Death*, 158–64.

22. See "Ta Tsing Leu Lee," *British Critics* 36 (1810): 217; also see John Barrow, "Ta Tsing Leu Lee," *Quarterly Review* 3, no. 6 (1810): 294–95. Likewise, see Pan Shicheng, *Da Qing lüli anyu* (*Commentaries on the Qing Code*) (Guangzhou: Haishan xianguan, 1847), *juan* 31:10a (glossing beating with the light bamboo as "shaming"); Liu-hung Huang, *A Complete Book Concerning Happiness and Benevolence: A Manual for Local Magistrates in Seventeenth-Century China*, trans. Djang Chu (Tucson: University of Arizona Press, 1994), 283, 273–74. For this penalty's history, see Yunsheng Xue, *Tang Ming lü hebian* (*The Tang and the Ming Codes Combined*), ed. Huai Xiaofeng and Li Ming (Beijing: Falü chubanshe, 1998), 6–9.

23. Voltaire, "Answer to Conseller Linguet, on Montesquieu and Grotius [in 1767]," *Annual Register* (1778): 166–67; John Barrow, *Travels in China* (London: Cadell and Davies, 1804), 27–28 (questioning Anson's evidence).

24. See Brook et al., *Death*, 164–65 (also on Quesnay's counterarguments). Similarly, Montesquieu transformed Leibniz's passing remark on Chinese "slavishness" into "a major component of a universal system" (Spence, *Chan's Great Continent*, 88).

25. Montesquieu, *Spirit of the Laws* (1766), 1:184.

26. John J. Clarke, *Oriental Enlightenment: The Encounter between Asian and Western Thought* (London: Routledge, 1997), 49–50 (on Quesnay); Alfred O. Aldridge, *The Dragon and the Eagle: The Presence of China in the American Enlightenment* (Detroit: Wayne State University Press, 1993), 155, 145–56 (on early American

appreciation of China). On the Physiocrats, see Adas, *Machines*, 92–93. On Montesquieu's influence, see Spence, *Chan's Great Continent*, 211–18.

27. Georg Wilhelm Friedrich Hegel, *The Philosophy of History* (1837), trans. J. Sibree (New York: Columbia University Press, 1900), 163, 144, 111–28.

28. Prasenjit Duara, *Rescuing History from the Nation* (Chicago: University of Chicago Press, 1995), 17–18.

29. Montesquieu, *Spirit of the Laws* (1766), 1:130–31 (book VI, chapter XVI), 118–36. His criticism of Chinese law (134) was contradicted by evidence (see Tian Tao and Zheng Qin, eds., *Da Qing lüli* [*The Great Qing Code*] [1740] [Beijing: Falü chubanshe, 1998], 365, 895). His inaccurate understanding of the Chinese punishment for robbery might have been based on remarks of Du Halde (Du Halde, *General History*, 1:6, 2:222). On classical thought about guilt and punishment, see Lawrence M. Levin, *The Political Doctrine of Montesquieu's Esprit des Lois: Its Classical Background* (New York: Columba University, 1936).

30. Montesquieu, *Spirit of the Laws* (1766), 1:118.

31. Elaine Freedgood, "Fictional Settlements: Footnotes, Metalepsis, the Colonial Effect," *New Literary History* 41, no. 2 (2010): 393–411, 399 (on such important functions of footnotes).

32. "Proceedings of the Anniversary Meeting of the Royal Asiatic Society, Held on Saturday, the 10th of May, 1834," *Journal of the Royal Asiatic Society of Great Britain and Ireland* 1 (1834): 157–73, 162. Montesquieu's grandson had kept Montesquieu's reading notes before destroying some of them during the French Revolution. See Roger Boesche, *Theories of Tyranny: From Plato to Arendt* (University Park: Pennsylvania State University Press, 1996), 191.

33. David Porter, *Ideographia: The Chinese Cipher in Early Modern Europe* (Stanford: Stanford University Press, 2001), 206; also see 2 and 202–23.

34. On its circulation and influence, see Marcello T. Maestro, *Voltaire and Beccaria as Reformers of Criminal Law* (1942; repr., New York: Octagon, 1972), 92–93, 60.

35. Cesare Beccaria, *An Essay on Crimes and Punishments, by the Marquis Beccaria of Milan, with a Commentary by M. de Voltaire*. New, corrected ed. (Edinburgh: James Donaldson, 1788), 24, 30, 60–63, 78, 107; Adolph Caso, *America's Italian Founding Fathers* (Boston: Branden Press, 1975), 11–21, 75–102. For a summary, see Maestro, *Voltaire and Beccaria*, 57–62, and Marcello Maestro, *Cesare Beccaria and the Origins of Penal Reform* (Philadelphia: Temple University Press, 1973), 22–33.

36. Beccaria, *Essay on Crimes*, 88 (quotation), 32–35; Beccaria, *On Crimes and Punishments*, 14–16. Cf. Montesquieu, *Spirit of the Laws* (1766), 118, 121–22, 130–32.

37. William Eden, *Principles of Law* (London: B. White, 1771), 51, 287. On Beccaria's influence on early American law, see Paul M. Spurlin, "Beccaria's *Essay on Crimes and Punishments* in Eighteenth-Century America," *Studies on Voltaire and the Eighteenth Century* 27 (1963): 1489–1504; Louis P. Masur, *Rites of*

Execution: Capital Punishment and the Transformation of American Culture, 1776–1865 (Oxford: Oxford University Press, 1989), 25–57. On his influence in Britain, see Hugh Dunthorne, "Beccaria and Britain," in *Crime, Protest and Police in Modern British Society*, ed. David Howell and Kenneth Morgan, 73–96 (Cardiff: University of Wales Press, 1999).

38. Maestro, *Voltaire and Beccaria*, 13; Maurice E. Lang, *Codification in the British Empire and America* (Clark, N.J.: Lawbook Exchange, 2005), 2–4.

39. Voltaire, *The Works of M. de Voltaire*, trans. and ed. Dr. Smollet et al., 35 vols. (London: J. Newbery, 1761–1765), 1:23–24; Voltaire, *A Treatise on Toleration; The Ignorant Philosopher; and A Commentary on the Marquis of Beccaria's Treatise on Crimes and Punishments*, trans. D. Williams (London, 1779), 23–24; Beccaria, *Essay on Crimes*, 204; Adas, *Machines*, 87–89.

40. On a different reading of the "example effect," see Hayot, *Hypothetical Mandarin*, 27–30.

41. Voltaire was not as uncritical of Chinese civilization as scholars have often implied. For example, he criticized China's centuries-long "stagnation" in science and practical arts, which he attributed to the peculiarity of the Chinese language and adherence to tradition; Voltaire, *Treatise on Toleration*, 19–22; Voltaire, *The Philosophical Dictionary* (Glasgow: Robert Urie, 1766), 95–96; Basil Guy, *The French Image of China before and after Voltaire* (Oxford: Voltaire Foundation, 1963), 219, 262–63. For Voltaire's criticism of French institutions, see Maestro, *Voltaire and Beccaria*, 35–50 (criticism of French justice), 100–23 (advocacy of legal reform).

42. William Blackstone, *Commentaries on the Laws of England*, 13th ed., 4 vols. (London: Cadell and Davies, 1800), 4:18; also quoted in Basil Montagu, ed., *The Opinions of Different Authors upon the Punishment of Death*, 3 vols. (London: Longman, 1809–1813), 1:16–17. Cf. Montesquieu, *Spirit of the Laws* (1766), 1:131–32. On Blackstone's influence, see Richard Posner, "Blackstone and Bentham," *Journal of Law and Economics* 19, no. 3 (1976): 569–606, 583–89.

43. Posner, "Blackstone and Bentham," 570. See Jeremy Bentham, *Fragment on Government . . . Being a Critique on Some Passages in Blackstone's Commentaries* (1776). See also Herbert L. A. Hart, *Essays on Bentham: Jurisprudence and Political Theory* (Oxford: Oxford University Press, 1983), 340–52.

44. Blackstone, *Commentaries*, 4:18, 238–39.

45. Posner, "Blackstone and Bentham," 583–86; Montagu, *Opinions*, 1:292, 302.

46. Vincent Cronin, *Catherine, Empress of All the Russians* (New York: Morrow, 1978), 174 (on her interest in Montesquieu and Beccaria), 181 (on the *Instructions*). See Catherine II, *The Memoirs of Catherine the Great*, trans. Mark Cruse and Hilde Hoogenboom (New York: Modern Library, 2005), xxvi, xxxi, 138.

47. *The Grand Instructions to the Commissioners Appointed to Frame a New Code of Law for the Russian Empire*, trans. Michael Tatischeff (London: T. Jefferys, 1768), 89, 78, also 182.

48. David Schimmelpenninck van der Oye, *Russian Orientalism: Asia in the Russian Mind from Peter the Great to the Emigration* (New Haven: Yale University Press, 2010), 51–52.

49. Aleksiei Leontiev, trans., *Kitaiskoe ulozhenie: Perevel sokrashchenno s Manzhurskago na Rossiiskoi iazyk Kollegii Inostrannykh diel Maiorskago Ranga (The Chinese Law Code, Translated in an Abbreviated Version by a Major of the College of Foreign Affairs from Manchu to Russian)*, 2 vols. (Saint Petersburg: Imperatorskoĭ Akademīi Nauk, 1778–1779); Aleksiei Leontiev, trans., *Taitsin gurun' i Ukheri koli to est' vse zakony i ustanovleniia kitaiskogo (a nyne man' chzhurskogo) pravitel' stva (Taitsin gurun' i Ukheri koli, or All the Laws and Regulations of the Chinese [Now Manchu] Government* [translated from Manchu to Russian]), 3 vols. (Saint Petersburg: Imperatorskoĭ Akademīi Nauk, 1781–1783). See also Alexander Lukin, *The Bear Watches the Dragon: Russia's Perceptions of China and the Evolution of Russian-Chinese Relations since the Eighteenth Century* (New York: M.E. Sharpe, 2003), 10, 12. About Leontiev and Russian Sinology, see Eric Widmer, *The Russian Ecclesiastical Mission in Peking During the Eighteenth Century* (Cambridge, Mass.: Harvard University Asia Center, 1976), 160–66; A. V. Strenina, "U istokov russkogo i mirovogo kitaevedeniia," *Sovetskaia etnografiia* 1 (1950): 170–77.

50. On Montesquieu's influence, see M. P. Masterson, "Montesquieu's Grand Design: The Political Sociology of 'Esprit des Lois,'" *British Journal of Political Science* 2, no. 3 (1972): 292–93; Paul M. Spurlin, *Montesquieu in America, 1760–1801* (New York: Octagon, 1961); Donald Lutz, "The Relative Influence of European Writers on Late Eighteenth-Century American Political Thought," *American Political Science Review* 78, no. 1 (1984): 189–97. On Beccaria's influence, see Marcello T. Maestro, "Benjamin Franklin and the Penal Laws," *Journal of the History of Ideas* 36, no. 3 (1975): 554; Maestro, *Voltaire and Beccaria*, 124–51; Caso, *America's Italian Founding Fathers*, 13–39.

51. Jeremy Bentham, *Papers Relative to Codification and Public Instruction* (London: Payne and Foss, 1817), 84. Also see Birtsch, "Reform Absolutism," 343–58. The Napoléonic Codes included the Penal Code, the Civil Code (1804), the Commercial Code (1807), and the Code of Civil Procedure (1806) and Code of Criminal Procedure (1808). For legal reforms in Meiji Japan and late-Qing China, see, e.g., Paul Heng-chao Chen, *The Formation of the Early Meiji Legal Order* (Oxford: Oxford University Press, 1981); Xu, *Trial of Modernity*, 25–84. The French codes were translated into Chinese in 1880, and alongside Montesquieu's *Spirit of the Laws*, into Japanese in 1874.

52. Robert Travers, *Ideology and Empire in Eighteenth-Century India: The British in Bengal, 1757–93* (New York: Cambridge University Press, 2007).

53. See chapters 1 and 2; Nickolas Dirks, *Castes of Mind: Colonialism and the Making of Modern India* (Princeton: Princeton University Press, 2001), 102–23; Ann

Laura Stoler, *Along the Archival Grain: Epistemic Anxieties and Colonial Common Sense* (Princeton: Princeton University Press, 2009), 17–53, esp. 50–51.

54. *Le Mercure Galant*, founded in 1672, was renamed *Mercure de France* in 1714 and once had Voltaire as its editor.

55. Lewis E. Gates, "Introduction," in *Selections from the Essays of Francis Jeffrey*, ed. Lewis E. Gates (Boston: Ginn & Co., 1894), xxxii (on its circulation and readership). On the *Edinburgh Review*'s establishment and influence, see Henry Brougham, *The Life and Times of Lord Henry Brougham*, 3 vols. (London: William Blackwood, 1871–1872), 1:245–70; Sir George Otto Trevelyan, *The Life and Letters of Lord Macaulay* (London: Longmans, Green & Co., 1881), 85 (on Macaulay's rise to fame by publishing in this journal around 1825). Brougham was one of its founders.

56. For Gilford's claim, see John Barrow, *An Autobiographical Memoir of Sir John Barrow* (London: John Murray, 1847), 506, 507 (on reviews' greater influence than pamphlets). See Jonathan Cutmore, *Conservatism and the Quarterly Review: A Critical Analysis* (London: Pickering & Chatto, 2007).

57. "Canton," *Chinese Courier and Canton Gazette*, October 6, 1831. See John Francis Davis, *Chinese Miscellanies: A Collection of Essays and Notes* (London: John Murray, 1865), iv.

58. "Ta Tsing Leu Lee," *Selected Reviews* 5, no. 25 (1811): 23–40; "Ta-Tsing Leu Lee, ec., Leggi fondamentali, e scelta d'alcuni Statuti Supplimetari del Codice Penale del Chinesi," *Annali di scienze e lettere* 8 (1811): 289–304; 9 (1812): 35–44; 10 (1812): 3–38. This Italian translation has recently been attributed to Giovanni Rasori, rather than Ugo Foscolo (see http://www.agichina24.it/punta-di-pennello/notizie /ugo-foscolo-la-milano-br-/del-primo-800-e-il-diritto-cinese).

59. For its Italian and French translations, see George Thomas Staunton, *Ta-Tsing-Leu-Lee o sia Leggi fondamentali del Codice penale della China*, trans. Giovanni Rasori, 3 vols. (Milan: Stamperia di Giovanni Silvestri, 1812) (for the anonymous translator's identity, see Piero Corradini, "La Chine et l'Italie au XIXe siècle," in *La Chine entre amour et haine: Actes du 8ème colloque de sinologie de Chantilly*, ed. Michel Cartier [Paris: Desclée De Bouwer 1998], 266; I am grateful to Dr. Monika Lehner and Georg Lehner at the University of Vienna for referring me to this source); *Ta-Tsing-Leu-Lée, ou les lois fondamentales du Code pénal de la Chine*, trans. Félix Renouard de Sainte-Croix, 2 vols. (Paris: Lenormant, 1812). Also see "Ta-Tsing-Leu-Lee, o sia Leggi fondamentali del Còdice penale della China," *Giornale enciclopedico di Firenze* 4 (1812): 23–24 (*GEDF*). For works citing these retranslations, see, e.g., Adolphe Chauveau and Faustin Hélie, *Théorie du Code pénal* (Brussels: Société Typographique Belge, 1837), vol. 1; L. Nigon de Berty, *Histoire abrégée de la liberté indivi-duelle chez les principaux peuples anciens et modernes* (Paris: Moutardier, 1834), 143–50; Évariste Régis Huc, *L'empire chinois: Faisant suite à l'ouvrage intitulé;*

Souvenirs d'un voyage dans la Tartarie et le Thibet, 2 vols. (Paris: Librairie de Gaume Frères, 1854), 2:293–301; Gian Domenico Romagnosi, *Collezione degli articoli di economia politica e statistica civile*, 2nd ed. (Prato: Dalla Tipografia Guasti, 1836), 124.

60. "Ta Tsing Leu Lee," *Eclectic Review* 6, no. 2 (1810): 946.

61. Francis Jeffrey, "Ta Tsing Leu Lee," *Edinburgh Review* 16, no. 32 (1810): 493–94; "Ta Tsing Leu Lee," *British Critics*, 223.

62. "Ta Tsing Leu Lee," *Monthly Review* 64 (1811): 123.

63. "Ta Tsing Leu Lee," *Critical Review* 21, no. 4 (1810): 347.

64. Lorenzo Arrazola, "Codigo: China," in *Enciclopedia española de derecho y administración* (*Spanish Encyclopedia of Law and Administration*), ed. Lorenzo Arrazola, 367–69 (Madrid: Imprenta de la Revista de Legislacion y Jurisprudencia, á Cargo de J. Morales, 1856). The *Edinburgh* reviewer also mentioned the legislations that allowed those maimed or aged under fifteen or above seventy to redeem themselves from all but capital punishments by a small fine. Capital offenders under ten or above eighty would be recommended to the emperor for clemency (Jeffrey, "Ta Tsing Leu Lee," 489–90; *TTLL*, 25).

65. "Ta Tsing Leu Lee," *British Critics*, 217.

66. "Ta Tsing Leu Lee," *Journal général de la littérature de France* 15, no. 1 (1812): 28–29; Arrazola, "Codigo," 369; "Ta Tsing Leu Lee," *Critical Review*, 344; Barrow, "Ta Tsing Leu Lee," 299.

67. Jeremy Bentham, *Principles of Legislation*, ed. Étienne Dumont (Boston: Wells and Lilly, 1830), 256.

68. Jeffrey, "Ta Tsing Leu Lee," 489–90.

69. George [Egor Fedorovich] Timkovski, *Travels of the Russian Mission through Mongolia to China, and Residence in Peking, in the Years 1820–1821*, 2 vols. (London: Longman, 1827), 1:345–46, 340–46 (on Chinese law and punishments).

70. "Ta Tsing Leu Lee," *Critical Review*, 345; *TTLL*, 434.

71. "Ta Tsing Leu Lee," *Critical Review*, 345; "Ta Tsing Leu Lee," *British Critics*, 218. Cf. "Ta Tsing Leu Lee," *Eclectic Review*, 1040. On the benefit of clergy, see Scott Christianson, *With Liberty for Some: 500 Years of Imprisonment in America* (Boston: Northeastern University Press, 1998), 21–23.

72. "Ta Tsing Leu Lee," *Critical Review*, 349–50.

73. "Ta Tsing Leu Lee," *Eclectic Review*, 1030; Jeffrey, "Ta Tsing Leu Lee," 490.

74. See Blackstone, *Commentaries*, 4:33–39, 195–96 (on false accusation).

75. "Ta Tsing Leu Lee," *Journal général de la littérature*, 28; Arrazola, "Codigo," 369.

76. "Ta Tsing Leu Lee," *British Critics*, 217–18; *TTLL*, 360.

77. Barrow, *Travels*, 366–37.

78. [John Barrow], "[Review of] *Voyages à Peking, Manille, et l'Isle de France, faits dans l'intervalle des années 1784 à 1801*. Par M. de Guignes (Paris, 1808)," *Quarterly Review* 2, no. 4 (1809): 272 (on de Guignes's discussion of Chinese law). See

John Barrow, *Voyage en Chine, formant le complément du voyage de Lord Macartney*, trans. J. Castera (Paris: Buisson, 1805).

79. He noted again that this feature ensured that every shade of aggravation or mitigation of the offender's guilt would be taken into account. See Barrow, "Ta Tsing Leu Lee," 295, 309.

80. "Ta Tsing Leu Lee," *British Critics*, 222–23; *TTLL*, 315.

81. "Ta Tsing Leu Lee," *British Critics*, 223.

82. "Ta Tsing Leu Lee," *Monthly Review*, 121; Jeffrey, "Ta Tsing Leu Lee," 496–98; "Ta Tsing Leu Lee," *Eclectic Review*, 1030; "Ta Tsing Leu Lee," *Journal général de la littérature*, 27–28; Arrazola, "Codigo," 368–69; Saluges, "Ta-Tsing-Leu-Lee, ou les lois fondamentales du Code pénal de la Chine," *Mercure de France: Journal littéraire et politique* 50 (1812): 210–18, 216.

83. Walter H. Medhurst, *China: Its State and Prospects* (Boston: Crocker & Brewster, 1838), 113; John L. Nevius, *China and the Chinese* (New York: Harper & Brothers, 1869), 72; James Dyer Ball, *Things Chinese*, 2nd ed. (London: Sampson Low, 1893), 258–59; James Bashford, *China: An Interpretation* (Cincinnati: Abingdon Press, 1916), 282.

84. Jeffrey, "Ta Tsing Leu Lee," 481–82.

85. See Lord Henry Cockburn, *Life of Lord Jeffrey, with a Selection from His Correspondence*, 2nd ed., 2 vols. (Edinburgh: Adam and Charles Black, 1852), 1:422 (on the review's authorship), 419–25 (listing 200 contributions by Jeffrey). About Jeffrey, see Philip Flynn, *Francis Jeffrey* (Newark: University of Delaware Press, 1978).

86. [Francis Jeffrey], "John Barrow's Travels in China," *Edinburgh Review* 5, no. 10 (1805): 262.

87. "Ta Tsing Leu Lee," *Eclectic Review*, 1041.

88. Jeffrey, "Ta Tsing Leu Lee," 488.

89. "Ta Tsing Leu Lee," *Journal général de la littérature*, 28; Saluges, "Ta-Tsing-Leu-Lee," 212–15 (quoting De Pauw).

90. *TTLL*, 516–17; Jeffrey, "Ta Tsing Leu Lee," 498–99.

91. "Ta Tsing Leu Lee," *Monthly Review*, 130; "Ta Tsing Leu Lee," *Literary Panorama* 10 (1811): 25.

92. Barrow, "Ta Tsing Leu Lee," 314, 311, 313.

93. Jeffrey, "Ta Tsing Leu Lee," 498; Barrow, *Travels*, 179–80.

94. Jeffrey, "Ta Tsing Leu Lee," 498–99.

95. George Thomas Staunton, *Miscellaneous Notices Relating to China, and Our Commercial Intercourse with That Country* [Part 2] (London, 1828), 268, 272 (quotations); see also 262–77.

96. George Thomas Staunton, *Miscellaneous Notices Relating to China, and Our Commercial Intercourse with That Country*, 2nd, enlarged ed. (London: John Murray, 1850), 387–88. Cf. *TTLL*, 517.

97. See recent studies, Keith J. M. Smith, *Lawyers, Legislators, and Theorists: Developments in English Criminal Jurisprudence 1800–1957* (Oxford: Clarendon Press, 1998); Lindsay Farmer, "Reconstructing the English Codification Debate: The Criminal Law Commissioners, 1833–45," *Law and History Review* 18, no. 2 (2000): 397–425; Peter R. Glazebrook, "Criminal Law Reform: England," in *Encyclopedia of Crime and Justice*, ed. Joshua Dressler, 400–12 (New York: Macmillan, 2002).

98. For the growing influence of the writings of Voltaire, Montesquieu, and others in Europe, see Sir Samuel Romilly, *Memoirs of the Life of Sir Samuel Romilly*, 2nd ed., 3 vols. (London: John Murray, 1840), 2:342; Robert J. Mackintosh, ed., *Memoirs of the Life of the Right Honourable Sir James Mackintosh*, 2nd ed. (London: E. Moxon, 1836), 1:42 (1788); Montagu, *Opinions*. The three belonged to the famous King of Clubs, which had Thomas Malthus.

99. Sir Samuel Romilly, *Observations on the Criminal Law of England as It Relates to Capital Punishments, and on the Mode in Which It Is Admitted* (London: Cadell and Davies, 1810); "House of Commons: Penal Laws [and Reform Bills by Romilly]," *Times*, February 10, 1810. This speech (on February 9) was published around March 12 and reprinted with corrections and a postscript on October 30. See Romilly, *Memoirs*, 2:304, 341; see 243–90 for his role in the reform. Only the last Bill (on stealing from vessels) was moved for debate (Smith, *Lawyers*, 59).

100. Glazebrook, "Criminal Law Reform," 404–11.

101. Henry Dagge, *Considerations on Criminal Law* (Dublin: H. Saunders, 1772), 125, 180, 240–42; *Hints for a Reform in the Criminal Law, in a Letter Addressed to Sir Samuel Romilly, by a Late Member of Parliament* (London: J. Mawman, 1811), 6.

102. Dagge, *Considerations on the Criminal Law*, 241.

103. Romilly, *Observations*, 3.

104. Ibid., 3, 6–9, 12–18, 22–23; Basil Montagu, ed., *The Debates in the House of Commons, During the Year 1811: Upon Certain Bills for Abolishing the Punishment of Death* (London: Longman, 1812), 5–6.

105. See "Trial by Jury," *North China Herald* 12, no. 372 (1874): 556–57; Sir James Mackintosh, "A Charge," in *The Miscellaneous Works of the Right Honourable Sir James Mackintosh*, ed. Robert James Mackintosh, 3 vols. (London: Longman, 1846), 3:304; "The Administration of Justice in China," *North China Herald* 18, no. 521 (1877): 438. For critiques of English law and jury trial, see Douglas Hay and Francis Snyder, eds., *Policing and Prosecution in Britain, 1750–1850* (Oxford: Oxford University Press, 1989); Douglas Hay, "Crime and Justice in Eighteenth- and Nineteenth-Century England," *Crime and Justice* 2 (1980): 45–84.

106. Romilly, *Observations*, 4–9, 69–71 (on Paley's arguments). For more about the debates, see Michael Lobban, *The Common Law and English Jurisprudence, 1760–1850* (Oxford: Oxford University Press, 1991), 185–222 (on codification); David Liberman, *The Province of Legislation Determined: Legal Theory in*

Eighteenth-Century Britain (Cambridge: Cambridge University Press, 1989), 99–256 (on legal reform).

107. Romilly, *Observations*, 20–21; see also 2–4, 15–27.

108. Montagu, *Opinions*, 3:106–11.

109. James Fitzjames Stephen, *The History of the Criminal Law of England*, 3 vols. (London: Macmillan and Co., 1883), 2:216 (quotation); Charles Noble Gregory, "Bentham and the Codifiers," *Harvard Law Review* 13, no. 5 (1900): 349–50.

110. Smith, *Lawyers*, 50 (on Bentham's reputation and Romilly's sparing references to him); Gregory, "Bentham and the Codifiers," 47–49; Leslie Stephen, *The Life of Sir James Fitzjames Stephen* (London: Smith, Elder & Co., 1895), 247.

111. See George H. Mason, "Preface," in *The Punishments of China: Illustrated by Twenty-two Engravings, with Explanations in English and French* (London: William Miller, 1801).

112. Bentham sometimes cited China as a negative illustration. See Bentham, *Principles of Legislation*, 306; Jeremy Bentham, *Principles of the Penal Code* (Boston: Weeks, 1840), 91.

113. *Hints for a Reform in Criminal Law*, 4–5, 7.

114. Ibid., 12–14, 26–28.

115. Romilly, *Observations*, 1; James Mackintosh, "Speech on Moving for a Committee to Inquire into the State of the Criminal Law," in *Miscellaneous Works*, 3:384 (quoting Montagu's pamphlet on capital punishments). Also see William Frankland, *The Speech of Wm. Frankland, Esq. in the House of Commons on Friday, the 29th of March, 1811* (London: Ridgway, 1811).

116. Montagu, *Debates*, 35–37; see also 3–139 (February 21 to April 8, 1811). See Montagu, *Opinions*, 3:2–139. Frankland was a Conservative member of Parliament for Thirsk from 1801 to 1815.

117. Montagu, *Debates*, 39–40 (emphasis added); Montagu, *Opinions*, 3:39–40.

118. Michel Foucault, "Governmentality," in *The Foucault Effect: Studies in Governmentality*, ed. Graham Burchell et al., 87–104 (Chicago: University of Chicago Press, 1991), 91; Nicholas Dirks, *The Scandal of Empire: India and the Creation of Imperial Britain* (Cambridge, Mass.: Harvard University Press, 2008), 211. See also Michel Foucault, *Discipline and Punish: The Birth of the Prison*, trans. Alan Sheridan (New York: Random House, 1995); Aijaz Ahmad, "*Orientalism* and After: Ambivalence and Metropolitan Location in the Work of Edward Said," in *Imperialism: Critical Concepts in Historical Studies*, ed. Peter J. Cain and Mark Harrison (London: Routledge, 2000), 256–308, 261 (on Foucault's Eurocentric assumptions). For late imperial China's social control by policing, see, e.g., "Ta Tsing Leu Lee," *Literary Panorama*, 24; Alison Dray-Novey, "Spatial Order and Police in Imperial Beijing," *Journal of Asian Studies* 52, no. 4 (1993): 885–922.

119. On Weber's depiction of patrimonial China and subsequent studies, see Max Weber, *The Religion of China: Confucianism and Taoism*, trans. Hans H. Gerth

(New York: Free Press, 1951); Max Weber, *Economy and Society: An Outline of Interpretative Sociology*, ed. Guenther Roth and Claus Wittich, 2 vols. (Berkeley: University of California Press, 1978), 2:1047; Wolfgang Schluchter, *Rationalism, Religion, and Domination: A Weberian Perspective* (Berkeley: University of California Press, 1989), 107–10; Steven Seidman, *Contested Knowledge: Social Theory Today* (London: Wiley-Blackwell, 2011), 54–56. See chapter 4 on Mill. One wonders how much Foucault's theorization was influenced by such earlier Orientalist imaginaries.

120. Montagu, *Debates*, 40. Bentham's *Principles of Legislation* was first written in 1780.

121. Robert Southey to John Rickman, 1812, in *The Collected Letters of Robert Southey, Part 4: 1810–1815*, ed. Ian Packer and Lynda Pratt, Letter 2194, http://www.rc.umd.edu/editions/southey_letters/Part_Four/HTML/letterEEd.26.2194.html#*

122. Farmer, "Reconstructing," 398–99 (quotation and summary of the arguments); Shael Herman, "The Fate and the Future of Codification in America," *American Journal of Legal History* 40, no. 4 (1996): 414–15, 417–24.

123. Weber, *Economy and Society*, 2:858.

124. See, e.g., Qing Nian, *Shuotie zhaiyao chaocun* (*Abstracts for Record of Legal Memoranda*), 14 *ce* (Kaifeng: Kaifeng fushu, 1831–1848); Yang Yuekun, comp., *Da Qing lü lici zuanxiu tiaoli* (*Rules for Revising the Great Qing Code*), 12 *juan* (Beijing: Da Qing lüliguan, 1807); Hong Hongxu, comp., *Cheng'an zhiyi* (*Doubtful Issues in Leading Cases*), 36 *juan* (Hangzhou: Sanyutang, 1736); *Xingbu tongxing tiaoli* (*Circulars of the Ministry of Justice*), 6 *juan* (1886).

125. Montagu, *Debates*, 70.

126. Ibid., 89–97, 107–12.

127. See the debates in the House of Lords of May 24, 1811, in "Criminal Law Bills," in *Parliamentary Debates* (May 13–July 24, 1811), ed. T. C. Hansard (London: Longman, Hurst, Rees, 1812), 296–303, esp. 297–99. Montagu, *Opinions*, 3:272–73. Also see Romilly to Lord Holland, April 11 and 13, 1811, in Holland Papers, British Library, Add MSS51826, ff. 146–47. Lord Ellenborough (Edward Law) became attorney general in 1801 and was chief justice of the King's Bench 1801–1818. He received his peerage in 1802.

128. "Criminal Law Bills," 209–303. See "House of Lords (May 24th): Criminal Laws," *Caledonian Mercury*, May 30, 1811, 4.

129. Henry Brougham, "Sir Samuel Romilly on English Criminal Law," *Edinburgh Review* 19 (1812): 394. Brougham was not a fan of China (Brougham, *Life and Times*, 1:268, 116).

130. This paraphrase is from "House of Lords (May 24th): Criminal Laws."

131. See the speech by George Canning in "Motion Respecting the System of Transportation, and the State of New South Wales [February 18, 1819]," in

The Parliamentary Debates from the Year 1803 to the Present Time [1819], ed. T. C. Hansard (London: Longman, 1819), 463–509, 502.

132. Mackintosh, *Miscellaneous Works*, 3:369–70, also 1:190–92 (on his appreciation of codification and Bentham's legislative schemes), 206 (critiquing Bentham and Mill).

133. Farmer, "Reconstructing," 423–25. See Barbara Shapiro, "Codification of the Laws in Seventeenth-Century England," *Wisconsin Law Review*, no. 2 (1974): 428–65; Gunther A. Weiss, "The Enchantment of Codification in the Common-Law World," *Yale Journal of International Law* 25 (2000): 435–532.

134. Smith, *Lawyers*, 58–61.

135. Mackintosh, *Miscellaneous Works*, 3:380, 379 (commending Romilly). For the British codification projects, see Farmer, "Reconstruction," 407–8; Chris Clarkson, "Recent Law Reform and Codification of the General Principles of Criminal Law in England and Wales: A Tale of Woe," in *Codification, Macaulay and the Indian Penal Code*, ed. Wing-Cheong Chan et al., 337–65 (Burlington, Vt.: Ashgate, 2011), 337–39 (on the death of codification there). On the law commissions, see Lobban, *Common Law*, 185–222; Rupert Cross, "The Reports of the Criminal Law Commissioners (1833–49) and the Abortive Bills of 1853," in *Reshaping the Criminal Law: Essays in Honour of Glanville Williams*, ed. P. R. Glazebrook (London: Stevens, 1978), 5–20; Lang, *Codification*, 9–68.

136. Stephen, *Life*, 246–47. On other factors that shaped the legal reform in Victorian England, see Martin Wiener, *Reconstructing the Criminal: Culture, Law, Policy in England, 1830–1914* (Cambridge: Cambridge University Press, 1990), 14–174.

137. In November 1810, the French Penal Code, promulgated in February, was still unavailable to British readers because of the war with France, and its first English translation appeared only in 1819 (James Mill, "The Code d'Instruction Criminelle," *Edinburgh Review* 17, no. 33 [1810]: 90; *The Penal Code of France, Translated into English* [London: H. Butterworth, 1819]). For more on French codification, see John W. Head, "Codes, Cultures, Chaos, and Champions: Common Features of Legal Codification Experiences in China, Europe, and North America," *Duke Journal of Comparative and International Law* 13, no. 1 (2004): 35–47.

138. David Skuy, "Macaulay and the Indian Penal Code of 1862," *Modern Asian Studies* 32, no. 2 (1998): 514.

139. Stephen, *Life*, 247–74 (on the codification); Keith J. M. Smith, *James Fitzjames Stephen: Portrait of a Victorian Rationalist* (Cambridge: Cambridge University Press, 1988), 138.

140. See James Stephen's address at the Social Science Association for 1872–1873, quoted in Lester Lelan, "Law and the Study of Law," *Canadian Monthly and National Review* 13, no. 1 (1878): 190–201, 199. Thomas Babington Macaulay, "Introductory Report upon the Indian Penal Code," in *The Complete Writings of*

Thomas Babington Macaulay: Miscellanies (New York: Houghton, Mifflin & Co., 1901), 551–734, 553.

141. Elizabeth Kolsky, "Codification and the Rule of Colonial Difference: Criminal Procedure in British India," *Law and History Review* 23, no. 3 (2005): 631–86, 652 (quotation); Nasser Hussain, *The Jurisprudence of Emergency: Colonialism and the Rule of Law* (Ann Arbor: University of Michigan Press, 2003), 35–68 (on British policies informed by the discourse of Oriental despotism).

142. Sir William Jones, *Institutes of Hindu Law: Or, the Ordinances of Menu, According to the Gloss of Cullúca, Comprising the Indian System of Duties, Religious and Civil* (London: J. Sewell, Cornhill, 1796), iii, quoted in *TTLL*, xxvi. James Mill, *The History of British India*, 4th ed., 6 vols. (London: James Madden, 1840), 2:135. See Bruce Mazlish, *James and John Stuart Mill* (New Brunswick, N.J.: Transaction, 1988), 122–23.

143. Partha Chatterjee, *The Black Hole of Empire: History of a Global Practice of Power* (Princeton: Princeton University Press, 2012). Also see his more recent interview, "Empire as a Practice of Power," http://www.humanityjournal .net/?s=empire+as+a+practice+of+power.

144. See, e.g., Hegel, *Philosophy of History*, 124, 138.

145. Macaulay, "Introductory Report," 553–55. Maine argued in 1879 that India was "a country singularly empty of law" (Maine, "Minutes on Codification in India" [July 17, 1879], quoted in Kolsky, "Codification," 652).

146. See, e.g., Gregory Blue, "China and Western Social Thought in the Modern Period," in *China and Historical Capitalism: Genealogies of Sinological Knowledge*, ed. Timothy Brook and Gregory Blue, 57–109 (Cambridge: Cambridge University Press, 2002); Le Comte, *Memoirs*, 314; Pak, *China and the West*, 55 (on Christian Wolff's admiration of the Chinese government). On the view of Mogul India as decadent and weak, see Dirks, *Scandal*, 199, 320–21.

147. Jeffrey, "Ta Tsing Leu Lee," 482, 487–89, 498–99; Barrow, "[Review of] *Voyages à Peking*," 272–73; Barrow, *Travels*, 366–67.

148. *Hansard's Parliamentary Debates*, 3d ser., 19:531, quoted in Kolsky, "Codification," 635.

149. Trevelyan, *Life*, 287. Macaulay was an admirer of Mackintosh's. See [Thomas B. Macaulay], "Review of *Memoirs of the Life of the Right Honourable Sir James Mackintosh*," *Edinburgh Review* 62, no. 125 (1835): 210–11 (on his views of Mackintosh). The authorship of this originally anonymous review was based on Trevelyan, *Life*, 335–42.

150. Quoted in Trevelyan, *Life*, 302–3. The Code of Criminal Procedure had 542 sections and formed "a pamphlet of 210 widely printed octavo pages," while the Penal Code consisted of 510 sections (compared with 432 sections or statutes in *Ta Tsing Leu Lee*). The post-1858 Indian Subcontinent of 200 or 300 million Indians were overseen by some 2,000 Europeans.

151. *TTLL*, xxiv–xxv, xxxv (on the Qing Code). Mackintosh was also accused of being a "rash theorist" or "ultra-philosopher" (Mackintosh, *Miscellaneous Works*, 3:366).

152. See, e.g., Elizabeth Kolsky, *Colonial Justice in British India: White Violence and the Rule of Law* (Cambridge: Cambridge University Press, 2010).

153. Farmer, "Reconstructing," 399.

154. Weber, *Economy and Society*, 2:865–66, 882–92, 813–14; see 891 and 865 for quotations. Cf. Blue, "China," 95–99 (critiquing Weber).

155. Weber, *Economy and Society*, 2:850–52, 852–55 (about Roman law's influence). For Weber's Sinological deficiency and flawed arguments, see Robert M. Marsh, "Weber's Misunderstanding of Traditional Chinese Law," *American Journal of Sociology* 106, no. 2 (2000): 283–84; Otto B. van der Sprenkel, "Max Weber on China," *History and Theory* 3, no. 3 (1964): 348–70.

156. Weber, *Economy and Society*, 2:844–46, 816–28; cf. 857.

157. Derk Bodde and Clarence Morris, *Law in Imperial China* (Cambridge, Mass.: Harvard University Press, 1967), 174; Brian E. McKnight, *The Enlightened Judgments: Ch'ing-Ming Chi* (Albany: SUNY Press, 1999), 15–16; Philip C. C. Huang, *Civil Justice in China: Representation and Practice in the Qing* (Stanford: Stanford University Press, 1996), 281–82; John M. Hobson, *The Eastern Origins of Western Civilisation* (Cambridge: Cambridge University Press, 2004), 16, 190–218, 289–91; Li Chen, "Legal Specialists and Judicial Administration in Late Imperial China, 1651–1911," *Late Imperial China* 33, no. 1 (June 2012): 1–54; Ruskola, *Legal Orientalism*.

4. SENTIMENTAL IMPERIALISM AND THE GLOBAL SPECTACLE OF CHINESE PUNISHMENTS

1. "Execution by Strangulation," *North China Herald* 16, no. 469 (1876): 421–22.

2. "Punishment of the Canton and Fuhkeen Vagabonds," ibid., 1, no. 4 (1850): 1.

3. For two excellent reviews of the vast relevant literature, see Daniel Wickberg, "What Is the History of Sensibilities? On Cultural Histories, Old and New," *American Historical Review* 112, no. 3 (2007): 661–84, and Barbara H. Rosenwein, "Worrying About Emotions in History," *American Historical Review* 107 (2001): 821–45.

4. Athena Athanasiou et al., "Towards a New Epistemology: The 'Affective Turn,'" *Historein* 8 (2008): 5–16.

5. Barbara H. Rosenwein, "Problems and Methods in the History of Emotions," *Passions in Context: International Journal for the History and Theory of Emotions* 1 (2010): 19–20.

6. Athanasiou et al., "Toward a New Epistemology," 5.

7. David Der-wei Wang, *The Monster That Is History: History, Violence, and Fictional Writing in Twentieth-Century China* (Berkeley: University of California Press, 2004), 15–116; Michael Berry, *A History of Pain: Trauma in Modern Chinese Literature and Film* (New York: Columbia University Press, 2008); Eric Hayot, *The Hypothetical Mandarin: Sympathy, Modernity, and Chinese Pain* (New York: Oxford University Press, 2009). See also Haiyan Lee, *Revolution of the Heart: The Genealogy of Love in China, 1900–1950* (Stanford: Stanford University Press, 2007).

8. Eugenia Lean, *Public Passions: The Trial of Shi Jianqiao and the Rise of Popular Sympathy in Republican China* (Berkeley: University of California Press, 2007). See also James L. Hevia, *English Lessons: The Pedagogy of Imperialism in Nineteenth-Century China* (Durham: Duke University Press, 2003), 102–21, 185–240, 282–314; Timothy Brook, Jérôme Bourgon, and Gregory Blue, *Death by a Thousand Cuts* (Cambridge, Mass.: Harvard University Press, 2008).

9. Adam Smith, *The Theory of Moral Sentiments* (London: A. Millar, 1759), 1–6; David Hume, *A Treatise of Human Nature*, 3 vols. (London: John Noon, 1739), 1:169; David Hume, *An Enquiry Concerning the Principles of Morals* (London: A. Millar, 1751), 78–99; Dipesh Chakrabarty, *Provincializing Europe: Postcolonial Thought and Historical Difference* (Princeton: Princeton University Press, 2000), 123.

10. Smith, *Theory of Moral Sentiments*, 2–3.

11. Chakrabarty, *Provincializing Europe*, 119, 126–27. For Rousseau's similar view of sympathy, see Lee, *Revolution of the Heart*, 225.

12. Uday S. Mehta, *Liberalism and Empire: A Study in Nineteenth-Century British Liberal Thought* (Chicago: University of Chicago Press, 1999), 16–17. For the transformation of liberalism over time, see Jennifer Pitts, *A Turn to Empire: The Rise of Imperial Liberalism in Britain and France* (Princeton: Princeton University Press, 2005).

13. I paraphrase Wickberg's definition of "culture of sensibility" here (Wickberg, "What Is the History of Sensibilities," 667–69). For this study, I have followed others to understand affect as precognitive responses, feelings as cognitive or conscious personal sensations, emotions as social-culturally informed expressions of feelings, and sentiments as further developed attitudes or opinions of emotions and their associated social and cultural assumptions. See Lynn Festa, *Sentimental Figures of Empire in Eighteenth-Century Britain and France* (Baltimore: Johns Hopkins University Press, 2006), 14–22. For recent debates, see Ruth Leys, "The Turn to Affect: A Critique," *Critical Inquiry* 37, no. 3 (2011): 434–72; Athanasiou et al., "Towards a New Epistemology," 5–12.

14. Karen Halttunen, "Humanitarianism and the Pornography of Pain in Anglo-American Culture," *American Historical Review* 100, no. 2 (1995): 303. See literature reviews by Wickberg and Rosenwein cited earlier. Works by Hume

and Smith were avidly read by legal reformers. See Samuel Romilly, *Memoirs of the Life of Sir Samuel Romilly*, 2nd ed., 3 vols. (London: John Murray, 1840), 1:397, 403, 2:342 (reading Voltaire, Burke, and Hume in 1810).

15. Vic A. C. Gatrell, *The Hanging Tree: Execution and the English People 1770–1868* (Oxford: Oxford University Press, 1994), 236, 7, 56; Pieter Spierenburg, *The Spectacle of Suffering: Execution and the Evolution of Repression* (Cambridge: Cambridge University Press, 1984); Louis P. Masur, *Rites of Execution: Capital Punishment and the Transformation of American Culture, 1776–1865* (Oxford: Oxford University Press, 1989).

16. See, e.g., Michel Foucault, *Discipline and Punish: The Birth of the Prison*, trans. Alan Sheridan (New York: Random House, 1995), 44–65.

17. Halttunen, "Humanitarianism," 303. See Elizabeth Barnes, "Affecting Relations: Pedagogy, Patriarchy, and the Politics of Sympathy," *American Literary History* 8, no. 4 (1996): 597–614.

18. Elizabeth Barnes, "Communicable Violence and the Problem of Capital Punishment in New England, 1830–1890," *Modern Language Studies* 30, no. 1 (2000): 7.

19. For the impact of sensibility on European legal reforms, see, e.g., Randall McGowen, "A Powerful Sympathy: Terror, the Prison, and Humanitarian Reform in Early Nineteenth-Century Britain," *Journal of British Studies* 25, no. 3 (1986): 312–34; Spierenburg, *Spectacle of Suffering*.

20. Foucault, *Discipline and Punish*, 92; Gatrell, *Hanging Tree*, 22–24, 25 (acknowledging the influence of sentimentalism). For other revisionist scholarship, see Michael Ignatieff, *A Just Measure of Pain: The Penitentiary in the Industrial Revolution, 1750–1850* (London: Macmillan, 1978); David Garland, *Punishment and Modern Society* (Chicago: University of Chicago Press, 1990).

21. John Stuart Mill, "Civilization: Signs of the Times," *London and Westminster Review* 3, no. 1 (1836): 13–14; see also 12–13.

22. For recent exceptions, see books by Hayot, Berry, and Brook et al. cited earlier.

23. Chakrabarty, *Provincializing Europe*, 119–20 (emphasis added).

24. Franciscus de Victoria (Vitoria), *De Indis et de ivre Belli Relectiones, Being Parts of Relectiones Theologicae XII*, trans. John Pawley Bate (Washington, D.C.: Carnegie Institution of Washington, 1917), 156–62, 96–100 (modern editors lauding Vitoria as a champion of Indian or human rights).

25. The Treaty of Westphalia in 1648 ended the religious wars in Europe and came to be remembered as the legal recognition of the nation-state system or even the start of modern international law.

26. Festa, *Sentimental Figures*, 53.

27. Randall McGowen, "Revisiting the Hanging Tree," *British Journal of Criminology* 40, no. 1 (2000): 9; McGowen, "Powerful Sympathy."

28. Rosenwein, "Worrying about Emotions," 35; Barbara H. Rosenwein, *Emotional Communities in the Early Middle Ages* (Ithaca: Cornell University Press, 2006), 20–29. Rosenwein argues that emotional communities are "an aspect of every social group in which people have a stake and interest" ("Problems and Methods," 12).

29. Foucault, *Discipline and Punish*, 3–5. See Brook et al., *Death*, 155–69.

30. Brook et al., *Death*, 200.

31. For the quotation, see Athanasiou et al. "Towards a New Epistemology," 9.

32. Tanja E. Aalberts, *Constructing Sovereignty between Politics and Law* (New York: Routledge, 2012), 132 (quoting Foucault).

33. Craig Clunas, *Chinese Export Watercolours* (London: Victoria and Albert Museum, 1984), 12, 38–77, 91; Brook et al., *Death*, 25; Carl L. Crossman, *The China Trade* (Princeton: Pyne, 1972), 15–38. Concerning a famous local watercolor painter Lamqua, see Patrick Conner, "Lamqua: Western and Chinese Painter," *Arts of Asia* 29, no. 2 (1999): 46–64.

34. Beth F. Tobin, *Picturing Imperial Power: Colonial Subjects in Eighteenth-Century British Painting* (Durham: Duke University Press, 1999), 14.

35. See Janet Wolff, *The Social Production of Art* (1981), quoted in Tobin, *Picturing Imperial Power*, 14; George H. Mason, ed., *The Punishments of China: Illustrated by Twenty-two Engravings, with Explanations in English and French* (London: W. Miller by W. Bulmer, 1801).

36. See its existing editions in libraries at WorldCat.org.

37. *Philadelphia Gazette*, October 23, 1801 (about these books at Samuel F. Bradford's bookstore, at No. 4 South Third Street), and February 13, 1802 (noticing *The Punishments of China* available at another bookstore).

38. "Review: *The Punishments of China* (Miller, 1801)," *Monthly Review* 35 (1801): 25 (suspecting its being fictitious representations). For the English comparative work citing *The Punishments of China* as an authority on Chinese law, see *The Criminal Recorder; or, Biographical Sketches of Notorious Public Characters*, 4 vols. (London: Albion Press, 1810), 3:19–22, 37, 42, 83, 88, 117, 198, 411–12. I saw an 1804 German edition in July 2005, at http://www.rootenbergbooks.com/Rootenberg_Books_Illustrated.html. For the French edition, see D. Bazin de Malpière, *La Chine: Mœurs, usages, costumes, arts et métiers, peines civiles et militaires, cérémonies religieuses, monuments et paysages*, 2 vols. (Paris: L'éditeur, 1825), also featured in the *Journal Asiatique*, as reported in the *Canton Register* 1, no. 31 (1828): 123.

39. For a few albums of nineteenth-century watercolor paintings of "Chinese" punishments in Euro-American librarians and museums, see http://turandot.chineselegalculture.org/VisualSet.php?ID=95& and http://turandot.chineselegalculture.org/VisualSet.php?ID=99&. I have found many such paintings at various other Web sites during the past ten years or so.

40. See George H. Mason, "Preface," in *The Costume of China* (London: William Miller, 1800); see also Clunas, *Chinese Export Watercolours*, 33–42 (dating the originals to 1780–1790, at the Victoria and Albert Museum).

41. Samuel Wells Williams, *The Middle Kingdom: A Survey of the Chinese Empire and Its Inhabitants*, 2 vols. (New York: Wiley & Putnam, 1848), 2:175.

42. Refer to two Westerners buying watercolors at the Yongtai Xingtong Studio in Guangzhou in Cheng Cunjie, *Shijiu shiji Zhongguo waixiao tongcao shuicaihua yanjiu* (*Study of Nineteenth-Century China Export Watercolor Paintings on Gouache Paper*) (Shanghai: Shanghai guji chubanshe, 2008), 109.

43. Clunas, *Chinese Export Watercolours*, 11–12, 72, 25.

44. Hayot, *Hypothetical Mandarin*, 79–80.

45. George H. Mason, "Preface," in *Punishments of China*. See Susan Sontag, *Regarding the Pain of Others* (New York: Picador, 2003), 83, 122. Cf. Judith Butler, *Frames of War: When Is Life Grievable?* (New York: Verso, 2010), 68–69, 96–99.

46. See Sir George Leonard Staunton, *An Authentic Account of an Embassy from the King of Great Britain to the Emperor of China*, 3 vols. (London: G. Nicol, 1797), 2:490. Cf. Andrea McKenzie, "'This Death Some Strong and Stout Hearted Man Doth Choose': The Practice of *Peine forte et dure* in Seventeenth- and Eighteenth-Century England," *Law and History Review* 23, no. 2 (2005): 1–43; Elizabeth Hanson, "Torture and Truth in Renaissance England," *Representations* 34 (1991): 53–84. On critiques of the English legal system, also see chapter 3.

47. Foucault, *Discipline and Punish*, 15, 37–41 (on torture); Lisa Silverman, *Tortured Subjects: Pain, Truth, and the Body in Early Modern France* (Chicago: University of Chicago Press 2001), 51–178. On European abolition of judicial torture by the 1780s, see John H. Langbein, *Torture and the Law of Proof* (Chicago: University of Chicago Press, 1976). About Chinese practice, see Nancy Park, "Imperial Chinese Justice and the Law of Torture," *Late Imperial China* 29, no. 2 (2008): 37–67.

48. See "Preface" and plate XXI in Mason, *Punishments of China*. The Qing Code stipulated that women could not wear gold ornaments with jewels unsuitable to their social status, but that those who violated this rule would subject their *male household head* (e.g., father or husband) to punishment of fifty to one hundred strokes of the bamboo. See Tian Tao and Zheng Qin, eds., *Da Qing lüli* (*The Great Qing Code*) (1740) (Beijing: Falü chubanshe, 1998), 289–90.

49. Mason, "Preface," in *Punishments of China*.

50. Chakrabarty, *Provincializing Europe*, 127 (citing Smith, *Theory of Moral Sentiments*, 45, 50).

51. Smith, *Theory of Moral Sentiments*, 9–11, 3, 5.

52. Adam Smith, *The Theory of Moral Sentiments*, 2nd ed. (London: A. Millar, 1761), 211–14 (part 3, chap. 2). It was the same in the third edition (1767) and fifth edition (1781). Cf. the sixth Dublin edition (1777), 192–93 (part 3, chap. 2). It was not rearranged and placed in the renamed chapter 3 of part 3 until the sixth

London edition (1790), 1:343–44. Many modern scholars have assumed that this passage appeared in the first edition in 1759, while others have suggested that it was not in the printed edition until 1790.

53. Edmund Burke, *The Works and Correspondence of the Right Honourable Edmund Burke*, 8 vols. (London: Francis & John Rivington, 1852), 7:380, 287–88 ("narrow circle of municipal justice"). See also Pitts, *Turn to Empire*, 77.

54. Hannah Arendt, *On Revolution* (New York: Penguin, 2006), 75–79; Luc Boltanski, *Distant Suffering: Morality, Media, and Politics* (New York: Cambridge University Press, 1999), 3–6 (for a nice summary), 5–13.

55. For this book, I have examined a large number of periodicals and newspapers, including such China-oriented ones as the *Indo-Chinese Gleaner* (1817–1822), *Malacca Observer* (1826–1829), *Canton Register* (1827–1843), *Chinese Repository* (1832–1851), *Canton Press* (1831–1833), *North China Herald* (1850–1943), *China Review* (1872–1901), and the *China Recorder and Missionary Journal* (1867–1941), as well as those based in Western metropoles such as the *Times*, *Quarterly Review*, *Journal of the Royal Asiatic Society*, the Paris-based *Journal Asiatique*, the *Boston Recorder*, *Chicago Tribune*, *New York Times*, *Washington Post*, and the *Los Angeles Times*. Also see chapter 5.

56. "Decapitated by Dozens," *Chicago Daily Tribune*, July 28, 1877.

57. See, e.g., "Punishment by Strangulation," *Canton Press*, April 14, 1838; "A Chinese Execution [at Peking Recounted by a Correspondent of *Le Soir*]," *Times*, March 28, 1870; "Chinese Cruelty: Inhumanities Perpetrated in the Flowery Kingdom," *Chicago Tribune*, July 30, 1877 (reprinted from the *San Francisco Chronicle*); Rev. Anson Smyth, "Chinese Punishment Contrasted with Our Dealing with Criminals," *New York Evangelist*, December 3, 1877; William Laird-Clowes, "Chinese Cruelty: To the Editor of the *Times*," *Times*, September 18, 1879; "Chinese Punishments," *Saturday Evening Post*, October 4, 1884; "Barbarous Chinese Punishment," *Chicago Daily Tribune*, June 18, 1888; James Gilmour, "A Chinese Execution in Mongolia," *Chinese Recorder and Missionary Journal* 20, no. 6 (1889): 248–54; "Executions in China," *Boston Daily Globe*, November 25, 1894; Philippe Berthelot, "Les supplices en Chine," *Je sais tout: Encyclopédie mondiale illustrée* 9 (October 15, 1905): 289–96.

58. Claire Margat, "Supplice Chinois in French Literature: From Octave Mirbeau's *Le Jardin des Supplices* to Georges Bataille's *Les Larmes d'Éros*," http://turandot .chineselegalculture.org/Essay.php?ID=38⊠ (accessed December 2006). Also see Brook et al., *Death*.

59. Athanasiou et al., "Toward a New Epistemology," 9–10.

60. "Executions among the Chinese," *Chinese Repository* 19, no. 1 (1850): 55–56.

61. "Decapitated by Dozens."

62. John H. Gray, *China: A History of the Laws, Manners, and Customs of the People*, 2 vols. (London: Macmillan and Co., 1878), 74, 46–74.

63. For the painful duty, see "Decapitated by Dozens"; "China" (on Chinese "vindictive barbarity"), *Times*, September 13, 1879; Henry Norman, *The People and Politics of the Far East* (London: Scribner, 1895), 226, 219. See also Walter H. Medhurst, *The Foreigner in Far Cathay* (New York: Scribner, 1872); Évariste Régis Huc, *A Journey through the Chinese Empire*, 2 vols. (New York: Harper, 1855). Also see Brook et al., *Death*, 178–208.

64. Sontag, *Regarding the Pain of Others*, 83, 122; Foucault, *Punish and Discipline*.

65. Brook et al., *Death*, 24; Jérôme Bourgon, "Chinese Executions: Visualizing Their Differences with European *Supplices*," *European Journal of East Asian Studies* 2, no. 1 (June 2003): 155, 161–67 (comparing Chinese and European executions).

66. See Amicus, "Execution of Criminals in China," *Indo-Chinese Gleaner* 1, no. 1 (May 1817): 16–17, reprinted as "Execution of Criminals in China," *Boston Recorder*, January 1, 1818, and "Notices of Modern China," *Chinese Repository* 4, no. 3 (1835): 383. Amicus was Morrison's pen name (Eliza A. Morrison, *Memoirs of the Life and Labours of Robert Morrison*, 2 vols. [London: Longman, 1839], 2:42).

67. "Journal of Occurrences—Decapitation," *Chinese Repository* 1, no. 7 1832): 291.

68. Amicus, "Execution of Criminals in China," 18.

69. "Chinese Culprit before a Magistrate," *Free Enquirer*, March 29, 1835 (extensively using the notes and pictures in *The Punishments of China*); "Chinese Punishments," *Free Enquirer*, April 19, 1835; "Chinese Punishment," *Family Magazine* 2 (April 1835): 349–52. These articles were then reprinted by other journals.

70. George E. Morrison, *An Australian in China*, 2nd ed. (London: Horace Cox, 1895), 103–4.

71. Sara Ahmed, *The Cultural Politics of Emotion* (New York: Routledge, 2004), 13–14, 93.

72. Mrs. John Henry Gray, *Fourteen Months in Canton* (London: Macmillan, 1880), 426–27 (emphasis added).

73. Judith Butler, *Bodies That Matter: On the Discursive Limits of "Sex"* (New York: Routledge, 1993), 2, 107; Ahmed, *Cultural Politics of Emotion*, 13–14, 93.

74. Mill, "Civilization," 1–2, 12. On the elusive meanings of "civilized" and "civilization," see Thomas Taylor Meadows, *The Chinese and Their Rebellions: With an Essay on Civilization* (London: Smith, Elder & Co., 1856), 519.

75. "The Trial of Francis Henry De la Motte, for High Treason," in *The Proceedings of the Old Bailey*, July 11, 1781, p. 2, ref. T17810711-1, http://www.oldbaileyonline.org/browse.jsp?id=t17810711-1&div=t17810711-1&terms=motte#highlight or http://www.oldbaileyonline.org/images.jsp?doc=178107110002 (accessed December 2006). On changes of such penal practices, see John M. Beattie, *Crime and the Courts in England, 1660–1800* (Oxford: Oxford University Press, 1986), 451.

76. Job Sibly, *The Trial at Large of Acou (a Chinese Tartar Sailor) for Murder: Tried at the Admiralty Sessions Holden at the Sessions' House in the Old Bailey, on Friday, July 11, 1806* (London: R. Butters, 1806), 20, 4. A pamphleteer described Chinese *lingchi* in scary details to argue that harsh penalties for treason under English law should be kept as effective deterrents; see *Thoughts on the Law of Forfeiture and Parliamentary Attainder for High Treason, as Applying to the Bill Now Pending in Parliament* (Dublin: Graisberry & Campbell, 1798), 22–23.

77. The capital crimes in England actually grew from 160 in the 1760s to 223 in 1819. See Gatrell, *Hanging Tree*, 22; Foucault, *Punish and Discipline*, 14. Regarding changes in sensibilities or penal practices more generally in Europe, see Spierenburg, *Spectacle of Suffering*.

78. Cf. Brook et al., *Death*, 24–26, 200.

79. William M. Reddy, *The Navigation of Feeling: A Framework for the History of Emotions* (Cambridge: Cambridge University Press, 2001), 129, also 128 (defining "emotives" as a type of "speech-act").

80. Thomas Taylor Meadows, *Desultory Notes on the Government and People of China* (London: Wm. H. Allen & Co., 1847), 207–10, 197–98 (for the first quotation); Medhurst, *Foreigner in Far Cathay*, 163 (for the second quotation); Harry S. Parkes, "Description of Proceedings in the Criminal Court of Canton, with an Account of an Execution at Canton by Frank Parish," *Transactions of the China Branch of the Royal Asiatic Society*, part 3 (1853): 43, 46, 53.

81. His account of the execution (on July 30, 1851), dated August 22, 1851, was appended to *The Chinese and Their Rebellions* (651–56) and was also published as "Description of an Execution at Canton," *Journal of the Royal Asiatic Society of Great Britain and Ireland* 16 (1856): 54–58. In the latter, he added a postscript about why he went to the execution. A shorter account based on his paper was read at the Royal Asiatic Society in London in January 1852 and published as "Executions in Canton," *Times*, January 1, 1852.

82. Norman, *People and Politics*, 219–30. For similar pictures taken in 1903, see Edward H. Parker, *China: Past and Present* (London: Chapman & Hall, 1903), 376–86.

83. Bourgon, "Chinese Executions," 160. See also James Elkins, *The Object Stares Back: On the Nature of Seeing* (New York: Simon & Schuster, 1996), 108–15 (reproducing some of these images). For the wide circulation of such images, see Brook et al., *Death*, 22–34, 222–51.

84. William F. Mayers et al., *The Treaty Ports of China and Japan* (London: Trubner and Co., 1867), 502–3; see also 254 and 310 (execution grounds), 174–76 (quoting Meadows's 1851 description).

85. Dr. Julius Berncastle, *A Voyage to China*, 2 vols. (London: W. Shoberl, 1850), 2:163–67.

86. Benjamin Lincoln Ball, *Rambles in Eastern Asia* (Boston: James French, 1856), 125, 78, 146, 356, 373–73, 404.

87. "Around the World: Administration of Justice in China," *New York Evangelist*, November 29, 1877.

88. Gray, *Fourteen Months in Canton*, 66–68, 135–37, 149–50, 424–29; L. M. Fay, "On the Execution of State Criminals," *China Review* 2, no. 3 (November 1873): 173–75; Mayers et al., *Treaty Ports*, 254.

89. Elijah C. Bridgman, "Letter from China," *Religious Intelligencer* 17, no. 45 (April 6, 1833): 708. Bridgman wrote his letter in Guangzhou on December 8, 1831.

90. K. Y. Solonin et al., eds., *The Bretschneider Albums: 19th Century Paintings of Life in China* (Reading, U.K.: Garnet, 1995), 7–9, and images 85, 89 ("Slicing") and 87 ("Decapitation").

91. Halttunen, "Humanitarianism," 304.

92. Eliza J. Gillett Bridgman, ed., *The Life and Labors of Elijah Coleman Bridgman* (New York: Randolph, 1864), 162–63.

93. Edward P. Tenney, *Contrasts in Social Progress* (London: Longmans, Green and Co., 1907), 314.

94. Brook et al., *Death*, 31.

95. Sontag, *Regarding the Pain of Others*, 102–3.

96. For the many instances of affrays, homicides, smuggling, and other illegalities, see, e.g., *PTYDP*, 319 (1766), 345 (1842), 714–30, 128–47 (on opium from 1798 to 1846).

97. Neil J. Smelser, "Psychological Trauma and Cultural Trauma," in *Cultural Trauma and Collective Identity*, ed. Jeffrey Alexander (Berkeley: University of California Press, 2004), 39.

98. Ibid., 41–42.

99. "Extract of a Letter from China, Dec. 6," *India Gazette*, January 31, 1785; *India Gazette*, April 23, 1785.

100. Josiah Quincy, *The Journals of Major Samuel Shaw* (Boston: Wm. Crosby and H. P. Nichols, 1847), 188–92; John Jay, *The Correspondence and Public Papers of John Jay, 1782–1793*, ed. Henry P. Johnston (New York: G. P. Putnam's Sons, 1891), 3:146–48 (May 1785). John Jay was secretary for foreign affairs in 1784–1790 and also became the first chief justice of the U.S. Supreme Court in 1789.

101. "A Letter from Macao [dated February 10, 1773]," *York Chronicle*, December 24, 1773.

102. See his narrative of this case in "Mémoire sur la position actuelle des Européens à la Chine, ses causes, et les moyens de l'améliorer," Archives Nationale, MS 6/2, ff. 109–55, reprinted in Louis Dermigny, ed., *Les mémoires de Charles de Constant sur le commerce à la Chine* (Paris: S.E.V.P.E.N., 1964), 382–412, 398.

103. "Extract of a Letter from China, Dec. 6"; Dermigny, *Les mémoires*, 396–97, 387 (on China as a "despotic state")

104. Alexander, "Toward a Theory of Cultural Trauma," 23.

105. The preponderance of the evidence suggests a likely case of murder (or intentional killing under Chinese law); see Joseph Askew, "Re-visiting New Territory: The Terranova Incident Re-examined," *Asian Studies Review* 28, no. 4 (2004): 357–67; Li Chen, "Universalism and Equal Sovereignty as Contested Myths of International Law in the Sino-Western Encounter," *Journal of the History of International Law* 13, no. 1 (January 2011): 97–102. For the archives, see FO1048/21/7–8 (1821); *YPZZD*, 1:28–32; cf. "Benjamin Wilcocks to John Quincy Adams," November 1, 1821, DFUSCC; *PRUSC*, esp. 10–11, 23–36.

106. Quoted in "American Intercourse with China," *Asiatic Journal and Monthly Register for British and Foreign India, China, and Australia*, n.s., 15, 60 (September–December 1834): 321; *PRUSC*, 16–17; *CBEIC*, 4:112 (1825).

107. John Francis Davis, *The Chinese: A General Description of the Empire of China and Its Inhabitants*, 2 vols. (London: Charles Knight & Co., 1836), 1:100; John Barrow, "Free Trade to China," *Quarterly Review* 100, no. 50 (1834): 462; Sir Henry Ellis, *A Series of Letters on the East India Question*, 2nd ed. (London: John Murray, 1830), 34.

108. "Execution of an Italian at Canton," *North American Review* 4, no. 1 (January 1835): 59; see also 68.

109. John Quincy Adams, "Adams' Lecture on the War with China," *Chinese Repository* 11, no. 5 (1842): 274–89.

110. *YPZZD*, 1:244–48 (DG17/12/23), 249 (edict); *Jiaqing Daoguang liangchao shangyudang* (*Edicts of the Jiaqing and Daoguang Reigns*), comp. Zhongguo Diyi Lishi Dang'anguan (Nanning: Guangxi shifan chubanshe, 2000), 43:39. See "[Execution in Macao for Opium Smuggling]," *Canton Register*, April 17, 1838, 62; "Punishment by Strangulation," *Canton Press*, April 14, 1838; "Journal of Occurrences: A Case of Strangulation," *Chinese Repository* 6, no. 12 (1838): 607–8.

111. *YPZZD*, 1:366–79 (DG18/8/21). See "Riot in Front of the Factories," in IOR/G/12/262 (December 12, 1838); FO17/30:227–28; "Suspension of Trade," *Chinese Repository* 7, no. 8 (1838): 445–46; "Attack on the Foreign Factories," *Canton Press*, December 15, 1838, 171; William C. Hunter, *The "Fan Kwae" at Canton before Treaty Days, 1825–1844* (London: Kegan Paul, Trench, 1882), 74–75 (quotations); *CRTC*, 324 (on the riotous foreigners).

112. See FO17/30:229–30; "Suspension of Trade," 447–50 (translated by John Morrison). About the American consul's report, see Kenneth S. Latourette, *The History of Early Relations between the United States and China, 1784–1844* (New Haven: Yale University Press, 1917), 112.

113. "Correspondence to the Editor," *Canton Press*, March 2, 1839, 606. On Lin's arrival in Guangzhou (March 10, 1839), see Hsin-pao Chang, *Commissioner Lin and the Opium War* (Cambridge, Mass.: Harvard University Press, 1964), 124–29.

114. See "Notice to Her Majesty's Subjects," March 4, 1839, FO17/31:23; IOR/L/ PS/9/193:61. For the foreign community's reactions, see Hunter, "Fan Kwae," 73; "Suspension of Trade," 450 (on the Chamber of Commerce).

115. FO17/31:25–26 (March 4), 30–31 (March 9), 32 (March 22, 1839); *Review of the Management of Our affairs in China, Since the Opening of the Trade in 1834* (London: Smith, Elder & Co., 1840), 31, 181.

116. See chapter 5; IOR/L/PS/9/193 (1839–1840):21.

117. "Attack on the Foreign Factories."

118. For Chinese depositions in the Huangzhuqi case, see *YPZZD*, 7:825–27; *Chouban yiwu shimo* (*A Full Account of the Management of Foreign Affairs*), comp. Wenqing et al., 8 *juan* (Shanghai: Shanghai guji chubanshe, 2002), 3:225–28 (*Xuxiu siku quanshu*, 416:225–28). Cf. "Papers Relating to the Murder of Six Englishmen in the Neighbourhood of Canton in the Month of December 1847," in *Parliamentary Papers*, House of Commons, 1847–48 (930), XLVIII.617 (London: T. R. Harrison, 1848), 22–23 (on "affray"), 24–26 (rendering *xiongfan* as "murder"). The unpunished killing of three Chinese in 1846 as well as the First Opium War had contributed to the local resentment. See "Papers Relating to Riot at Canton in July 1846," in *Parliamentary Papers*, House of Commons, 1847 (808), XL.331 (London: T. R. Harrison, 1847), 68–69, 82–87, 42–46.

119. "Papers Relating to the Murder," 26–27 (Davis to Qiying, December 12); *Da Qing Xuanzong Chenghuangdi shilu* (*Veritable Records of the Daoguang Emperor*), 12 vols. (Taipei: Huawen shuju, 1964), 12:7836–39.

120. "Papers Relating to the Murder," 22–29, 34–36 (Qiying to Davis, December 17); FO682/1980:64. For the Chinese investigation, see *YPZZD*, 7:825–28; *Chouban yiwu shimo*, 3:227–28; *Chouban yiwu shimo buyi* (*Supplement to "A Full Account of the Management of Foreign Affairs"*), comp. Guo Tingyi (Taipei: Zhongyang yanjiuyuan jindaishi yanjiusuo, 1966), 1:198–201.

121. See, e.g., "The Murders at Canton," *Times*, February 21, 1848; "Execution of Murderers," *Chinese Repository* 17, no. 1 (1848): 54–55.

122. "The Chinese Murders," *New York Evangelist*, March 23, 1848; "[Report of the Execution of the Chinese]," *Albion*, March 18, 1848; "Fresh Misunderstandings— Six British Subjects Murdered," *Indian News and Chronicle of Eastern Affairs*, January 25, 1848.

123. "Papers Relating to the Murder," 37 (Johnston to Davis, December 21, 1847).

124. "Execution of Murderers," 55.

125. "Papers Relating to the Murder," 37.

126. Ibid., 44–47 (Guangzhou merchants), 75–76 (petition from sixty-two Shanghai merchants). For other petitions, see *Correspondence between the Foreign Office and the Commercial Association of Manchester, Relative to Outrages Committed on British Subjects in China, in 1846, 1847, 1848* (London: Harrison and Sons, 1846–1848), 3–5.

127. John Y. Wong, *Deadly Dreams: Opium, Imperialism, and the Arrow War (1856–1860) in China* (Cambridge: Cambridge University Press, 1998), 464, 472–74, 484–85.

128. "Ministerial Banquet at the Mansion-House," *Times*, March 21, 1857; "House of Commons [Debates on March 3, 1857]," *Times*, March 4, 1857. Concerning the *Arrow* incident as the manufactured casus belli, see Wong, *Deadly Dreams*, 4–5, 26–27, 69–127, 459–63.

129. *Morning Post*, February 28, 1857; "China," Letters to the Editor, *Times*, April 6, 1857.

130. Parkes, "Description of Proceedings," 43–56, 56; John Bowring, "Recollections of Crime and Criminals in China," *Cornhill Magazine* 12 (1865): 235–42. See also "Chinese Humanity," Letters to the Editor, *Times*, May 5, 1857; "[Comment on the War with China]," *Morning Post*, February 28, 1857 (citing earlier accounts); also see Wong, *Deadly Dreams*, 226–29.

131. Wong, *Deadly Dreams*, 226.

132. Ibid., 292 (on the attorney general), 174–92 (on the issue of legality). For the election debates, see Angus Hawkins, *Parliament, Party, and the Art of Politics in Britain, 1855–59* (Stanford: Stanford University Press, 1987), 52–72; Edward D. Steele, *Palmerston and Liberalism, 1855–1865* (Cambridge: University of Cambridge Press, 1991), 57–60, 157–69.

133. Baron Jean-Baptiste-Louis Gros, *Négociations entre la France et la Chine, en 1860* (Paris: Librairie Militaire, 1864), 136–37; Maurice Hérisson, *Journal d'un interprète en Chine* (Paris: Paul Ollendorff, 1886), 353–55.

134. "Correspondence Respecting Affairs in China, 1859–60," in *Parliamentary Papers*, House of Commons, 1861 (2754), LXVI.1 (London: Harrison and Sons, 1861), 214–15 (Elgin to Russell); Sir James Hope Grant, *Incidents in the China War of 1860*, comp. Henry Knollys (London: William Blackwood and Sons, 1875), 202–5.

135. "Correspondence Respecting Affairs in China, 1859–60," 214. For foreign witness accounts, see, e.g., Armand Lucy, *Lettres intimes sur la campagne de Chine* (Marseille: Barile, 1861); Robert Swinhoe, *Narrative of the North China Campaign of 1860* (London: Smith, Elder & Co., 1861); Hérisson, *Journal*, 306–56. For a recent study, see James L. Hevia, *English Lessons: The Pedagogy of Imperialism in Nineteenth-Century China* (Durham: Duke University Press, 2003), 74–102. For the foreign detainees' accounts, see Henry Brougham Loch, *Personal Narrative of Occurrences during Lord Elgin's Second Embassy to China in 1860* (London: John Murray, 1869), 371–75; "A Chinese Inquisition [of Parkes]," *New York Times*, January 15, 1861. For Chinese refutations, see FO1080/82/1–2 (XF10/8/16).

136. Robert K. Douglas, *Society in China* (London: A.D. Innes & Co., 1894), 96, 94–108.

137. For the treaties, see, e.g., "Correspondence Relative to the Earl of Elgin's Special Missions to China and Japan, 1857–59," in *Parliamentary Papers*, House

of Commons, 1859 (2571), XXXIII.1 (London: Harrison and Sons, 1859), 346–57. Also see "Correspondence Respecting Affairs in China, as Regards Negotiations with Chinese Authorities," in *Parliamentary Papers*, House of Commons, 1860 (2587), LXIX.45 (London: Harrison and Sons, 1860); "Correspondence Respecting Affairs in China, 1859–60."

138. John Stuart Mill, *On Liberty* (London: John W. Parker and Son, 1859), 128–30.

139. John Stuart Mill, *Considerations of Representative Government* (London: Parker, Son, and Bourn, 1861), 80. See Mehta, *Liberalism and Empire*.

140. Ann Laura Stoler, "On Degrees of Imperial Sovereignty," *Public Culture* 18, no. 1 (2006): 128.

141. Butler, *Frames of War*, 24, 34, 74–75.

142. On the demands of executing Chinese officials under foreign supervision, see FO233/123:259–71 (1898–1900); "Demand Punishment of China," *New York Times*, August 4, 1900; "China: Punishment of the Officials after the Boxers Movement," *Times*, November 19, 1901. Also see Hevia, *English Lessons*, 31–48 (on the Second Opium War), 74–118 (looting), 186–281 (on the Boxer Rebellion).

143. Meadows, *Chinese*, 519.

144. "Enlightened Barbarism," *New York Times*, October 1, 1891; Gray, *Fourteen Months in Canton*, 68.

145. Ann Laura Stoler, *Along the Archival Grain: Epistemic Anxieties and Colonial Common Sense* (Princeton: Princeton University Press, 2009), 255–56, 259.

5. LAW AND EMPIRE IN THE MAKING
OF THE FIRST OPIUM WAR

1. "The Opium Trade and War," *Eclectic Review* 7 (May 1840): 700 (emphasis in original). This London-based journal for highly literate readers of middle- or lower-middle-class background was comparable in influence to the *Edinburgh*, the *Quarterly*, and the *Westminster Review*. For harsher criticism of the war, see Joseph Sturge, "Chinese War," *Times*, March 20, 1840.

2. "Minute by Governor-General," April 7, 1840, in Minutes and Letters of Lord Auckland, British Library, Add MSS 37715:1–2; WWC, 53:946 (April 9, 1840) (Palmerston quoting merchants' memorial). For similar ideas in the press, see "The Quarrel between Great Britain and China," *Monthly Chronicle* 1 (May 1840): 95 (citing a British journal); "War with China, and the Opium Question," *Blackwood's Edinburgh Magazine* 67 (March 1840): 849.

3. Hsin-pao Chang, *Commissioner Lin and the Opium War* (Cambridge, Mass.: Harvard University Press, 1964), 15; see also 2–14. For "the standard reference" quote, see John Y. Wong, *Deadly Dreams: Opium, Imperialism, and the Arrow War (1856–1860) in China* (Cambridge: Cambridge University Press, 1998), 14, 378, 428.

Polachek calls Chang's book an "excellent study of the diplomatic background to the 1839 war" (James M. Polachek, *The Inner Opium War* [Cambridge, Mass.: Harvard University Press, 1992], 103).

4. Chang, *Commissioner Lin*, 215, 214. For critiques of this theory, see Lydia H. Liu, *The Clash of Empires: The Invention of China in Modern World Making* (Cambridge, Mass.: Harvard University Press, 2004); Wong, *Deadly Dreams*; James L. Hevia, *Cherishing Men from Afar: Qing Guest Ritual and the Macartney Embassy of 1793* (Durham: Duke University Press, 1995).

5. Chang was influenced by Morse in his narrative about the *Lady Hughes* case (Chang, *Commissioner Lin*, 13–14). Others, such as Fay and Melancon, repeated the traditional portrayal of earlier Sino-Western legal disputes.

6. For an excellent critique of these conventional interpretations, see Wong, *Deadly Dreams*, 472, 470–86, 484–85 (critiquing Chang's emphasis on free trade and cultural clashes). Cf. Glenn Melancon, *Britain's China Policy and the Opium Crisis: Balancing Drugs, Violence and National Honour, 1833–1840* (Burlington, Vt.: Ashgate, 2003), 137–39, 5–6; Glenn Melancon, "Honour in Opium? The British Declaration of War on China, 1839–1840," *International History Review* 21, no. 4 (2000): 870; Harry G. Gelber, *Opium, Soldiers and Evangelicals: Britain's 1840–42 War with China, and Its Aftermath* (New York: Palgrave Macmillan, 2004).

7. Michael Greenberg, *British Trade and the Opening of China 1800–42* (Cambridge, Mass.: Harvard University Press, 1951), 104–43 (on the opium trade). On the EIC monopoly, see John F. Richards, "Opium and the British Indian Empire: The Royal Commission of 1895," *Modern Asian Studies* 36, no. 2 (2002): 375–76.

8. *YPZZD*, 1:4–130, 43–45, 72 (on Hong merchants); John Slade, *Narrative of the Late Proceedings and Events in China* (Canton: Canton Register Press, 1839), 27.

9. *YPZZD*, 1:49–349; JMC, 330, 243–45. See Chang, *Commissioner Lin*, 22–31 (on British traders' resistance); Peter W. Fay, *The Opium War, 1840–1842* (Chapel Hill: University of North Carolina Press, 1975), 59–61.

10. Chang, *Commissioner Lin*, 32, 41 (showing a net silver outflow of over 2.2 million taels in 1821–1830, and about 10 million in 1831–1833), 39–45.

11. Xu was a subdirector of the court of imperial sacrifice and a former Guangdong provincial judge. For his proposal (dated May 17, 1836, rescripted on June 10, and forwarded to Deng on July 2) and comments by Deng and others, see *YPZZD*, 1:200–209; Slade, *Narrative*, 1–5, 10–18 (appendix); Chang, *Commissioner Lin*, 85–88.

12. Zhu learned from *The History of Formosa* about European colonialism. His memorial of September 19 is translated in Slade, *Narrative*, 18–26 (appendix). See similar arguments by Xu Qiu of the Ministry of War (Slade, *Narrative*, 26–35 [appendix]) and by Censor Yuan Yuling (*YPZZD*, 1:213–17 [DG16/10/4]).

13. *YPZZD*, 1:254–57 (DG18/4/10) (for Huang's memorial), 258–349 (DG18/4/10–7/22) (for the debate), 1:270–78 (for Lin's memorial, dated DG/18/5/19). For those

sympathetic to Huang, see *YPZZD*, 1:287, 313, 319, 323, 335, 337. Also see Chang, *Commissioner Lin*, 92–93.

14. *YPZZD*, 1:332–33, 391 (DG/18/9/11); see also 204, 394, and 424 (DG18/11/15) (on Lin's appointment).

15. Polachek, *Inner Opium War*, 102, 113–35 (on the legalization debate and factional politics).

16. Staunton and some other British politicians acknowledged this in 1840 and 1843. See discussion below.

17. JMC, 324–26 (letter 152, January 9, 1838), 338 (letter 161, June 18, 1838), 330–40.

18. "Correspondence," *Canton Press*, March 2, 1839, 606; "Attack on the Foreign Factories," *Canton Press*, December 15, 1838.

19. FO17/31:25–26 (March 4), 30–31 (March 9), 32 (March 22, 1839); IOR/L/PS/9/193:61; *Review of the Management of Our affairs in China, Since the Opening of the Trade in 1834* (London: Smith, Elder & Co., 1840), 31, 181. Also see chapter 4.

20. "Crisis in the Opium Traffic," *Chinese Repository* 7, no. 12 (1839): 609; IOR/L/PS/9/193:21, 23 (Elliot to Palmerston, March 30, 1839, enclosing the *Canton Press*).

21. FO682/1972:1–43. For Lin's two edicts, see IOR/L/PS/9/193:21–44; CRTC, 349–55. Also see JMC, 359–62. For standard references, see Chang, *Commissioner Lin*, 121–88; Fay, *Opium War*, 142–61.

22. WWC, 704 (April 7, 1840).

23. On this shift, see works by Antony Anghie, *Imperialism, Sovereignty, and the Making of International Law* (Cambridge: Cambridge University Press, 2004); Martti Koskenniemi, *The Gentle Civilizers of Nations: The Rise and Fall of International Law 1870–1960* (Cambridge: Cambridge University Press, 2002); Partha Chatterjee, *The Black Hole of Empire: History of a Global Practice of Power* (Princeton: Princeton University Press, 2012), 187–95.

24. Wheaton cited Vattel to define a "sovereign state" as "any nation or people, whatever may be of the form of its internal constitution, which governs itself independently of foreign powers" (Henry Wheaton, *Elements of International Law* [Philadelphia: Carey, Lea & Blanchard, 1836], 51; Emmerich de Vattel, *The Law of Nations* [1758], trans. Joseph Chitty [London: Stevens & Sons, 1834], 2, 40).

25. Palmerston to Elliot (March 1839), in CRTC (1840), 418 (May 23, 1839); "Memorials Addressed to Her Majesty's Government by British Merchants Interested in the Trade with China," in *Parliamentary Papers*, House of Commons and Lords, 1840 (242) (London: T. R. Harrison, 1840), 11 (November 2, 1839); Hugh H. Lindsay, *Letter to the Right Honourable Viscount Palmerston on British Relations with China* (London: Saunders and Otley, 1836), 6.

26. Palmerston to Elliot, March 23, 1839, quoted in WWC, 686. See Melbourne's speech of May 12, 1840, in "War with China . . . Parliamentary Debate," *Chinese*

Repository 9, no. 5 (1840): 253–54. In 1832, the EIC Board of Directors reminded the Select Committee that China had "the right exclusively to regulate the grounds on which any intercourse would be permitted with other countries" (cited in WWC, 673–74).

27. WWC, 716–17.

28. Vattel, *Law of Nations*, 38–40.

29. Hugo Grotius, *The Free Sea; or, A Disputation Concerning the Right Which the Hollanders Ought to Have to the Indian Merchandise for Trading* (1609), ed. David Armitage (Indianapolis: Liberty Fund, 2004), 43, 53.

30. James Matheson, *The Present Position and Prospects of the British Trade with China* (London: Smith, Elder, 1836), 35, 44; see also 33–49. This pamphlet was reviewed in "Free Intercourse with China and Christendom; with Remarks," *Chinese Repository* 5, no. 6 (1836): 241–57.

31. Lindsay, *Letter*, 3–7 (quotations), 12–18 (on planning). On his 1832 voyage and the translation issue, see chapter 2; Liu, *Clash of Empires*; Robert A. Bickers, "The Challenger: Hugh Hamilton Lindsay and the Rise of British Asia, 1832–1865," *Transactions of the Royal Historical Society*, 6th ser., 22 (2012): 141–69. Lindsay was chair of the Chamber of Commerce in China when protesting the Chinese executions in 1838 and early 1839.

32. Charles H. Alexandrowicz, *An Introduction to the History of the Law of Nations in the East Indies (16th, 17th and 18th Centuries)* (Oxford: Clarendon Press, 1967), 10–11. Concerning the recognition doctrine, see Anghie, *Imperialism*; Koskenniemi, *Gentle Civilizers*. Besides various French and Italian versions, Wheaton's treatise had English or American editions in 1855, 1857, 1863, 1864, 1866, 1878, 1880, 1889, 1904, 1916, 1929, 1936.

33. Wheaton, Elements *of International Law* (1836), 45, 46.

34. Koskenniemi, *Gentle Civilizers*, 114–15.

35. Wheaton, *Elements of International Law* (1836), 244–45.

36. YPZZD, 1:643–46 (DG19/6/24, or August 3, 1839), 661–62. For translation, see "Letter to the Queen of England," *Chinese Repository* 8, no. 10 (1840): 497–503, 500 (quotation); J. Lewis Shuck, *Portfolio Chinensis; or, A Collection of Authentic Chinese State Papers* (Macao: New Washington Press of F. F de Cruz, 1840), 128–49.

37. Lin Zexu, *Lin Zexu quanji* (*Complete Works of Lin Zexu*), 10 vols. (Fuzhou: Haxia wenyi chubanshe, 2002), 10:352–55. For the original passages, see Vattel, *Law of Nations*, 39, 172, 292. Also see Immanuel C. Y. Hsu, *China's Entrance into the Family of Nations* (Cambridge, Mass.: Harvard University Press, 1960), 123–25; Liu, *Clash of Empires*, 118–19. On Parker, see Edward V. Gulick, *Peter Parker and the Opening of China* (Cambridge, Mass.: Harvard University Press, 1973).

38. See, e.g., Lin to Elliot, April 8, 1839, FO17/31:159b–162a. For the translated intelligence, see Lin, *Lin Zexu quanji*, 10:8–373 (including Davis's book).

39. "Threatened War with China in Consequence of the Villainous Conduct of the Villainous Shopocracy [from *the Northern Star*]," *Southern Star and London and Brighton Patriot*, January 26, 1840; "The High Commissioner's Second Letter to the Queen of England," *Times*, June 11, 1840. Chang, *Commissioner Lin*, 136–38.

40. "Threatened War with China,"13.

41. See, e.g., Julie Lovell, *The Opium War: Drugs, Dreams and the Making of China* (London: Picador, 2011).

42. Cf. Gelber, *Opium, Soldiers* (asserting that the opium trade lacked moral stigma in Britain).

43. Britain's opium trade lasted until 1917; John K. Fairbank, "The Creation of the Treaty System," in *The Cambridge History of China: Volume 10, Late Ch'ing 1800–1911, Part 1*, ed. John K. Fairbank (New York: Cambridge University Press, 1978), 213. Opium was "probably the largest commerce of the time in any single commodity" (Greenburg, *British Trade*, 104).

44. For Marx's use of "opium war" to refer to the two Anglo-Chinese wars, see Karl Marx, "The British and Chinese Treaty," *New York Daily Tribune*, October 15, 1858; Karl Marx, "Free Trade and Monopoly," *New York Daily Tribune*, September 25, 1858. See Tan Chung, *China and the Brave New World: A Study of the Origins of the Opium War, 1840–41* (New Delhi: Allied Publishers, 1978) (attributing the term "Opium War" to Marx).

45. Algernon S. Thelwall, *The Iniquities of the Opium Trade with China* (London: Allen & Co., 1839), 1–2. He wrote it upon the request of several British East India merchants. His sources included Martin's statistics, Medhurst's account of the harm of opium smoking, and memorials of Xu Naiji, Zhu Zun, and Xu Qiu.

46. "Iniquities of the Opium Trade with China," *Times*, May 24, 1839; August 15, 1839. News about the opium seizure was reported in early August ("Opium Trade with China," *Times*, August 7, 1839).

47. For the meetings, see, e.g., "The Opium Trade: Public Meeting at Leeds," *Leeds Mercury*, February 22, 1840; see also Joseph Sturge, *A Visit to the United States in 1841* (London: Hamilton, 1842), appendix G: lxiii.

48. "The Dispute with China," *Manchester Times and Gazette*, October 19, 1839; "The Opium Traffic," *Freeman's Journal*, December 17, 1839; "The Opium Trade with China [Reprinting from *Bombay Times* of May 23]," *Times*, September 27, 1839.

49. For the quotations, see "The Opium Smugglers," *Liverpool Mercury*, September 27, 1839; "From the Details . . . ," *Times*, August 21, 1839.

50. WWC, 739.

51. Ibid., 824 (April 8, 1840).

52. See Sir Stephen Lushington's speech, WWC, 856. Lushington (1782–1873), a veteran Whig member of Parliament for Tower Hamlets (1832–1841), was against the slave trade and capital punishment.

53. WWC, 716.

54. Ibid., 927.

55. Quoting Robert Bruce, superintendent of a tea plantation in Assam, India, Lord Sandon showed how opium turned its "fine race of people [into] the most abject, servile, crafty, and demoralized race" (WWC, 879).

56. See the speech of George Palmer (1772–1853), member of Parliament for South Sussex (1836–1847) and former partner of the London agent of a major opium firm, Dent & Co., on April 8, 1840, in WWC, 836.

57. WWC, 747–48.

58. "The Quarrel between Great Britain and China," 95. Also see the *Guardian*, as quoted critically in "The Dispute with China," *Manchester Times and Gazette*, October 19, 1839.

59. Hugo Grotius, *Commentary on the Law of Prize and Booty* (ca. 1604), trans. Gwladys L. Williams, ed. Martine Julia van Ittersum (Indianapolis: Liberty Fund, 2005), 102–7; Hugo Grotius, *The Rights of War and Peace* (1625), ed. Richard Tuck (Indianapolis: Liberty Fund, 2005), 393–96; Vattel, *Law of Nations*, 482–84 (echoing Grotius's just-war theory).

60. Grotius, *Commentary*, 103, 102–7 (on defense of life or property, recovery of debt, and punishment of wrongdoing)

61. See Barbara Arneil, "The Wild Indian's Venison: Locke's Theory of Property and English Colonialism in America," *Political Studies* 44, no. 1 (March 1996): 66–74. Also see recent studies of Locke's property theory cited in Karl Widerquist, "Lockean Theories of Property: Justifications for Unilateral Appropriation," *Public Reason* 2, no. 1 (June 2010): 4–6.

62. For contemporary views of the political importance of property, see "The Whig Dissolution," *Blackwood's Edinburgh Magazine* 309, no. 50 (July 1841): 4.

63. FO17/31:131–32, also 122b–23b (April 6, 1839); CRTC, 388–89.

64. FO17/31:38–43; CRTC, 365–67; Slade, *Narrative*, 32–37, 74–78; JMC, 358–62 (Matheson to Jardine, May 1, 1839), 383 (Matheson to Smith, September 24, 1839); Hunter, *"Fan Kwae,"* 16–19. See also FO682/1972:1–21 (March–May 1839); Chang, *Commissioner Lin*, 144–51, 118.

65. Elliot to Palmerston, January 2, 1839, in CRTC, 328. This dispatch did not reach London until May 13, and Palmerston replied that Elliot had no authority to expel the opium traders from Chinese territory. Palmerston failed to get a new China bill passed in Parliament in 1838 to give the superintendents effective judicial power in China. For the failed China bill, see "Draft: An Act to Authorize the Establishing of a Court or Courts with Criminal and Admiralty and Civil Jurisdiction in China," FO17/28:12a–22a (submitted to House of Commons March 13, 1838), 25–33 (for revisions).

66. FO17/30:286, 287–311 (Lin's edicts) (received on August 5); IOR/L/PS/9/193:17.

67. Elliot to Palmerston, April 6, 1839, FO17/31:118b–127; Elliot to Blake, March 23, 1839, FO17/31:36. See Elliot's correspondence with his wife of March 21–23, in

Susanna Hoe and Derek Roebuck, *The Taking of Hong Kong: Charles and Clara Elliot in China Waters* (London: Routledge, 1999), 70–73.

68. FO17/35:14–15; JMC, 361–62; Hoe and Roebuck, *Taking of Hong Kong*, 73–74. See also IOR/L/PS/9/193:235 (for Lin's suspicion of Dent's fleeing); "Proceedings at Canton Relative to the Trade in Opium [from the *Canton Press*, March 23 and 30, 1839]," *Times*, August 13, 1839; Chang, *Commissioner Lin*, 144–51.

69. Elliot's circular notices (from the *Canton Register*), March 22 and 23, 1839, FO17/35:60–61; see Blake to Maitland, March 31, 1839, FO17/35:135a.

70. FO17/31:1–260 (March–May 29, 1839); CRTC, 355–418.

71. Robert Blake, *Jardine Matheson: Traders of the Far East* (London: Weidenfeld, 1999), 91.

72. FO17/31:10–11 (March 30, 1839); IOR/L/PS/9/193:235, 237 (April 6, 1839); FO17/31:120b, 125b; CRTC, 385.

73. For the public notice, see *China: Copies of All Communications between the Board of Treasury or the India Board, or Any Other Public Department and the Parties or Their Agents Who Are Holders of Certificates or Bills Granted by the Chief Superintendent at Canton for Opium Surrendered to the Chinese Authorities*, House of Commons, March 23, 1840, 10.

74. See, e.g., "The Chinese and Our 'Great Plenipotentiary,'" *Fraser's Magazine* 24 (November 1841): 620.

75. Charles to Clara Elliot, April 4, 1839, in Hoe and Roebuck, *Taking of Hong Kong*, 74–75. See Elliot to Palmerston, March, 30, 1839 (received August 20), FO17/31:10a–b; CRTC, 357.

76. IOR/F/4/1737/70429, no. 9 (Draft 164-1839), enclosures 2 (Elliot to Auckland), 7 (Elliot to Palmerston). What he did in 1839 was fully consistent with the same considerations.

77. See Matheson's letter in JMC, 364–68; Greenburg, *British Trade*, 204 (for the quotation); Chang, *Commissioner Lin*, 162, 165–67.

78. Samuel Wells Williams, *The Middle Kingdom: A Survey of the Chinese Empire and Its Inhabitants*, 2 vols. (New York: Wiley & Putnam, 1848), 2:524.

79. *China: Copies of All Communications*, 4.

80. See the replies of the Treasury and the Foreign Office, ibid., 5 (November 11, 1839), and 8 ("Treasury Minute," December 3, 1839). For Elliot's lack of authority, see "Chinese and Our 'Great Plenipotentiary,'" 620.

81. Also see Elliot to Palmerston, April 2, 1839 (received August 29), FO17/31:13.

82. WWC, 753, 778–79.

83. Ibid., 717.

84. Elliot cited Chinese officials' connivance, proposal to legalize opium, and inability to eliminate the contraband as reasons for condemning Lin's opium destruction (FO17/31:121–26; see also 1–14, 118–142; CRTC, 385–91, 386–91).

85. The £4.2 million of Britain's annual revenue from the China trade included £3.6 million from Chinese tea, or 15 percent of total British customs duties in 1839. See WWC, 670, 836–37; FO17/35:66–67 (July 4, 1839); "Memorials Addressed to Her Majesty's Government," 11–12.

86. Robert M. Martin, *Statistics of Colonies of the British Empire . . . From the Official Records of the Colonial Office* (London: Wm. H. Allen, 1839), 366 (including Malwa opium), 359. Martin's figure of 200 million Spanish dollars was based on an average of 1,200 dollars per chest, but the price dropped to about 500 dollars in early 1839. For the conversion to sterling pounds, I used the exchange rate of 4s. 10d. per Spanish dollar at the time of the opium seizure; see *China: Copies of All Communication*, 7.

87. Wong, *Deadly Dreams*, 411–12 (quotation), 376–81 (on the triangular trade), 397–432 (increased opium importation), 331–85 (British trade deficit); Chang, *Commissioner Lin*, 17, 219–23; Richard, "Opium Industry in British India," 151–53.

88. For cautionary voices, see speeches by Graham (WWC, 671–72) and Frederick Thesiger (WWC, 757). About the calls for aggressive policies, see the speech by Charles Buller (WWC, 782); Hugh H. Lindsay, *Is the War with China a Just One?* 2nd ed. (London: James Ridgway, 1840), 3–5; Lindsay, *Letter*, 19; Hugh H. Lindsay, *Remarks on Occurrences in China since the Opium Seizure in March 1839 to the Latest Date* (London: Sherwood, Gilbert and Piper, 1840); Hugh H. Lindsay, *The Rupture with China, and Its Causes . . . In a Letter to Lord Viscount Palmerston by a Resident in China* (London: Sherwood, Gilbert, 1840).

89. For the interviews and lobbying activities, see Smith to Palmerston, August 18, 1839, FO17/35:14–16 (forwarding letters about opium payment, dated April 3, 4, and 8, 1839); Johnston to Palmerston, September 9, 1839, FO17/35:45–48 (about China merchants' deputation to London); JMC, 380 (interview in late August); FO17/35:68–70 (Smith to Palmerston, September 18); JMC, 386–87 (interview on September 27), 389–93, 407 (interview on October 14), 388, 411 (interview in February 1840). See Melancon, "Honor in Opium?" 864 (interview on August 7, 1839). Smith was a senior partner of Magniac Smith & Co., an agent of Jardine Matheson.

90. FO17/35:187–88, October 8, 1839. About the lobbying, see FO17/35:24 (John Macvicar to Palmerston, August 23, 1839), FO17/35:53–56 (Liverpool merchants, September 17), FO17/35:104–6 (thirty-nine Manchester firms); FO17/35:120–21 (sixty-nine Leeds firms, October 4); FO17/35:190–91 (Bristol firms, October 10). See Fay, *Opium War*, 190–92.

91. See the merchants' memorial to Palmerston, in FO17/35:190–91 (received October 11, 1839); "Memorials Addressed to Her Majesty's Government," 9–10. See also Carl A. Trocki, *Opium, Empire and the Global Political Economy* (London: Routledge, 1999), xiii (for the quotation); "Opium Trade and War," 706; Samuel Warren, *The Opium Question* (London: J. Ridgway, 1840).

92. "Memorials Addressed to Her Majesty's Government," 11, 16–17, 20–21 (on military operations).

93. See the petitions of Calcutta merchants to Palmerston on July 4, 1839 (FO17/35:66–67), and to the Privy Council ("Opium Trade with China," *Times*, September 30, 1839). The Indian government refused to suspend the opium auctions even after it learned of the Chinese seizure (FO17/35:63a–64a [April 17, May 27, 1839]).

94. See the speeches by John Hobhouse (Aril 9, 1840, WWC, 890–92) and Thomas Staunton (April 7, 1840, WWC, 743)

95. WWC, 752.

96. Graham to Stanley, March 18, 31, 1840, *The Papers of Sir James Graham, Part I, General Series, 1820–1860* (Brighton, Sussex: Harvester Press Microform Publications, 1984); William E. Gladstone, *The Gladstone Diaries, Volume 3: 1840–1847*, ed. M. R. D. Foot and H. C. G. Matthew (Oxford: Clarendon Press, 1974), 3:16–18 (esp. for the meeting on March 25, 1840).

97. "The Opium Trade and War," 700, 699–702.

98. Gladstone, *Gladstone Diaries*, 3:16–17 (about the Tories' private meeting on March 18, 1840).

99. WWC, 246–47.

100. Jardine to Matheson, April 2–5, 1840, in JMC, 421–23.

101. John Cam Hobhouse, *Recollections of a Long Life, with Additional Extracts from His Private Diaries*, ed. by his daughter, Lady Dorchester, 6 vols. (London: John Murray, 1909), 5:257.

102. George Thomas Staunton, *Remarks on the British Relations with China, and the Proposed Plans for Improving Them* (London: E. Lloyd, 1836), 13–14; cf. 31, 35, 2, 8, 10. Lindsay testified to a Parliamentary committee in 1832.

103. WWC, 740–41.

104. For his source of information, see, e.g., Elliot to Palmerston, April 6, 1839, FO17/31:122b–23a. For Gladstone's challenge of Lindsay's credibility, see WWC, 807, 805 (citing Charles King's pamphlet).

105. WWC, 741–42.

106. John Hobhouse Diaries (1839–1844), April 7, 1840, British Library, Add MSS 56562:103b–104a.

107. WWC, 742, 744.

108. John Hobhouse Diaries, April 7, 1840, Add MSS 56562:103b. He was president in 1835–1841 and 1846–1851. About Staunton's authority on China affairs, see WWC, 894; John Barrow, "Free Trade to China," *Quarterly Review* 100, no. 50 (1834): 431.

109. WWC, 717, 894.

110. "Singapore," *Canton Press*, February 23, 1839 (reprinting from the *Singapore Free Press*, December 27, 1838, which in turn was critiquing a recent commentary in the *Canton Register*).

111. "The Opium Trade and War," 712–13.
112. The grace period had been extended from the originally one-year period. Lin to Elliot (through Guangzhou prefect), April 8, 1839, FO17/31/158b–59a; CRTC, 395. See *YPZZD*, 1:646 (DG19/6/24); Sasaki Masaya, ed., *Yapian zhanzheng qian zhongying jiaoshe wenshu* (*Sino-British Correspondence in Chinese before the Opium War*) (Taipei: Wenhai chubanshe, 1976), 223 (DG19/7/20); *Bombay Courier*, December 24, 1839, reprinted in "War with China," *Morning Chronicle*, February 13, 1840.
113. WWC, 808–10, 868–69.
114. Ibid., 777–79.
115. See the Speech of Macaulay in the House of Commons in WWC, 812. For the press, see, e.g., Lindsay, *Remarks*, 4; "The Chinese and Our 'Great Plenipotentiary,'" 612–27.
116. WWC, 811–12. Lord Sandon noted that only about two persons could fairly be said to be unrelated to the illegal traffic (WWC, 875). Viscount Sandon (Dudley Ryder, 1798–1882) was member of Parliament for Liverpool (1831–1847) and later held office under Palmerston as chancellor of the Duchy of Lancaster and Lord Privy Seal in 1855–57.
117. WWC, 915. The original is in FO17/30:243 (Elliot to Palmerston, January 30, 1839, received May 31, 1839); CRTC, 342. For similar comments, also see CRTC, 327–28 (January 2, 1839), and Elliot to Deng, December 23/25, 1838, FO17/30:233b.
118. WWC, 810 (quoted by Gladstone); Elliot to Palmerston, March 30, 1839, in FO17/31:3b.
119. "The Chinese and Our 'Great Plenipotentiary,'" 620; Hoe and Roebuck, *Taking of Hong Kong*, 73.
120. FO17/35:243–53, 244. Campbell was connected with Matheson's business.
121. See the extract of Palmerston's instructions to Henry Pottinger on May 31, 1841, enclosed in Palmerston to John Abel Smith, April 6(?), 1843, at West Sussex Record Office, Add MSS 22409. See also articles 4 and 6 of the Treaty of Nanjing (*HCT*, 1:8–9).
122. Williams, *Middle Kingdom*, 2:523.
123. Blake, *Jardine Matheson*, 91 (quotation) (describing the situation like a picnic); Chang, *Commissioner Lin*, 151–59, 229–30 (a British surgeon's letter); Williams, *Middle Kingdom*, 2:523; JMC, 386; Hoe and Roebuck, *Taking of Hong Kong*, 73 (Elliot told his wife "never [to] fear that the Chinese will hurt a hair of my poor head"). Matheson and Palmerston called it "durance" or "duress" (JMC, 357, 380).
124. Blake to Maitland, April 1, 1839, FO17/35:138; Maitland to President in Council of India, June 13, 1849, FO17/35:144; Hoe and Roebuck, *Taking of Hong Kong*, 73–76. See Elliot to Backhouse, March 26, 1839, FO17/30:313.
125. "Quarrel between Great Britain and China," 95. See Blake, *Jardine Matheson*, 91.

126. George Thomas Staunton, *Corrected Report of the Speech of Sir George Staunton, on Sir James Graham's Motion on the China Trade, in the House of Commons, April 7, 1840* (London: Edmund Lloyd, 1840), 11–15. See "The War against China," *Times*, March 23, 1840.

127. Lushington also saw China as "an anomaly in the history of nations." See WWC, 855–56.

128. Ibid., 739–42, 856–64.

129. Charles Marjoribanks, *Letter to the Right Hon. Charles Grant, President of the Board of Controul, on the Present State of British Intercourse with China* (London: J. Hatchard & Son, 1833), 50–53. See Sir James Brabazon Urmston, *Observations on the China Trade and on the Importance and Advantages of Removing It from Canton to Some Other Parts of the Coast of That Empire* (London: A. H. Baily & Co., 1834), 21; "Petition to Parliament," *Canton Register*, January 17, 1831.

130. Chatterjee, *Black Hole*, 194, 185–96. Also see Giorgio Agamben, *State of Exception* (Chicago: University of Chicago Press, 2005).

131. See relevant discussions in chapters 1 and 2. For the calls for a treaty, see Sir George Thomas Staunton, *Corrected Report of the Speeches of Sir George Staunton on the China Trade (June 4 and 13, 1833 in the Commons)* (London: Edmund Lloyd, 1833), 23–26; Lindsay, *Letter*, 12; Barrow, "Free Trade to China."

132. John L. Cranmer-Byng, *An Embassy to China: Lord Macartney's Journal, 1793–1794*, in *Britain and the China Trade, 1635–1842*, vol. 8, ed. Patrick Tuck (New York: Routledge, 2000), 208–13.

133. "The Opium and the China Question," *Blackwood's Edinburgh Magazine* 47, no. 296 (June 1840): 732, 738.

134. John Barrow, "Chinese Affairs," *Quarterly Review* 65, no. 130 (June 1840): 581. For the authorship, see John Barrow, *An Autobiographical Memoir of Sir John Barrow* (London: John Murray, 1847), 502–3. For his view in 1834, see Barrow, "Free Trade to China," 437–53, 445 (on Chinese rights).

135. Jardine to Matheson, September 25–27, 1839, in JMC, 386.

136. "Memorials Addressed to Her Majesty's Government," 18–21 (dated October 21, 1839).

137. Elliot to Palmerston, April 13, 1839, FO17/31:124–35.

138. CRTC, 384; Elliot to Palmerston, April 3, 1839, FO17/31:113a–14a.

139. Elliot to Palmerston, April 3, 1839, FO17/32:112–16, 116b (postscript). For the rest of the first package, see FO17/31:1–112 (thirty enclosures).

140. FO17/32:114a, 116a.

141. Chang, *Commissioner Lin*, 193–94; Fay, *Opium War*, 193.

142. On the meeting of September 27, see Jardine to Matheson, September 25–27, 1839, in JMC, 386–87 (letter 180). For the two memos, see Jardine to Palmerston, October 26 (received October 29) and October 27, 1839 (received

November 2), in FO17/35:281–82, 285–88, and IOR/L/PS/9/193 (1839–1840): 411–16, 423–28. Le Pichon and others misstated that Jardine's memos were not sent until December 1839. Jardine's letter of December 19 to Matheson was almost identical to these two memos, except that Hong Kong might have been left out in the extract; cf. JMC, 43–44; Blake, *Jardine Matheson*, 93. Jardine's advice was similar to and probably derived from Lindsay's 1836 letter.

143. Palmerston to Smith, November 28, 1842, West Sussex Record Office, Add MSS 22409; see also Palmerston's letter to Smith, April 6, 1843 (on their discussion of opium indemnities), Add MSS 22409.

144. Drafts to India Board, September 20, 1839, FO17/35:49–50. Hobhouse discussed sending out a squadron to China as early as September 16 (see John Hobhouse Diaries, Add MSS 56561:134a [September 16], 138b [September 26, 1839], 144b).

145. Palmerston to Melbourne, September 23, 1839, in Lloyd C. Sanders, *Lord Melbourne's Papers* (London: Longmans, 1890), 456–58. Also at Lamb Papers, M859/6, Box 12, f. 13, cited in Melancon, *Britain's China Policy*, 112. Hsin-pao Chang was unaware of this letter.

146. Compare details in Palmerston's letter and in Lindsay, *Letter*, 5, 12–14. At a cabinet meeting, Hobhouse noted that Palmerston's war plan was based on Lindsay's (John Hobhouse Diaries, October 1, 1839, Add MSS 56561:144a–145b).

147. Palmerston's early plan already included "the blockade of the river at Canton and the coast to the N.E. including perhaps taking possession of Amoy." See W. Crawford to R. Crawford, August 8, 1839, Jardine Matheson Archive, B1/10, f. 35, cited in Melancon, "Honor in Opium?" 864. For Palmerston's efforts to keep the meetings secret, see Smith to Palmerston, September 18, 1839, in FO17/35:68–70.

148. John Hobhouse Diaries, October 1, 1839, Add MSS 56561:144a–145b. For military preparation in the next few weeks, see ibid., 148b, 154a–55b (October 2, 11, November 2–3, 1839).

149. Palmerston to Elliot, Secret, October 18, 1839, FO17/29:43–46, esp. 43b (for the quotation) and 45.

150. See Lord Auckland's remarks about the war on April 7, 1840, in Minutes and Letters of Lord Auckland, Add MSS 37715:1. For the cabinet meeting of February 15, 1940, at which Palmerston read his letter to Chinese ministers, see John Hobhouse Diaries, February 13, 1840, Add MSS 56562:68b–69a (February 15, 1840). For the letter, see Pei-kai Cheng, Michael Lestz, and Jonathan Spence, *The Search for Modern China: A Documentary Collection* (New York: Norton, 1999), 123–27.

151. John Hobhouse Diaries, Add MSS 56562:90, 95a (March 12–13, 19, 1840). On the military planning, see Minutes and Letters of Lord Auckland, Add MSS 37715:1–29 and ADD MSS 37717:7a–8a.

152. "The Chinese and Our 'Great Plenipotentiary,'" 612–19; "The Opium and the China Question," 718–38, esp. 732 (quotations); "War with China, and the Opium Question," 369.

153. Cases of James Flint, Francis Scott, and Francis Terranova were also noted. For the quotations, see "The Chinese and Our 'Great Plenipotentiary,'" 616; "The Opium and the China Question," 732, 738.

154. WWC, 718–19.

155. Ibid., 719.

156. John Hobhouse Diary, February 7, 1840, Add MSS 56562:103b; Arthur C. Benson and Viscount Esher, eds., *The Letters of Queen Victoria (Illustrated Edition)*, 3 vols. (Teddington, Middlesex, U.K.: Echo Library, 2008), 1:235 (John Russell to Queen Victoria, April 8, 1840).

157. For doubts about the tale, see Chatterjee, *Black Hole*; also see Nicholas B. Dirks, *The Scandal of Empire: India and the Creation of Imperial Britain* (Cambridge, Mass.: Harvard University Press, 2008).

158. Staunton, *Corrected Report* (1840), 14–15.

159. John Hobhouse Diaries, November 2, 1839, Add MSS 56561:154b. See the 2,400 pages of correspondence between British commanders in India and China on the war in 1841, National Archive (London), WO461/1.

160. Palmerston noted that unless the Chinese actions were responded to with firmness and energy, trade with China could no longer be conducted with security to life and property or with credit and advantage to the British or Western nations (WWC, 925–47, 944–45, quoting a similar American memorial; "War with China . . . Parliamentary Debate," 249–51).

161. Gladstone, *Gladstone Diaries*, 3:21.

162. See FO682/1975:71–74 (August 1842), 682/1976:92–99 (June–July 1843).

163. Dirks, *Scandal*, xii–xiii.

164. See Hobhouse's speech, in WWC, 898.

165. Elliot to Palmerston, April 6, 1839 (received September 21), FO17/31:126–27; CRTC, 385–86. See Elliot to Palmerston, FO17/31:112, 114–16.

166. "Memorials Addressed to Her Majesty's Government," 20 (quotation from Henderson), 16. See the *Hampshire Telegraph*, quoted in "War with China, and the Opium Question," 383.

167. "The Chinese and Our 'Great Plenipotentiary,'" 619; for a similar argument by Macaulay, see WWC, 720.

168. Palmerston to Smith, November 28, 1842, West Sussex Record Office, Add MSS 22409.

169. Wong, *Deadly Dreams*, 476.

170. Staunton to Palmerston, February 20, 1840, IOR/L/PS/193:513–14.

171. See "Suppression of the Opium Trade, April 4, 1843," in *Hansard's Parliamentary Debates*, 3rd ser. (London: Thomas Curson Hansard, 1843), 68:417–18, 411. For his

advice on the postwar China policy, see Staunton to Aberdeen, December 19, 1842, in Correspondence with Lord Aberdeen, British Library, Add MSS 43240, CCII:100a–101a.

172. Aberdeen to Pottinger, December 29, 1842, quoted by Peel in "Suppression of the Opium Trade," 68:464. On treaty negotiations, see FO681/1974:5, 31–33, 40, 59; FO/682/1975:9 (opium legalization), 11–153; FO682/1976:32–121, 112 (opium). Also see FO682/1980:15–16 (Davis's seeking opium legalization in 1847).

173. *Hansard's Parliamentary Debates*, 66:547–74 (February 14, 1843), esp. 566–68 (Palmerston), 571–72 (Staunton and Inglis); 68:362 (April 4, 1843, Ashley).

174. John Quincy Adams, "Lecture on the War with China," *Albion*, September 11, 1841, 433–35; John Quincy Adams, "Lecture on the War with China," *Albion*, December 18, 1841, 441–44.

175. Wheaton, *Elements of International Law* (1866), 22, 178 (quotations). See Liu, *Clash of Empires*, 108–39; Rune Svarverud, *International Law as World Order in Late Imperial China: Translation, Reception and Discourse, 1847–1911* (Leiden: Brill, 2007). Cf. QGJJD, 098135 (TZ3/7/29) (Yixin's memorial requesting promulgation of the Chinese translation).

176. Thelwall, *Iniquities*; Charles W. King, *Opium Crisis: A Letter Addressed to Charles Elliot* (London: Suter, 1839). See also "Opium Traffic"; "Threatened War with China."

177. Gladstone, *Gladstone Diaries*, 3:29 (May 14, 1840), 49, 133, 136, 144, 280 (1843). He read pamphlets of Thelwall and King.

178. For criticism of the opium traders, see "Suppression of the Opium Trade," 68:362–71 (Ashley), 384–92 (Trevelyan), 415–23 (Staunton).

179. See Memorandum forwarded by Staunton, in Correspondence with Lord Aberdeen, Add MSS 43240, Vol. CCII, 43240 (October 1842–April 1843): f. 104a–b.

180. The motion was made by Lord Sandon; see "Suppression of the Opium Trade,"68:416–19, 421–23 (Staunton). Cf. Speeches by Colebrook, Elphinstone, Lindsay, and Peel, ibid., 68:449, 456, 461–68.

181. "Correspondence Respecting Affairs in China, as Regards Negotiations with Chinese Authorities," in *Parliamentary Papers*, House of Commons, 1860 (2587), LXIX.45 (London: Harrison and Sons, 1860), 393–97 (Elgin to Reed, September 13, 1858), esp. 394–95.

182. On the Second Opium War, see Wong, *Deadly Dreams*, 152–260. For the violence and looting, see Hevia, *English Lessons*, 49–281. For anti-Chinese policies, see Diana L. Ahmad, *The Opium Debate and Chinese Exclusion Laws in the Nineteenth-Century American West* (Reno: University of Nevada Press, 2007); Daniel E. Bender, *American Abyss: Savagery and Civilization in the Age of Industry* (Ithaca: Cornell University Press, 2009), 55–60, 90–97; Kay J. Anderson,

Vancouver's Chinatown: Racial Discourse in Canada, 1875–1980 (Montreal: McGill-Queen's University Press, 1995).

183. It was spread by a series of Arthur Ward's novels and translated into more than twenty languages and adapted to films and other media in the 1910s to 1960s. See Hevia, *English Lessons*, 317–26, 324 (for the quotations).

184. Samuel P. Huntington, *The Clash of Civilizations and the Remaking of World Order* (New York: Simon & Schuster, 1997).

185. Ann Laura Stoler and Frederick Cooper, "Between Metropole and Colony: Rethinking a Research Agenda," in *Tensions of Empire: Colonial Cultures in a Bourgeois World*, ed. Frederick Cooper and Ann Laura Stoler (Berkeley: University of California Press, 1997), 7. For the politics of difference construction, see Kathleen Wilson, *The Island Race: Englishness, Empire, and Gender in the Eighteenth Century* (London: Routledge, 2002), 146–48; Thomas R. Metcalf, *Ideologies of the Raj* (New York: Cambridge University Press, 1997), 66–159; Takashi Fujitani, *Race for Empire, Koreans as Japanese and Japanese as Americans during World War II* (Berkeley: University of California Press, 2011), 49–54, 77; Rande W. Kostal, *A Jurisprudence of Power: Victorian Empire and the Rule of Law* (Oxford: Oxford University Press, 2008), 468–73.

CONCLUSION

1. Liang Qichao, *Liang Qichao faxue wenji* (*Liang Qichao's Essays on Jurisprudence*), ed. Fan Zhongxin (Beijing: Zhongguo zhengfa daxue chubanshe, 1997), 120–82 (1904), esp. 175–78, 124, and 160.

2. Xianzheng Bianchaguan Dang'an, Archival no. 52, First National Historical Archives (Beijing); Xiuding Falüguan Dang'an, Archival nos. 7, 13, 18, First National Historical Archives (Beijing).

3. Edward H. Parker, "The Principles of Chinese Law and Equity," *Law Quarterly Review* 22, no. 2 (1906): 190–212, 191. Wu started from January 1874 and took his final exams in 1876 on topics including "the Institute of Gaius and Justinian, Roman law and jurisprudence, and constitutional law and legal history." He was called to the bar on January 26, 1877. See Linda Pomerantz-Zhang, *Wu Tingfang (1842–1922): Reform and Modernization in Modern Chinese History* (Hong Kong: Hong Kong University Press, 1992), 33–34.

4. Benjamin Schwartz, *In Search of Wealth and Power: Yen Fu and the West* (Cambridge, Mass.: Harvard University Press, 1964), 159–60, 161–64.

5. Lu Xun, *Nahan* (*Crying out*), *Yao* (*Medicine*), and *A Q zhengzhuan* (*The True Story of Ah Q*). For recent studies of this, see the analysis and works cited in Haiyan Lee, *Revolution of the Heart: The Genealogy of Love in China, 1900–1950* (Stanford: Stanford University Press, 2007), 225–40.

6. Shu-mei Shih, *The Lure of the Modern: Writing Modernism in Semicolonial China, 1917–1937* (Berkeley: University of California Press, 2001), 36, 32–37.

7. For foreign jurists still acknowledging the long history and sophistication of Chinese law in the early 1900s, see Harald Gutherz, "Zhongguo xin xinglü lun" (On the Chinese New Criminal Code), in *Xin Xinglü xiuzheng'an huilu* (*A Collection of Memoranda on the Proposed Revisions of the Draft New Criminal Code*), comp. Lao Naixuan (Beijing, 1910); Charles Sumner Lobingier, "The Need of Law Reform in China," *American Review of Reviews* 37 (1908): 218–19. For the late-Qing Chinese debates on codification, see *Xinglü cao'an qianzhu* (*Commentaries on the Draft Criminal Code*) (Xianzheng bianchaguan, ca. 1910).

8. About contemporary China's self-Orientalizing legal reform, see Teemu Ruskola, *Legal Orientalism: China, the United States, and Modern Law* (Cambridge, Mass.: Harvard University Press, 2013), 198–236.

9. Arif Dirlik, "Chinese History and the Question of Orientalism," *History and Theory* 35, no. 4 (1996): 114; Arif Dirlik, *Culture and History in Postrevolutionary China: The Perspective of Global Modernity* (Hong Kong: Chinese University Press, 2011), 15–28 (on the analytical problematic of global modernity).

10. Dipesh Chakrabarty, *Provincializing Europe: Postcolonial Thought and Historical Difference* (Princeton: Princeton University Press, 2000), 42.

Glossary

anchashi	按察使
Aomen tongzhi	澳门同知
baogu xianqi	保辜限期
bing	稟
binglü	兵律
bude zhengti	不得政体
bu xiaoxin zhihui	不小心知会
Celeng	策楞
cheng'an	成案
Chen Huiqian	陈辉千
Chen Yazhen	陈亚振
chiling	饬令
chuli	处理
chu wu hairen zhiyi	初无害人之意
chuzi wuxin	出自无心
Daoguang	道光
Da Qing Lüli	大清律例
datong	大同
Deng Tingzhen	邓廷桢
dingli	定例
Dixiehua	的些华 (口旁)
dousha	斗杀
dutong	督同
enwei bingji	恩威并济
fadu	法度
fangwei dujian	防微杜渐

fawai shi'en	法外施恩
gonglü	工律
guoji minsheng	国计民生
guoshisha	过失杀
guoshi sharen	过失杀人
gusha	故杀
haijiang	海疆
haiwai ru xiyang deng guo,	海外如西洋等国, 千百年后, 中国恐受其累
qianbai nian hou,	
Zhongguo kongshou qilei	
hangshang	行商
hanjian	汉奸
He Laojin	何老金
heming	核明
huairou	怀柔
Huang Juezi	黄爵滋
Huangpu	黄埔
Huangzhuqi	黄竹岐
huitong	会同
hulü	户律
hu'ou	互殴
jiagun	夹棍
Jian Ya'er	简亚二
Kangxi	康熙
koutou	叩头
li	例
lilü	吏律
lilü	礼律
linchuan	邻船
lingchi	凌迟
Lin Weixi	林维喜
Lin Zexu	林则徐
Li Tingfu	李廷富
Li Yajian	李亚健
lü	律
minglilü	名例律
miuqie	谬怯
Mo Lunzhi	莫伦志
Muteng'e	穆腾额
Pang Shangpeng	庞尚鹏 (1524–1580)
Qianlong	乾隆

qienuo	怯懦
qinchai	钦差
Qiying	耆英
rouyuan xushang	柔远恤商
Ruan Yuan	阮元
sangfutu	丧服图
shangshen guofa	上申国法
shengshi tongwen	盛世同文
Shuchang	舒常
songshi miben	讼师秘本
Sun Shiyi	孙士毅
tianchao guofa	天朝国法
tiaoli	条例
tingji	廷寄
tongshi	通事
tongxing	通行
waiyang	外洋
Wang Yunfa	王运发
Wu Guifang	吴桂芳
wuxin biming	无心毙命
wuxin wushang	无心误伤
Wu Yake	吴亚科
xianxing zhengfa	现行正法
xiashun yiqing	下顺夷情
xietong	协同
xing	刑
Xingbu	刑部
xinglü	刑律
Xinjiang	新疆
Xu Guangjin	徐广缙
Xu Naiji	许乃济
Xu Qiu	许球
yangren	洋人
Yao Fen	姚棻
yiqiu	夷酋
yiren	夷人
yishi rouyuan zhichu	以示柔远之处
Yuanmingyuan	圆明园
Yuan Yulin	袁玉麟
Yue Jun	岳濬
zanzhi	拶指

zaoyi	造意
Zhang Minggang	张鸣冈
zhisuo jingwei	知所敬畏
Zhu Zun	朱嶟
zouzhe	奏摺

BIBLIOGRAPHY

ARCHIVES AND MANUSCRIPTS CONSULTED

Chinese Official Records, 1500s–1900s

The First National Historical Archives, Beijing
Gongzhongdang Quanzong (Archives of Palace Memorials)
Junjichu Lufu Zouzhe (Grand Council Copies of Memorials) (JJCLFZZ)
Junjichu Shangyudang (Grand Council Copies of Edicts)
Junjichu Suishou Dengjidang (Grand Council Register of Edicts and Memorials)
Xianzheng Bianchaguan Dang'an (Archives of the Constitutional Commission)
Xiuding Falüguan Dang'an (Archives of the Law Revision Commission)

The National Palace Museum, Taipei
Qingdai Gongzhongdang Ji Junjichu Dangzhejian (Qing Palace Memorials and
  Archives of the Grand Council) (QGJJD)

Euro-American Official Records

The British Library, London
IOR/F/4/1737/70429, India Office Records and Private Papers, Board's Collections,
  1837–1840.
IOR/G/12/1–291, India Office Records, East India Company Factory Records, China
  (1500s–1838)
IOR/G/12/90–93, Records of the Cathcart Embassy and the Macartney Embassy

IOR/L/PS/9/193–202, Secret Department China Correspondence (1831–1854)

IOR/R/10/1–21, Factory Records, China (II), Diary and Consultation (1623–1803)

IOR/R/10/22–31, Secret Consultations of Select Committee of Supercargoes (1796–1834)

IOR/R/10/33–66, Court's Letters to the Council or Select Committee of Supercargoes (1784–1827)

IOR/R/10/67–74, Miscellaneous Correspondence and Papers of the Canton Factory, etc.

Add MSS 37715–17, China Books. Copies of Minutes and Letters of Lord Auckland (1840–1842)

Add MSS 43161–62, Letterbook: Official Correspondence of Lord Aberdeen, as Foreign Secretary, with British Ambassadors and Ministers in China, vol. CXXIII (June 1841–June 1846)

Add MSS 43240, Correspondence with Lord Aberdeen, vol. CCII (Oct. 1842–April 1843)

Add MSS 52414, Despatches of General Hugh Grant from China (1860–1861)

Add MSS 56561–65, John Hobhouse Diaries (1839–1844)

The National Archives, Kew, London

Foreign Office Records

FO17/1–150, General Correspondence, China (1815–1848)

FO83/2247, Law Officers' Reports, China (1833–1844)

FO228, Embassies and Consular Reports, China (1834–1894)

FO233/123, Copybooks of Chinese Language Documents

FO233/189, Copybooks of Chinese Language Documents (1750s–1808)

FO682/1972–1981, Chinese Language Diplomatic Correspondence and Other Documents (1839–1848)

FO881/832, China: Memorandum, War with China, 1839–1842, Confidential Print (1859)

FO881/914, China: Despatches Regarding the War with China, Confidential Print (Jan.–Dec. 1860)

FO931, Kwangtung Provincial Archives (1838–1850s)

FO932, Chinese Secretary's Office, Chinese Registers of Correspondence (1840–1938)

FO1048, Chinese Secretary's Office, Chinese Language Correspondence and Papers (1793–1834)

FO1080/1–100, Chinese Secretary's Office, Embassy and Legation, China, Miscellanea (1833–1860)

War Office Records

WO32/8230 (1860)

WO461/1 (1840–1843)

Public Record Office

PRO30/22/30, Correspondence of Lord John Russell to Lord Palmerston, 1859–1860
PRO30/29/23/11, Memorandum on the War with China to the Duke of Wellington
(1841)

National Archives, Washington, D.C., and College Park, Maryland
Department of State, Consular Despatches/Diplomatic Despatches, 1790–1906
Despatches from U.S. Consuls in Canton, 1790–1906 (DFUSCC).
Despatches from U.S. Ministers to China, 1843–1906

Arquivo Nacional da Torre do Tombo, Lisbon
Chinese official correspondence concerning Macao, 1693–1886 (a copy in microfilm
is also available at the Arquivo Históricao de Macau; for the sake of convenience,
citations in notes of *PTYDP* refer to Liu Fang and Zhang Wenqin, eds. *Putaoya
dongpota dang'anguan chang Qingdai Aomen zhongwen dang'an huibian [Collections
of Chinese Documents on Qing-Dynasty Macao at the National Archives of Portugal].*
Macao: Aomen jijinhui, 1999)

West Sussex Record Office, Chichester, West Sussex
Add MSS 22/409, Letters from Palmerston to John Abel Smith (1842–1843)

William R. Perkins Library, Duke University, North Carolina
Sir George Leonard and George Thomas Staunton Papers [diaries, letters, etc.], 1743–
1885 (SP). Also available in *China through Western Eyes: Manuscripts of Traders,
Travellers, Missionaries and Diplomats, 1792–1987* (Marlborough, U.K.: Adam
Matthew Publications, 1996), part 2, reels 27–30.

NEWSPAPERS AND MAGAZINES CITED

The Albion: A Journal of News, Politics and Literature (New York)
American Beacon, and Norfolk & Portsmouth Daily Adventure
The American Reviews of Reviews (New York)
The Analectic Magazine (Philadelphia)
Annali di scienze e lettere (Milan, Venice)
The Annual Register (London)
The Asiatic Journal and Monthly Miscellany (London)
*The Asiatic Journal and Monthly Register for British and Foreign India, China, and
Australia*, 2nd ser. (1830–1843, London)

The Asiatic Journal and Monthly Register for British India and Its Dependencies (1816–1829, London)

The BBC News

Blackwood's Edinburgh Magazine

The Bombay Times

The Boston Daily Globe

The Boston Recorder

The British Critic (London)

The British Review (London)

The Calcutta Gazette; or, Oriental Advertiser

The Caledonian Mercury (Edinburgh)

The Canadian Monthly and National Review (Toronto)

The Canton Press

The Canton Register

The Charter (London)

The Chicago Daily Tribune

The Chicago Tribune

The China Review; or, Notes and Queries on the Far East (Hong Kong)

The Chinese Courier and Canton Gazette

The Chinese Repository (Guangzhou)

The Christian Examiner and General Review (Boston)

The Columbian Centinel (Boston)

The Cornhill Magazine (London)

The Critical Review (Edinburgh)

The Daily Mail (London)

The Eclectic Review (London)

The Edinburgh Review

The Evangelical Magazine and Missionary Chronicle (London)

The Family Magazine (New York)

Fraser's Magazine (London)

The Free Enquirer (New York)

The Freeman's Journal (Dublin)

The Genius of Liberty (Leesburg, Virginia)

The Gentleman's Magazine (London)

The India Gazette (Calcutta)

The Indian News and Chronicle of Eastern Affairs (London)

The Indo-Chinese Gleaner (Malacca)

Je sais tout: Encyclopédie mondiale illustrée (Paris)

Journal of the Royal Asiatic Society of Great Britain and Ireland (London)

The Leeds Mercury

The Liverpool Mercury

The London Westminster Review
The Manchester Times and Gazette
Mercure de France: Journal littéraire et politique (Paris)
The Monthly Chronicle (London)
The Monthly Review (London)
The Monthly Visitor (London)
The Morning Post (London)
Newsweek (New York)
The New York Daily Tribune
New York Evangelist
The New York Times
The North American Review (Boston)
The North China Herald (Shanghai)
The Northern Star (Yorkshire)
The Pall Mall Gazette (London)
The Phrenological Journal and Science of Health (New York)
The Providence Gazette (1795–1811, Providence, Rhode Island)
The Quarterly Review (London, reprinted in New York)
The Religious Intelligencer (New Haven)
The Saturday Evening Post (Philadelphia)
The Singapore Free Press
The Southern Star and London and Brighton Patriot
The Telegraph (London)
The Times (London)
Transactions of the China Branch of the Royal Asiatic Society (London)
The Universal Register (London)
Waldie's (Philadelphia)
The Washington Post
The York Chronicle

OTHER PRINTED SOURCES AND
SECONDARY LITERATURE

Aalberts, Tanja E. *Constructing Sovereignty between Politics and Law*. New York: Routledge, 2012.
Adas, Michael. *Machines as the Measure of Men*. Ithaca: Cornell University Press, 1989.
Agamben, Giorgio. *State of Exception*. Chicago: University of Chicago Press, 2005.
Ahmad, Aijaz. "*Orientalism* and After: Ambivalence and Metropolitan Location in the Work of Edward Said." In *Imperialism: Critical Concepts in Historical Studies*, edited by Peter J. Cain and Mark Harrison, 256–308. London: Routledge, 2000.

Ahmad, Diana L. *The Opium Debate and Chinese Exclusion Laws in the Nineteenth-Century American West*. Reno: University of Nevada Press, 2007.

Ahmed, Sara. *The Cultural Politics of Emotion*. New York: Routledge, 2004.

Alabaster, Ernest. *Notes and Commentaries on Chinese Criminal Law and Cognate Topics*. London: Luzac, 1899.

Aldridge, Alfred O. *The Dragon and the Eagle: The Presence of China in the American Enlightenment*. Detroit: Wayne State University Press, 1993.

Alexandrowicz, Charles H. *An Introduction to the History of the Law of Nations in the East Indies (16th, 17th and 18th Centuries)*. Oxford: Clarendon Press, 1967.

Alford, William P. "Of Arsenic and Old Laws: Looking Anew at Criminal Justice in Late Imperial China." *California Law Review* 72 (1984): 1180–1250.

——. "The Inscrutable Occidental? Implications of Robert Unger's Uses and Abuses of the Chinese Past." *Texas Law Review* 64, no. 5 (1986): 915–72.

——. "Law, Law, What Law? Why Western Scholars of Chinese History and Society Have Not Had More to Say about Its Law." *Modern China* 23, no. 4 (1997): 398–419.

Ames, Glenn J. *The Globe Encompassed: The Age of European Discovery, 1500–1700*. Upper Saddle River, N.J.: Pearson Prentice Hall, 2008.

Anderson, Benedict. *Imagined Communities: Reflections on the Origin and Spread of Nationalism*. New York: Verso, 2001.

Anderson, Kay J. *Vancouver's Chinatown: Racial Discourse in Canada, 1875–1980*. Montreal: McGill-Queen's University Press, 1995.

Anghie, Antony. *Imperialism, Sovereignty, and the Making of International Law*. Cambridge: Cambridge University Press, 2004.

Anson, George. *A Voyage round the World, in the Years 1740–44, by George Anson*. Edited by Richard Walter. London: John and Paul Knapton, 1748.

Archivio storico italiano: Appendice. Vol. 3. Florence: G.P. Vieusseux, 1846.

Arendt, Hannah. *On Revolution*. New York: Penguin, 2006.

Armitage, David. *The Ideological Origins of the British Empire*. New York: Columbia University Press, 2000.

Arneil, Barbara. "The Wild Indian's Venison: Locke's Theory of Property and English Colonialism in America." *Political Studies* 44, no. 1 (March 1996): 66–74.

Arrazola, Lorenzo. "Codigo: China." In *Enciclopedia española de derecho y administración (Spanish Encyclopedia of Law and Administration)*, edited by Lorenzo Arrazola, 367–69. Madrid: Imprenta de la Revista de Legislacion y Jurisprudencia, á Cargo de J. Morales, 1856.

Askew, Joseph. "Re-visiting New Territory: The Terranova Incident Re-examined." *Asian Studies Review* 28, no. 4 (2004): 351–71.

Athanasiou, Athena, et al. "Towards a New Epistemology: The 'Affective Turn.'" *Historein* 8 (2008): 5–16.

Auber, Peter. *China: An Outline of Its Government, Laws, and Policy*. London: Parbury, 1834.

Balfour, Edward. *The Cyclopædia of India and of Eastern and Southern Asia*. 3 vols. London: Bernard Quaritch, 1885.

Ball, Benjamin Lincoln. *Rambles in Eastern Asia*. 2nd ed. Boston: James French, 1856.

Ball, James Dyer. *Things Chinese*. 2nd ed. London: Sampson Low, 1893.

Barlow, Tani. "~~Colonialism's~~ Career in China Studies." In *Formations of Colonial Modernity in East Asia*, edited by Tani Barlow, 373–412. Durham: Duke University Press, 1997.

Barnes, Elizabeth. "Affecting Relations: Pedagogy, Patriarchy, and the Politics of Sympathy." *American Literary History* 8, no. 4 (1996): 597–614.

——. "Communicable Violence and the Problem of Capital Punishment in New England, 1830–1890." *Modern Language Studies* 30, no. 1 (2000): 7–26.

Barnhart, James David. "Violence and the Civilizing Mission: Native Justice in French Colonial Vietnam, 1858–1914." Ph.D. diss., University of Chicago, 1999.

Barrow, John. *Travels in China*. London: Cadell and Davies, 1804.

——. *Voyage en Chine, formant le complément du voyage de Lord Macartney*. Translated by J. Castera. Paris: Buisson, 1805.

——. *Some Account of the Public Life, and a Selection from the Unpublished Writings, of the Earl of Macartney*. 2 vols. London: Cadell and Davies, 1807.

——. *An Autobiographical Memoir of Sir John Barrow*. London: John Murray, 1847.

Barry, Michael. *A History of Pain: Trauma in Modern Chinese Literature and Film*. New York: Columbia University Press, 2013.

Bashford, James W. *China: An Interpretation*. Cincinnati: Abingdon Press, 1916.

Beattie, John M. *Crime and the Courts in England, 1660–1800*. Oxford: Oxford University Press, 1986.

Beccaria, Cesare. *On Crimes and Punishments*. 1764. Translated by David Young. Indianapolis: Hackett, 1986.

——. *An Essay on Crimes and Punishments, by the Marquis Beccaria of Milan, with a Commentary by M. de Voltaire*. New, corrected ed. Edinburgh: James Donaldson, 1788.

Beck, Theodric R. *Elements of Medical Jurisprudence*. 2 vols. Albany: Webster and Skinner, 1823.

Bellomo, Manlio. *The Common Legal Past of Europe, 1000–1800*. Translated by Lydia G. Cochrane. Washington, D.C.: Catholic University of America Press, 1995.

Bender, Daniel E. *American Abyss: Savagery and Civilization in the Age of Industry*. Ithaca: Cornell University Press, 2009.

Benson, Arthur C., and Viscount Esher, eds. *The Letters of Queen Victoria (Illustrated Edition)*. 3 vols. Teddington, Middlesex, U.K.: Echo Library, 2008.

Bentham, Jeremy. *A Fragment on Government: Being an Examination of What Is Delivered, on the Subject of Government in General in the Introduction to Sir William Blackstone's Commentaries*. London: T. Payne, 1776.

——. *Papers Relative to Codification and Public Instruction*. London: Payne and Foss, 1817.

——. *Principles of Legislation.* Edited by Étienne Dumont. Translated by John Neal. Boston: Wells and Lilly, 1830.

——. *The Rationale of Punishment.* Translated by [Étienne] Dumont. London: Robert Heward, 1830. Originally published by Étienne Dumont in French in 1811, based on MS of 1770s.

——. *Principles of the Penal Code.* Boston: Weeks, 1840.

Benton, Lauren. "Colonial Law and Cultural Difference: Jurisdictional Politics and the Formation of the Colonial State." *Comparative Studies in Society and History* 41, no. 3 (2000): 563–88.

——. *Law and Colonial Cultures: Legal Regimes in World History, 1400–1900.* Cambridge: Cambridge University Press, 2002.

Berncastle, Dr. Julius. *A Voyage to China.* 2 vols. London: W. Shoberl, 1850.

Berry, Michael. *A History of Pain: Trauma in Modern Chinese Literature and Film.* New York: Columbia University Press, 2008.

Berty, L. Nigon de. *Histoire abrégée de la liberté individuelle chez les principaux peuples anciens et modernes.* Paris: Moutardier, 1834.

Bhabha, Homi. *The Location of Culture.* New York: Routledge, 2006.

Bhattacharyya-Panda, Nandini. *Appropriation and Invention of Tradition: The East India Company and Hindu Law in Early Colonial Bengal.* Oxford: Oxford University Press, 2008.

Bickers, Robert A., ed. *Ritual and Diplomacy: The Macartney Mission to China, 1792–1794.* London: Wellsweep Press, 1993.

——. "The Challenger: Hugh Hamilton Lindsay and the Rise of British Asia, 1832–1865." *Transactions of the Royal Historical Society*, 6th ser., 22 (2012): 141–69.

Biggar, Henry P., ed. *The Precursors of Jacques Cartier, 1497–1534: A Collection of Documents Relating to the Early History of the Dominion of Canada.* Ottawa: Government Printing Bureau, 1911.

Birtsch, Günter. "Reform Absolutism and the Codification of Law: The Genesis and Nature of the Prussian General Code (1794)." In *Rethinking Leviathan: The Eighteenth-Century State in Britain and Germany*, edited by John Brewer and Eckhart Hellmuth, 343–58. Oxford: Oxford University Press, 1999.

Blackstone, Sir William. *Commentaries on the Laws of England.* 13th ed. 4 vols. London: Cadell and Davies, 1800.

Blair, Emma H., and James A. Robertson, eds. *The Philippine Islands, 1493–1898.* 55 vols. Cleveland: Arthur H. Clark Co., 1903–1909.

Blake, Robert. *Jardine Matheson: Traders of the Far East.* London: Weidenfeld, 1999.

Blondel, Lucien Antoine, and Jacques Louis César Alexandre Randon. *Relation de l'expédition de Chine en 1860: Rédigée au dépôt de la guerre.* Paris: Imprimerie imperiale, 1862.

Blue, Gregory. "China and Western Social Thought in the Modern Period." In *China and Historical Capitalism: Genealogies of Sinological Knowledge*, edited by Timothy Brook and Gregory Blue, 57–109. Cambridge: Cambridge University Press, 2002.

Bocarro, Antonio, ed. *Decada 13 da historia da India*. 2 vols. Lisbon: Academia das Ciências de Lisboa, 1876.

Bodde, Derk, and Clarence Morris. *Law in Imperial China*. Cambridge, Mass.: Harvard University Press, 1967.

Boesche, Roger. *Theories of Tyranny: From Plato to Arendt*. University Park: Pennsylvania State University Press, 1996.

Boltanski, Luc. *Distant Suffering: Morality, Media, and Politics*. New York: Cambridge University Press, 1999.

Botsman, Daniel V. *Punishment and Power in the Making of Modern Japan*. Princeton: Princeton University Press, 2005.

Bourgon, Jérôme. "Uncivil Dialogue: Law and Custom Did Not Merge into Civil Law under the Qing." *Late Imperial China* 23, no. 1 (June 2002): 50–90.

——. "Abolishing 'Cruel Punishments': A Reappraisal of the Chinese Roots and Long-Term Efficiency of the Xinzheng Legal Reforms." *Modern Asian Studies* 37, no. 4 (2003): 851–62.

——. "Chinese Executions: Visualizing Their Differences with European *Supplices*." *European Journal of East Asian Studies* 2, no. 1 (June 2003): 153–84.

Boxer, Charles R. *The Christian Century in Japan: 1549–1650*. Berkeley: University of California Press, 1951.

Bridgman, Eliza J. Gillett, ed. *The Life and Labors of Elijah Coleman Bridgman*. New York: Anson D. F. Randolph, 1864.

A Brief Account of the Privileges and Immunities Granted by the French King to the East-India Company, &c. of France. London: Ambrose Isted, 1671.

Brook, Timothy. *Vermeer's Hat: The Seventeenth Century and the Dawn of the Global World*. London: Profile Books, 2009.

Brook, Timothy, Jérôme Bourgon, and Gregory Blue. *Death by a Thousand Cuts*. Cambridge, Mass.: Harvard University Press, 2008.

Brougham, Henry. *The Life and Times of Lord Henry Brougham*. 3 vols. London: William Blackwood, 1871–1872.

Bruce, James. *Letters and Journals of James Bruce, Earl of Elgin*. Edited by T. Walrond. London: Spottiswoode and Co., 1872.

Buoye, Thomas M. Review of *The Great Qing Code*, translated by William C. Jones. *Journal of Asian Studies* 54, no. 4 (1994): 1242–43.

——. "Suddenly Murderous Intent Arose: Bureaucratization and Benevolence in Eighteenth-Century Qing Homicide Reports." *Late Imperial China* 16, no. 2 (1995): 62–97.

Butler, Judith. *Bodies That Matter: On the Discursive Limits of "Sex."* New York: Routledge, 1993.

——. *Precarious Life: The Powers of Mourning and Violence.* New York: Verso, 2006.

——. *Frames of War: When Is Life Grievable?* New York: Verso, 2010.

Cameron, Charles H. *An Address to Parliament on the Duties of Great Britain to India, in Respect of the Education of the Natives and Their Official Employment.* London: Longman, Brown, 1853.

Campbell, Archibald. *A Voyage Round the World, from 1806 to 1812.* New York: Van Winkle, Wiley & Co., 1817.

Campbell, Donald. *A Journey Overland to India.* London: Cullen and Co., 1795.

Cannon, Garland, ed. *The Letters of Sir William Jones.* 2 vols. Oxford: Clarendon Press, 1970.

——. "Sir William Jones's Indian Studies." *Journal of the American Oriental Society* 91, no. 3 (1971): 418–25.

Caso, Adolph. *America's Italian Founding Fathers.* Boston: Branden Press, 1975.

Cassel, Pär. *Grounds of Judgment: Extraterritoriality and Imperial Power in Nineteenth-Century China and Japan.* Oxford: Oxford University Press, 2012.

Catherine II. *The Memoirs of Catherine the Great.* Translated by Mark Cruse and Hilde Hoogenboom. New York: Modern Library, 2005.

A Century of Japanese Photography. Compiled by the Japan Photographers Association. New York: Pantheon, 1980.

Chakrabarty, Dipesh. *Provincializing Europe: Postcolonial Thought and Historical Difference.* Princeton: Princeton University Press, 2000.

Chang, Hsin-pao. *Commissioner Lin and the Opium War.* Cambridge, Mass.: Harvard University Press, 1964.

Chang, Hsiu-jung, and Anthony Farrington, eds. *The English Factory in Taiwan, 1670–1685.* Taipei: National Taiwan University, 1995.

Chang, T'ien-tse. "Malacca and the Failure of the First Portuguese Embassy to Peking." *Journal of Southeast Asian History* 3, no. 2 (1962): 45–64.

——. *Sino-Portuguese Trade from 1514 to 1644.* 1934. Reprint, New York: AMS Press, 1973.

Chan Lau, Kit-ching. "The Abrogation of British Extraterritoriality in China 1942–43." *Modern Asian Studies* 11, no. 2 (1977): 257–91.

Chanock, Martin. *Law, Custom, and Social Order: The Colonial Experience in Malawi and Zambia.* Portsmouth, N.H.: Heinemann, 1998.

Chatterjee, Partha. *The Black Hole of Empire: History of a Global Practice of Power.* Princeton: Princeton University Press, 2012.

Chauveau, Adolphe, and Faustin Hélie. *Théorie du Code pénal.* Vol. 1. Brussels: Société Typographique Belge, 1837.

——. *Théorie du Code pénal.* 4th ed. Paris: Imprimerie et librairie générale de jurisprudence, 1861.

Chen, Li. "Law, Empire, and Historiography of Modern Sino-Western Relations: A Case Study of the *Lady Hughes* Controversy in 1784." *Law and History Review* 27, no. 1 (2009): 1–53.

——. "Universalism and Equal Sovereignty as Contested Myths of International Law in the Sino-Western Encounter." *Journal of the History of International Law* 13, no. 1 (January 2011): 75–116.

——. "Legal Specialists and Judicial Administration in Late Imperial China, 1651–1911." *Late Imperial China* 33, no. 1 (June 2012): 1–54.

——. Affective Sovereignty, International Law, and China's Legal Status in the Nineteenth Century." In *The Scaffold of Sovereignty: A Global Interdisciplinary Approach*, edited by Stefanos Geroulanos, Zvi Ben-Dor Benite, and Nichole Jerr. New York: Columbia University Press, forthcoming.

Chen, Li, and Madeleine Zelin, eds. *Chinese Law: Knowledge, Practice and Transformation, 1530s–1950s*. Leiden: Brill, 2015.

Chen, Xiaomei. *Occidentalism: Theory of Counter-Discourse in Post-Mao China*. New York: New York University Press, 1994.

Cheng Cunjie. *Shijiu shiji Zhongguo waixiao tongcao shuicaihua yanjiu* (*Study of Nineteenth-Century China Export Watercolor Paintings on Gouache Paper*). Shanghai: Shanghai guji chubanshe, 2008.

Cheng, Pei-kai, Michael Lestz, and Jonathan Spence. *The Search for Modern China: A Documentary Collection*. New York: Norton, 1999.

Cheong, Weng Eang. *The Hong Merchants of Canton: Chinese Merchants in Sino-Western Trade, 1684–1798*. London: Routledge, 1997.

China: Copies of All Communications between the Board of Treasury or the India Board, or Any Other Public Department and the Parties or Their Agents Who Are Holders of Certificates or Bills Granted by the Chief Superintendent at Canton for Opium Surrendered to the Chinese Authorities. House of Commons, March 23, 1840.

Chouban yiwu shimo (*A Full Account of the Management of Foreign Affairs*). Compiled by Wenqing et al. 8 *juan*. In *Xuxiu siku quanshu*, vols. 414–21. Shanghai: Shanghai guji chubanshe, 2002.

Chow, Rey. *Not Like a Native Speaker: On Languaging as a Postcolonial Experience*. New York: Columbia University Press, 2014.

Christianson, Scott. *With Liberty for Some: 500 Years of Imprisonment in America*. Boston: Northeastern University Press, 1998.

Chung, Tan. *China and the Brave New World: A Study of the Origins of the Opium War, 1840–41*. New Delhi: Allied Publishers, 1978.

——. "Imperialism in Nineteenth-Century China (1): Foreign Mud on Good Earth; British Opium Enterprise vis-a-vis China." *China Report* 17, no. 2 (1981): 9–41.

Çırakman, Aslı. "From Tyranny to Despotism: The Enlightenment's Unenlightened Image of the Turks." *International Journal of Middle East Studies* 33 (2001): 49–68.

Clarke, John J. *Oriental Enlightenment: The Encounter between Asian and Western Thought.* London: Routledge, 1997.

Clarkson, Chris. "Recent Law Reform and Codification of the General Principles of Criminal Law in England and Wales: A Tale of Woe." In *Codification, Macaulay and the Indian Penal Code*, edited by Wing-Cheong Chan et al., 337–65. Burlington, Vt.: Ashgate, 2011.

Clunas, Craig. *Chinese Export Watercolours.* London: Victoria and Albert Museum, 1984.

Cockburn, Lord Henry. *Life of Lord Jeffrey, with a Selection from His Correspondence.* 2nd ed. 2 vols. Edinburgh: Adam and Charles Black, 1852.

The Code Napoléon: Verbally translated from the French, to which is prefixed an introductory discourse, containing a succinct account of the civil regulations, comprised in the Jewish law, the ordinances of Menu, the Ta Tsing Leu Lee, the Zend Avesta, the laws of Solon, the twelve tables of Rome, the laws of the Barbarians, the Assises of Jerusalem, and the Koran. Translated by Bryant Barrett. 2 vols. London: W. Reed, 1811.

Cohen, Jerome A., et al., eds. *Essays on China's Legal Tradition.* Princeton: Princeton University Press, 1980.

Cohen, Paul A. *Discovering History in China: American Historical Writings on the Recent Chinese Past.* New York: Columbia University Press, 1986.

Cohn, Bernard S. *Colonialism and Its Forms of Knowledge: The British in India.* Princeton: Princeton University Press, 1996.

Coke, Edward. *The First Part of the Institutes of the Laws of England.* 1624. 8th ed. 2 vols. Vol. 1. London: J. & W. T. Clarke, 1823.

Colebrooke, H. T. *A Digest of Hindu Law, on Contracts and Successions: With a Commentary by Jagannát'ha Tercapanchánana, Translated from the Original Sanscrit.* 1797. 3rd ed. 2 vols. Vol. 1. Madras: J. Higginbotham, 1864.

Comaroff, John. "Colonialism, Culture, and the Law: A Foreword." *Law & Social Inquiry* 26, no. 2 (2001): 305–14.

Conklin, Alice L., and Ian C. Fletcher, eds. *European Imperialism, 1830–1930: Climax and Contradiction.* Boston: Houghton Mifflin, 1999.

Conner, Patrick. "Lamqua: Western and Chinese Painter." *Arts of Asia* 29, no. 2 (1999): 46–64.

Cooper, Frederick, and Ann Laura Stoler, eds. *Tensions of Empire: Colonial Cultures in a Bourgeois World.* Berkeley: University of California Press, 1997.

Cordier, Henri. "Le consulat de France à Canton au XVIIIe siècle." *T'oung Pao* 9, no. 1 (1908): 47–96.

Correspondence between the Foreign Office and the Commercial Association of Manchester, Relative to Outrages Committed on British Subjects in China, in 1846, 1847, 1848. London: Harrison and Sons, 1846–1848.

"Correspondence Relating to China [01/1834–09/1839]." In *Parliamentary Papers.* London: House of Commons, 1840 (CRTC).

"Correspondence Relative to the Earl of Elgin's Special Missions to China and Japan, 1857–59." In *Parliamentary Papers*, House of Commons, 1859 (2571), XXXIII.1. London: Harrison and Sons, 1859.

"Correspondence Respecting Affairs in China, as Regards Negotiations with Chinese Authorities." In *Parliamentary Papers*, House of Commons, 1860 (2587), LXIX.45. London: Harrison and Sons, 1860.

"Correspondence Respecting Affairs in China, 1859–60." In *Parliamentary Papers*, House of Commons, 1861 (2754), LXVI.1. London: Harrison and Sons, 1861.

Cortesão, Armando. *Primeira embaixada europeia à China (Ouzhou diyige fuhua shijie).* 1945. Reprint, Macao: Instituto Cultural de Macau, 1990.

Cranmer-Byng, John L. "The First English Sinologists—Sir George Staunton and the Reverend Robert Morrison." In *Symposium on Historical, Archaeological and Linguistic Studies on Southern China, South-East Asia and the Hong Kong Region*, edited by E. C. Drake, 247–60. Hong Kong: Hong Kong University Press, 1967.

——. *An Embassy to China: Lord Macartney's Journal, 1793–1794.* In *Britain and the China Trade, 1635–1842*, vol. 8, edited by Patrick Tuck. New York: Routledge, 2000.

Cranmer-Byng, John L., and John E. Wills Jr. "Trade and Diplomacy with Maritime Europe, 1644–c. 1800." In *China and Maritime Europe, 1500–1800*, edited by John E. Wills Jr., 183–254. Cambridge: Cambridge University Press, 2011.

"Criminal Law Bills." In *Parliamentary Debates* [May 13–July 24, 1811], edited by T. C. Hansard, 296–303. London: Longman, Hurst, Rees, 1812.

The Criminal Recorder; or, Biographical Sketches of Notorious Public Characters. 4 vols. London: Albion Press, 1810.

Cronin, Vincent. *Catherine, Empress of All the Russians.* New York: Morrow, 1978.

Cross, Rupert. "The Reports of the Criminal Law Commissioners (1833–49) and the Abortive Bills of 1853." In *Reshaping the Criminal Law: Essays in Honour of Glanville Williams*, edited by P. R. Glazebrook, 5–20. London: Stevens, 1978.

Crossley, Pamela. *A Translucent Mirror: History and Identity in Qing Imperial Ideology.* Berkeley: University of California Press, 2002.

Crossley, Pamela, and Evelyn S. Rawski. "A Profile of the Manchu Language in Ch'ing History." *Harvard Journal of Asiatic Studies* 53, no. 1 (1993): 63–102.

Crossman, Carl. L. *The China Trade.* Princeton: Pyne, 1972.

Cutmore, Jonathan. *Conservatism and the Quarterly Review: A Critical Analysis.* London: Pickering & Chatto, 2007.

——. *Contributors to the Quarterly Review: A History, 1809–1825.* London: Pickering & Chatto, 2008.

Dagge, Henry. *Considerations on Criminal Law.* Dublin: H. Saunders, 1772.

Dai Yixuan. *Mingshi Folangji zhuan jianzheng (Corrections for the Section on Portugal in the Ming History).* Beijing: Shehui kexueyuan chubanshe, 1984.

Da Qing Xuanzong Chenghuangdi shilu (Veritable Records of the Daoguang Emperor). 12 vols. Taipei: Huawen shuju, 1964.

Davenport, Frances G., ed. *European Treaties Bearing on the History of the United States and Its Dependencies to 1648.* Washington, D.C.: Carnegie Institution of Washington, 1917.

Davis, John Francis. *The Chinese: A General Description of the Empire of China and Its Inhabitants.* 2 vols. London: Charles Knight & Co., 1836.

———. *Chinese Miscellanies: A Collection of Essays and Notes.* London: John Murray, 1865.

de Guignes, Chrétien-Louis-Joseph. "Détail d'une affaire survenue entre les Européens et les Chinois, en 1784, à l'occasion de deux hommes tués à Wampou par un coup de canon" (Details of a Case Arising between Europeans and Chinese, in 1784, on the Occasion of Two Men Killed at Huangpu by a Cannon). In *Voyages à Peking, Manille et l'île de France faits dans l'intervalle des années 1784 à 1801*, 292–97. Paris: Imprimerie imperiale, 1808.

de Malpière, D. Bazin. *La Chine: Mœurs, usages, costumes, arts et métiers, peines civiles et militaires, cérémonies religieuses, monuments et paysages.* 2 vols. Paris: L'éditeur, 1825.

Deng, Jianpeng. "Classification of Litigation and Implications for Qing Judicial Practice." In Chen and Zelin, *Chinese Law*, 17–46.

Dermigny, Louis. *La Chine et l'Occident: Le commerce à Canton au XVIIIe siècle, 1719–1833.* 3 vols. Paris: S.E.V.P.E.N., 1964.

———, ed. *Les mémoires de Charles de Constant sur le commerce à la Chine.* Paris: S.E.V.P.E.N., 1964.

Dikötter, Frank. *The Tragedy of Liberation: A History of the Chinese Revolution, 1945–57.* London: Bloomsbury, 2013.

Dirks, Nicholas B. *Castes of Mind: Colonialism and the Making of Modern India.* Princeton: Princeton University Press, 2001.

———. *The Scandal of Empire: India and the Creation of Imperial Britain.* Cambridge, Mass.: Harvard University Press, 2008.

Dirlik, Arif. "Chinese History and the Question of Orientalism." *History and Theory* 35, no. 4 (1996): 96–118.

———. *Culture and History in Postrevolutionary China: The Perspective of Global Modernity.* Hong Kong: Chinese University Press, 2011.

Douglas, Robert K. *Society in China.* London: A.D. Innes & Co., 1894.

Downing, C. Toogood. *The Fan-Qui in China, in 1836–7.* 3 vols. London: Henry Colburn, 1838.

Doyle, Jack P. "Two Sixteenth-Century Jesuits and a Plan to Conquer China: Alonso Sánchez and Jose de Acosta; An Outrageous Proposal and Its Rejection." In *Rechtsdenken: Schnittpunkte West und Ost; Recht in den Gesellschafts- und Staatstragenden Institutionen Europas und Chinas*, edited by Harald Holz and Konrad Wegmann, 253–73. Münster: LIT Verlag, 2005.

Dray-Novey, Alison. "Spatial Order and Police in Imperial Beijing." *Journal of Asian Studies* 52, no. 4 (1993): 885–922.

Drayton, Richard. "Knowledge and Empire." In Marshall, *The Oxford History of the British Empire*, 231–52.

———. *Nature's Government: Science, Imperial Britain, and the "Improvement" of the World*. New Haven: Yale University Press, 2000.

Duara, Prasenjit. *Rescuing History from the Nation*. Chicago: University of Chicago Press, 1995.

Dubois, Page. *Torture and Truth*. New York: Routledge, 1990.

Du Halde, Jean Baptiste. *Description géographique, historique, chronologique et physique de l'empire de la Chine et de la Tartarie chinoise*. Paris: P. G. Le Mercier, 1735.

———. *The General History of China: Containing a Geographical, Historical, Chronological, Political and Physical Description of the Empire of China*. Translated by Richard Brookes. 4 vols. London: J. Watts, 1736.

Dunthorne, Hugh. "Beccaria and Britain." In *Crime, Protest and Police in Modern British Society*, edited by David Howell and Kenneth Morgan, 73–96. Cardiff: University of Wales Press, 1999.

Eden, William. *Principles of Law*. London: B. White, 1771.

Edwards, R. Randle. "Ch'ing Legal Jurisdiction over Foreigners." In Cohen et al., *Essays on China's Legal Tradition*, 222–69.

———. "Imperial China's Border Control Law." *Journal of Chinese Law* 1, no. 33 (1987): 33–62.

Elkins, James. *The Object Stares Back: On the Nature of Seeing*. New York: Simon & Schuster, 1996.

Elliott, Mark C. *The Manchu Way: The Eight Banners and Ethnic Identity in Late Imperial China*. Stanford: Stanford University Press, 2001.

Ellis, Sir Henry. *Journal of the Proceedings of the Late Embassy to China*. London: John Murray, 1817.

———. *A Series of Letters on the East India Question*. 2nd ed. London: John Murray, 1830.

Elman, Benjamin A. *On Their Own Terms: Science in China 1550–1900*. Cambridge, Mass.: Harvard University Press, 2005.

Ensor, George. *Defects of the English Laws and Tribunals*. London: J. Johnson & Co., 1812.

Epstein, James. *Scandal of Colonial Rule: Power and Subversion in the British Atlantic during the Age of Revolution*. New York: Cambridge University Press, 2012.

Esherick, Joseph W. *The Origins of the Boxer Uprising*. Berkeley: University of California Press, 1988.

Fairbank, John K. "Synarchy under the Treaties." In *Chinese Thought and Institutions*, edited by John K. Fairbank, 163–203. Chicago: University of Chicago Press, 1957.

———. *Trade and Diplomacy on the China Coast: The Opening of the Treaty Ports, 1842–1854*. Cambridge, Mass.: Harvard University Press, 1964.

——. "The Creation of the Treaty System." In *The Cambridge History of China: Volume 10, Late Ch'ing 1800–1911, Part 1,* edited by John K. Fairbank, 213–63. New York: Cambridge University Press, 1978.

——. *China Watch.* Cambridge, Mass.: Harvard University Press, 1987.

Fairbank, John K., and Edwin O. Reischauer. *China: Tradition and Transformation.* Boston: Houghton Mifflin, 1989.

Fairbank, John K., and Ssu-yu Teng. "On the Ch'ing Tributary System." *Harvard Journal of Asiatic Studies* 6, no. 2 (June 1941): 135–246.

Fan, Fa-ti. "Hybrid Discourse and Textual Practice: Sinology and Natural History in the Nineteenth Century." *History of Science* 38, no. 1 (2000): 25–56.

——. *British Naturalists in Qing China: Science, Empire, and Cultural Encounter.* Cambridge, Mass.: Harvard University Press, 2004.

Farmer, Lindsay. "Reconstructing the English Codification Debate: The Criminal Law Commissioners, 1833–45." *Law and History Review* 18, no. 2 (2000): 397–425.

Farrington, Anthony, ed. *The English Factory in Japan, 1613–1623.* 2 vols. London: British Library, 1991.

——. *Trading Places: The East India Company and Asia, 1600–1834.* London: British Library, 2002.

Fay, Peter W. "The French Catholic Mission in China during the Opium War." *Modern Asian Studies* 4, no. 2 (1970): 115–28.

——. *The Opium War, 1840–1842.* Chapel Hill: University of North Carolina Press, 1975.

Ferguson, Donald. *Letters from Portuguese Captives in Canton, Written in 1534 and 1536.* Bombay: Education Society, 1902.

Festa, Lynn. *Sentimental Figures of Empire in Eighteenth-Century Britain and France.* Baltimore: Johns Hopkins University Press, 2006.

Fisher, David R. *The History of Parliament: The House of Commons, 1820–1832.* 7 vols. Cambridge: Cambridge University Press, 2009.

Fitzgerald, John. *Awakening China: Politics, Culture, and Class in the Nationalist Revolution.* Stanford: Stanford University Press, 1996.

Fitzmaurice, Andrew. *Humanism and America: An Intellectual History of English Colonization, 1500–1625.* Cambridge: Cambridge University Press, 2003.

Flynn, Philip. *Francis Jeffrey.* Newark: University of Delaware Press, 1978.

Forbes, Robert B. *Remarks on China and the China Trade.* Boston: S.N. Dickinson, 1844.

——. *Personal Reminiscences.* Rev. ed. Boston: Little, Brown, 1882.

Foucault, Michel. "Governmentality." In *The Foucault Effect: Studies in Governmentality,* edited by Graham Burchell et al., 87–104. Chicago: University of Chicago Press, 1991.

——. *Discipline and Punish: The Birth of the Prison.* Translated by Alan Sheridan. New York: Random House, 1995.

Foulke, William D. *Fighting the Spoilsmen: Reminiscences of the Civil Service Reform.* New York: G. P. Putnam's Sons, 1919.

Frankland, William. *The Speech of Wm. Frankland, Esq. in the House of Commons on Friday, the 29th of March, 1811: On the Second Reading of Several Bills, Brought In by Sir Samuel Romilly, for Making Alterations in the Criminal Law.* London: Ridgway, 1811.

Freedgood, Elaine. "Fictional Settlements: Footnotes, Metalepsis, the Colonial Effect." *New Literary History* 41, no. 2 (2010): 393–411.

Fu, Lo-shu. *A Documentary Chronicle of Sino-Western Relations (1644–1820).* 2 vols. Tucson: University of Arizona Press, 1966.

Fujitani, Takashi. *Race for Empire: Koreans as Japanese and Japanese as Americans during World War II.* Berkeley: University of California Press, 2011.

Fuma, Susumu. "Litigation Masters and the Litigation Systems of Ming and Qing China." *International Journal of Asian Studies* 4, no. 1 (2007): 79–111.

Fung, Edmund S. K. "The Chinese Nationalists and the Unequal Treaties 1924–1931." *Modern Asian Studies* 21, no. 4 (1987): 793–819.

García Ortega, J. *El derecho penal estudiado en sus principios, en sus aplicaciones legislaciones de los diversos pueblos del mundo (Study of Criminal Law in Its Principles and Legislative Applications of the Different Peoples of the World).* Vol. 3. Madrid: Góngora, 1880.

Garland, David. *Punishment and Modern Society.* Chicago: University of Chicago Press, 1990.

Gascoigne, John. *Science in the Service of Empire: Joseph Banks, the British State and the Uses of Science in the Age of Revolution.* Cambridge: Cambridge University Press, 1998.

Gates, Lewis E. "Introduction." In *Selections from the Essays of Francis Jeffrey,* edited by Lewis E. Gates, vi–xlv. Boston: Ginn & Co., 1894.

Gatrell, Vic A. C. *The Hanging Tree: Execution and the English People 1770–1868.* Oxford: Oxford University Press, 1994.

Gelber, Harry G. *Opium, Soldiers and Evangelicals: Britain's 1840–42 War with China, and Its Aftermath.* New York: Palgrave Macmillan, 2004.

——. *The Dragon and the Foreign Devils: China and the World, 1100 B.C. to the Present.* London: Bloomsbury, 2007.

Genette, Gérard. *Paratexts: Thresholds of Interpretation.* Translated by Jane E. Lewin. Cambridge: Cambridge University Press, 1997.

Geroulanos, Stefanos, Zvi Ben-Dor Benite, and Nichole Jerr, eds. *The Scaffold of Sovereignty: A Global Interdisciplinary Approach.* New York: Columbia University Press, forthcoming.

Gibbon, Edward. *The Decline and Fall of the Roman Empire.* 6 vols. London: Strahan and Cadell, 1781–1788.

Gladstone, William E. *The Gladstone Diaries, Volume 3: 1840–1847.* Edited by M. R. D. Foot and H. C. G. Matthew. Oxford: Clarendon Press, 1974.

Glazebrook, Peter R. "Criminal Law Reform: England." In *Encyclopedia of Crime and Justice*, edited by Joshua Dressler, 400–412. New York: Macmillan, 2002.

Goldman, David B. *Globalisation and the Western Legal Tradition*. Cambridge: Cambridge University Press, 2008.

Gongzhongdang Qianlongchao zouzhe (*Secret Palace Memorials of the Qianlong Period*). 75 vols. Taipei: National Palace Museum Press, 1982–1988.

Gooch, George P., ed. *The Later Correspondence of Lord John Russell, 1840–1878*. 2 vols. Vol. 1. London: Longmans, 1925.

The Grand Instructions to the Commissioners Appointed to Frame a New Code of Law for the Russian Empire. Translated by Michael Tatischeff. London: T. Jefferys, 1768.

Grant, Sir James Hope. *Incidents in the China War of 1860*. Compiled by Henry Knollys. London: William Blackwood and Sons, 1875.

Gray, John H. *China: A History of the Laws, Manners, and Customs of the People*. 2 vols. London: Macmillan and Co., 1878.

Gray, Mrs. John Henry. *Fourteen Months in Canton*. London: Macmillan, 1880.

Greenberg, Michael. *British Trade and the Opening of China 1800–42*. Cambridge, Mass.: Harvard University Press, 1951.

Greene, Jack P. "Empire and Identity from the Glorious Revolution to the American Revolution." In *The Oxford History of the British Empire: The Eighteenth Century*, edited by Peter J. Marshall, 2:208–30. Oxford: Oxford University Press.

Gregory, Charles Noble. "Bentham and the Codifiers." *Harvard Law Review* 13, no. 5 (1900): 344–57.

Gros, Jean -Baptiste-Louis, Baron. *Négociations entre la France et la Chine, en 1860*. Paris: Librairie Militaire, 1864.

Grotius, Hugo. *The Free Sea; or, A Disputation Concerning the Right Which the Hollanders Ought to Have to the Indian Merchandise for Trading*. 1609. Edited and with an introduction by David Armitage. Indianapolis: Liberty Fund, 2004.

——. *Commentary on the Law of Prize and Booty*. Ca. 1604. Translated by Gwladys L. Williams. Edited by Martine Julia van Ittersum. Natural Law and Enlightenment Classics. Indianapolis: Liberty Fund, 2005.

——. *The Rights of War and Peace*. 1625. Edited by Richard Tuck. Natural Law and Enlightenment Classics. Indianapolis: Liberty Fund, 2005.

Gulick, Edward V. *Peter Parker and the Opening of China*. Cambridge, Mass.: Harvard University Press, 1973.

Guo Tingyi, ed. *Chouban yiwu shimo buyi* (*Supplement to "A Complete Account of Management of Foreign Affairs"*). Taipei: Zhongyang yanjiuyuan jindaishi yanjiusuo, 1966.

Gutherz, Harald. "Zhongguo xin xinglü lun" (On the Chinese New Criminal Code). In *Xin Xinglü xiuzheng'an huilu* (*A Collection of Memoranda on the Proposed Revisions of the Draft New Criminal Code*), compiled by Lao Naixuan. Beijing, 1910.

Gutzlaff, Charles. *A Sketch of Chinese History, Ancient and Modern: Comprising a Retrospect of the Foreign Intercourse and Trade with China*. 2 vols. New York: John P. Haven, 1834.

Guy, Basil. *The French Image of China before and after Voltaire*. Oxford: Voltaire Foundation, 1963.

Hales, Sir Matthew. *Pleas of the Crown, in Two Parts*. London: Giles Jacob, 1716.

Halhed, Nathaniel Brassey. *A Code of Gentoo Laws, or, Ordinations of the Pundits, from a Persian Translation, Made from the Original, Written in the Shanscrit Language*. London, 1776.

Hall, Catherine. "Introduction: Thinking the Postcolonial, Thinking the Empire." In *Cultures of Empire: Colonizers in Britain and the Empire in the Nineteenth and Twentieth Centuries*, edited by Catherine Hall, 1–36. Manchester: Manchester University Press, 2000.

Hall, Stuart. "Who Needs 'Identity'?" In *Identity: A Reader*, edited by Paul du Gay, Jessica Evans, and Peter Redman, 15–30. London: Sage, 2000.

Halttunen, Karen. "Humanitarianism and the Pornography of Pain in Anglo-American Culture." *American Historical Review* 100, no. 2 (1995): 303–34.

Hansen, Valerie. *Negotiating Daily Life in Traditional China: How Ordinary People Used Contracts 600–1400*. New Haven: Yale University Press, 1995.

Hanson, Elizabeth. "Torture and Truth in Renaissance England." *Representations* 34 (1991): 53–84.

Harbsmeier, Christoph. *Language and Logic*. Cambridge: Cambridge University Press, 1998.

Hardin, Russell. *David Hume: Moral and Political Theorist*. Oxford: Oxford University Press, 2007.

Hart, Herbert L. A. *Essays on Bentham: Jurisprudence and Political Theory*. Oxford: Oxford University Press, 1983.

Hart, Roger. *Imagined Civilizations: China, the West, and Their First Encounter*. Baltimore: Johns Hopkins University Press, 2013.

Hawkins, Angus. *Parliament, Party, and the Art of Politics in Britain, 1855–59*. Stanford: Stanford University Press, 1987.

Hay, Douglas. "Crime and Justice in Eighteenth- and Nineteenth-Century England." *Crime and Justice* 2 (1980): 45–84.

Hay, Douglas, and Francis Snyder, eds. *Policing and Prosecution in Britain, 1750–1850*. Oxford: Oxford University Press, 1989.

Hayot, Eric. *The Hypothetical Mandarin: Sympathy, Modernity, and Chinese Pain*. New York: Oxford University Press, 2009.

He Wenxian. *Wenming de chongtu yu zhenghe—Tongzhi zhongxing shiqi zhongwai guanxi chongjian (Clash and Reintegration of Civilizations: Reconstructing Sino-Foreign Relations during the Tongzhi Restoration)*. Xiamen: Xiamen daxue chubanshe, 2006.

Head, John W. "Codes, Cultures, Chaos, and Champions: Common Features of Legal Codification Experiences in China, Europe, and North America." *Duke Journal of Comparative and International Law* 13, no. 1 (2004): 1–93.

Hegel, Georg Wilhelm Friedrich. *The Philosophy of History*. 1837. Translated by J. Sibree. Rev. ed. New York: Colonial Press, 1900.

Heinrich, Larissa N. *The Afterlife of Images: Translating the Pathological Body between China and the West*. Durham: Duke University Press, 2008.

Hérisson, Maurice. *Journal d'un interprète en Chine*. Paris: Paul Ollendorff, 1886.

Herman, Shael. "The Fate and the Future of Codification in America." *American Journal of Legal History* 40, no. 4 (1996): 407–37.

Hertslet, Edward, and Godfrey E. P. Hertslet, eds. *Hertslet's China Treaties: Treaties, &c., between Great Britain and China; and between China and Foreign Powers; and Orders in Council, Rules, Regulations, Acts of Parliament, Decrees, &c., Affecting British Interests in China, in Force on the 1st January, 1908*. 3rd ed. 2 vols. London: His Majesty's Stationery Office, 1908. (*HCT*)

Hevia, James L. *Cherishing Men from Afar: Qing Guest Ritual and the Macartney Embassy of 1793*. Durham: Duke University Press, 1995.

——. *English Lessons: The Pedagogy of Imperialism in Nineteenth-Century China*. Durham: Duke University Press, 2003.

——. *The Imperial Security State: British Colonial Knowledge and Empire-Building in Asia*. Cambridge: Cambridge University Press, 2012.

Hints for a Reform in the Criminal Law, in a Letter Addressed to Sir Samuel Romilly, by a Late Member of Parliament. London: J. Mawman, 1811.

Hobhouse, John Cam. *Recollections of a Long Life, with Additional Extracts from His Private Diaries*. Edited by his daughter, Lady Dorchester. 6 vols. London: John Murray, 1909.

Hobson, John M. *The Eastern Origins of Western Civilisation*. Cambridge: Cambridge University Press, 2004.

Hoe, Susanna, and Derek Roebuck. *The Taking of Hong Kong: Charles and Clara Elliot in China Waters*. London: Routledge, 1999.

Hoebel, E. Adamson. *The Law of Primitive Man*. Cambridge, Mass.: Harvard University Press, 1954.

Hong Hongxu, comp. *Cheng'an zhiyi (Doubtful Issues in Leading Cases)*. 36 juan. Hangzhou: Sanyutang, 1736.

Hostetler, Laura. *Qing Colonial Enterprise: Ethnography and Cartography in Early Modern China*. Chicago: University of Chicago Press, 2005.

Houghton, Walter E., ed. *The Wellesley Index to Victorian Periodicals, 1824–1900*. Toronto: University of Toronto Press, 1966–1989.

Hsu, Dao-lin. "Crime and Cosmic Order." *Harvard Journal of Asiatic Studies* 30 (1970): 111–25.

Hsu, Immanuel C. Y. *China's Entrance into the Family of Nations*. Cambridge, Mass.: Harvard University Press, 1960.

Huang Hongzhao. *Aomen tongzhi yu jindai Aomen* (*The Subprefect Office of Macao and Modern Macao*). Guangzhou: Guangdong renmin chubanshe, 2006.

Huang, Liu-hung. *A Complete Book Concerning Happiness and Benevolence: A Manual for Local Magistrates in Seventeenth-Century China*. Translated by Djang Chu. Tucson: University of Arizona Press, 1994.

Huang, Philip C.C. *Civil Justice in China: Representation and Practice in the Qing*. Stanford: Stanford University Press, 1996.

Huc, Évariste Régis. *L'empire chinois: Faisant suite à l'ouvrage intitulé; Souvenirs d'un voyage dans la Tartarie et le Thibet*. Vol. 2. Paris: Librairie de Gaume Frères, 1854.

——. *A Journey through the Chinese Empire*. 2 vols. New York: Harper, 1855.

Hume, David. *A Treatise of Human Nature*. 3 vols. London: John Noon, 1739.

——. *An Enquiry Concerning the Principles of Morals*. London: A. Millar, 1751.

Hunter, William C. *The "Fan Kwae" at Canton before Treaty Days, 1825–1844, by an Old Resident*. London: Kegan Paul, Trench, 1882.

Huntington, Samuel P. *The Clash of Civilizations and the Remaking of World Order*. New York: Simon & Schuster, 1997.

Hussain, Nasser. *The Jurisprudence of Emergency: Colonialism and the Rule of Law*. Ann Arbor: University of Michigan Press, 2003.

Ignatieff, Michael. *A Just Measure of Pain: The Penitentiary in the Industrial Revolution, 1750–1850*. London: Macmillan, 1978.

Innes, Joanna, and John Styles. "The Crime Wave: Recent Writings on Crime and Criminal Justice in Eighteenth-Century England." *Journal of British Studies* 25, no. 4 (1986): 380–435.

Ives, George. *A History of Penal Methods: Criminals, Witches, Lunatics*. London: S. Paul, 1914.

Jay, John. *The Correspondence and Public Papers of John Jay, 1782–1793*. Edited by Henry P. Johnston. Vol. 3. New York: G. P. Putnam's Sons, 1891.

Jensen, Lione M. *Manufacturing Confucianism: Chinese Traditions and Universal Civilization*. Durham: Duke University Press, 1997.

Jiaqing Daoguang liangchao shangyudang (*Edicts of the Jiaqing and Daoguang Reigns*). Compiled by Zhongguo Diyi Lishi Dang'anguan. 55 vols. Nanning: Guangxi shifan chubanshe, 2000.

Jin Guoping. *Zhongpu guanxi shidi kaozheng* (*An Evidentiary Study of the Historical Geography in Sino-Portuguese Relations*). Macao: Aomen jijinhui, 2000.

——, ed. *Xifang Aomen shiliao xuancui* (*Selected Western Historical Sources on Macao*). Guangzhou: Guangdong renmin chubanshe, 2005 (*XFAMS*).

Jin Guoping and Wu Zhiliang, eds. *Correspondência oficial trocada entre as autoridades de Cantão e os procuradores do Senado: Fundo das chapas sínicas em português (1749–1847) (Yue'ao gongdu lucun)*. 8 vols. Macao: Fundação Macau, 2000 (*COT*).

Johnson, Wallace. *The Tang Code, Volume I: General Principles*. Princeton: Princeton University Press, 1979.

Jones, Sir William. *Institutes of Hindu Law: Or, the Ordinances of Menu, According to the Gloss of Cullúca, Comprising the Indian System of Duties, Religious and Civil.* London: J. Sewell, Cornhill, 1796.

Jones, William C., trans. *The Great Qing Code.* New York: Oxford University Press, 1994.

Kalmo, Hent, and Quentin Skinner, eds. *Sovereignty in Fragments: The Past, Present and Future of a Contested Concept.* Cambridge: Cambridge University Press, 2010.

Kayaoğlu, Turan. *Legal Imperialism: Sovereignty and Extraterritoriality in Japan, the Ottoman Empire, and China.* Cambridge: Cambridge University Press, 2010.

Keeton, George W. *The Development of Extraterritoriality in China.* 2 vols. London: Longmans, 1928.

Kidd, Samuel. *Catalogue of the Chinese Library of the Royal Asiatic Society.* London: John W. Parker, 1838.

King, Charles W. *Opium Crisis: A Letter Addressed to Charles Elliot.* London: Suter, 1839.

Kitson, Peter J. *Forging Romantic China: Sino-British Cultural Exchange 1760–1840.* Cambridge: Cambridge University Press, 2013.

Kolsky, Elizabeth. "Codification and the Rule of Colonial Difference: Criminal Procedure in British India." *Law and History Review* 23, no. 3 (2005): 631–86.

——. *Colonial Justice in British India: White Violence and the Rule of Law.* Cambridge: Cambridge University Press, 2010.

Koo, V. K. Wellington. *The Status of Aliens in China.* New York: Columbia University Press, 1912.

Koskenniemi, Martti. *The Gentle Civilizer of Nations: The Rise and Fall of International Law 1870–1960.* Cambridge: Cambridge University Press, 2002.

Kostal, Rande W. *A Jurisprudence of Power: Victorian Empire and the Rule of Law.* Oxford: Oxford University Press, 2008.

Kuhn, Philip A. *Soulstealers: The Chinese Sorcery Scare of 1768.* Cambridge, Mass.: Harvard University Press, 1990.

Lach, Donald F. *Asia in the Making of Europe, Volume II: A Century of Wonder.* Chicago: University of Chicago Press, 1994.

Lalu, Premesh. "The Grammar of Domination and the Subjection of Agency: Colonial Texts and Modes of Evidence." *History and Theory* 39, no. 4 (2000): 45–68.

——. *The Deaths of Hintsa: Postapartheid South Africa and the Shape of Recurring Pasts.* Cape Town: HSRC Press, 2009.

Lang, Maurice E. *Codification in the British Empire and America.* Clark, N.J.: Lawbook Exchange, 2005.

Langbein, John H. *Torture and the Law of Proof.* Chicago: University of Chicago Press, 1976.

Latourette, Kenneth S. *The History of Early Relations between the United States and China, 1784–1844.* New Haven: Yale University Press, 1917.

Lean, Eugenia. *Public Passions: The Trial of Shi Jianqiao and the Rise of Popular Sympathy in Republican China*. Berkeley: University of California Press, 2007.

Le Comte, Louis. *Memoirs and Remarks . . . Made in above Ten Years Travels through the Empire of China*. 1696. London: Olive Payne, 1737.

Lee, Haiyan. *Revolution of the Heart: The Genealogy of Love in China, 1900–1950*. Stanford: Stanford University Press, 2007.

Lee, Sidney, ed. *Dictionary of National Biography*. London: Macmillan, 1898.

Leontiev, Aleksiei, trans. *Kitaiskoe ulozhenie: Perevel sokrashchenno s Manzhurskago na Rossiiskoi iazyk Kollegii Inostrannykh diel Maiorskago Ranga* (*The Chinese Law Code, Translated in an Abbreviated Version by a Major of the College of Foreign Affairs from Manchu to Russian*). 2 vols. Saint Petersburg: Imperatorskoĭ Akademīi Nauk, 1778–1779.

——. *Taitsin gurun' i Ukheri koli to est' vse zakony i ustanovleniia kitaiskogo (a nyne man' chzhurskogo) pravitel' stva* (*Taitsin gurun' i Ukheri koli, or All the Laws and Regulations of the Chinese [Now Manchu] Government* [translated from Manchu to Russian]). 3 vols. Saint Petersburg: Imperatorskoĭ Akademīi Nauk, 1781–1783.

Le Pichon, Alain, ed. *China Trade and Empire: Jardine, Matheson & Co. and the Origins of British Rule in Hong Kong, 1827–1843*. Oxford: Oxford University Press, 2006.

Levin, Lawrence M. *The Political Doctrine of Montesquieu's Esprit des Lois: Its Classical Background*. New York: Columbia University, 1936.

Leys, Ruth. "The Turn to Affect: A Critique." *Critical Inquiry* 37, no. 3 (2011): 434–72.

Li Guilian. *Jindai Zhongguo fazhi yu faxue* (*Modern Chinese Law and Jurisprudence*). Beijing: Beijing daxue chubanshe, 2002.

Li, Huaiyin. *Reinventing Modern China: Imagination and Authenticity in Chinese Historical Writing*. Honolulu: University of Hawai`i Press, 2012.

Li Li. *Chutu wenwu yu xianqin fazhi* (*Excavated Artifacts and the Legal System of the Qin Dynasty*). Beijing: Daxiang chubanshe, 1997.

Li Wenhai. *Cong minzu chenlun dao minzu zhenxing* (*From the National Decline to the National Revival*). Beijing: Renmin daxue chubanshe, 2012.

Li Zhiyun. *Cheng'an xubian erke* (*A Second Collection of Leading Cases*). 1763.

Liang, Linxia. *Delivering Justice in Qing China: Civil Trials in the Magistrate's Court*. Oxford: Oxford University Press, 2008.

Liang Qichao. "Lun Zhongguo chengwenfa bianzhi zhi yan'ge deshi" (On the Merits and Demerits of China's Legal Codification in History). In *Liang Qichao faxue wenji* (*Liang Qichao's Essays on Jurisprudence*), edited by Fan Zhongxin, 120–82. 1904. Reprint, Beijing: Zhongguo zhengfa daxue chubanshe, 1997.

——. "Zhongguo Fali xue fada shilun" (History of the Development of Chinese Jurisprudence). In *Liang Qichao faxue wenji* (*Liang Qichao's Essays on Jurisprudence*), edited by Zhongxin Fan, 68–119. 1904. Reprint, Beijing: Zhongguo zhengfa daxue chubanshe, 1997.

Liang Tingnan. *Yifen wenji* (*Recollections of the Foreign Threat*). 1850s. Reprint, Beijing: Zhonghua shuju, 1958.

———. *Yue haiguan zhi* (*Gazetteer of the Guangdong Customs Station*). Taipei: Chengwen chubanshe, 1966.

Liberman, David. *The Province of Legislation Determined: Legal Theory in Eighteenth-Century Britain*. Cambridge: Cambridge University Press, 1989.

Lie Dao, ed. *Yapian zhanzheng shi lunwen zhuanji* (*Essays on the History of the Opium War*). Beijing: Sanlian shudian, 1958.

Lieber, Francis. *Manual of Political Ethics: Designed Chiefly for the Use of Colleges and Students at Law*. 2 vols. Boston: Charles C. Little and James Brown, 1838–1839.

Lin Zexu. *Lin Zexu quanji* (*Complete Works of Lin Zexu*). 10 vols. Fuzhou: Haixia wenyi chubanshe, 2002.

Lindsay, Hugh Hamilton. *Letter to the Right Honourable Viscount Palmerston on British Relations with China*. London: Saunders and Otley, 1836.

———. *Is the War with China a Just One?* 2nd ed. London: James Ridgway, 1840.

———. *Remarks on Occurrences in China since the Opium Seizure in March 1839 to the Latest Date*. London: Sherwood, Gilbert and Piper, 1840.

———. *The Rupture with China, and Its Causes . . . In a Letter to Lord Viscount Palmerston by a Resident in China* [Sept.–Oct. 1839]. London: Sherwood, Gilbert, 1840.

Linebaugh, Peter. *The London Hanged: Crime and Civil Society in the Eighteenth Century*. 2nd ed. London: Verso, 2003.

Liu Fang and Zhang Wenqin, eds. *Putaoya dongpota dang'anguan chang Qingdai Aomen zhongwen dang'an huibian* (*Collections of Chinese Documents on Qing-Dynasty Macao at the National Archives of Portugal*). Macao: Aomen jijinhui, 1999 (*PTYDP*).

Liu, Lydia H. *Translingual Practice: Literature, National Culture, and Translated Modernity—China, 1900–1937*. Stanford: Stanford University Press, 1995.

———. *The Clash of Empires: The Invention of China in Modern World Making*. Cambridge, Mass.: Harvard University Press, 2004.

Liu, Shihshun. *Extraterritoriality: Its Rise and Decline*. New York: Columbia University Press, 1925.

Liu, Yong. *The Dutch East India Company's Tea Trade with China, 1757–1781*. Leiden: Brill, 2007.

Ljungstedt, Andrew. *An Historical Sketch of the Portuguese Settlements in China*. London: J. Munroe, 1836.

Lobban, Michael. *The Common Law and English Jurisprudence, 1760–1850*. Oxford: Oxford University Press, 1991.

Lobingier, Charles Sumner. "The Need of Law Reform in China." *American Review of Reviews* 37 (1908): 218–19.

Loch, Henry Brougham. *Personal Narrative of Occurrences during Lord Elgin's Second Embassy to China in 1860*. London: John Murray, 1869.

Locke, John. *Two Treatises of Government*. 1680–1690. Clark, N.J.: Lawbook Exchange, 2006.

Lockey, Brian C. *Law and Empire in English Renaissance Literature.* Cambridge: Cambridge University Press, 2009.

Logan, Robert K. *The Alphabet Effect: The Impact of the Phonetic Alphabet on the Development of Western Civilization.* New York: Morrow, 1986.

Lovell, Julie. *The Opium War: Drugs, Dreams and the Making of China.* London: Picador, 2011.

Lucy, Armand. *Lettres intimes sur la campagne de Chine.* Marseille: Barile, 1861.

Lukin, Alexander. *The Bear Watches the Dragon: Russia's Perceptions of China and the Evolution of Russian-Chinese Relations since the Eighteenth Century.* New York: M.E. Sharpe, 2003.

Lutz, Donald. "The Relative Influence of European Writers on Late Eighteenth-Century American Political Thought." *American Political Science Review* 78, no. 1 (1984): 189–97.

Macauley, Melissa. *Social Power and Legal Culture: Litigation Masters in Late Imperial China.* Stanford: Stanford University Press, 1998.

Macaulay, Thomas Babington. "Introductory Report upon the Indian Penal Code." In *The Complete Writings of Thomas Babington Macaulay: Miscellanies,* 551–734. New York: Houghton, Mifflin & Co., 1901.

MacCormack, Geoffrey. "Issues of Causation in Homicide Decisions of the Qing Board of Punishments from the Eighteenth and Nineteenth Centuries." *Bulletin of the School of African and Oriental Studies* 73, no. 2 (2010): 285–310.

Macfarlane, Charles. *A History of British India from the Earliest English Intercourse to the Present Time.* London: Routledge, 1853.

Mackintosh, Sir James. *The Miscellaneous Works of the Right Honourable Sir James Mackintosh.* Edited by Robert James Mackintosh. 3 vols. London: Longman, 1846.

Mackintosh, Robert James, ed. *Memoirs of the Life of the Right Honourable Sir James Mackintosh.* 2nd ed. London: E. Moxon, 1836.

MacMillan, Ken. *Sovereignty and Possession in the English New World: The Legal Foundations of Empire, 1576–1640.* Cambridge: Cambridge University Press, 2009.

Maestro, Marcello T. *Voltaire and Beccaria as Reformers of Criminal Law.* 1942. Reprint, New York: Octagon, 1972.

———. *Cesare Beccaria and the Origins of Penal Reform.* Philadelphia: Temple University Press, 1973.

———. "Benjamin Franklin and the Penal Laws." *Journal of the History of Ideas* 36, no. 3 (1975): 551–62.

Maine, Sir Henry Sumner. *Ancient Law: Its Connection with the Early History of Society, and Its Relation to Modern Ideas.* 2nd ed. New York: Charles Scribner, 1864.

Malcolm, Elizabeth L. "The Chinese Repository and Western Literature on China 1800 to 1850." *Modern Asian Studies* 7, no. 2 (1973): 165–78.

Malthus, Thomas Robert. *An Essay on the Principle of Population.* London: J. Johnson, 1803.

Mao Haijian. *Tianchao de bengkui: Yapian zhanzheng zai yanjiu* (*Collapse of the Heavenly Dynasty: Reexamining the Opium War*). 2nd ed. Beijing: Sanlian shudian, 2005.

Margat, Claire. "Supplice Chinois in French Literature: From Octave Mirbeau's *Le Jardin des Supplices* to Georges Bataille's *Les Larmes d'Éros*." 2005. http://turandot. chineselegalculture.org/Essay.php?ID=38 (accessed December 2006).

Marjoribanks, Charles. *Letter to the Right Hon. Charles Grant, President of the Board of Controul, on the Present State of British Intercourse with China*. London: J. Hatchard & Son, 1833.

Marsh, Robert M. "Weber's Misunderstanding of Traditional Chinese Law." *American Journal of Sociology* 106, no. 2 (2000): 281–302.

Marshall, Peter J. *The Making and Unmaking of Empires: Britain, India, and America, c. 1750–1783*. Oxford: Oxford University Press, 2005.

——. "Introduction." In Marshall, *Oxford History of the British Empire*, 2:1–27.

——, ed. *The Oxford History of the British Empire: The Eighteenth Century*. 4 vols. Oxford: Oxford University Press, 2009.

M'Arthur, John. *Principles and Practice of Naval and Military Courts Martial*. 4th ed. 2 vols. London: J. Butterworth, 1813.

Martin, Robert M. *Statistics of Colonies of the British Empire . . . From the Official Records of the Colonial Office*. London: Wm. H. Allen, 1839.

Mason, George H., ed. *The Costume of China*. London: William Miller, 1800.

——, ed. *The Punishments of China: Illustrated by Twenty-two Engravings, with Explanations in English and French*. London: W. Miller by W. Bulmer, 1801.

Masterson, M. P. "Montesquieu's Grand Design: The Political Sociology of 'Esprit des Lois.'" *British Journal of Political Science* 2, no. 3 (1972): 283–318.

Masur, Louis P. *Rites of Execution: Capital Punishment and the Transformation of American Culture, 1776–1865*. Oxford: Oxford University Press, 1989.

Matheson, James. *The Present Position and Prospects of the British Trade with China*. London: Smith, Elder, 1836.

Mayers, William F., et al. *The Treaty Ports of China and Japan*. London: Trubner and Co., 1867.

Mazlish, Bruce. *James and John Stuart Mill*. New Brunswick, N.J.: Transaction, 1988.

McClintock, Anne. *Imperial Leather: Race, Gender and Sexuality in the Colonial Contest*. New York: Routledge, 1995.

McGowen, Randall. "A Powerful Sympathy: Terror, the Prison, and Humanitarian Reform in Early Nineteenth-Century Britain." *Journal of British Studies* 25, no. 3 (1986): 312–34.

——. "Revisiting the Hanging Tree." *British Journal of Criminology* 40, no. 1 (2000): 1–13.

McKenzie, Andrea. "'This Death Some Strong and Stout Hearted Man Doth Choose': The Practice of *Peine forte et dure* in Seventeenth- and Eighteenth-Century England." *Law and History Review* 23, no. 2 (2005): 1–43.

McKnight, Brian E. *The Enlightened Judgments: "Ch'ing-Ming Chi."* Albany: SUNY Press, 1999.

McLynn, Frank J. *Crime and Punishment in Eighteenth-Century England.* New York: Routledge, 1989.

Meadows, Thomas Taylor. *Desultory Notes on the Government and People of China, and on the Chinese Language.* London: Wm. H. Allen & Co., 1847.

——. *The Chinese and Their Rebellions: With an Essay on Civilization.* London: Smith, Elder & Co., 1856.

Medhurst, Walter Henry. *China: Its State and Prospects.* Boston: Crocker & Brewster, 1838.

——. *The Foreigner in Far Cathay.* New York: Scribner, 1872.

Mehta, Uday S. *Liberalism and Empire: A Study in Nineteenth-Century British Liberal Thought.* Chicago: University of Chicago Press, 1999.

——. "Liberal Strategies of Exclusion." In Cooper and Stoler, *Tensions of Empire,* 59–86.

Melancon, Glenn. "Honour in Opium? The British Declaration of War on China, 1839–1840." *International History Review* 21, no. 4 (2000): 855–74.

——. *Britain's China Policy and the Opium Crisis: Balancing Drugs, Violence and National Honour, 1833–1840.* Burlington, Vt.: Ashgate, 2003.

"Memorials Addressed to Her Majesty's Government by British Merchants Interested in the Trade with China." In *Parliamentary Papers,* House of Commons and Lords, 1840 (242). London: T. R. Harrison, 1840.

Metcalf, Thomas R. *Ideologies of the Raj.* New York: Cambridge University Press, 1997.

Miklowitz, David J. *Bipolar Disorder: A Family-Oriented Treatment Approach.* New York: Guilford Press, 2008.

Mill, James. *The History of British India.* 4th ed. 6 vols. London: James Madden, 1840.

Mill, John Stuart. *On Liberty.* London: John W. Parker and Son, 1859.

——. *Considerations of Representative Government.* London: Parker, Son, and Bourn, 1861.

Milne, Rev. William C. *Life in China.* New York: Routledge, 1857.

Ming Qing huanggong Huangpu midang tujian (Illustrated Secret Archives on Huangpu in the Ming and Qing Imperial Palaces). Compiled by Zhongguo Diyi Lishi Dang'anguan and Guangzhou Huangpuqu Renmin Zhengfu. Guangzhou: Jinan daxue chubanshe, 2006 (*MQHQH*).

Ming Qing shiqi Aomen wenti dang'an wenxian huibian (Archival Material on Macao in the Ming-Qing Period). Compiled by Zhongguo Diyi Lishi Dang'anguan et al. 6 vols. Beijing: Renmin chubanshe, 1999(*MQSQA*).

Mogridge, George [Old Humphrey]. *The Celestial Empire, or Points and Pickings of Information about China and the Chinese.* London: Grant and Griffith, 1844.

Montagu, Basil, ed. *The Opinions of Different Authors upon the Punishment of Death.* 3 vols. London: Longman, 1809–1813.

——. *The Debates in the House of Commons, During the Year 1811: Upon Certain Bills for Abolishing the Punishment of Death.* London: Longman, 1812.

Montauban, Cousin de. *Montuobang zhengzhan Zhongguo huiyilu (Souvenirs du Général Cousin de Montauban).* Translated by Wang Dazhi Wang and Chen Juan. Shanghai: Zhongxi shuju, 2011.

Montesquieu, M. de Secondat, Baron de. *The Spirit of the Laws.* Translated by Thomas Nugent. 4th ed. 4 vols. London: J. Nourse and P. Vallant, 1766.

——. *The Spirit of the Laws.* 2 vols. Glasgow: J. Duncan & Son, 1793.

Moon, Penderel. *Warren Hastings and British India.* New York: Macmillan, 1949.

Moore, Sally F. *Law as Process: An Anthropological Approach.* London: Routledge, 1977.

Morrison, Eliza A. *Memoirs of the Life and Labours of Robert Morrison.* 2 vols. London: Longman, 1839.

Morrison, George E. *An Australian in China.* 2nd ed. London: Horace Cox, 1895.

Morrison, Robert. *A Memoir of the Principle Occurrences during an Embassy from the British Government to the Court of China in the Year 1816.* London: Hatchard & Son, 1820.

Morse, Hosea B. *The International Relations of the Chinese Empire.* 3 vols. New York: Longmans, 1910.

——, ed. *The Chronicles of the East India Company Trading to China, 1635–1834.* 5 vols. Oxford: Clarendon Press, 1926–1929 (*CBEIC*).

Mosca, Matthew W. *From Frontier Policy to Foreign Policy: The Question of India and the Transformation of Geopolitics in Qing China.* Stanford: Stanford University Press, 2013.

"Motion Respecting the System of Transportation, and the State of New South Wales." In *The Parliamentary Debates from the Year 1803 to the Present Time*, edited by T. C. Hansard, 463–509. London: Longman, 1819.

Muldoon, James. *Empire and Order: The Concept of Empire, 800–1800.* New York: Palgrave MacMillan, 1999.

Mungello, David E. *Curious Land: Jesuit Accommodations and the Origin of Sinology.* Honolulu: University of Hawai`i Press, 1989.

——, ed. *The Chinese Rites Controversy.* Nettetal, Ger.: Steyler Verlag, 1994.

——. *The Great Encounter of China and the West, 1500–1800.* Lanham, Md.: Rowman & Littlefield, 2005.

Munn, Christopher. *Anglo-China: Chinese People and British Rule in Hong Kong, 1841–1880.* London: Routledge, 2001.

Navarrete, Domingo. *The Travels and Controversies of Friar Domingo Navarrete, 1618–1686.* Cambridge: Cambridge University Press, 1962.

Needham, Joseph. *Science and Civilisation.* Vol. 2. Cambridge: Cambridge University Press, 1965.

Neighbors, Jennifer M. "Criminal Intent and Homicide Law in Qing and Republican China." Ph.D. diss., University of California, Los Angeles, 2004.

Nevius, Helen S. *Our Life in China.* New York: Robert Carter and Brothers, 1869.

Nevius, John L. *China and the Chinese.* New York: Harper & Brothers, 1869.

The New Annual Register for the Year 1785. London, 1786.

Newsinger, John. "Elgin in China." *New Left Review* 15 (2002): 119–40.

Niranjana, Tejaswini. *Siting Translation: History, Post-Structuralism, and the Colonial Context.* Berkeley: University of California Press, 1992.

Noble, Charles F. *A Voyage to the East Indies in 1747 and 1748.* London, 1765.

Norman, Henry. *The People and Politics of the Far East.* London: Scribner, 1895.

Ollé, Manel. *La invención de China: Percepciones y estrategias Filipinas respecto a China durante el siglo xvi.* Wiesbaden: Harrassowitz, 2000.

Osterhammel, Jürgen. *Die Entzauberung Asiens: Europa und die asiatischen Reiche im 18. Jahrhundert.* Munich: C.H. Beck, 1998.

Pagden, Anthony. *Lords of All the World: Ideologies of Empire in Spain, Britain and France, c. 1500–c. 1800.* New Haven: Yale University Press, 1995.

Pak, Hyobom. *China and the West: Myths and Realities in History.* Leiden: Brill, 1974.

Palencia-Roth, Michael. "The Presidential Addresses of Sir William Jones: The Asiatick Society of Bengal and the ISCSC." *Biogenes* 55, no. 2 (2008): 103–15.

Pan Shicheng (z. Deshe). *Da Qing lüli anyu (Commentaries on the Qing Code).* 104 *juan.* Guangzhou: Haishan xianguan, 1847.

"Papers Relating to the Murder of Six Englishmen in the Neighbourhood of Canton in the Month of December 1847." In *Parliamentary Papers*, House of Commons, 1847–48 (930), XLVIII.617. London: T. R. Harrison, 1848.

"Papers Relating to Riot at Canton in July 1846." In *Parliamentary Papers*, House of Commons, 1847 (808), XL.331. London: T. R. Harrison, 1847.

Papers Relative to the Establishment of a Court of Judicature in China, Presented to the House of Commons, 1838. London: J. Harrison & Son, 1838.

Papers Respecting the Negotiation with His Majesty's Ministers on the Subject of the East-India Company's Charter and the Government of His Majesty's Indian Territories for Further Term after the 22d April 1834. London, 1833.

Pargiter, Frederick E., ed. *Centennial Volume of the Royal Asiatic Society of Great Britain and Ireland, 1823–1923.* London: Royal Asiatic Society, 1923.

Park, Nancy. Review of *The Great Qing Code*, by William C. Jones. *American Journal of Legal History* 39, no. 4 (1995): 514–15.

——. "Imperial Chinese Justice and the Law of Torture." *Late Imperial China* 29, no. 2 (2008): 37–67.

Parker, Edward H. *China: Past and Present.* London: Chapman & Hall, 1903.

——. "The Principles of Chinese Law and Equity." *Law Quarterly Review* 22, no. 2 (1906): 190–212.

——. *China: Her History, Diplomacy and Commerce from the Earliest Times to the Present Day.* 2nd ed. New York: E. P. Dutton, 1917.

The Penal Code of France, Translated into English. London: H. Butterworth, 1819.

Perdue, Peter C. *China Marches West: The Qing Conquest of Central Eurasia.* Cambridge, Mass.: Harvard University Press, 2010.

Peterson, Willard J. "Learning from Heaven: The Introduction of Christianity and Other Western Ideas into Late Ming China." In *China and Maritime Europe, 1500–1800,* edited by John E. Wills Jr., 78–134. Cambridge: Cambridge University Press, 2011.

Petitjean, Patrick, Catherine Jami, and Anne Marie Moulin, eds. *Science and Empire: Historical Studies about Scientific Development and European Expansion.* Dordrecht: Kluwer Academic, 1992.

Peyrefitte, Alain. *The Collision of Two Civilisations: The British Expedition to China in 1792–4.* Translated by Jon Rothschild. London: Harvill, 1993.

Philastre, P. L. F. *Le code annamite, nouvelle traduction complète.* 1876. Reprint, Taipei: Ch'eng-wen Pub. Co., 1967.

Pires, Tomé. *The Suma Oriental of Tomé Pires: An Account of the East, from the Red Sea to Japan . . . in 1512–1515.* 1944. Edited by Armando Cortesão. 2 vols. Burlington, Vt.: Ashgate, 2010.

Pitts, Jennifer. *A Turn to Empire: The Rise of Imperial Liberalism in Britain and France.* Princeton: Princeton University Press, 2005.

Plamper, Jan. "The History of Emotions: An Interview with William Reddy, Barbara Rosenwein, and Peter Stearns." *History and Theory* 49 (2010): 237–65.

Polachek, James M. *The Inner Opium War.* Cambridge, Mass.: Harvard University Press, 1992.

Political Relations Between the United States and China. U.S. Department of State, no. 71. Submitted to the 26th Cong., 2nd sess., January 25, 1841. Washington, D.C.: GPO, 1841. Printed edition of DFUSCC, 1790–1834 (*PRUSC*).

Pomerantz-Zhang, Linda. *Wu Tingfang (1842–1922): Reform and Modernization in Modern Chinese History.* Hong Kong: Hong Kong University Press, 1992.

Pomeranz, Kenneth. *The Great Divergence: China, Europe, and the Making of the Modern World Economy.* Princeton: Princeton University Press, 2001.

Porter, David. *Ideographia: The Chinese Cipher in Early Modern Europe.* Stanford: Stanford University Press, 2001.

Posner, Richard. "Blackstone and Bentham." *Journal of Law and Economics* 19 no. 3 (1976): 569–606.

Pratt, Mary Louise. *Imperial Eyes: Travel Writing and Transculturation.* New York: Routledge, 1992.

Pritchard, Earl H. "The Origin of Extraterritoriality in China." *Northwest Science* 4, no. 4 (1930): 108–14.

——. "The Instructions of the East India Company to Lord Macartney on His Embassy to China and His Reports to the Company, 1792–4. Part I." *Journal of the Royal Asiatic Society of Great Britain and Ireland* 2 (1938): 201–38.

——. *The Crucial Years of Early Anglo-Chinese Relations, 1750–1800*. 1936. Reprinted in *Britain and the China Trade, 1635–1842*, edited by Patrick Tuck. New York: Routledge, 2000.

Pritchard, R. E. *Peter Mundy, Merchant Adventurer*. Oxford: Bodleian Library, University of Oxford, 2011.

Qian Daqun. *Tanglü yanjiu* (*Study of Tang Law*). Beijing: Falü chubanshe, 1999.

Qianlongchao junjichu suishou dengjidang (*Register of the Grand Council in the Qianlong Reign*). Compiled by Zhongguo Diyi Lishi Dang'anguan. 46 vols. Guilin: Guangxi shifan daxue chubanshe, 2000.

Qianlongchao shangyudang (*Imperial Edicts of the Qianlong Emperor*). Compiled by Zhongguo Diyi Lishi Dang'anguan. 18 vols. Beijing: Dang'an chubanshe, 1991 (*QLCSYD*).

Qing Nian. *Shuotie zhaiyao chaocun* (*Abstracts for Record of Legal Memoranda*). 14 ce. Kaifeng: Kaifeng fushu, 1831–1848.

Qing shilu (*Veritable Records of the Qing Dynasty*). 60 vols. Beijing: Zhonghua shuju, 1986.

Qinggong Guangzhou shisanhang dang'an jingxuan (*Selected Imperial Records of the Thirteen Hongs of Guangzhou*). Compiled by Zhongguo Diyi Lishi Dang'anguan and Guangzhou Liwanqu Renmin Zhengfu. Guangzhou: Guangdong jingji chubanshe, 2002.

Qinggong Yue Gang Ao shangmao dang'an quanji (*Complete Records from the Qing Imperial Archives on the Foreign Trade at Canton, Hong Kong, and Macao*). Compiled by Zhongguo Diyi Lishi Dang'anguan. 8 vols. Beijing: Zhongguo shudian, 2002 (*QGYGA*).

Quincy, Josiah. *The Journals of Major Samuel Shaw*. Boston: Wm. Crosby and H. P. Nichols, 1847.

Rabinow, Paul, ed. *The Foucault Reader*. New York: Pantheon, 1984.

Radzinowicz, Leon. *A History of English Criminal Law and Its Administration from 1750: Volume 1, The Movement for Reform, 1750–1833*. London: Stevens & Sons, 1948.

Reddy, William M. *The Navigation of Feeling: A Framework for the History of Emotions*. Cambridge: Cambridge University Press, 2001.

Review of the Management of Our Affairs in China, Since the Opening of the Trade in 1834. London: Smith, Elder & Co., 1840.

Richard, John F. "Opium and the British Indian Empire: The Royal Commission of 1895." *Modern Asian Studies* 36, no. 2 (2002): 375–402.

——. "The Opium Industry in British India." *Indian Economic and Social History Review* 39, nos. 2, 3 (2002): 149–80.

Richards, Thomas. *Imperial Archives: Knowledge and the Fantasy of Empire*. New York: Verso, 1998.

Rienstra, M. Howard, ed. *Jesuit Letters from China, 1583–84*. Minneapolis: University of Minnesota Press, 1986.

Rocher, Ludo, and Rosane Rocher. *The Making of Western Indology: Henry Thomas Cole-brooke and the East India Company*. London: Routledge, 2008.

Rocher, Rosane. *Orientalism, Poetry, and the Millennium: The Checkered Life of Nathaniel Brassey Halhed, 1751–1830*. Delhi: Varanasi, 1983.

Rogaski, Ruth. *Hygienic Modernity: Meanings of Health and Disease in Treaty-Port China*. Berkeley: University of California Press, 2004.

Romagnosi, Gian Domenico. *Collezione degli articoli di economia politica e statistica civile*. 2nd ed. Prato: Dalla Tipografia Guasti, 1836.

Romilly, Sir Samuel. *Observations on the Criminal Law of England as It Relates to Capital Punishments, and on the Mode in Which It Is Admitted*. London: Cadell and Davies, 1810.

——. *Memoirs of the Life of Sir Samuel Romilly*. 2nd ed. 3 vols. London: John Murray, 1840.

Rosenwein, Barbara H. "Worrying about Emotions in History." *American Historical Review* 107 (2001): 821–45.

——. *Emotional Communities in the Early Middle Ages*. Ithaca: Cornell University Press, 2006.

——. "Problems and Methods in the History of Emotions." *Passions in Context: International Journal for the History and Theory of Emotions* 1 (2010): 1–32.

Rothman, Natalie E. *Brokering Empire: Transimperial Subjects between Venice and Istanbul*. Ithaca: Cornell University Press, 2012.

Rowe, William T. *Hankow: Commerce and Society in a Chinese City, 1796–1889*. Stanford: Stanford University Press, 1984.

Ruskola, Teemu. "Legal Orientalism." *Michigan Law Review* 101, no. 1 (2002): 179–234.

——. "Canton Is Not Boston: The Invention of American Imperial Sovereignty." *American Quarterly* 57, no. 3 (2005): 859–84.

——. *Legal Orientalism: China, the United States, and Modern Law*. Cambridge, Mass.: Harvard University Press, 2013.

Said, Edward W. *Culture and Imperialism*. New York: Knopf, 1993.

——. *Orientalism*. New York: Random House, 1994.

Sanders, Lloyd, C., ed. *Lord Melbourne's Papers*. London: Longmans, 1890.

Sasaki Masaya, ed. *Yapian zhanzheng qian zhongying jiaoshe wenshu (Sino-British Correspondence in Chinese before the Opium War)*. Taipei: Wenhai chubanshe, 1976.

Schimmelpenninck van der Oye, David. *Russian Orientalism: Asia in the Russian Mind from Peter the Great to the Emigration*. New Haven: Yale University Press, 2010.

Schluchter, Wolfgang. *Rationalism, Religion, and Domination: A Weberian Perspective*. Berkeley: University of California Press, 1989.

Schwartz, Benjamin. *In Search of Wealth and Power: Yen Fu and the West*. Cambridge, Mass.: Harvard University Press, 1964.

Scogin, Hugh T., Jr. "Civil 'Law' in Traditional China: History and Theory." In *Civil Law in Qing and Republican China*, edited by Kathryn Bernhardt et al., 13–42. Stanford: Stanford University Press, 1994.

Scully, Eileen P. *Bargaining with the State from Afar: American Citizenship in Treaty Port China, 1844–1942.* New York: Columbia University Press, 2001.

Seaman, Ezra C. *Essays on the Progress of Nations in Civilization, Productive Industry, Wealth and Population.* New York: Charles Scribner, 1868.

Seidman, Steven. *Contested Knowledge: Social Theory Today.* London: Wiley-Blackwell, 2011.

"Select Committee on Commercial Relations with China." In *Parliamentary Papers*, V.1. London: House of Commons, 1847.

Semedo, Alvaro. *The History of That Great and Renowned Monarchy of China.* London: John Crook, 1655.

Shapiro, Barbara. "Codification of the Laws in Seventeenth-Century England." *Wisconsin Law Review*, no. 2 (1974): 428–65.

Shaw, John. *Charters Relating to the East India Company from 1600 to 1761.* Madras: R. Hill, 1887.

Shaw, Samuel. "Samuel Shaw to Jay (New York, 19th May 1785)." In *The Correspondence and Public Papers of John Jay, 1782–1793*, edited by Henry P. Johnston, 143–49. New York: G. P. Putnam's Sons, 1891.

Shelvocke, Captain George. *Voyage Round the World by Way of the Great South Sea* [1719–1722]. Vol. 11. London: J. Senex, 1726.

Shen Jiaben. *Lidai xingfa kao (On the Laws and Punishments of Various Dynasties).* Beijing: Zhonghua shuju, 2006.

Shih, Shu-mei. *The Lure of the Modern: Writing Modernism in Semicolonial China, 1917–1937.* Berkeley: University of California Press, 2001.

Shiliao xunkan (Historical Documents Published Every Ten Days). 1930–1931. Edited by Gugong Bowuyuan. 40 vols. Taipei: Guofeng chubanshe, 1963.

Shuck, J. Lewis. *Portfolio Chinensis; or, A Collection of Authentic Chinese State Papers.* Macao: New Washington Press of F. F de Cruz, 1840.

Sibly, Job. *The Trial at Large of Acou (a Chinese Tartar Sailor) for Murder: Tried at the Admiralty Sessions Holden at the Sessions' House in the Old Bailey, on Friday, July 11, 1806.* London: R. Butters, 1806.

Siku quanshu (The Complete Library of Four Treasures). 1772–1783. Reprint, Taipei: Shangwu yinshuguan, 1986.

Silverman, Lisa. *Tortured Subjects: Pain, Truth, and the Body in Early Modern France.* Chicago: University of Chicago Press 2001.

Singer, Aubrey. *The Lion and the Dragon: The Story of the First British Embassy to the Court of the Emperor Qianlong in Peking, 1792–94.* London: Barrie & Jenkins, 1992.

Singer, Brian. *Montesquieu and the Discovery of the Social.* London: Palgrave MacMillan, 2013.

Skuy, David. "Macaulay and the Indian Penal Code of 1862." *Modern Asian Studies* 32, no. 2 (1998): 513–57.

Slade, John. *Narrative of the Late Proceedings and Events in China*. Canton: Canton Register Press, 1839.

Smelser, Neil J. "Psychological Trauma and Cultural Trauma." In *Cultural Trauma and Collective Identity*, edited by Jeffrey Alexander, 31–59. Berkeley: University of California Press, 2004.

Smith, Adam. *The Theory of Moral Sentiments*. London: A. Millar, 1759.

Smith, Keith J. M. *James Fitzjames Stephen: Portrait of a Victorian Rationalist*. Cambridge: Cambridge University Press, 1988.

——. *Lawyers, Legislators, and Theorists: Developments in English Criminal Jurisprudence 1800–1957*. Oxford: Clarendon Press, 1998.

Smith, Philip C. F. *The Empress of China*. Philadelphia: Philadelphia Maritime Museum, 1984.

Solonin, K. Y., et al., eds. *The Bretschneider Albums: 19th Century Paintings of Life in China*. Reading, U.K.: Garnet, 1995.

Sommer, Matthew. *Sex, Law, and Society in Late Imperial China*. Stanford: Stanford University Press, 2000.

Sontag, Susan. *Regarding the Pain of Others*. New York: Picador, 2003.

Souza, George B. *The Survival of Empire: Portuguese Trade and Society in China and the South China Sea, 1630–1754*. Cambridge: Cambridge University Press, 2004.

Spence, Jonathan D. *The Chan's Great Continent*. New York: Norton, 1998.

——. *The Search for Modern China*. 2nd ed. New York: Norton, 1999.

Spierenburg, Pieter. *The Spectacle of Suffering: Execution and the Evolution of Repression*. Cambridge: Cambridge University Press, 1984.

Spivak, Gayatri Chakravorty. "Can the Subaltern Speak?" In *Marxism and the Interpretation of Culture*, edited by Cary Nelson and Lawrence Grossberg, 277–316. Urbana: University of Illinois Press, 1988.

——. "The Politics of Translation." In *Outside in the Teaching Machine*, 179–200. New York: Routledge, 1993.

Sprenkel, Otto B. van der. "Max Weber on China." *History and Theory* 3, no. 3 (1964): 348–70.

Spurlin, Paul M. *Montesquieu in America, 1760–1801*. New York: Octagon, 1961.

——. "Beccaria's *Essay on Crimes and Punishments* in Eighteenth-Century America." *Studies on Voltaire and the Eighteenth Century* 27 (1963): 1489–1504.

St. André, James. "'But Do They Have a Notion of Justice?' Staunton's 1810 Translation of the Great Qing Code." *Translator* 10, no. 1 (2004): 1–33.

Staunton, Sir George Leonard. *An Authentic Account of an Embassy from the King of Great Britain to the Emperor of China*. 3 vols. London: G. Nicol, 1797.

Staunton, Sir George Thomas. *Ta Tsing Leu Lee; Being the Fundamental Laws, and a Selection from the Supplementary Statute of the Penal Code of China*. London: Cadell and Davies, 1810 (*TTLL*).

——. *Ta-Tsing-Leu-Lee, o sia, Leggi fondamentali del Codice penale della China, stampato e promulgato a Pekin coll'autorità di tutti gl'imperatori Ta-Tsing, della presente dinastia.* Translated by Giovanni Rasori. 3 vols. Milan: Stamperia di Giovanni Silvestri, 1812.

——. *Ta-Tsing-Leu-Lée, ou les lois fondamentales du Code pénal de la Chine.* Translated by Félix Renouard de Sainte-Croix. 2 vols. Paris: Lenormant, 1812.

——. *Miscellaneous Notices Relating to China, and Our Commercial Intercourses with That Country.* London: John Murray, 1822.

——. *Notes of Proceedings and Occurrences during the British Embassy to Pekin, in 1816.* London: Havant Press, 1824.

——. *Miscellaneous Notices Relating to China, and Our Commercial Intercourse with That Country* [Part 2]. London, 1828.

——. *Corrected Report of the Speeches of Sir George Staunton on the China Trade, in the House of Commons, June 4, and June 13, 1833: With an Appendix by George Thomas Staunton.* London: Edmund Lloyd, 1833.

——. *Remarks on the British Relations with China, and the Proposed Plans for Improving Them.* London: E. Lloyd, 1836.

——. *Corrected Report of the Speech of Sir George Staunton, on Sir James Graham's Motion on the China Trade, in the House of Commons, April 7, 1840.* London: Edmund Lloyd, 1840.

——. *Miscellaneous Notices Relating to China, and Our Commercial Intercourse with That Country, Including a Few Translations from the Chinese Language.* 2nd, enlarged ed. London: John Murray, 1850.

——. *Memoirs of the Chief Incidents of the Public Life of Sir George Thomas Staunton.* London: L. Booth, 1856.

——. *Ta-Tsing-Leu-Lee, ó las leyes fundamentales del Código penal de la China.* Translated by D. Francisco de la Escosura y Escosura. Havana: Imprenta del Gobierno y Capitania General, 1862.

——. *Ta-Tsing-Léu-Lée, ó las leyes fundamentales del Código penal de la China.* Translated by Juan de Dios Vico y Brabo. Madrid: Imprenta de la Revista de Legislación, 1884.

Steele, Edward D. *Palmerston and Liberalism, 1855–1865.* Cambridge: Cambridge University Press, 1991.

Steiner, Eve. "Codification in England." *Statute Law Review* 25, no. 3 (2004): 209–22.

Stephen, James Fitzjames. *The History of the Criminal Law of England.* 3 vols. London: Macmillan and Co., 1883.

Stephen, Leslie. *The Life of Sir James Fitzjames Stephen.* London: Smith, Elder & Co., 1895.

Stifler, Susan Reed. "The Language Students of the East India Company's Canton Factory." *Journal of the North China Branch of the Royal Asiatic Society* 69 (1938): 46–82.

Stokes, Eric. *The English Utilitarians and India.* New York: Oxford University Press, 1990.

Stoler, Ann Laura. "'In Cold Blood': Hierarchies of Credibility and the Politics of Colonial Narratives." *Representations*, no. 37 (1992): 151–89.

——. "Colonial Archives and the Arts of Governance." *Archival Science* 2 (2002): 87–109.

——. "On Degrees of Imperial Sovereignty." *Public Culture* 18, no. 1 (2006): 125–46.

——. *Along the Archival Grain: Epistemic Anxieties and Colonial Common Sense.* Princeton: Princeton University Press, 2009.

Stoler, Ann Laura, and Frederick Cooper. "Between Metropole and Colony: Rethinking a Research Agenda." In Cooper and Stoler, *Tensions of Empire*, 1–37.

Sturge, Joseph. *A Visit to the United States in 1841.* London: Hamilton, 1842.

Su Yigong. *Ming Qing lüdian yu tiaoli (Laws and Regulations in the Ming and Qing Periods).* Beijing: Zhongguo zhengfa daxue chubanshe, 1998.

"Suppression of the Opium Trade, April 4, 1843." In *Hansard's Parliamentary Debates*, 3rd ser., vol. 68, 362–469. London: Thomas Curson Hansard, 1843.

Svarverud, Rune. *International Law as World Order in Late Imperial China: Translation, Reception and Discourse, 1847–1911.* Leiden: Brill, 2007.

Swinhoe, Robert. *Narrative of the North China Campaign of 1860.* London, Smith, Elder & Co., 1861.

Tai, Ta-Van. "Vietnam's Code of the Lê Dynasty (1428–1788)." *American Journal of Comparative Law* 30, no. 3 (1982): 523–54.

Tan, Carol G. S. *British Rule in China: Law and Justice in Weihaiwei, 1898–1930.* London: Wildy, Simmonds & Hill, 2008.

Tao Jun and Tao Nianlin. *Da Qing lüli zengxiu tongzuan jicheng (Comprehensive Edition of the Revised Qing Code).* 22 juan. Shanghai: Wenyuan shanfang, 1900.

Tarducci, Francesco. *John and Sebastian Cabot.* Translated by Henry F. Brownson. Whitefish, Mont.: Kessinger, 2007.

"Ta-tsing-leu-lee, o sia Leggi fondamentali del Còdice penale della China." *Giornale enciclopedico di Firenze* 4 (1812): 23–24 *(GEDF)*.

Temple, Sir Richard Carnac, ed. *The Travels of Peter Mundy in Europe and Asia, 1608–1667.* vol. 3, part 2 (London: Hakluyt Society, 1919).

Tenney, Edward P. *Contrasts in Social Progress.* London: Longmans, Green and Co., 1907.

Thelwall, Algernon S. *The Iniquities of the Opium Trade with China.* London: Allen & Co., 1839.

Thoughts on the Law of Forfeiture and Parliamentary Attainder for High Treason, as Applying to the Bill Now Pending in Parliament. Dublin: Graisberry & Campbell, 1798.

Three Reports of the Select Committee [of the EIC] . . . *Laid before the Lords of the Committee of Privy Council.* London: J.S. Jordan, 1793.

Tian Tao and Zheng Qin, eds. *Da Qing lüli (The Great Qing Code).* 1740. Beijing: Falü chubanshe, 1998.

Timkovski, George [Egor Fedorovich]. *Travels of the Russian Mission through Mongo-lia to China, and Residence in Peking, in the Years 1820–1821.* 2 vols. Vol. 1. London: Longman, 1827.

Timmermans, Glenn H. "Sir George Thomas Staunton and the Translation of the Qing Legal Code." *Chinese Cross Currents* 2, no. 1 (2005): 26–57.

Tobin, Beth F. *Picturing Imperial Power: Colonial Subjects in Eighteenth-Century British Painting.* Durham: Duke University Press, 1999.

Travers, Robert. *Ideology and Empire in Eighteenth-Century India: The British in Bengal, 1757–93.* New York: Cambridge University Press, 2007.

Trevelyan, Sir George Otto. *The Life and Letters of Lord Macaulay.* London: Long-mans, Green & Co., 1881.

Trocki, Carl A. *Opium, Empire and the Global Political Economy.* London: Routledge, 1999.

Tuck, Richard. *Natural Rights Theories: Their Origin and Development.* Cambridge: Cambridge University Press, 1998.

——. *The Rights of War and Peace: Political Thought and the International Order from Grotius to Kant.* Oxford: Oxford University Press, 1999.

Urmston, Sir James Brabazon. *Observations on the China Trade and on the Importance and Advantages of Removing It from Canton to Some Other Parts of the Coast of That Empire.* London: A. H. Baily & Co., 1834.

Valk, M. H. van der. *Interpretations of the Supreme Court at Peking, Years 1915 and 1916.* Batavia: Sinological Institute, University of Indonesia, 1949.

Van der Sprenkel, Sybille. *Legal Institutions of Manchu China.* London: Athlone Press, 1962.

Van Dyke, Paul A. *The Canton Trade: Life and Enterprise on the China Coast, 1700–1845.* Hong Kong: Hong Kong University Press, 2006.

Van Dyke, Paul A. (trans.), and Cynthia Viallé (rev.). *The Canton-Macao Dagregisters, 1762.* Macao: Instituto Cultural do Governoro da R.A.E. de Macao, 2006.

——. *The Canton-Macao Dagregisters, 1764.* Macao: Instituto Cultural do Governoro da R.A.E. de Macao, 2009.

Vattel, Emmerich de. *The Law of Nations.* 1758. Translated by Joseph Chitty. London: Stevens & Sons, 1834.

Venuti, Lawrence. *The Scandals of Translation.* New York: Routledge, 1998.

Venturi, Franco. "Oriental Despotism." *Journal of the History of Ideas* 24, no. 1 (1963): 133–42.

Victoria [Vitoria], Franciscus de. *De Indis et de ivre Belli Relectiones, Being Parts of Relectiones Theologicae XII.* 1557. Translated by John Pawley Bate. Reprinted by James B. Scott. Originally edited by Ernest Nye. Washington, D.C.: Carnegie Institution of Washington, 1917.

Voltaire [François-Marie Arouet]. *The Works of M. de Voltaire.* Translated and edited by Dr. Smollet et al. 35 vols. Vol. 1. London: J. Newbery, 1761–1765.

——. *The Philosophical Dictionary*. Glasgow: Robert Urie, 1766.

——. *A Treatise on Toleration; The Ignorant Philosopher; and A Commentary on the Marquis of Beccaria's Treatise on Crimes and Punishments*. Translated by D. Williams. London, 1779.

Wakeman, Frederic E., Jr. "The Canton Trade and the Opium War." In *The Cambridge History of China: Volume 10, Late Ch'ing 1800–1911, Part 1*, edited by John K. Fairbank, 163–212. London: Cambridge University Press, 1992.

——. *Strangers at the Gate: Social Disorder in South China, 1839–1861*. Berkeley: University of California Press, 1997.

Waley-Cohen, Joanna. *Exile in Mid-Qing China: Banishment to Xinjiang, 1758–1820*. New Haven: Yale University Press, 1991.

——. "China and Western Technology in the Late Eighteenth Century." *American Historical Review* 98, no. 5 (1993): 1525–44.

——. *The Sextants of Beijing: Global Currents in Chinese History*. New York: Norton, 1999.

——. "Collective Responsibility in Qing Criminal Law." In *The Limits of the Rule of Law in China*, edited by Karen Turner et al., 112–31. Seattle: University of Washington Press, 2000.

Walravens, Hartmut. *Julius Klaproth (1783–1835): Briefe und Dokumente*. Wiesbaden: Harrassowitz, 1999.

——. *Zur Geschichte der Ostasienwissenschaften in Europa: Abel Rémusat (1788–1832) und das Umfeld Julius Klaproths (1783–1835)*. Wiesbaden: Harrassowitz, 1999.

Wang, Ching-Chun. "China Still Waits the End of Extraterritoriality." *Foreign Affairs* 15, no. 4 (July 1937): 745–49.

Wang, David Der-wei. *The Monster That Is History: History, Violence, and Fictional Writing in Twentieth-Century China*. Berkeley: University of California Press, 2004.

Wang Hongzhi. "Majia'erni shihua de fanyi wenti" (The Problem of Translation of the Macartney Embassy to China). *Zhongyang yanjiuyuan jindaishi yanjiusuo jikan* 63 (2009): 97–145.

Wang Zhi. *Chongyatang gao (Drafts from the Chongya Hall)*. 8 vols. 1759.

"War with China." In *Hansard's Parliamentary Debates*, 3rd ser., vol. 53, 3rd sess., 13th Parliament, March–May 1840. London: Thomas Curson Hansard, 1840 (WWC).

Warren, Samuel. *The Opium Question*. London: J. Ridgway, 1840.

Weber, Max. *Economy and Society: An Outline of Interpretative Sociology*. Edited by Guenther Roth and Claus Wittich. 2 vols. Berkeley: University of California Press, 1978.

Wei, Betty Peh-t'i. *Ruan Yuan, 1764–1849: The Life and Work of a Major Scholar-Official*. Hong Kong: Hong Kong University Press, 2006.

Weiss, Gunther A. "The Enchantment of Codification in the Common-Law World." *Yale Journal of International Law* 25 (2000): 435–532.

Wheaton, Henry. *Elements of International Law: With a Sketch of the History of the Science*. Philadelphia: Carey, Lea & Blanchard, 1836.

——. *Elements of International Law*. 8th ed. Reprint with notes by Richard Henry Dana. Boston: Little, Brown, 1866.

Wickberg, Daniel. "What Is the History of Sensibilities? On Cultural Histories, Old and New." *American Historical Review* 112, no. 3 (2007): 661–84.

Widerquist, Karl. "Lockean Theories of Property: Justifications for Unilateral Appropriation." *Public Reason* 2, no. 1 (June 2010): 3–26.

Widmer, Eric. *The Russian Ecclesiastical Mission in Peking During the Eighteenth Century*. Cambridge, Mass.: Harvard University Asia Center, 1976.

Wiener, Martin. *Reconstructing the Criminal: Culture, Law, Policy in England, 1830–1914*. Cambridge: Cambridge University Press, 1990.

Wild, Anthony. *The East India Company: Trade and Conquest from 1600*. London: HarperCollins, 2000.

Williams, Patrick, ed. *Edward Said*. 4 vols. London: Sage, 2001.

Williams, Robert A. *The American Indian in Western Legal Thought: The Discourses of Conquest*. Oxford: Oxford University Press, 1992.

Williams, Samuel Wells. *The Middle Kingdom: A Survey of the Chinese Empire and Its Inhabitants*. 2 vols. New York: Wiley & Putnam, 1848.

——. *General Index of Subjects Contained in the Twenty Volumes of the Chinese Repository*. Reprint. Tokyo: Maruzen Co., 1851.

Wills, John E., Jr. *Embassies and Illusions: Dutch and Portuguese Envoys to K'ang-Hsi, 1666–1687*. Cambridge, Mass.: Harvard University Press, 1984.

——. "Maritime Europe and the Ming." In *China and Maritime Europe, 1500–1800: Trade, Settlement, Diplomacy, and Missions*, edited by John E. Wills Jr., 24–77. Cambridge: Cambridge University Press, 2011.

Wilson, Kathleen. *The Sense of the People: Politics, Culture, and Imperialism in England, 1715–1785*. Cambridge: Cambridge University Press, 1995.

——. *The Island Race: Englishness, Empire, and Gender in the Eighteenth Century*. London: Routledge, 2002.

——, ed. *A New Imperial History: Culture, Identity and Modernity in Britain and the Empire, 1660–1840*. Cambridge: Cambridge University Press, 2004.

Winterbotham, William. *An Historical, Geographical, and Philosophical View of the Chinese Empire*. London: J. Ridgeway, 1795.

Witek, John W. *Controversial Ideas in China and in Europe: A Biography of Jean-François Fouquet, S.J., 1665–1741*. Rome: Institutum Historicum S.I., 1982.

——. "Catholic Missions and the Expansion of Christianity, 1644–1800." In *China and Maritime Europe, 1500–1800: Trade, Settlement, Diplomacy, and Missions*, edited by John E. Wills Jr., 135–82. Cambridge: Cambridge University Press, 2011

Wittfogel, Karl. *Oriental Despotism: A Comparative Study of Total Power*. New Haven: Yale University Press, 1957.

Wong, John Y. *Deadly Dreams: Opium, Imperialism, and the Arrow War (1856–1860) in China*. Cambridge: Cambridge University Press, 1998.

Wong, R. Bin. *China Transformed: Historical Change and the Limits of European Experience*. Ithaca: Cornell University Press, 1997.

Wright, David. "The Translation of Modern Western Science in Nineteenth-Century China, 1840–1895." *Isis* 89, no. 4 (1998): 653–73.

Wu, Silas H. L. *Communication and Imperial Control in China: Evolution of the Palace Memorial System, 1693–1735*. Cambridge, Mass.: Harvard University Press, 1970.

Xia Li. *Di erci yapian zhanzheng shi* (*History of the Second Opium War*). Shanghai: Shanghai shudian chubanshe, 2007.

Xingbu tongxing tiaoli (*Circulars of the Ministry of Justice*). 6 *juan*. 1886.

Xinglü cao'an qianzhu (*Commentaries on the Draft Criminal Code*). Xianzheng bianchaguan. ca.1910.

Xu Dishan, ed. *Dazhong Ji: Yapian zhanzhen qian zhongying jiaoshe shiliao* ([*Chinese*] *Sources for Sino-British Relations before the Opium War*). Shanghai: Shangwu yinshuguan, 1928.

Xu Minglong. *Huang Jialue yu zhaoqi faguo hanxue* (*Huang Jialue and Early French Sinology*). Beijing: Zhonghua shuju, 2004.

——. "Mengdesijiu dui liyi zhizheng de jiedu" (Montesquieu's Understanding of the Rites Controversy). *Shijie lishi* 4 (2011): 28–38.

Xu, Xiaoqun. *Trial of Modernity: Judicial Reform in Early Twentieth-Century China, 1901–1937*. Stanford: Stanford University Press, 2008.

Xue Yunsheng. *Tang Ming lü hebian* (*The Tang and the Ming Codes Combined*). Edited by Huai Xiaofeng and Li Ming. Beijing: Falü chubanshe, 1998.

Yang Yifan. *Hongwu falü dianji kaozheng* (*Evidentiary Study of the Law Books of the Hongwu Reign* [1368–1398]). Beijing: Falü chubanshe, 1992.

Yang Yuekun, comp. *Da Qing lü lici zuanxiu tiaoli* (*Rules for Revising the Great Qing Code*). 12 *juan*. Beijing: Da Qing lüliguan, 1807.

Yapian zhanzheng dang'an shiliao (*Archival Sources of the Opium War*). Compiled by Zhongguo Diyi Lishi Dang'anguan. 7 vols. Tianjin: Tianjin guji chubanshe, 1992 (*YPZZD*).

Yin Guangren and Zhang Rulin, eds. *Ao'men jilue jiaozhu* (*Annotated Edition of the Brief Records of Macao*). 1751. Annotated by Zhao Chunchen. Macao: Aomen wenhuasi shu, 1992 (*AMJLJZ*).

Yingshi Majia'erni fanghua dang'an shiliao huibian (*Archival Records about the Macartney Embassy to China*). Compiled by Zhongguo Diyi Lishi Dang'an guan. Beijing: Guoji wenhua chuban gongsi, 1996.

Young, Robert. *White Mythologies: Writing History and the West*. New York: Routledge, 2001.

Zelin, Madeleine. *The Merchants of Zigong: Industrial Entrepreneurship in Early Modern China*. New York: Columbia University Press, 2006.

Zelin, Madeleine, Jonathan Ocko, and Robert Gardella, eds. *Contract and Property in Early Modern China*. Stanford: Stanford University Press, 2004.

Zhang Jinfan. *Zhongguo falü de chuantong yu jindai zhuanxing* (*Tradition and Modern Transformation of Chinese Law*). 2nd ed. Beijing: Falü chubanshe, 2005.

Zhu Kejing, comp. *Rouyuan xinshu* (*A New Book on Cherishing Men from Afar*). 4 *juan*. Changsha, 1881.

Zhu Qingqi et al., eds. *Xing'an huilan sanbian* (*Conspectus of Legal Cases in Three Installments*). 1886. Reprint, Beijing: Beijing guji chubanshe, 2003.

INDEX

Page ranges in **bold** refer to entire chapters; page numbers in *italics* refer to maps, photographs, or illustrations.

Studies of the Weatherhead East Asian Institute
Columbia University

Selected Titles
(Complete list at: http://www.columbia.edu/cu/weai/weatherhead-studies.html)

The Age of Irreverence: A New History of Laughter in China, by Christopher Rea. University of California Press, 2015

The Nature of Knowledge and the Knowledge of Nature in Early Modern Japan, by Federico Marcon. University of Chicago Press, 2015

The Fascist Effect: Japan and Italy, 1915–1952, by Reto Hoffman. Cornell University Press, 2015

The International Minimum: Creativity and Contradiction in Japan's Global Engagement, 1933–1964, by Jessamyn R. Abel. University of Hawai'i Press, 2015

Empires of Coal: Fueling China's Entry Into the Modern World Order, 1860–1920, by Shellen Xiao Wu. Stanford University Press, 2015

Casualties of History: Wounded Japanese Servicemen and the Second World War, by Lee K. Pennington. Cornell University Press, 2015

City of Virtues: Nanjing in an Age of Utopian Visions, by Chuck Wooldridge. University of Washington Press, 2015

The Proletarian Wave: Literature and Leftist Culture in Colonial Korea, 1910–1945, by Sunyoung Park. Harvard University Asia Center, 2015.

Neither Donkey Nor Horse: Medicine in the Struggle Over China's Modernity, by Sean Hsiang-lin Lei. University of Chicago Press, 2014.

When the Future Disappears: The Modernist Imagination in Late Colonial Korea, by Janet Poole. Columbia University Press, 2014.

Bad Water: Nature, Pollution, and Politics in Japan, 1870–1950, by Robert Stolz. Duke University Press, 2014.

Rise of a Japanese Chinatown: Yokohama, 1894–1972, by Eric C. Han. Harvard University Asia Center, 2014.

Beyond the Metropolis: Second Cities and Modern Life in Interwar Japan, by Louise Young. University of California Press, 2013.

From Cultures of War to Cultures of Peace: War and Peace Museums in Japan, China, and South Korea, by Takashi Yoshida. Merwin Asia, 2013.

Imperial Eclipse: Japan's Strategic Thinking About Continental Asia Before August 1945, by Yukiko Koshiro. Cornell University Press, 2013.

The Nature of the Beasts: Empire and Exhibition at the Tokyo Imperial Zoo, by Ian J. Miller. University of California Press, 2013.

Public Properties: Museums in Imperial Japan, by Noriko Aso. Duke University Press, 2013.

Reconstructing Bodies: Biomedicine, Health, and Nation-Building in South Korea Since 1945, by John P. DiMoia. Stanford University Press, 2013.

Taming Tibet: Landscape Transformation and the Gift of Chinese Development, by Emily T. Yeh. Cornell University Press, 2013.

Tyranny of the Weak: North Korea and the World, 1950–1992, by Charles K. Armstrong. Cornell University Press, 2013.

The Art of Censorship in Postwar Japan, by Kirsten Cather.University of Hawai'i Press, 2012.

Asia for the Asians: China in the Lives of Five Meiji Japanese, by Paula Harrell. Merwin Asia, 2012.

Lin Shu, Inc.: Translation and the Making of Modern Chinese Culture, by Michael Gibbs Hill. Oxford University Press, 2012.

Occupying Power: Sex Workers and Servicemen in Postwar Japan, by Sarah Kovner. Stanford University Press, 2012.

Redacted: The Archives of Censorship in Postwar Japan, by Jonathan E. Abel. University of California Press, 2012.

Empire of Dogs: Canines, Japan, and the Making of the Modern Imperial World, by Aaron Herald Skabelund. Cornell University Press, 2011.

Planning for Empire: Reform Bureaucrats and the Japanese Wartime State, by Janis Mimura. Cornell University Press, 2011.

Realms of Literacy: Early Japan and the History of Writing, by David Lurie. Harvard University Asia Center, 2011.

Russo-Japanese Relations, 1905–17: From Enemies to Allies, by Peter Berton. Routledge, 2011.

Behind the Gate: Inventing Students in Beijing,
    by Fabio Lanza. Columbia University Press,
    2010.
*Imperial Japan at Its Zenith: The Wartime
    Celebration of the Empire's 2,600th
    Anniversary, by* Kenneth J. Ruoff. Cornell
    University Press, 2010.
Ethnic Conflict in Western China, by Ben
    Hillman and Gray Tuttle. Columbia
    University Press, 2016

GPSR Authorized Representative: Easy Access System Europe, Mustamäe tee 50, 10621 Tallinn, Estonia, gpsr.requests@easproject.com